Brunngasse 36
CH-3011 Bern
www.ta-swiss.ch

TA-SWISS 73/2020

Nils Braun-Dubler, Hans-Peter Gier, Tetiana Bulatnikova, Manuel Langhart, Manuela Merki, Florian Roth, Antoine Burret, Simon Perdrisat

Blockchain: Capabilities, Economic Viability, and the Socio-Technical Environment

Bibliografische Information der Deutschen Nationalbibliothek
Die Deutsche Nationalbibliothek verzeichnet diese Publikation in der Deutschen Nationalbibliografie; detaillierte bibliografische Daten sind im Internet über http://dnb.dnb.de abrufbar.

Zitiervorschlag
Braun-Dubler N., Gier H.-P., Bulatnikova T., Langhart M., Merki M., Roth F., Burret A., Perdrisat S. (2020).
Blockchain: Capabilities, Economic Viability, and the Socio-Technical Environment.
In TA-SWISS Publikationsreihe (Hrsg.): TA 73/2020. Zürich: vdf.

ISBN 978-3-7281-4016-6 (Printausgabe)

Download open access:
ISBN 978-3-7281-4017-3 / DOI 10.3218/4017-3

www.vdf.ethz.ch
verlag@vdf.ethz.ch

Preface

In October of 2016, the TA-SWISS Foundation issued a call for a study on the topic of blockchain technology. At the time, the cryptocurrency Bitcoin – the technology's first application – was surging: its development was increasingly fast and its value rising. In addition, the Zug region had dubbed itself "Crypto Valley", and it was generally assumed that Switzerland would play an important role in developing this new currency. Nevertheless, TA-SWISS wanted to look beyond cryptocurrencies and expanded the topic of the study to include the underlying technology: the blockchain.

Already before the call for tenders was issued, the Steering Committee had held intense discussions on the scope of the study and the questions it should answer. These preliminary debates were an apt reflection of the uncertainties linked to blockchain technology: finding a way to address the topic and understanding the technology are both difficult – indeed, it remains a riddle to the average layperson. Moreover, the numerous media reports at the time indicated a certain hype surrounding the blockchain. The Steering Committee decided to first take inventory and to itemize information pertaining to blockchain technology; this approach would provide the public sector, public administration bodies, and the political sphere with a broad knowledge base and was deemed more relevant than a standard TA study with a series of recommendations.

From May 2017 to September 2018, the first project group began working on the complex topic, concentrating on technological as well as economic and ecological aspects of blockchain technology. The project group conducted a broad-based study consisting of an initial, introductory part that provides a very good general introduction into how blockchains function, followed by a second section with twelve case studies. In the case studies, a careful comparison is drawn between standard applications and blockchain applications, enabling the project group to establish that blockchain applications are often less efficient than standard applications, and that they should be promoted only in certain contexts.

After the study was presented at their 2018 retreat, the TA-SWISS Steering Committee expressed the wish to supplement the information in the first report by placing blockchain technology in a social context: for instance, the sociological and cultural settings in which the technology has flourished and the observed consequences should be explored. A second project group was therefore charged with contextualising the technology. The two sociologists in the project group selected for the study interviews held with blockchain technology professionals from Switzerland and abroad. Their report provides an overview of the blockchain's origins, while also focussing on aspects of standardisation, which is what enabled the blockchain to become a part of everyday discourse.

Upon project conclusion, the TA-SWISS Steering Committee decided against formulating recommendations on the topic – partly on account of the complexity of the issue but also due to the lack of a so-called "killer application" that would have an actual impact on our society. The two partial studies should be considered together; they offer a broad overview of how the technology functions as well as of its opportunities and risks.

Elisabeth Ehrensperger

Vorwort

Im Oktober 2016 schrieb die Stiftung TA-SWISS eine neue Studie zum Thema Blockchain aus. Zu diesem Zeitpunkt erlebte der Bitcoin, die erste Anwendung der Blockchain, einen rasanten Aufschwung: Die Kryptowährung entwickelte sich immer schneller und gewann an Wert. Die Region Zug taufte sich «Crypto Valley», und es wurde davon ausgegangen, dass die Schweiz bei der Entwicklung dieser neuen Währung eine wichtige Rolle spielen würde. TA-SWISS wollte sich jedoch nicht auf die Kryptowährungen beschränken und weitete das Thema der Studie auf die der Währung zugrundeliegende Technologie aus: die Blockchain.

Bereits vor der Ausschreibung gab es innerhalb des Leitungsausschusses intensive Diskussionen über den Umfang der Studie und die Fragen, die diese beantworten sollte. Darin spiegelte sich die Ungewissheit, die in Bezug auf die Blockchain-Technologie herrscht: Es ist nicht einfach, eine Herangehensweise zu finden und die Technologie zu verstehen – für Laien bleibt sie ein Rätsel. Gleichzeitig bezeugten zahlreiche Medienberichte in dieser Zeit den Hype um die Blockchain. Der Leitungsausschuss hielt es für sachdienlicher, eine erste Bestandsaufnahme bzw. eine Auslegeordnung in Bezug auf die Blockchain-Technologie zu erarbeiten, um der Öffentlichkeit, den Verwaltungen und der Politik eine breite Wissensgrundlage zur Verfügung stellen zu können, als dies mit einer Standard-TA-Studie mit einer Reihe von Empfehlungen zu versuchen.

Von Mai 2017 bis September 2018 hat sich eine erste Projektgruppe des komplexen Themas angenommen und sich auf die technologischen sowie auf die ökonomischen und ökologischen Aspekte der Blockchain konzentriert. Die Projektgruppe präsentierte am Ende eine breit angelegte Studie, bestehend aus einem ersten einleitenden Teil, der ein sehr gutes Grundverständnis der Funktionsweise der «Blockketten» liefert, gefolgt von einem zweiten Teil mit zwölf Fallstudien. In diesen Fallstudien wird ein sorgfältiger Vergleich zwischen der Standardanwendung und der Blockchain-Anwendung gemacht. Die Projektgruppe stellt dabei fest, dass Blockchain-Anwendungen oft noch weniger leistungsfähig sind als Standardanwendungen und dass sie einzig in bestimmten Kontexten zu fördern sind.

Infolge der Präsentation der Studie an der LA-Klausur 2018 äusserte der Leitungsausschuss von TA-SWISS den Wunsch, die bestehende Arbeit sei durch eine gesellschaftliche Kontextualisierung der Blockchain-Technologie zu ergänzen: In welchem soziologischen und kulturellen Kontext hat sich diese Technologie entwickelt, mit welchen Folgen usw.? Dazu wurde eine zweite Projektgruppe beauftragt. Die beiden Soziologen der gewählten Projektgruppe gingen den oben erwähnten Fragen u.a. in Gesprächen mit Akteuren auf diesem Gebiet aus dem In- und Ausland nach und reichten eine Arbeit ein, die einen Überblick über die Entstehung der Blockchain liefert. Dieser Bericht fokussiert zudem auf Aspekte der Standardisierung, die der Blockchain ermöglichten, sich im täglichen Diskurs durchzusetzen.

Bei Abschluss des Projektes hat sich der Leitungsausschuss von TA-SWISS entschieden, keine Empfehlungen zum Thema zu formulieren – mit Verweis auf die Komplexität des Themas, aber auch das Fehlen einer sogenannten «Killerapplikation», welche tatsächlichen Einfluss auf unsere Gesellschaft haben könnte. Die beiden Teilstudien sind als komplementär zu betrachten und bieten eine breite Sicht auf die Technologie ebenso wie auf deren Chancen und Risiken.

Elisabeth Ehrensperger

Préface

En octobre 2016, la Fondation TA-SWISS met au concours une nouvelle étude de choix technologiques sur le thème de la blockchain. À ce moment-là, le Bitcoin, première application de la blockchain, est en plein essor : la crypto-monnaie se développe de plus en plus rapidement et prend de la valeur. En Suisse, la région de Zoug se baptise « Crypto Valley » et certains prennent le pari que le pays jouera un rôle important dans le développement de ces nouvelles monnaies. Ne souhaitant pas se limiter aux seules cryptomonnaies, TA-SWISS prend le parti d'étendre le sujet de son étude à la technologie sous-jacente qu'est la blockchain.

Avant la mise au concours, les discussions au sein du comité directeur sont intenses lorsqu'il s'agit de définir les contours de l'étude et les questions auxquelles elle devra répondre. Elles reflètent l'incertitude qui règne autour de cette technologie : elle est difficile à aborder et à comprendre et reste mystérieuse pour les non-initiés. En même temps, le « hype » autour de la blockchain est bien réel comme en témoignent les nombreux articles de presse que l'on peut lire à ce moment-là. En lieu et place d'une étude TA standard, la question se pose de réaliser plutôt un état de l'art de la technologie qui n'aboutirait pas à une série de recommandations, comme c'est le cas pour la plupart des études de TA-SWISS, mais à une base de connaissance riche qui puisse être mise à la disposition du grand public, des administrations et du monde politique.

De mai 2017 à septembre 2018, un premier groupe de projet s'attaque à ce thème complexe et se concentre sur les aspects technologiques, économiques et écologiques de la blockchain. Au final, le groupe de projet présente une étude riche, composée d'une première partie introductive qui donne une très bonne base de compréhension du fonctionnement des chaines de blocs, puis d'une seconde partie où sont énumérées douze études de cas. Dans ces études de cas, une comparaison minutieuse est effectuée entre application standard et application blockchain. Le groupe de projet fait ainsi le constat que les applications blockchain sont souvent encore moins performantes que les applications standards. Dans certains contextes bien précis uniquement, elles sont à promouvoir.

Suite à la présentation de l'étude, le comité directeur de TA-SWISS souhaite poursuivre le travail et y apporter des éléments de contextualisation : dans quel contexte sociologique et culturel s'est développé cette technologie, avec quelles conséquences, etc. ? Pour ce faire, une seconde équipe de projet est mandatée. Composée de deux sociologues, elle se penche sur ces questions en menant une série d'entretiens en Suisse et à l'étranger avec des acteurs du domaine. Cette seconde équipe présente un travail qui détaille l'historique qui a permis à la blockchain d'émerger. Il se concentre également sur les aspects de normalisation qui ont permis à la blockchain de s'imposer dans le discours quotidien.

À la fin de ce projet, le comité directeur de TA-SWISS a décidé de ne pas émettre de recommandations sur ce thème. Il a noté la difficulté de la thématique mais également l'absence actuelle d'applications déployées à grande échelle qui pourraient avoir un impact véritable sur la société. Les deux études sont complémentaires et présentent une vue large de la technologie, ainsi que des chances et des risques qui y sont associés.

Elisabeth Ehrensperger

Premessa

Nell'ottobre 2016 la Fondazione TA-SWISS ha emesso il bando per un nuovo studio sul tema «blockchain». Era il periodo in cui il bitcoin, prima applicazione della blockchain, stava vivendo un vero e proprio boom: la popolarità della criptovaluta cresceva vertiginosamente, registrando valori sempre più elevati. La regione di Zugo si era ribattezzata «Crypto Valley» e già si ipotizzava che la Svizzera avrebbe svolto un ruolo importante nello sviluppo della nuova moneta. TA-SWISS non voleva però limitare lo studio all'ambito delle criptovalute e decise quindi di estenderlo alla tecnologia alla base del bitcoin: la blockchain.

L'incertezza che aleggiava attorno alla tematica della blockchain si è manifestata chiaramente già prima dell'emissione del bando nelle intense discussioni interne al comitato di direzione sull'estensione delle attività da svolgere e le questioni da affrontare: non è facile definire un approccio a questa tecnologia e comprenderne i meccanismi, tant'è che per i non addetti ai lavori resta un mistero. Contemporaneamente i media si facevano portavoce dell'ondata di entusiasmo che investiva la blockchain. Il comitato di direzione ha quindi ritenuto più utile mappare innanzitutto la situazione elaborandone una panoramica per fornire ai cittadini, alle amministrazioni e agli esponenti politici un'ampia base di conoscenze, piuttosto che proporre uno dei classici studi di TA con una serie di raccomandazioni.

Un primo gruppo di progetto ha affrontato questa complessa tematica dal maggio 2017 al settembre 2018, concentrandosi sugli aspetti tecnologici, economici ed ecologici della blockchain. Al termine delle attività il gruppo di progetto ha presentato una disamina ad ampio raggio composta da una prima parte introduttiva, che fornisce un'ottima comprensione di base del funzionamento delle «catene di blocchi», seguita da una seconda parte composta da dodici studi di casi-tipo con un accurato confronto tra applicazioni standard e applicazioni blockchain. Il gruppo di progetto vi constata che spesso le applicazioni blockchain sono meno potenti delle applicazioni standard e che quindi vanno privilegiate solo in determinati contesti.

In seguito alla presentazione dello studio il comitato di direzione di TA-SWISS ha auspicato, nella riunione a porte chiuse del 2018, che il lavoro svolto venisse integrato da una contestualizzazione sociale della tecnologia blockchain: in quale contesto socioculturale si è sviluppata, con quali conseguenze, ecc.?

Questi approfondimenti sono stati affidati a un secondo gruppo di progetto. I due sociologi del gruppo prescelto hanno affrontato le domande citate per es. in discussioni con protagonisti del settore in Svizzera e all'estero, producendo un lavoro che fornisce una panoramica sull'origine della blockchain. Questo rapporto si concentra anche sugli aspetti della standardizzazione che hanno consentito alla blockchain di affermarsi nel dibattito pubblico.

A conclusione del progetto il comitato di direzione di TA-SWISS ha deciso di non formulare raccomandazioni sull'argomento, appellandosi sia alla complessità del tema, sia anche alla mancanza di una cosiddetta killer application che possa produrre un impatto reale sulla nostra società. I due studi parziali sono da considerarsi complementari e offrono un'ampia panoramica della tecnologia, delle opportunità e dei rischi che presenta.

Elisabeth Ehrensperger, Direttrice TA-SWISS

Table of Contents

Preface 3

Vorwort 5

Préface 7

Premessa 9

Figures 17

Tables 21

The Technical Capabilities of Blockchain and its Economic Viability 23

Summary 25

Zusammenfassung 29

Résumé 33

Sintesi 37

1. Introduction 41

2. Basics of Cryptography 45

2.1. Hashing 46

2.2. 2^{256} or The Power of Big Numbers 49

2.3. Public key cryptosystems and digital signatures 50

2.3.1. Public key cryptosystems 50

2.3.2. Digital signatures in blockchain technology 52

2.3.3. Safety of private keys 53

2.4. Zero-knowledge proof 55

2.4.1. Zero-knowledge proof explained 56

2.4.2. Zk-Snarks & blockchain 58

2.5. Quantum computing 58

2.6. Conclusion 60

3. Blockchain Technology 61

3.1. The origin of blockchain technology 63

3.2. How a blockchain works 65

3.2.1. The genesis block 65

3.2.2. Participating in a blockchain 67

3.2.3. Relaying transactions in the network 68

3.2.4. Validation 70

3.2.5. Multi-signatures 71

3.2.6. Creating a block 72

3.2.7. Building the chain 73

3.2.8. Reaching consensus 74

3.3. Who can participate? 76

3.3.1. Permissionless chains 76

3.3.2. Permissioned chains 78

3.3.3. Software protocol governance 79

3.4. Incentives 81

3.4.1. Transactions fees 82

3.4.2. Block rewards 86

3.5. Consensus protocols 87

3.5.1. Proof-of-work (PoW) 87

3.5.2. Proof-of-stake (PoS) 94

3.5.3. Proof-of-authority (PoA) 97

3.5.4. Practical Byzantine Fault Tolerance (PBFT) 98

3.6. Smart contracts 102

3.7. Scalability 107

3.8. Interoperability of blockchains 110

3.9. Privacy versus transparency 111

3.10. Patents 113

4. Potential Benefits 117

4.1. Where blockchains can generate trust in business processes 117

4.1.1. Replacing intermediaries 117

4.1.2. Automating verification processes 118

4.2. How relationships are typically affected 118

4.2.1. Business to business relationships (B2B) 118

4.2.2. Business to consumer relationships (B2C) 119

4.2.3. Consumer to consumer relationships (C2C) 119

4.2.4. Government to citizen relationships (G2C) 120

4.3. Transaction cost theory 120

4.3.1. Financial transaction costs 122

4.3.2. Costs of legal certainty 125

4.3.3. Time costs 126

5. Technical Challenges 129

5.1. Tokenisation of assets 129

5.1.1. Tokenisation for different asset types 129

5.1.2. Tokenisation processes 131

5.1.3. Cryptocurrencies 132

5.1.4. Fiat currencies and lifecycle-less assets 134

5.1.5. Assets with a lifecycle 136

5.2. Delivery versus payment 136

5.3. Voting 137

5.3.1. Voting tokens 139

5.3.2. Open voting 140

5.3.3. Confidential voting 141

5.3.4. Anonymous voting 142

6. Use Cases 143

6.1. Pure blockchain use cases 145

6.1.1. Public register (land and commercial registers) 145

6.1.2. Cryptocurrencies 151

6.1.3. Crowdfunding (Initial Coin Offering) 168

6.1.4. Private payment systems (World Food Programme) 173

6.2. Blockchain with smart contracts 177

6.2.1. Gambling (vDice) 177

6.2.2. Insurance (Etherisc) 183

6.2.3. e-ID (City of Zug) 189

6.2.4. Public e-voting (Follow my Vote) 198

6.2.5. Trade financing (Batavia) 204

6.2.6. Exchanges (Lykke) 209

6.3. Blockchain with smart contracts and IOT 215

6.3.1. Proof of provenance (Provenance, Ambrosus, Chronicled) 215

6.3.2. Energy (Brooklyn Microgrid and Tal.Markt/Elblox) 222

7. Legal, Social, Political, and Ecological Aspects 231

7.1. Legal Aspects 231

7.1.1. MME: Framework for legal and risk assessment 233

7.1.2. FINMA: Applicability of financial regulation for ICOs 236

7.1.3 Transfer of tokens on the blockchain 237

7.1.4. Economic reflections 239

7.2. Ecological aspects 241

7.2.1. Main ecological problem: proof-of-work-based mining 241

7.2.2. Potential ecological gains through accountability 243

7.3. Social and political aspects 245

7.3.1. Change in trust 245

7.3.2. Transparency 247

7.3.3. Missing intermediaries 248

7.3.4. Collective ownership 249

7.3.5. Decentralisation 249

7.3.6. Participation 250

Conclusions 251

Appendices 259

Blockchain: A New Socio-Technical Environment **263**

Summary 265

Zusammenfassung 268

Résumé 271

Sintesi 274

8. Blockchain as a Historical Construct **277**

8.1. Cryptography and decentralised networks in the post-war period 277

8.2. Consequences of the growth of electronic communications 278

8.3. Designing privacy 280

8.4. Consequences of public access to the global computer network 281

9. The Design and Implementation of the Bitcoin Protocol **285**

9.1. The publicising of the Bitcoin project 285

9.2. The collective design process of the Bitcoin protocol 287

9.3. Community ownership of the Bitcoin project 289

10. Blockchain as a Distributed Ledger Technology **291**

10.1. Other applications of the Bitcoin protocol 291

10.2. The objectification of blockchain 292

10.3. The emergence of permissioned distributed ledger techniques 294

10.4. Other distributed ledger techniques 296

11. Blockchain Socialisation Patterns **299**

11.1. Exogenous socialisation patterns 299

11.2. Endogenous socialisation patterns 308

12. Designing Through Blockchain **319**

12.1. The emergence of a new sector 319

12.2. New regulation techniques 324

12.3. Identity paradigms 326

Conclusions 329

Contributors 333

Glossary **335**

References **343**

Supervisory Group **383**

Project Management TA-SWISS **383**

Figures

Figure 1 Distribution of blockchain companies in Switzerland (June 2018). 44

Figure 2 Message encryption using a private key. 52

Figure 3 Illustration of the zero-knowledge proof. 56

Figure 4 The essence of blockchain technology. 62

Figure 5 A transaction initiated by a user of the blockchain is propagated through the network. 69

Figure 6 Transaction from a multisig wallet. 72

Figure 7 A Merkle tree. 73

Figure 8 The correlation between the number of nodes and the number of transactions. 77

Figure 9 Average Bitcoin transaction fee in USD per day from October 2016 through September 2017. 83

Figure 10 Average Bitcoin transaction fee in BTC per day from October 2016 through September 2017. 84

Figure 11 Average Ethereum transaction fee in USD per day from October 2016 through September 2017. 84

Figure 12 Average gas price per day over a 12-month period. 85

Figure 13 A 256-bit string in a hexadecimal format for Bitcoin block #486913. 88

Figure 14 The increase in the Bitcoin difficulty over 12 months. 91

Figure 15 The Bitcoin hash rate in exa-hashes per second (millions of tera hashes). 91

Figure 16 Ethereum difficulty over 12 months. 92

Figure 17 Ethereum hash rate over 12 months. 93

Figure 18 Illustration of a simple insurance contract. 104

Figure 19 Smart lock model. 105

Figure 20 The number of patent applications submitted to the USPTO. 113

Figure 21 A voting contract. 139

Figure 22 Details of a voting contract. 140

Figure 23 Voting transaction details. 141

Figure 24 Use cases grouped by transaction costs. 144

Figure 25 Bitcoin price development in USD during 2017. 153

Figure 26 Ether price development in USD during 2017. 154

Figure 27 Coinmap.org screenshot of the Bitcoin-accepting venue heat map on 6 March 2018. 155

Figure 28 The market capitalisation and quantity of ICOs since 2014. 169

Figure 29 Largest ICOs by market capitalisation. 171

Figure 30 Overview of the process with a conventional e-ID. 191

Figure 31 The uPort processes. 193

Figure 32 Example of a Web of Trust. 195

Figure 33 An example of applying a Web of Trust. 197

Figure 34 A unique and anonymous voter registration process. 203

Figure 35 A conventionally-secured trade finance process. 206

Figure 36 A blockchain-secured trade finance process. 208

Figure 37 Market structures with traditional and blockchain-based processes. 226

Figure 38 BCP Classification and Risk Assessment Method. 235

Figure 39 Bitcoin balance maintenance using UTXOs. 259

Figure 40 The number of UTXOs over nearly two years. 260

Figure 41 Screenshot of a message from Satoshi Nakamoto on 6 November 2018 287

Figure 42 Articles found on Google Scholar by Keyword. The total may exceed 100% as multiple keywords can be used in an article. 300

Figure 43 Number of posts on Reddit.com from 2014 to 2019 ... 301

Figure 44 Number of scientific articles found on the Web of Science bibliographic databases (https://clarivate.com/products/web-of-science/) for “Blockchain” and “Distributed Ledger” ... 302

Figure 45 ICO Market 2017–2018 ... 310

Figure 46 The main forks of Bitcoin ... 314

Figure 47 A soft fork: blocks violating new rules are made stale by the upgraded mining majority ... 315

Figure 48 A hard fork: Non-upgraded nodes reject the new rules, diverging the chain ... 315

Figure 49 Total market capitalisation according to CryptomarketCap ... 320

Figure 50 Warning message for the Status mobile app on Android PlayStore. ... 321

Figure 51 Tweet from the Open Money Initiative showing a woman hiding money in her hair ... 322

Figure 52 In each blockchain you write a message that identifies your key in the other blockchain. This proves you have access to both keys. ... 327

Tables

Table 1 Transformation of a string using the SHA-256 hash function. 47

Table 2 Example of a Bitcoin public-private key pair example. 53

Table 3 The number of calculations per time unit possible with quantum computers. 59

Table 4 Transaction fees and mining time for Ether. 85

Table 5 Transaction fees and mining time for Bitcoin 86

Table 6 Block rewards. 86

Table 7 The number of published patents worldwide. 114

Table 8 Top 10 topics of published patents worldwide. 114

Table 9 Top 5 companies of published patents worldwide. 115

Table 10 Comparing Bitcoin and Ether to mainstream currencies. 152

Table 11 Mean values and standard deviation of Bitcoin and Ether prices. 154

Table 12 Permissioned and permissionless public and private blockchains. 295

The Technical Capabilities of Blockchain and its Economic Viability

Institut für Wirtschaftsstudien Basel

Nils Braun-Dubler
Hans-Peter Gier
Tetiana Bulatnikova
Manuel Langhart
Manuela Merki
Florian Roth

In Cooperation with banking concepts and MME

Summary

It is likely that blockchain technology will become one of the most important underlying technologies for decentralised business transactions. The cryptocurrency Bitcoin is the best-known application of the blockchain – but Bitcoin is actually only a poor example of the technology's potential. Blockchains simplify collective ownership, ensure end-to-end verifiable proof-of-provenance, and can be used to combat corruption. In essence, the blockchain is a decentralised database – or a distributed ledger technology – whose strength becomes evident mainly when used in combination with so-called smart contracts: this makes it possible to do away with intermediaries in many contexts and to reduce transaction costs when concluding contracts. The present study describes the opportunities and risks associated with blockchain technology and formulates recommended actions for mitigating the negative impacts of the new technology while also tapping into its potential for Switzerland.

A blockchain is a decentralised database that is replicated on the servers or computers of independent legal entities. New information or transactions must always be signed by senders using their private key. Miners then bundle the transactions in blocks and cryptographically secure them, with the new block always referencing the previous block. The miners work like accountants: they assess submitted transactions for validity, transform them into blocks and control the validity of the previous blocks in the chain. The miners are compensated for their work, typically by receiving a transaction fee and/or a lump sum payment.

The decentralised character of the database means that there is no single correct version for all users in the network (asynchronicity). Instead, a consensus mechanism provides the basis for the users in a network to agree on the validity of the next block in the chain, which results in the creation of a single valid blockchain for a given network. The most common consensus protocol is called 'proof-of-work', and it rewards the user whose computer is fastest at solving a cryptographic puzzle.

Strengths and opportunities

The greatest advantage of the blockchain is its immutability, which is ensured via cryptographic hashes and a smart incentive system. In addition, because a distributed ledger has no single point of failure, it has robust protection against standard IT hacking attempts. These features create trust between participants, who may not know each other well – or at all.

Economic advantages can be assessed from the standpoint of transaction cost theory and can be traced to three different sources. Firstly, doing away with intermediaries would directly reduce transaction costs. Secondly, legal certainty would increase due to the transparency and immutability of the secured information. Thirdly, time could be saved if legal enforcement were automated in conjunction with smart contracts.

In a societal context, blockchain technology could make collective ownership and participation in cooperatives less expensive and thus more common. In countries where the rule of law is weak, transactions could, for instance, be modelled on Swiss law by using blockchain-based contracts. In addition, the technology could reduce corruption if governmentally recognised property rights were stored in a decentralised network and cannot be altered retroactively.

Weaknesses and risks

Currently, the greatest disadvantage associated with many blockchains is the ecological impact. The 'proof-of-work' consensus mechanism consumes a massive amount of energy due to its competitive nature. Despite intense discussions in the blockchain community, a complete transition to an eco-friendly 'proof-of-work' protocol has not yet succeeded.

The role of opinion leaders in the tech world – in particular, the founders of a blockchain – is a societal challenge that should not be underestimated. Indeed, a majority of participants can use a so-called 'hard fork' to retroactively change the rules in a blockchain, meaning the minority is not adequately protected. Moreover, blockchains and smart contracts are theoretically highly transparent, but they are largely incomprehensible to non-specialists; the average layperson is therefore unable to identify weak links. The societal risks of disruption caused by job loss among intermediaries cannot be calculated, as the number of jobs created (e.g., in the blockchain ecosystem) remains uncertain.

The effect of pseudo-anonymity of the blockchain is also not clear-cut. On the one hand, protecting privacy is highly desirable, while, on the other hand, this privacy can be misused for criminal purposes. In addition, pseudo-anonymity implies that all transactions can be viewed once the identity behind a pseudonym is revealed. This, combined with immutability, also means the 'right to be forgotten' cannot be enforced.

Applications

The applications presented in the study range from public land registers, payment systems in refugee camps, lotteries, insurance policies, and e-voting on to proofs-of-provenance and energy supply systems. Interestingly, the best-known blockchain application – cryptocurrencies – is not particularly promising. Successful cryptocurrencies tend towards deflation, while others are prone to inflation. Independent of this aspect, the fixed amount of money in a cryptocurrency combined with unregulated exchange results in greater volatility. Relative price stability is, however, a key component of a successful, reliable currency.

Disruptive changes are anticipated first in financial services, where many digital representations of ownership already exist. Proofs-of-provenance are also expected to become significantly more transparent due to a steep decline in costs. In conjunction with decentralised transaction options, this could, in particular, render emissions trading systems less expensive and more transparent.

Interestingly, Switzerland is well-positioned to benefit from the blockchain, although the country is currently active as a trusted mediator in a variety of contexts, a role that the new technology could potentially render obsolete. Trust will not, however, be entirely supplanted by the blockchain but will be shifted to other areas, for instance, the storage and safeguarding of collective property in duty-free warehouses, vaults or bunkers. The liberal business regulations in Switzerland are also advantageous and have attracted blockchain pioneers, resulting in the creation of a productive community in the Zug-Zurich region. Combined with the country's liberal arbitration practices, this means there is now a chance that many smart contracts will name Switzerland as the place of jurisdiction. Regarding the financial sector – in the medium-term, also the insurance sector – companies must be prepared to 'cannibalise' their own business models in order to master the looming structural change.

Limits

The technical limits of blockchain applications primarily concern three aspects: (1) Scalability is limited, as each block makes the chain 'heavier' and slows down the decentralised network. As a result, large quantities of data (such as images and videos) cannot be stored on the blockchain. (2) Objects in real life have a lifecycle, for instance, rights lapse, foodstuffs expire. Smart contracts that imitate this lifecycle must assign third parties additional rights without causing unwanted hierarchies in the process. (3) There is no globally recognised, secure digital identity, although this would be an essential factor for cross-border blockchains that are in compliance with money laundering laws.

Finally, a system based on blockchain technology means that society must be prepared to embrace a new way of thinking. In our current system, we assume that an individual person is responsible – and can be held accountable – for any errors that occur; moreover, many people instinctively have greater confidence in a system that is actively monitored by a human being. Because human error is excluded, blockchain technology is ultimately more reliable; indeed, the probability-based approach of the technology means that the likelihood of error is vanishingly small. Nevertheless, a minimal risk is inherent in the system, yet no human being will be held accountable.

Zusammenfassung

Die Blockchain-Technologie wird wahrscheinlich eine der bedeutendsten Hintergrundtechnologien für den dezentralisierten Handel werden. Ihre bekannteste Anwendung ist die Kryptowährung Bitcoin. Gerade Bitcoin reflektiert jedoch die Anwendungspotenziale nur sehr ungenügend. Blockchains vereinfachen den kollektiven Besitz, sorgen für lückenlos nachvollziehbare Herkunftsnachweise (‹Proof-of-Provenance›) und können zur Korruptionsbekämpfung eingesetzt werden. Im Kern ist die Blockchain eine dezentrale Datenbank, deren Macht vor allem in Kombination mit intelligenten Verträgen (‹smart contracts›) zum Tragen kommt, wodurch vielerorts Mittelsmänner überflüssig werden und die Transaktionskosten für Vertragsabwicklungen reduziert werden. Die vorliegende Studie zeigt die Chancen und Risiken der Blockchain-Technologie auf und formuliert konkrete Handlungsempfehlungen, welche die negativen Auswirkungen mindern und das Potenzial der Technologie für die Schweiz erschliessen sollen.

Eine Blockchain ist eine dezentrale Datenbank, welche auf Servern oder Computern von unabhängigen Rechtspersonen repliziert wird. Neue Informationen bzw. Transaktionen müssen vom Sender mit dessen privaten Schlüssel signiert werden. Transaktionen werden in der Folge von Minern in Blocks gebündelt und kryptografisch versiegelt, wobei auf den vorhergehenden Block referenziert wird. Die Miner verhalten sich wie Buchhalter: Sie prüfen die eingereichten Transaktionen auf ihre Gültigkeit, verarbeiten diese zu Blocks und kontrollieren die Gültigkeit der bisherigen Blockchain. Für diese Aktivität werden die Miner entschädigt (typischerweise mittels Transaktionsgebühr und/oder Blockentschädigung).

Die Dezentralität der Datenbank bringt es mit sich, dass es nicht eine einzige korrekte Version bei allen Teilnehmern des Netzwerks gibt (Asynchronität). Stattdessen muss ein Konsensmechanismus vorhanden sein, auf dessen Basis sich das Netzwerk über die Gültigkeit des nächsten Blocks der Kette einigt, wodurch das Netzwerk zu einer einzigen gültigen Blockchain konvergiert. Das am häufigsten verwendete Konsensprotokoll heisst Proof-of-Work und entschädigt denjenigen, dessen Rechner ein kryptografisches Rätsel am schnellsten lösen kann.

Stärken und Chancen

Die grösste Stärke einer Blockchain ist deren Unveränderbarkeit, welche durch Kryptografie und ein intelligentes Anreizsystem sichergestellt wird. Ein dezentrales Register verfügt zudem nicht über eine einzelne Schwachstelle (‹single point of failure›), dadurch ist es robust gegenüber klassischen IT-Attacken. Durch diese Eigenschaften wird Vertrauen zwischen Akteuren geschaffen, welche sich gegenseitig nicht oder kaum kennen.

Der ökonomische Nutzen lässt sich aus Sicht der Transaktionskostentheorie bewerten und kann in drei Quellen unterteilt werden. Erstens kann das Weglassen von Mittelsmännern die finanziellen Kosten einer Transaktion direkt senken. Zweitens können die Transparenz und Unveränderbarkeit der gesicherten Information die Rechtssicherheit erhöhen. Drittens kann eine Zeitersparnis realisiert werden, wenn in Kombination mit intelligenten Verträgen die Rechtsdurchsetzung automatisiert wird.

Gesellschaftlich könnte Kollektiveigentum und Mitbestimmung an gemeinsamem Eigentum günstiger und damit verbreiteter werden. In Ländern mit schwachem Rechtsstaat können Transaktionen mittels blockchainbasierter Verträge beispielsweise auf Schweizer Recht abgestützt werden. Auch kann der Korruption entgegengewirkt werden, wenn staatlich anerkannte Eigentumsrechte dezentral und rückwirkend unveränderbar aufbewahrt werden.

Schwächen und Risiken

Das zurzeit grösste Problem vieler Blockchains ist ökologischer Natur. Der Proof-of-Work-Konsensmechanismus ist aufgrund seines kompetitiven Charakters extrem energieintensiv. Trotz intensiver Diskussionen in der Blockchain-Gemeinschaft gelang bisher noch keiner Proof-of-Work-Blockchain der vollständige Wechsel zu einer ressourcenschonenden Alternative.

Als gesellschaftliche Herausforderung sollte die Rolle der technologischen Meinungsführer (insbesondere der Gründer einer Blockchain) nicht unterschätzt werden. Die Mehrheit kann nämlich beispielsweise einen sogenannten ‹hard fork› durchführen, d.h. die Regeln einer Blockchain rückwirkend ändern (mangelhafter Minderheitenschutz). Auch ist zu beachten, dass Blockchains und intelligente Verträge zwar theoretisch extrem transparent sind, dass diese aber für einen Normalbürger kaum lesbar sind und Schwachpunkte dadurch nicht identifizierbar sind. Die gesellschaftlichen Risiken der Disruption durch Wegfall von Stellen bei Mittelsmännern lassen sich nicht beziffern, da unklar bleibt, wie viele andere Stellen (z.B. im Blockchain-Ökosystem) entstehen.

Ambivalent ist die Wirkung der Pseudoanonymität einer Blockchain. Der Schutz der Privatsphäre ist einerseits ein hohes Gut und kann andererseits auch für kriminelle Zwecke missbraucht werden. Weiter hat die Pseudoanonymität zur Folge, dass man alle Transaktionen betrachten kann, sobald man die Identität eines Pseudonyms kennt. Kombiniert mit der Unveränderbarkeit bedeutet dies auch, dass kein ‹Recht auf Vergessen› durchgesetzt werden kann.

Anwendungsgebiete

Die in der Studie vorgestellten Anwendungsbeispiele reichen von öffentlichen Grundbüchern, Zahlungssystemen in Flüchtlingslagern, Glückspielen, Versicherungen, öffentlichem e-Voting bis hin zu Herkunftsnachweisen und Energieversorgung. Interessanterweise ist das bekannteste Anwendungsbeispiel, die Kryptowährung, nicht sonderlich vielversprechend. Die erfolgreichen Kryptowährungen tendieren zur Deflation, während die anderen zur Inflation neigen. Die starre Geldmenge, kombiniert mit einem unreglementierten Handel, führt ferner unabhängig davon zu einer erhöhten Volatilität. Relative Preisstabilität ist jedoch ein zentraler Erfolgsfaktor einer verlässlichen Währung.

Disruptive Veränderungen sind zuerst bei den Finanzdienstleistungen zu erwarten, wo bereits heute viele digitale Repräsentationen von Eigentum existieren. Auch bei den Herkunftsnachweisen ist eine starke Erhöhung der Transparenz dank stark sinkender Kosten zu erwarten. Kombiniert mit den dezentralen Handlungsmöglichkeiten, könnte dies insbesondere günstigere und transparentere Emissionshandelssysteme ermöglichen.

Interessanterweise ist die Ausgangslage der Schweiz gut, um von der Blockchain zu profitieren, obwohl das Land in vielen Bereichen als vertrauenswürdiger Mittler auftritt – eine Rolle, welche durch das neue System obsolet werden könnte. Das Vertrauen wird jedoch durch die Blockchain nicht vollständig ersetzt, sondern es verschiebt sich in andere Gebiete, z.B. zur Aufbewahrung und Kontrolle des Zustands der Kollektivgüter in Zollfreilagern, Tresoren oder Bunkern. Auch profitiert die Schweiz von einem liberalen Regulierungsrahmen, welcher Blockchain-Pioniere in die Schweiz (Zug-Zürich) lockt und so eine sich befruchtende Gemeinschaft schuf. In Kombination mit der liberalen Schiedsgerichtspraxis besteht nun die Chance, dass viele intelligente Verträge den Gerichtsstand Schweiz wählen. Im Kontext der Finanz- und mittelfristig auch

Versicherungsbranche müssen die Firmen bereit sein, auch eigene Geschäftsmodelle zu ‹kannibalisieren›, um gestärkt aus dem sich anbahnenden Strukturwandel hervorzugehen.

Grenzen

Die technischen Grenzen der Anwendung von Blockchain-Technologie betreffen primär drei Aspekte: (1) Die Skalierbarkeit ist eingeschränkt, da jeder Block die Blockchain ‹schwerer› werden lässt, was ein dezentrales Netzwerk träge werden lässt. Entsprechend können auch grosse Datenmengen (Bilder, Video etc.) nicht auf der Blockchain gespeichert werden. (2) Objekte im realen Leben haben einen Lebenszyklus (z.B. Rechte erlöschen, Lebensmittel verderben etc.). Intelligente Verträge, welche diese Lebenszyklen nachbilden, müssen Drittpersonen zusätzliche Rechte zuweisen, ohne dabei unerwünschte Hierarchien zu schaffen. (3) Es fehlt eine weltweit anerkannte, sichere digitale Identität, welche für geldwäschereigesetzkompatible, grenzüberschreitende Blockchains zentral wären.

Des Weiteren muss sich die Gesellschaft mit einem solchen System auf eine neue Geisteshaltung einlassen. Traditionell gehen wir heute davon aus, dass für jeden Fehler jemand Verantwortung trägt und zur Rechenschaft gezogen werden kann. Auch vertrauen viele Leute instinktiv einem System mehr, in welchem eine Person aktiv eine Kontrollfunktion wahrnimmt. Die Blockchain-Technologie ist in letzter Konsequenz sicherer, weil menschliche Fehler nicht auftreten. Der probabilistische Ansatz sorgt dafür, dass es unfassbar unwahrscheinlich ist, dass Fehler auftreten. Trotzdem, ein minimales Restrisiko ist systeminhärent und niemand wird die Verantwortung dafür übernehmen.

Résumé

La technologie blockchain est susceptible de devenir l'une des technologies de base les plus importantes pour les échanges commerciaux décentralisés. Son application la plus célèbre est la cryptomonnaie Bitcoin. Mais le Bitcoin à lui seul n'est pas représentatif de son potentiel applicatif. Les blockchains simplifient la propriété collective, fournissent une preuve d'origine sans faille (proof-of-provenance) et peuvent être utilisées pour lutter contre la corruption. La blockchain est en réalité une base de données décentralisée dont le potentiel se déploie avant tout lorsqu'elle est combinée à des contrats intelligents (smart contracts). Un certain nombre d'intermédiaires deviennent ainsi superflus et les coûts de transaction pour le traitement des contrats diminuent. La présente étude décrit les chances et les risques de la technologie blockchain et formule des recommandations d'action concrètes pour en limiter les effets négatifs et en exploiter le potentiel pour la Suisse.

Une blockchain est une base de données décentralisée répliquée sur des serveurs ou des ordinateurs d'entités juridiques indépendantes les unes des autres. Les nouvelles informations ou transactions doivent être signées par l'expéditeur avec sa clé privée. Les transactions sont ensuite regroupées en blocs par les mineurs et scellées à l'aide d'outils cryptographiques, en établissant une référence au bloc précédent. Les mineurs agissent comme des comptables : ils vérifient la validité des transactions soumises, les transforment en blocs et contrôlent la validité des blocs précédents dans la chaîne. Les mineurs sont rémunérés pour cette activité (généralement par le biais de frais de transaction et/ou d'une compensation forfaitaire).

La nature décentralisée de la base de données implique qu'il n'existe pas de version unique correcte pour tous les participants au réseau (asynchronie). Au contraire, elle suppose l'existence d'un mécanisme de consensus qui permet au réseau de se mettre d'accord sur la validité du bloc suivant dans la chaîne, ce qui aboutit à la création d'une seule blockchain valide pour un réseau donné. Le protocole de consensus le plus couramment utilisé est appelé preuve de travail (proof-of-work) et récompense la personne dont l'ordinateur est capable de résoudre le plus rapidement un puzzle cryptographique.

Atouts et opportunités

Le plus grand atout d'une blockchain est son immuabilité, qui est assurée par la cryptographie et par un système d'incitation intelligent. De plus, un registre décentralisé ne comporte pas de point de défaillance unique (single point of failure), ce qui le rend résistant aux attaques informatiques classiques. Ces caractéristiques créent un rapport de confiance entre des acteurs qui ne se connaissent pas ou peu.

L'avantage économique peut être évalué du point de vue de la théorie des coûts de transaction et peut être subdivisé en trois sources. Premièrement, le fait de se passer d'intermédiaires peut directement réduire le coût financier d'une transaction. Deuxièmement, la transparence et l'immuabilité des informations sécurisées peuvent accroître la sécurité juridique. Troisièmement, il est possible de gagner du temps en automatisant l'application de la législation et en la combinant avec des contrats intelligents.

Au niveau sociétal, la propriété collective et la codétermination en propriété commune pourraient devenir moins coûteuses et donc se développer. Dans les pays où l'état de droit est faible, les transactions peuvent par exemple s'appuyer sur le droit suisse au moyen de contrats basés sur la blockchain. Il est également possible de combattre la corruption si les droits de propriété reconnus par l'État sont conservés de manière décentralisée et ne peuvent pas être altérés rétroactivement.

Faiblesses et risques

Actuellement, le plus grand problème de nombreuses blockchains est d'ordre écologique. Le mécanisme de consensus basé sur la preuve du travail consomme une grande quantité d'énergie en raison de sa nature compétitive. Malgré des discussions intensives au sein de la communauté en question, aucune blockchain de preuve de travail n'a encore vraiment réussi à passer à une alternative permettant d'économiser les ressources.

Le rôle des leaders d'opinion technologiques, en particulier celui des fondateurs d'une blockchain, est un défi sociétal qui ne devrait pas être sous-estimé. Par exemple, si une majorité le décide, elle peut procéder à un « hard fork », c'est-à-dire modifier rétroactivement les règles d'une blockchain, au mépris de la protection de la minorité. Il faut aussi souligner que si les blockchains et les contrats intelligents sont extrêmement transparents en théorie, ils sont à peine lisibles pour un citoyen ordinaire, ce qui rend leurs points faibles difficiles à identifier. Les risques sociétaux de disruption liés à la perte d'emplois des intermédiaires ne peuvent être quantifiés car le nombre de postes créés par ailleurs reste incertain (par exemple dans l'écosystème de la blockchain).

L'effet du pseudo anonymat d'une blockchain est ambivalent. La protection de la vie privée est un bien précieux qui peut aussi être utilisée à des fins criminelles. En outre, le pseudo anonymat signifie que toutes les transactions peuvent être consultées dès que l'identité cachée sous un pseudonyme est connue. Combiné à l'immuabilité, cela signifie également qu'il n'existe aucun « droit à l'oubli ».

Domaines d'application

Les exemples d'applications présentés dans l'étude vont des registres fonciers publics aux systèmes de paiement dans les camps de réfugiés, en passant par les jeux de hasard, les assurances, le vote électronique public, les preuves d'origine et l'approvisionnement en énergie. Il est intéressant de noter que l'exemple d'application la plus connue, la cryptomonnaie, n'est pas particulièrement prometteuse. Les cryptomonnaies qui ont du succès ont tendance à être déflationnistes tandis que les autres ont tendance à être inflationnistes. Indépendamment de cela, la rigidité de la masse monétaire combinée à des échanges commerciaux non réglementés conduit en outre à une volatilité accrue. Toutefois, la stabilité relative des prix est un facteur clé de succès pour une monnaie fiable.

Des changements disruptifs sont d'abord à prévoir dans les services financiers, où il existe déjà de nombreuses représentations numériques de la propriété. Les preuves d'origine sont également susceptibles de devenir nettement plus transparentes grâce à une forte baisse des coûts ce qui, combiné aux options d'action décentralisées, pourrait notamment rendre les systèmes d'échange de droits d'émission plus favorables et plus transparents.

Il est intéressant de noter que la Suisse est bien placée pour tirer profit de la blockchain bien que, dans de nombreux domaines, le pays ait un rôle de médiateur fiable que le nouveau système pourrait rendre obsolète. La confiance n'est toutefois pas complètement supplantée par la blockchain et se trouve au contraire transposée dans d'autres domaines tels que la conservation et le contrôle de l'état des biens publics dans des ports francs, des chambres fortes ou des bunkers. La Suisse bénéficie également d'un cadre réglementaire libéral qui attire des pionniers de la blockchain, créant ainsi un terrain fertile pour cette communauté dans notre pays (Zoug-Zurich). Si l'on y ajoute notre pratique d'arbitrage libérale, il y a des chances pour que la Suisse soit désormais choisie comme lieu de juridiction pour de nombreux contrats intelligents. Dans le secteur financier et, à moyen terme, le secteur des assurances, les entreprises doivent être prêtes à « cannibaliser » leurs propres modèles d'entreprise afin de sortir plus fortes du changement structurel qui est sur le point de se produire.

Limites

Les limites techniques d'application de la technologie de la blockchain concernent principalement trois aspects : (1) La scalabilité est limitée car chaque bloc rend la blockchain plus « lourde », ce qui ralentit le réseau décentralisé. Par conséquent, de grandes quantités de données (images, vidéo, etc.) ne peuvent être stockées sur la blockchain. (2) Les objets dans la vie réelle ont un cycle de vie (par exemple, les droits expirent, les denrées alimentaires s'avarient, etc.). Les contrats intelligents qui imitent ces cycles de vie doivent accorder des droits supplémentaires à des tiers sans pour autant créer de hiérarchies indésirables. (3) Il manque une identité numérique sûre et reconnue au niveau international, qui serait au centre des blockchains transfrontalières compatibles avec la législation sur le blanchiment de capitaux.

D'autre part, un tel système présuppose que la société adopte un nouvel état d'esprit. Aujourd'hui, nous partons du principe que, derrière toute erreur, il y a une personne responsable qui peut être tenue de rendre des comptes. De plus, beaucoup de gens font instinctivement davantage confiance à un système sur lequel un être humain exerce activement une fonction de contrôle. Pourtant, la technologie de la blockchain est en réalité plus sûre parce qu'elle exclut toute erreur humaine. Selon l'approche probabiliste, il est presque inconcevable que des erreurs se produisent. Malgré tout, un risque résiduel minimal est inhérent au système et aucun être humain n'en assumera la responsabilité.

Sintesi

La tecnologia blockchain diventerà probabilmente una delle più importanti tecnologie alla base del commercio decentralizzato. La criptovaluta bitcoin, pur essendone l'applicazione più famosa, è solo una pallida espressione del suo potenziale effettivo. La blockchain semplifica la proprietà collettiva, fornisce certificati di origine tracciabili senza soluzione di continuità («proof of provenance») e può essere utilizzata per combattere la corruzione. In sostanza la blockchain è un database decentralizzato, la cui potenza si esprime soprattutto in combinazione con i contratti intelligenti («smart contracts») poiché in molti casi rende superflui gli intermediari e riduce i costi di transazione nell'esecu-zione dei contratti.

Una blockchain è un database decentralizzato che viene replicato sui server o sui computer di persone giuridiche indipendenti. Il mittente deve firmare le nuove informazioni o transazioni con la sua chiave privata. Le transazioni vengono poi raggruppate in blocchi dai cosiddetti minatori e dotate di un sigillo crittografico che appone un riferimento al blocco precedente. I minatori si comportano come dei contabili: controllano l'attendibilità delle transazioni inviate, le trasformano in blocchi e verificano la validità della blockchain fino al punto raggiunto. Per l'attività svolta i minatori ricevono un compenso, in genere in forma di commissione di transazione e/o di premio di blocco.

Data la natura decentralizzata della banca dati, non ne esiste un'unica versione corretta condivisa da tutti i partecipanti alla rete (asincronia). Essa è sostituita da un meccanismo di consenso che la rete utilizza per concordare la validità del blocco successivo della catena, grazie al quale la rete converge verso una sola blockchain valida. Il protocollo di consenso più diffuso viene definito «proof of work» e premia chi ha il computer più rapido a risolvere i puzzle crittografici.

Punti di forza e opportunità

Il principale punto di forza della blockchain è la sua immutabilità, garantita dalla crittografia e da un sistema di incentivi intelligente. A ciò si aggiunge che il registro decentralizzato non presenta un singolo punto di vulnerabilità («single point of failure»), il che lo rende resistente nei confronti dei classici attacchi informatici. Queste caratteristiche favoriscono l'instaurarsi di un'atmosfera di fiducia tra i vari partecipanti, sebbene si conoscano poco o nulla.

Il vantaggio economico si può valutare dal punto di vista della teoria dei costi di transazione e suddividere in tre fonti. Primo, escludere gli intermediari consente di ridurre in modo diretto i costi finanziari delle transazioni. Secondo, la trasparenza e l'immutabilità delle informazioni protette incrementano la certezza del diritto. Terzo, l'applicazione automatizzata della legge grazie alla combinazione con i contratti intelligenti consente di risparmiare tempo.

Dal punto di vista sociale la tecnologia blockchain potrebbe favorire la diffusione della proprietà collettiva e la cogestione della proprietà comune riducendone i costi. Nei Paesi in cui lo Stato di diritto è debole, per le transazioni legate a contratti blockchain-based ci si potrebbe appoggiare per es. al diritto svizzero. Anche la lotta alla corruzione potrebbe guadagnare in efficacia, se i diritti di proprietà statalmente riconosciuti venissero conservati in modo decentralizzato e non fossero alterabili retroattivamente.

Punti deboli e rischi

Al momento il problema principale di molte blockchain è essenzialmente di natura ecologica, in quanto la natura competitiva del meccanismo di consenso «proof of work» lo rende molto dispendioso di energia. Nonostante le accese discussioni all'interno della relativa comunità, finora nessuna blockchain con protocollo PoW è riuscita a completare il passaggio a un'alternativa a basso consumo di risorse.

A livello di sfida sociale, è bene non sottovalutare il ruolo degli opinion leader tecnologici (in particolare dei fondatori di una blockchain). La maggioranza può infatti imporre una cosiddetta «hard fork», cioè modificare retroattivamente le regole di una determinata blockchain (insufficiente tutela della minoranza). Va inoltre osservato che, sebbene in teoria le blockchain e i contratti intelligenti siano estremamente trasparenti, per i comuni cittadini è quasi impossibile decifrarli e dunque identificarne eventuali punti deboli. Non è possibile quantificare i rischi sociali «distruttivi» dovuti alla perdita di posti di lavoro nel settore degli intermediari, poiché non è ancora chiaro quanti altri nuovi posti di lavoro verrebbero a crearsi (ad esempio nell'ecosistema della blockchain).

L'effetto dello pseudoanonimato delle blockchain è ambivalente. Da un lato la tutela della privacy è un bene prezioso, dall'altro può essere sfruttata in modo improprio per scopi criminali. Inoltre lo pseudoanonimato comporta la criticità che basta conoscere l'identità di uno pseudonimo per poter vedere tutte le transazioni a esso legate. In combinazione con la'immodificabilità del database, ciò rende impossibile avvalersi del «diritto all'oblio».

Campi di applicazione

Gli esempi applicativi presentati nello studio spaziano dai registri fondiari pubblici ai sistemi di pagamento nei campi profughi, al gioco d'azzardo, alle assicurazioni, al voto elettronico pubblico e ai certificati di origine fino all'approvvigionamento energetico. È interessante notare che il caso di applicazione più noto, ossia la criptovaluta, non è molto promettente. Le criptovalute di successo tendono alla deflazione, mentre le altre valute all'inflazione. Indipendentemente da ciò, la rigidità dell'offerta di moneta abbinata a un trading non regolamentato comporta anche una maggiore volatilità. La relativa stabilità dei prezzi è invece un fattore di successo cruciale per una moneta affidabile.

La previsione di cambiamenti «distruttivi» riguarda innanzitutto il comparto dei servizi finanziari, dove già oggi esistono svariate rappresentazioni digitali della proprietà. Il forte calo dei costi induce a ipotizzare un deciso incremento della trasparenza anche per quanto riguarda i certificati di origine. Abbinato alle opzioni di negoziazione decentrate, ciò potrebbe incentivare in particolare la diffusione sistemi di scambio delle quote di emissione più economici e trasparenti.

È interessante notare che la Svizzera si trova in una situazione favorevole per sfruttare la blockchain a proprio vantaggio, nonostante il ruolo di mediatore affidabile svolto dal Paese in molti settori, che il nuovo sistema potrebbe rendere obsoleto. La tecnologia blockchain non rende comunque superflui i rapporti di fiducia, ma tende piuttosto a trasferirli in altri ambiti, come la custodia e il controllo delle condizioni dei beni pubblici in depositi franchi doganali, camere blindate e bunker. La Svizzera beneficia peraltro di un quadro normativo liberale, che ha attratto sul proprio territorio (Zugo-Zurigo) i pionieri della blockchain e favorito la creazione di una comunità feconda. Questo quadro, combinato con la pratica liberale dell'arbitrato, dischiude l'opportunità che per molti contratti intelligenti venga eletta la Svizzera a foro competente. Nel settore finanziario e, a medio termine, anche in quello assicurativo le imprese dovranno essere disposte a «cannibalizzare» i propri modelli di business per uscire rinforzate dal cambiamento strutturale che si va delineando.

Limiti

I limiti tecnico-applicativi della tecnologia blockchain riguardano principalmente tre aspetti: (1) la scalabilità è limitata perché ogni blocco «appesantisce» ulteriormente la blockchain, il che rallenta la rete decentralizzata e rende inoltre impossibile memorizzare nella blockchain grandi quantità di dati (immagini, video, ecc.). (2) Nella realtà le cose hanno un ciclo di vita (ad es. i diritti decadono, il cibo si deteriora, ecc.). I contratti intelligenti che riproducono questi cicli vitali devono assegnare diritti aggiuntivi a terzi, senza però creare gerarchie indesiderate. (3) Non esiste un'identità digitale sicura riconosciuta a livello globale, che invece è essenziale per blockchain transfrontaliere compatibili con la legge sul riciclaggio di denaro.

Inoltre un sistema di questo genere costringe la società ad aprirsi a una nuova mentalità. Oggi diamo ancora per scontato che per ogni errore esista un responsabile che possa essere chiamato a risponderne. A ciò si somma il fatto che molte persone tendono d'istinto a fidarsi più dei sistemi controllati attivamente da esseri umani. In ultima analisi però la tecnologia blockchain è più sicura proprio perché esclude l'errore umano. L'approccio probabilistico rende estremamente remota l'eventualità che si verifichino errori. Tuttavia nel sistema è comunque insito un minimo rischio di cui nessuno è responsabile.

1. Introduction

Over the past two years, a technology available since the launch of Bitcoin in January 2009 has been hyped as a revolution in information technology. Blockchain is the core technology behind buzzwords such as cryptocurrency, ICO[1], smart contract, Internet 4.0, the contractual web, and the internet of money. Because of this excitement surrounding blockchain, many wonder whether it can hold up to its promise of 'changing money, business, and the world', as Don Tapscott, author and blockchain proponent, advocates. If blockchain changes the world, then we must analyse how different aspects of life will eventually be affected by it. What will be its impact on business and the economy, what new legislation is needed? Does it have an effect on the environment, and will society change due to blockchain?

At its core, blockchain is a decentralised database that allows the enhancement of trust by cryptographically securing all transactions verifiably and permanently. This is why The Economist called blockchain 'the trust machine' (The Economist, 2015). Many transactions require the trust of its users, as delivery and payment do not always occur simultaneously. A simple, direct exchange of goods, say an apple for an orange, is 'trust-less' because the exchange can occur without needing someone else to record, track, or verify the interchange of fruit. However, a trade involving 10,000 pairs of jeans from a Chinese garment factory for delivery to Switzerland in four months requires trust from both sides. Today, many interactions require some form of verification from intermediaries. In this trade example, the intermediary third party is a bank. As another example, when buying fair-trade bananas, we trust the distribution company that the bananas were produced under fair-trade terms. As with any service provider, intermediaries are compensated for their service. This expense becomes part of the transaction costs involved in the exchange of goods and services. If trust can be shifted from intermediaries to an

---

[1] ICO stands for 'initial coin offerings', a form of blockchain based crowd funding. For a more detailed explanation, see the Glossary or Chapter 6.1.3.

automated technology, such as blockchain, then transaction costs would be lowered when exchanging goods for money, investing, and for proofs of existence, integrity, authenticity, or provenance.

To realise more of its potential, blockchain can be combined with smart contracts and the Internet of Things (IoT). Smart contracts are self-executing contractual agreements written in computer code, thereby circumventing legal uncertainties of normal written contracts and further reducing transaction costs. Examples include insurances written as smart contracts that automatically execute payment to the insured when certain conditions are met. IoT devices can act as sensors integrated with software to report relevant parameters to a database like blockchain. More potent smart contracts are possible by combining them with IoT devices, such as a smart contract to ensure the authenticity of pharmaceuticals by recording and evaluating IoT sensor data against a blockchain to solve the trust issue created by counterfeit drugs in developing countries.

Because blockchain is a new technology, there remain numerous challenges to address, including technical (e.g., scalability and interoperability of blockchains), ecological (e.g., immense power consumption is required for operating current public blockchain solutions), and legal (e.g., written requirements for a legally valid transfer of tokens).

This study assesses both the challenges and potential of blockchain with the complementary technologies of smart contracts and IoTs from a theoretically technical perspective as well as through 12 use cases covering a broad spectrum of industries and applications. From electronic ID and land registries to gambling and electronic voting as well as supply-chain management and microgrids, the use cases illustrate that many of the current implementations of blockchain offer only marginal benefits over state-of-the-art centralised solutions. However, these implementations may have far more significant economic potential and societal benefits once the remaining legal and technological challenges have been resolved. For a deeper understanding of the technologies used and the issues faced, we offer insights into the most important aspects of blockchain technology and the basics of cryptography, which forms the backbone of blockchains. Finally, we look at the legal, ecological, and social aspects of blockchain technology to complement the perspective of economic potential and business opportunities.

The legal issues revolve around how blockchain-based digital assets (tokens) are classified to fit into current legal and regulatory frameworks. The main challenges exist in the application of anti-money-laundering laws and the necessary changes to existing laws for the legal transfer of tokens. Ecologically, blockchains are an enormous burden due to required processing power. However, this is a temporary problem that newer iterations of the technology should no longer exhibit. The ecological upside depends on the greater accountability that unchangeable blockchain records offer. The social impact of blockchain results from structural changes that reduced transaction costs could bring to many industries as well as through the number of blockchain projects that aim to do social good.

From our extensive analysis of many facets of blockchain, we distill the overall potential along with the challenges the technology faces. This, in turn, allows us to propose multiple concrete recommendations to businesses, governments, and the general public.

As an introduction to one use case environment, we briefly review where Switzerland currently stands in terms of blockchain. Since blockchain remains a nascent industry, the number of start-ups and blockchain-based start-up funding (initial coin offerings or ICO) are reasonable measures of the market attractiveness. In Switzerland, most start-ups are concentrated in and around Zug and Zurich. Figure 1 shows that, beyond Zug and Zurich, the only other small cluster of companies exist on the shores of Lake Geneva (cantons Geneva and Vaud). This suggests that Switzerland as a country is not yet a 'crypto-nation'. Rather, it is Zug with its numerous blockchain start-ups, blockchain-related service providers, and its proximity to the second largest Swiss cluster in Zurich that constitutes a blockchain innovation centre of world renown, called Crypto Valley. In Zug, the culture of privacy protection, confidentiality, and legal certainty of all Switzerland is paired with a generally business-friendly environment and the supportive and open-minded cantonal and communal authorities. These are the main reasons why Zug is so attractive for blockchain companies. Moreover, with every additional company settling down in Zug, the network effects become larger, therefore constantly attracting more and more companies into Crypto Valley.

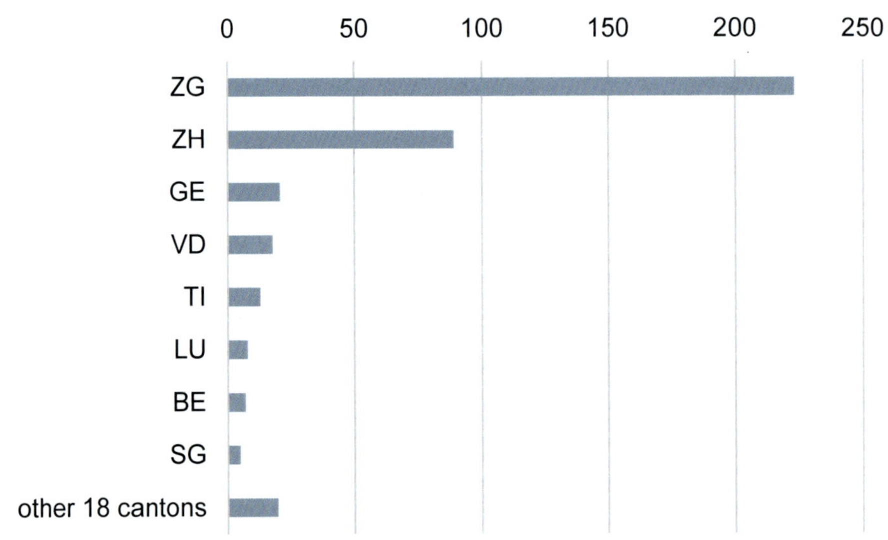

Source: cryptovalley.directory and IWSB.

Figure 1. Distribution of blockchain companies in Switzerland (June 2018).

2. Basics of Cryptography

Blockchain and smart contract technology hold the promise of providing trust between parties unknown to one another. At its core, this trust relies on cryptography, which has a long history of advances in IT security on the one hand along with loophole and security-breaking discoveries on the other. This race is still on, and there are no signs that it will soon come to an end. Currently, the progress with quantum computers that could break existing security algorithms are of major concern and spur new research on quantum-resilient security algorithms. In addition to security, this development reflects the broader debate between two public interests: the extent to which privacy should be guaranteed and the instruments of law enforcement agencies.

Although essential for acceptance of blockchain technology, the variety of cryptographic security aspects is too broad to be fully explored within the scope of this study. It also requires in-depth mathematical knowledge. Instead, we would like the interested reader to become familiar with the basics of cryptography relevant to blockchain technology and the terms most often used. We highlight four essential aspects:

1. the concept of hashing,
2. the probability of collisions,
3. public key cryptosystems,
4. the safety of the private key.

These concepts are not specific to blockchain technology as they are already widely in use throughout the digital landscape. We focus less on the underlying maths but illustrative examples to better understand the fundamentals of blockchain and smart contract technologies.[2]

---

[2] For further reading, we recommend Antonopoulos (2017).

2.1. Hashing

A hash function is an algorithm that converts data of any size into a *fixed length data string*. One of the most used hash functions is the *Secure Hash Algorithm 256* or *SHA256*, which generates a string of 256 bits. If the data are a video larger than a Gigabyte, a multi-megabyte picture or a text message of only a few bytes, the output is always a constant 256 bits. For the sake of convenience, the 256 bit-string is normally represented with 64 hexadecimal characters in the hash output (Table 1).

For any algorithm, an identical input generates the same result. So, in the hashing case, the same input data always generates the same hash output value.[3] However, there is one essential difference with other algorithms. While in many algorithms a minor change of the input value results in nearby output values, at least in predictable orders of magnitude, the slightest change in the input data of a secure hash algorithm results in an entirely different hash value, even if it the change is only a single colour value of a pixel in an image, a comma or space in a text document or the third digit after the comma in a number, as is demonstrated in Table 1.

[3] For this reason, hashes are often used as an identifier in big databases, which are known as hash tables.

Table 1. Transformation of a string using the SHA-256 hash function.

Input	SHA-256 output (256-bit binary format)	64-symbol hex representation[4]
Hello World	101001011001000110100110110101000000101111110100001000000100000000100101000000001000101110011001111001111101101111011000110010000110101100010110001100101101111110000010111100110110100011001010110101011110110010011101111110110011010110110011111000101000110111 0	a591a6d40bf420404a011733cfb7b190d62c65bf0bcda32b57b277d9ad9f146e
Hello, World	0000001101100111010110101100010100111111111110011100110100010101001101011100110011000111110111111100110111111010001011000100010110001100010100100001100000110111000111110100000110001101110000001001101101111001011010001100110101100000111111011111101000101001 01	03675ac53ff9cd1535ccc7dfcd-fa2c458c5218371f418dc136f2d19ac1fbe8a5

Source: Banking Concepts.

This characteristic results in two consequences:

- Applying the same hash function to the same input data, e.g., a data file, makes it possible to verify whether the input data has been altered.

---

[4] The hexadecimal system uses 16 symbols (the numbers 0–9 and characters a-f). As each hexadecimal digit represents four binary digits (bits), it allows a more human-friendly representation of binary-coded values. One hexadecimal digit represents 4 bits, which is half of a byte (8 bits). For example, a single byte can have values ranging from 00000000 to 11111111 in binary form, and this can be more conveniently represented as 00 to FF in hexadecimal.

- For a secure hash algorithm, it is *impossible to predict* the exact hash value or a range of hash values for a given change in the input data.

The second aspect above represents the essential characteristic of a good hash function and is of utmost importance for the security of the blockchain. If it would be possible to predict the outcome of a change of the input data, even by order of magnitude, or detect certain patterns in the hash values from permutations of the input data, e.g., a change appears only in the first ten digits of a 256-bit string, then a blockchain would no longer be secure. In other words, a defining criterion for a good hash function is that the hash value is *randomly and evenly* distributed over the output range.

The randomness of the output also implies that if, for instance, we want to generate a 256-bit string with a certain characteristic, e.g., a certain number of consecutive zeros at the beginning of the string, such as 000000001110100..., then we can only try by repeatedly applying different inputs. As will be demonstrated later, this is one reason why mining processes for the most prominent cryptocurrencies of Bitcoin and Ether are so energy intensive.

Another important characteristic of a secure hash function is that it works only in one direction, so it is impossible to generate the input data from a given hash value. The first reason for this is that, theoretically, there could be more than one input for one hash value. In other words, it is possible that different input data generate the same hash value. This scenario is referred to as a *collision*. However, as will be seen later, the likelihood of a collision is extremely low. The second reason is an explosion of possible variants that would need to be tested to identify the correct input data. Even if we knew that the input string had 'only' 256-bit or 32 ASCII-8 characters, we would still require quantum computers[5] to have a chance at identifying the correct input data. Attempts to identify the input data for a given hash value are called *pre-image attacks*.

---

[5] Quantum computers are described in Chapter 2.5.

2.2. 2^{256} or the power of big numbers

Cryptography operates through *probabilities*. Relying on probabilities, even when low, often causes uneasiness if the associated risks cannot be translated into our everyday life. To illustrate the power of big numbers in cryptography, we take the SHA256 algorithm described above and calculate how many combinations can be built from a 256-bit string.

$2^{256} \approx 1.16 * 10^{77} =$ 115 000 000 000 000 000 000 000 000 000 000 000 000 000 000 000 000 000 000 000 000 000 000 000 000 000 000

Since this number is so large that it is abstract to our understanding, we approximate it with real-world examples based on atoms. The human body consists mostly of water with approximately 10^{19} atoms. Most of the earth consists of iron and, taking this as a base, the earth has about 10^{49} atoms. There exist an estimated 10^{11} to 10^{12} stars in our galaxy and 10^{23} stars in the universe. The number of atoms in the known universe containing billions of galaxies is estimated between 10^{78} and 10^{82}. *So, as a rough approximation, a 256-bit string is enough to identify every atom in the known universe uniquely.*

From this comparison, we can then easily imagine that the probability of generating the same hash value from different inputs is extremely low.

- A collision is as likely as picking the same atom in the known universe (Antonopoulos, 2017b) with an occurrence of 1 of 2^{128} chance.
- A collision is as likely as it is to win the jackpot of the Euro Millions lottery more than nine times in a row.[6]

This unlikelihood offers a key implication for blockchain technology.

Traditional identifiers in commercial or public applications or registers assign every person or object a unique identifier, which is tested on its uniqueness *before* being used. For blockchain, account numbers are generated independently from a blockchain, so this technology relies on the fact that the

6 The chance of winning the jackpot one time is 1 in 139,838,160. Winning nine times sequentially is 1 in $2.04 * 10^{73}$.

likelihood of generating two identical numbers is very low. The same number, then, can also be used on multiple blockchains.

This concept is quite different from what we are familiar. Imagine if a bank assigned us the same account number previously given to another person and all money flowing into this account could be used by each of us independently. What would we do? As an honest person, we would ask the bank to correct the error or, in case our money was spent, reclaim possible damage. This scenario is not possible with blockchain technology. If a collision occurred, i.e., the same account number is generated twice, both account owner could still use any of the money. However, blockchain technology relies on the assumption that this will not happen due to an extremely low probability. During December 2017, a quick Internet search suggested that no proven collision for Bitcoin has yet been reported. A research project exists that generates trillions of keys to gain random access to Bitcoin funds, and has yet to demonstrate any success (Roberts, 2017). For even stronger security scenarios, cryptography is not limited to 256-bit as hash functions with 384- and 512-bit are already in place.[7] As will be described later, this small risk can be further mitigated by using permission instead of permissionless blockchains.

2.3. Public key cryptosystems and digital signatures

2.3.1. Public key cryptosystems

All blockchain systems are based on public-key cryptography, an asymmetric key cryptosystem dating back to the 1970s.[8] Today, it is used in various appli-

[7] An overview of the adoption of SHA functions can be found online at: https://www.csoonline.com/article/3256088/hacking/why-arent-we-using-sha3.html

[8] A major breakthrough was an article by Whitfiled Diffie and Martin Hellman (1976), in which they disclosed a method of public key distribution over unsecured networks, which later became known as the Diffie-Hellman key exchange.

cations, such as RSA, PGP, and SSH, to encrypt messages or secure the communication between servers and clients over insecure networks.[9]

In a public key cryptosystem, a pair of keys that are mathematically linked is generated. One part of the key-pair is public (the public key), and the other part must remain strictly secret (the private key). The algorithm that generates the key pair is designed such that with today's computers it is practically infeasible for an attacker to derive the private key from a given public key.[10]

A key pair can be used for two purposes:

- secure communication,
- a digital signature.

For secure communication, the public key of the recipient is used to *encrypt* confidential data, and the private key of the recipient is used to *decrypt* the data. So, once encrypted with a public key, the data can only be decrypted with the corresponding private key of the recipient. Even the sender would not be able to decrypt the message if the original input is not stored (e.g., a voice message not stored locally by the sender). Figure 2 illustrates message encryption using a private key.

In a blockchain, the digital signature property of a public key cryptosystem is also used. With a digital signature, data are signed with the private key of the sender, and everyone can verify its validity with the public key of the sender. A digital signature simultaneously provides authentication (who is the sender?), data integrity (has the data been manipulated after sending?), and non-repudiation (the finality of a transaction), all of which are essential to blockchains.

The difference between encryption and a digital signature is essential. Confidentiality is achieved by encrypting a message or transaction with the *public*

---

[9] The security of systems depends on the lengths of the keys in use. An impression of the variety of recommendations is provided by Bluecrypt at https://www.keylength.com

[10] The safety of private keys is addressed in the following chapter.

key of the recipient, and a digital signature uses the *private key* to sign data and provide authentication. Blockchain technology is based on digital signatures.

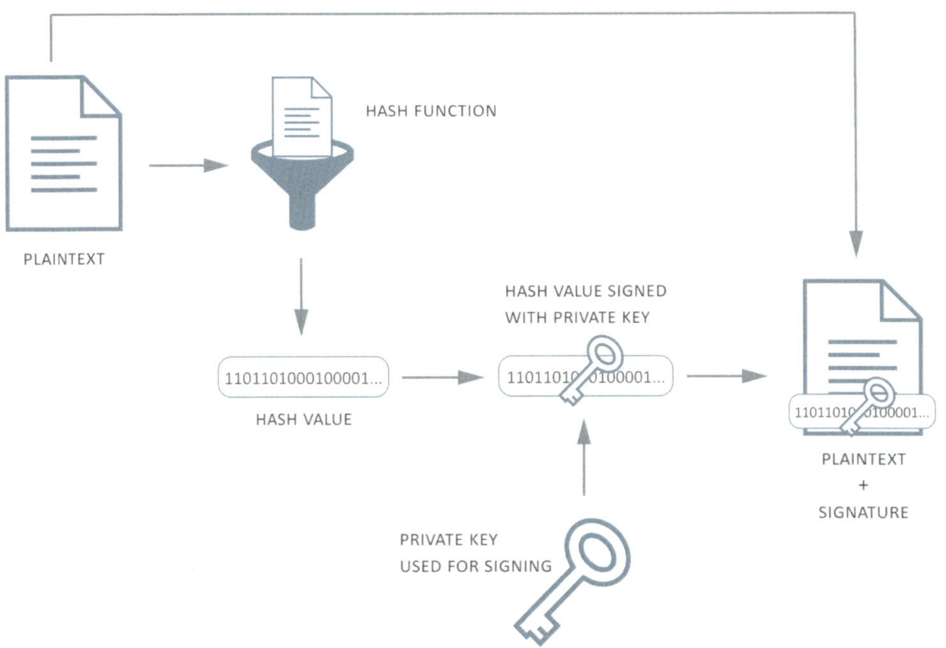

Source: Banking Concepts.

Figure 2. Message encryption using a private key.[11]

2.3.2. Digital signatures in blockchain technology

Digital signatures are decisive to blockchain technology as they are needed to prove ownership of an asset. Before using a blockchain, a public-private key-pair, called a wallet, must first be created. Table 2 shows such a key-pair.

---

[11] As Figure 2 summarises, signing data of a transaction occurs through the hashing of the input data and combining it with the private key from a mathematical algorithm.

Table 2. Example of a Bitcoin public-private key pair example.

Public key (Base58 encoded)	Private key
1P8BaU4QekeuaZUxLhrMdHzrRnYzzbzFZr	L4bHA722WFFVuUabqL1fGbkmkvpPySh5MedyhHoTYogxoLPydsr9

Source: Banking Concepts.

Various algorithms to generate key pairs exist and are normally provided by the software with which the user gains access to a blockchain, also called wallet applications. Users are prompted to note the private key or, more commonly, as the manual recording might be error-prone, a recovery passphrase consisting of up to 24 different words. These passphrases are called brain wallets. The private key is typically stored in a secure environment on the computer or the mobile device. Some wallet applications, however, store the private key on a server of the provider.

When Bitcoin or Ether are transferred from one owner to another, the sender signs the transaction with a private key before it is broadcasted to the rest of the network. The peers in the network that receive the transaction can verify with thc public key that the sender is the legitimate owner. After this signature verification, the transaction is considered valid and is relayed to other peers, ultimately ending up in the blockchain. Once the tokens are legitimately sent and recorded on the blockchain, the recipient can 'unlock' the assets because only can they produce a valid signature from the tokens that have been sent to their address. If someone tries to create a bogus transaction by sending funds from an address they do not own, then the signature is shown as invalid, and the transaction is rejected. Alternatively, if a malicious actor tries to alter a transaction by removing the recipient address and substituting it with their own or by changing the amount sent, then the signature is marked invalid.

2.3.3. Safety of private keys

In a system where digital signatures are used for claiming ownership, anyone who has the private key of a user can spend their funds, for example. The protection of the private key is decisive to the safety of blockchains and, hence, to the funds the user owns. Often, users are not aware of the importance of a private key because, despite explicit instructions and warnings, private keys are photographed, stored in unsecured files or given to service providers, such as with crypto-exchanges, which can theoretically access the user's funds on a blockchain – and have been subject to fraud and hacker attacks.[12] People rely on the notion that assets are protected by law and could be legally reclaimed through providing enough evidence. This assumption does not hold for blockchain technology. Blockchain technology assumes that the owner of a private key is eligible for any transaction, regardless of whether the key has been stolen. It is much harder, if not impossible, to reclaim ownership of assets that have been transferred with a legitimate private key. There is not much of difference when relying on a service provider to manage a user's private key for transferring money at a bank, which many crypto-enthusiasts claim they cannot trust and would like to take out of the equation. Apart from this, such services providers are far less regulated than banks.

The same importance applies for lost keys. If the private key is lost, then funds can no longer be accessed, making them impossible to recover. To mitigate this fundamental risk of use, some applications offer key recovery services.[13] The idea behind these services is either to hold redundant copies of the private key or give other people access to the assets with multiple collective signatures.[14]

Another security risk can arise from the use of the brain wallets,[15] which use 12 or 24 words from a dictionary with 2048 words to generate a better memorable and less error-prone recovery phrase for the private key. While the probability of a pre-image attack remains low, human negligence is still likely to be more dangerous.

---

[12] The collapse of the Japanese bitcoin exchange Mt. Gox is the most prominent example of such an attack. See McMillan (2014) for a more information on the collapse of Mt. Gox.

[13] See, for example, https://bitgo.freshdesk.com/support/solutions/folders/27000052895 and https://nem.io/project/nem-key-recovery-service-krs/

[14] A similar approach is the use of an algorithm that creates a set of recovery words for each private key to be split among trusted parties. When creating the recovery set, it can be defined how many of the recovery words are needed to recreate the private key.

[15] For a detailed account of the risks, see Courtois, Song, and Castellucci (2016).

So, from a technical perspective, how safe is the private key of a public key cryptosystem? How likely is it that someone can discover a private key by iterating through billions or trillions of trials? To assess this risk, we must remember that, strongly simplified, today's computers process information linearly. So, public key infrastructures 'link public and private keys using factors of a number that is the product of two incredibly large prime numbers. To determine the private key from the public key alone, one would have to figure out the factors of this product of primes. Even if a classical computer tested a trillion keys a second, it would take up to 785 million times longer than the roughly 14 billion years the universe has existed so far' (Sharma, 2017). However, it is often cited that quantum computing, because of its exponential computing power, might impose a substantial risk to existing public key cryptosystems, such as RSA.[16] Because quantum computing remains a generic risk and not specific to blockchain technology, we will explain its principles and summarise the risk with a discussion in Chapter 2.5.

2.4. Zero-knowledge proof

Over the last few years as an alternative to public key cryptography, researchers developed methods to prove the ownership of assets without revealing the public key. More generally speaking, these approaches try to prove to a verifier that the owner has some secret knowledge without revealing the secret (or only a portion of it). These methods have become known as zero-knowledge proof or ZKP. The basic principle has been available known for more than three decades, and it regained popularity over the last few years due to blockchain technology and some preceding algorithmic discoveries (Ben-Sasson, Chiesa, Tromer, & Virza, 2015) known as zk-SNARKs. As discussed later, these discoveries have far-reaching consequences on the anonymity of transactions by shifting the trade-off between transparency and crime prevention and the right for privacy to a new level.

[16] For instance, see Eperiesi-Beck (2017) and Nordrum (2016).

2.4.1. Zero-knowledge proof explained

In a zero-knowledge proof process, there is the prover and the verifier. A prover can prove to the verifier that they possess certain knowledge (announced in a statement) without revealing the actual knowledge to the verifier. Three criteria must be met by an algorithm to qualify for zero-knowledge proof (Schor, 2018):

- *Completeness*. If the statement is true, then an honest verifier can be convinced of it by an honest prover.
- *Soundness*. If the prover is dishonest, then they cannot convince the verifier of the soundness of the statement through lying.
- *Zero-knowledge*. If the statement is true, then the verifier will have no idea what the statement is.

A zero-knowledge proof can be easily explained through several well-known examples. The following are two cases, which are the most intuitive to illustrate the principles.

Alibaba's cave

This example is taken from a YouTube video by Scott Twomby (2016) and illustrated in Figure 3. A prover (P) wants to prove to a verifier (V) that they know the password to a secret door at the back of a cave without telling the verifier the password.

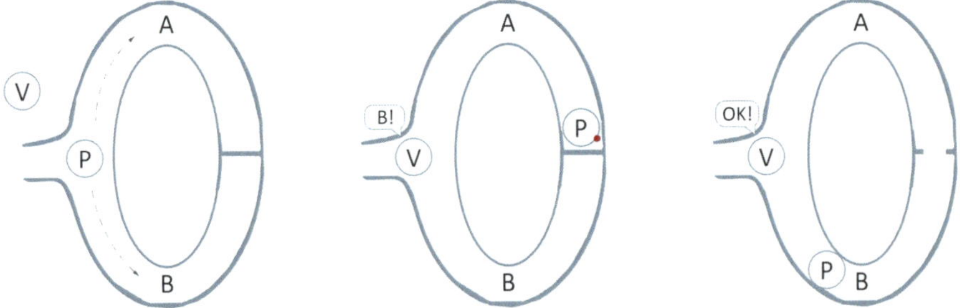

Source: Banking Concepts based on Scott Twomby (2016).

Figure 3. Illustration of the zero-knowledge proof.

'The Prover goes down any of the paths A and B, suppose they initially decide to go through path A and reach the secret door at the back. When they do so, the verifier V comes in at the entrance, with no knowledge of which path the prover took and declares that they want to see the prover appear from path B.

In the diagram, as you can see, the prover does indeed appear in path B. But what if this was dumb luck? What if the prover didn't know the pass code, and took the path B, was stuck at the door and by sheer fortune, the verifier told him to appear from path B, the one they were originally on anyway?

So, to test the validity, the experiment is done multiple times. If the prover can appear at the correct path every single time, it proves to the verifier that the prover indeed knows the password even though the verifier does not know what the password actually is' (Blockgeeks.com, n.d.).

Colour blind friend

'We have a colour-blind friend who owns two pens, which are identical except that one is green and the other one is blue (including the ink). Our friend cannot distinguish between them, and we want to convince him that the pens are indeed different. Of course, we cannot do this by simply telling him the colours, because he cannot assess whether we're lying or not.

So, what can we do? (Why not take a minute and try to work out the answer yourself ...) Well, we can ask him to take a piece of paper and draw two lines on it in another room. When doing this, he can freely decide whether to use the same pen for both lines or one pen for each. From his perspective, the result looks the same either way. Then he comes back in with the paper, and I tell him whether he used one pen or two. Of course, if the pens were the same colour, I would have no way of knowing. So, the fact that I get it right proves they are different.

Well, not quite. There is a problem with this logic. Even if the pens were identical, I would still have a 50% chance of giving the right answer, because there are only two possibilities (he used one pen or two). So, one lucky guess proves nothing at all. In order to strengthen my case, the game must be played over multiple rounds. After every round, my chance of being consistently right goes down by half. So, with 5 rounds, I have a 1 in 32 chances of successfully faking. With 10 rounds, It is 1 in 1024, and with 20 rounds, 1 in 1048576 – in other words, one in a million. Depending on my friend's relative level of boredom and suspicion, he can reach any probabilistic level of proof that he desires, although never absolute certainty' (Greenspan, 2016).

As we can see in the examples above, zero-knowledge proof relies on the fact that, due to the number of iterations required, the probability of lying about a statement tends exponentially toward zero. The verifier can define any level of confidence at the cost of playing more rounds. There is no absolute certainty in zero-knowledge proof. Just as in cryptography, there are unimaginably small probabilities, which can be reasonably assumed are several orders of magnitudes smaller than the probability of a human making an error in a verification process. However, this claim does not consider the uneasiness of such small probabilities as the logical part of the brain are trained to operate digitally.

2.4.2. Zk-Snarks and blockchain

From the examples above, the verification process of zero-knowledge proof always requires a simultaneous interaction between the prover and the verifier. Without diving into technical details, the major recent inventions of zk-Snarks were that a zero-knowledge proof could be algorithmically achieved, and, more importantly, it can be achieved without simultaneous interaction. This opens a new dimension of anonymity, which, as will be seen later, has a substantial impact on the adoption of blockchain technology for privacy reasons as well as for reducing abuse from criminal purposes.

2.5. Quantum computing

Because blockchain technology fosters the use of private key infrastructures, another aspect of the security that attracts public discussion is quantum computing. Quantum computers take advantage of quantum physics. As opposed to traditional computers, which process one bit at a time, a quantum computer processes qubits, which allow multiple calculations on a bit per time along an exponential curve. Table 3 outlines the potential capabilities of quantum computing.

Table 3. The number of calculations per time unit possible with quantum computers.

2 qubits	equals to	2^2	equals to	4
10 qubits	equals to	2^{10}	equals to	1024
30 qubits	equals to	2^{30}	equals to	≈1 billion

Source: Banking Concepts.

'The capacity to compute using qubits renders quantum computers many orders of magnitude faster than classical computers. Google showed a D-Wave quantum annealing computer could be https://www.wired.co.uk/article/google-quantum-computing-d-wave[17] than classical computers at certain specialized tasks. And Google and IBM are working on their own quantum computers' (Sharma, 2017).

However, quantum computers require special algorithms to solve problems, and research on such algorithms has only recently gained pace. In 2017, a report in the *MIT Technology Review* (Juskalian, 2017) notes that production availability is expected within the next four to five years. Other research shows that even today, 'the most popular public-key algorithms, [ ] can be efficiently broken by a sufficiently strong hypothetical quantum computer' (Wikipedia, 2018a).

On the other hand, work on 'quantum-safe' cryptography is also underway. In 2016, the U.S. National Institute of Standards and Technology (NIST) started 'Open Quantum Safe', a project for developing and prototyping quantum-resistant cryptography (Wikipedia, 2018a). This class of research is referred to as post-quantum cryptography and is expected to replace public key cryptosystems and public key signatures in a modular way wherever they are used today.

[17] Quotation links to Reynolds (2015).

2.6. Conclusion

A few conclusions that may be drawn from the basics of cryptography are summarised as follows:

- Cryptography relies on low probabilities. For humans, it is hard to translate these probabilities into real-world experience. As we rely on human control, the probability of human errors proves to be much higher than any error that might occur from cryptographic methods.
- Although collisions and pre-image attacks are highly unlikely, diversification of accounts and addresses appear to be an appropriate means to psychologically coping with this uneasiness for working with cryptographic technologies. In addition, insurances could be provided for losses occurring from a collision or pre-image attack, which should be inexpensive due to the extremely low probabilities.
- While quantum computing may pose a potential risk for blockchain security, it is not blockchain specific and will broadly affect computer system security. Hence, the risks of quantum computing attacks must be approached from a global scale, as otherwise no electronic transaction would be safe in the future. As discussed, quantum computing-resilient algorithms are already a focus of researchers, and it can be expected that, as quantum computing progresses, quantum computing resilience will also advance.

3. Blockchain Technology

Blockchain technology is also referred to as a trust engine[18] or trust machine as it enables business between parties unknown to each other without involving a trusted intermediary to organise the exchange of assets.[19]

Blockchain technology derives its trust from two concepts (see Figure 4):

1. The continuous validation of transactional data, their packaging into blocks in constant time intervals and their cryptographical linkage in a continuously growing chain. A cryptographical linkage makes it impossible to alter a transaction without rechaining all the blocks added to the chain after the altered transaction. This chaining of blocks process is from where the term 'blockchain technology' is derived.
2. The replication of the blockchain data across a set of computers owned by different individuals or businesses. Computers that participate in a blockchain are called nodes. A consensus protocol built into the blockchain software ensures how the blockchain data are synchronised between the nodes. The more nodes participating, the harder it becomes to tamper with the data, which is why the technology is also referred to as distributed ledger technology (DLT).

---

[18] See https://www.ubs.com/microsites/blockchain-report/en/home.html

[19] Blockchain technology does not replace trust completely as it cannot enforce promises (e.g., the repayment of a loan), but it facilitates the concurrent exchange of assets and the handling of collateral.

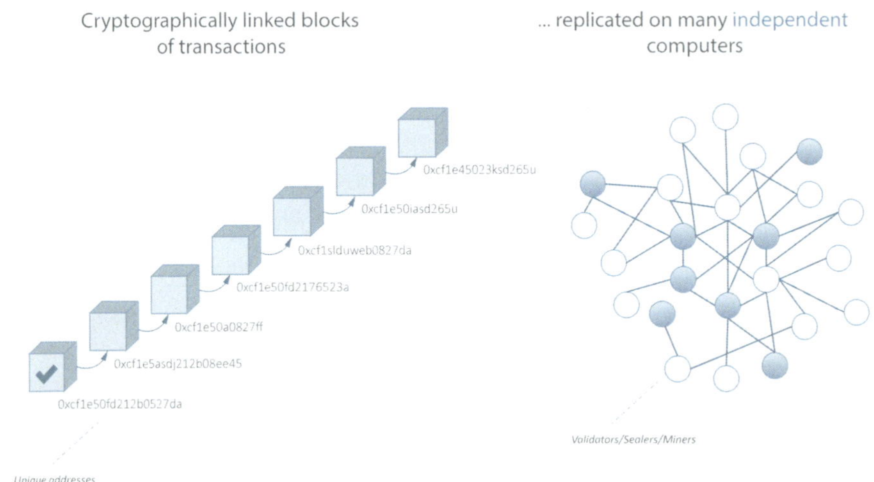

Source: Banking Concepts.

Figure 4. The essence of blockchain technology.

A blockchain is *a decentralised database* that is *replicated* on many servers or computers owned or governed by *independent* legal entities.

Trust in a blockchain depends on two factors:

1. The low probability that one person or a group of persons have enough power to alter a transaction, recalculate all blocks after the transaction and force the remaining participants to accept these changes. A smaller chance of this scenario results in a higher level of trust.
2. The governance mechanisms for the changes of the software and consensus protocol. With better checks and balances in the development of the software supporting the distributed ledger, a higher level of trust is established. A drawback to having proper checks and balances is that needed changes to the software protocol may take longer and errors might not be corrected quickly. However, this result is part of the nature of democratic decision-making.

Blockchain or distributed ledger technology is a radical shift from a world where one person or company control software to one where groups of people, companies or entire communities determine the evolution of the software.

New systems must be designed from scratch, and upgrades of the software are likely to take longer in order to reach consensus. Internal control systems, even those required by law, cannot be applied easily to blockchain technology as the final responsibility of development lies with a community. The industry remains in the early stages of understanding the implications of blockchain technology and how to design these systems that will both generate economic benefits and be controllable. In this chapter, we explain this paradigm shift from a technical perspective, beginning with understanding when and why the concept was first created.

3.1. The origin of blockchain technology

The concept of a blockchain first appeared in 2008 to solve the so-called double-spend problem for the Bitcoin payment system. Similar to the more than 1,000 cryptocurrencies available today, a Bitcoin is a digital token that can be used for payment purposes. As a digital entity and without further control, Bitcoin could be easily reproduced or *double spent*.[20]

The initial purpose of the blockchain was to ensure that tokens could be spent only once, and that a payment transaction, once validated, could not be repudiated. To achieve this, every Bitcoin transaction is validated by the network and placed into a public, distributed ledger. In this ledger, all transactions are grouped into blocks and cryptographically secured and linked. These linked blocks form the *blockchain*. Data can only be added to the database (i.e., the distributed ledger) through insertion to the next block, which, in Bitcoin, is built on average every 10 minutes. The cryptographical securing and linking of the blocks makes it substantially harder to tamper with the data because, in order to change a previous transaction, all subsequent blocks must be recalculated, relinked, and accepted by all network ledger participants.

Every participant of the network can download the ledger and revalidate every transaction with minuscule effort to be sure that no one manipulated the own-

[20] As opposed to physical money that cannot be easily reproduced and where there are judges and courts to arbitrate case of disputes.

ership of the tokens. In order to send Bitcoin to another party, the sender must specify the amount, sign the data using a private key, encrypt it using the address (public key) of the recipient, and send the transaction to the network where it is validated. This validation process for Bitcoins consists of two functions: The first checks whether the sender is the legitimate owner and, if correct, creates a hash value of the transaction ID number. The second combines all hash values to be included in a block of transactions.

As many as 4,000 transactions may be included in a Bitcoin block. However, the exact number of transactions per block varies as a block can contain no transactions. The quantity of blocks and block generation rate also varies for different blockchains. For example, a block in Ethereum is generated approximately every 15 seconds and consists of 20 transactions on average (Etherscan.io, n.d.-d).

The second essential purpose of Bitcoin was established through the concept of how the distributed copies of the ledger are synchronised, i.e., how consensus of the valid chain is achieved and how the participant is selected to be allowed to create a valid block. This mechanism is called consensus protocol and has a substantial impact on the security and ecological aspects, as will be discussed in later chapters.

While Bitcoin is the first and most well-known blockchain and cryptocurrency, it is limited to the transfer of only Bitcoin. However, blockchain systems are not limited to cryptocurrencies. On the other end of the spectrum, Ethereum is the first and most popular open source platform supporting smart contracts. The label Ethereum is often applied with two meanings: The Ethereum permissionless blockchain, called *Ethereum Main Net*, is where traded Ether is mined and can be used by everyone to run decentralised applications with their smart contracts. The open source *Ethereum software* can be downloaded and used to create new permissionless or permissioned blockchains. This distinction is important for the clear assessment of blockchain projects.

When describing the characteristics of blockchains in the following chapters, we refer to Bitcoin *and* Ethereum first. In our examples, we refer to the blockchain software as well as to these 'public' chains. Where necessary, we identify differences to other blockchain systems. Other than proprietary blockchain protocols, such as Ripple[21] and Corda,[22] the majority of all publicly known blockchain projects today use open source protocols grouped into the Hyperledger[23] umbrella project, which started in December 2015 and is supported by the Linux Foundation.

3.2. How a blockchain works

In this section, we overview how a blockchain is set up and how transactions are processed by a blockchain.

3.2.1. The genesis block

Every blockchain begins with a first block set by the initiator of the blockchain. This block is called the *genesis block* and represents the *constitution* of a blockchain. In this block, all important parameters for the functioning of a blockchain are defined. After being set, the parameters can no longer be changed without the consent of all blockchain participants. When the genesis block is changed later through consent, it undergoes a fork. Changing the genesis block means a new constitution comes into existence. The genesis block can contain a variety of parameters necessary to the constitution. The main parameters are described in the following.

Block time

The block time defines how frequently new blocks are added to the chain and may vary from a few seconds to few minutes. The block time is the expected average time a user must wait for the transaction to be validated, provided the blockchain is not overloaded and transactions must wait on being validated in a later block. Depending on the consensus protocol, which represents the method for validating transactions, the times may slightly vary between block

---

[21] See https://ripple.com

[22] See https://www.r3.com

[23] Note: there were earlier uses of the name Hyperledger.

insertions. However, the block time does not depend on the number of transactions to be validated since, on the one hand, the number of transactions that fit into a block is limited and, on the other hand, even without a single transaction, a new block is added to the blockchain in the frequency defined by the block time. For Bitcoin and Ethereum Main Net, the average block times are set to 10 minutes and 15 seconds, respectively.

Block size

The block size defines the maximum number of bytes a block can contain. As the blockchain grows with every block added, the maximum size of a block plays an important role of how many people can participate in a blockchain, as it determines the disk capacity required for its operation. The block size for Bitcoin is 1MB and, as of December 2017, the size of the entire Bitcoin blockchain reached approximately 150 GB. As of June 2018, the average daily size of a Bitcoin block ranged from 0.5 to 1MB (Blockchain.com, n.d.-a).

For Ethereum, the block size is defined slightly different as a limit in an 'energy unit', called *gas*, a block might contain. The energy units needed for a transaction are estimated from the number of bytes and the complexity of the functions[24] a transaction contains, so the principle remains the same. As the block time for Ethereum is substantially shorter, the size of one block is also smaller, and, as of the second half of 2017, ranged from 20 to 25KB per block (Etherscan.io, n.d.-a). As of December 2017, the total size of the Ethereum database was 40GB. However, during the first five months of 2018, it grew much faster to 75GB (Etherscan.io, n.d.-c).

Block times and block size determine how fast the blockchain database grows, which must be considered when designing a blockchain. Another consequence is that the blockchain is not designed to store large amounts of data, such as text documents, pictures, and videos. These types of data must remain off chain while the hashes representing these data files that ensures their integrity can be stored on the chain.

[24] In Ethereum, the price also depends on computational complexity of a transaction due to the introduction of smart contracts. Hence, the usage of other system components, such as the CPU, is considered for determining the gas needed for one transaction.

Pre-allocated coins and block rewards

The majority of blockchains, including Bitcoin and Ethereum, created a cryptocurrency when they started. For these blockchains, cryptocurrency is needed to pay for the transactions that are validated and stored on the blockchain as well as to incentivise participants to run a node.

The genesis block defines the reward structure and the built-in inflation value for the cryptocurrency. A genesis block can pre-allocate coins for a defined purpose, e.g., 100m coins for the developers of a blockchain or for users that bring a certain amount of traffic onto the network. The way these coins are distributed is defined in the initial documentation of the blockchain and made transparent. In addition, block rewards are defined that either distribute pre-allocated coins or mint new coins for every block that is successfully validated. The block rewards go to the validator (or miner) of the block thereby establishing an incentive to participate in the network.

If a blockchain is configured to mint new coins for every block, then the coin is inflated, which is why block rewards are also considered the built-in inflation of a cryptocurrency. To limit this inflation, some blockchains, such as Bitcoin, reduce the block rewards over time, but in order to be enforced, the conditions for the reduction must be set initially in the genesis block.

3.2.2. Participating in a blockchain

To participate in a blockchain, a user must operate a node, which means the user maintains a copy of the blockchain database and runs software to interact in the network. Not every user who submits a transaction to a blockchain is obliged to run a node. There are service providers that offer applications through which transactions may be submitted to the blockchain without running an individual node. The general idea of blockchain technology, however, is that every participant has the right to hold a copy of the database and can read and validate transactions.

To run a node, a participant must download blockchain software, which is available in variants with different convenience features and user interfaces. Once installed, the node connects to the blockchain network and downloads a copy of the existing database, i.e., the entire history of blocks. This process is also called syncing the blockchain and requires a minimum of local disk space. Depending on the bandwidth and speed of the hard disk, the time to fully synchronise the blockchain ranges from a few hours to an entire day. Once the blockchain is synchronised, a user can read from the blockchain and submit transactions.

For the operating nodes, there are validating and non-validating nodes. Validating nodes must hold a full copy of the blockchain and are also called miners, validators, or sealers, depending on the consensus protocol used. In this study, we use the neutral term 'validator' for the non-consensus protocol-specific function. Depending on the consensus protocol, a user can decide or apply to become a validating node. Non-validating nodes are used for querying the information stored on the blockchain. The number of nodes may range from a few to a couple thousand depending on the level of trust and manageability the initiator of the blockchain would like to achieve (see Chapter 3.3 for more details).

3.2.3. Relaying transactions in the network

Any *transaction* that is initiated by either a user or another system is *submitted* to one of the blockchain nodes.[25] The receiving node first stores the transactions in a pool of *unverified transactions*. The blockchain application chooses the node to which a transaction is submitted first. Advanced applications consider that nodes can go offline, and they determine on a case-by-case basis to which node it submits the transaction.

The receiving node *forwards* the transaction to adjacent nodes called *peers* (see Figure 5), and this forwarding continues until all nodes know about the transaction. Due to the time needed for relaying the transactions and the size of the network, it can take from a few seconds to minutes until all nodes know about a transaction. This implies that not every node knows about all submitted transactions simultaneously, so that different validating nodes could incorporate different transactions into the next block.

---

[25] For the remainder of the report, we use the term 'transaction' for signing a transfer or deploying software code.

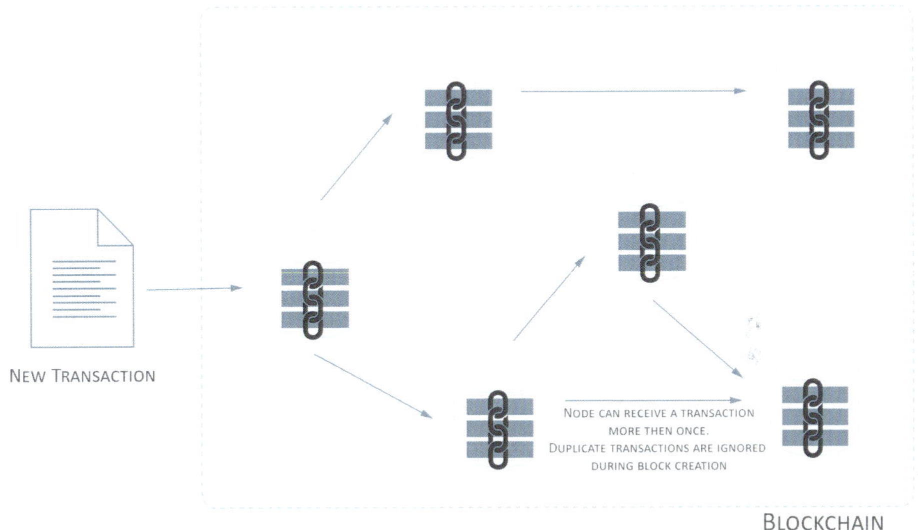

Source: Banking Concepts.

Figure 5. A transaction initiated by a user of the blockchain is propagated through the network.

There is a maximum number of peers allowed in a blockchain. For example, the maximum number of peers in the Bitcoin protocol is 125. Eight of these are outgoing peers, to which a transaction can be relayed, and 117 are incoming peers, from which messages can be received.[26] In Ethereum, the number of peers is limited to 25 by default but can be increased or decreased by the node. These limitations help reduce the traffic between the nodes and aim at improving the security of the network by increasing the cost for a group of nodes to co-operate and take control over a public blockchain.[27]

---

[26] For more information, see Bitcoin Stack Exchange (n.d.).

[27] Bitcoin nodes only attempt outgoing connections that are in ranges of IP addresses not close together. Specifically, for IPv4, it does not connect to any two nodes that are in the same block of 16 adjacent IP addresses. This means that any node running with a popular area of the Internet, such as a virtual private server host or virtual machines on an Amazon EC2 node, likely see substantially less incoming activity than one running in a less densely populated area. This can

It can also happen that a node goes offline, unintendedly or purposefully, e.g., for maintenance or energy saving. In this case, when the node comes back online, the blocks and the unverified transactions must first be synchronised before it can begin validating transactions.

3.2.4. Validation

As mentioned previously, the submitted transactions are first stored in a pool of unverified transactions. From this pool, the validators select transactions individually to validate them. On a blockchain, every transaction requires a signature of the initiator of the transaction. Validating a transaction, therefore, represents verifying the signature of the owner. This signature confirms that the signer is the eligible owner of a token or the author of a contract or document.[28] In advanced blockchains that support smart contracts, additional contractual conditions can be validated as being true or false.

As described above, the digital signature is generated by using the transaction data (e.g., sending tokens or a document) and hashing it with the user's private key. After the data are signed, the public key of the user could be used to verify the transaction, i.e., prove that exactly this transaction was initiated by exactly this user. At the same time, the digital signature ensures that the data can no longer be altered. Therefore, a change in the amount sent to a recipient or a change in the recipient would automatically lead to a different hash value, immediately detecting a fraud attempt. A simple check shows the signature as invalid.[29]

Another advantage of digital signatures is that, as soon as the user signs the transaction, they cannot claim it was not their signature, as they are the only

be interpreted as an attempt to raise the cost of a large-scale Sybil attacks against the network by increasing the diversity of IP addresses needed to gain an extremely large number of connections. (A Sybil attack in computer security is an attack wherein a reputation system is subverted by forging identities in peer-to-peer networks.)

[28] For more information, see (Ethereum Stack Exchange, 2016).

[29] The message of a standard transaction transferring Ether, Bitcoin, or any other token typically includes the recipient address, the amount, and metadata representing the token.

one who knows the private key. Of course, the key can be lost or stolen, but in this case, the user also loses all connected assets.

Blockchains use two approaches to maintaining balances: Bitcoin leverages the concept of unspent transactions, and Ethereum uses accounts. While the differences are technical, for interested readers, we include examples in the appendix of how these concepts work.

3.2.5. Multi-signatures

In the business world, multiple signatures are required for a payment to occur or a contract to come into effect (e.g., the mechanism of dual control, four-eye principle or joint accounts). Especially for public registries, notaries are often needed to verify and sign contracts in addition to the parties involved.

Most blockchains today allow the creation of accounts with more than one associated private key and require a quorum of these keys to make a transaction. Such addresses are called *multi-signature* wallets and contracts or, simply, *multisig*. Validators also verify if and how many signatures are required for a transaction to be valid. A prerequisite for a multisig account is that all the participants already have their accounts on the blockchain. Creating a multisig account requires designating the owners of the account by their public key and defining the number of signatures required to make a transaction. For example, creating a multisig wallet with five owners can have specified that only three signatures are required to make a transaction. In this case, any three of the five can make a transaction, and it will be deemed valid. The major difference compared to a standard single signature account is that multisig accounts do not have a private key as the transactions are signed with the private keys of the owners.[30]

---

30 For more technical information, see Amati (2016), Bitcoin Stack Exchange (2013), and Horwitz (2018).

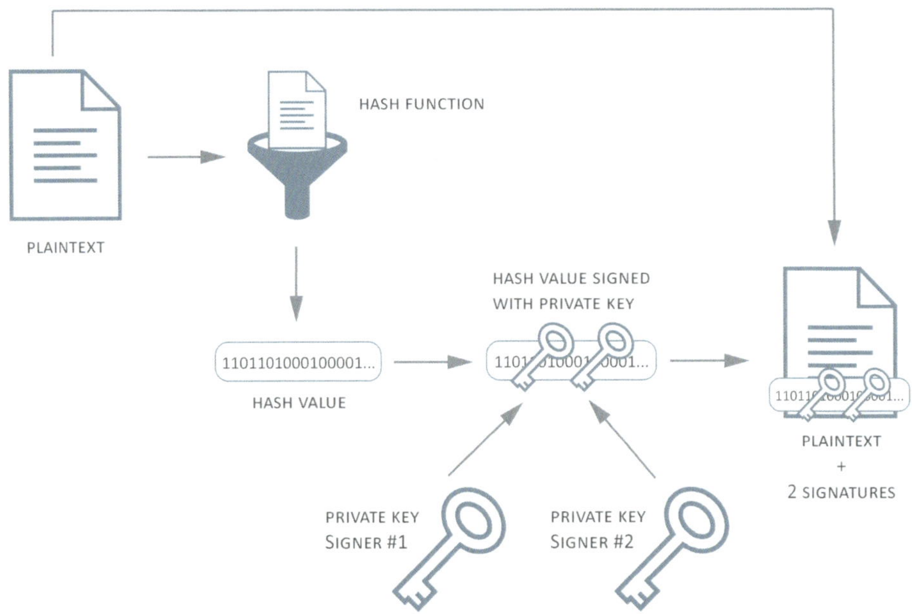

Source: Banking Concepts.

Figure 6. Transaction from a multisig wallet.

3.2.6. Creating a block

After validation, each transaction is *cryptographically secured (hashed)* and combined into a block. A block is built like a tree of transactions, also called a Merkle tree (see Figure 7). First, the transactions are grouped into pairs and hashed, which are then paired and hashed. This step is repeated until a single hash remains, referred to as the Merkle root or root hash.

The criteria with which miners decide which transactions to incorporate into a block are the transaction fees the initiator of the transaction is willing to pay.[31] Theoretically, the miners are free as to which and how many validated trans-

[31] See Chapter 3.4: Incentives.

actions are included in a block. In practice, the network delay means they cannot know about all the transactions at the same time, so the miners usually include different transactions in their blocks.

3.2.7. Building the chain

The blocks are eventually cryptographically *linked to form the blockchain.* This blockchain knows only one direction, i.e., *blocks* can be added but *never deleted.* Linking a block cryptographically means to take the block hash of the previous block, the root hash of the current block, a time stamp, and, in some cases, an additional number, called a nonce (which stands for a number used only once). All three or four elements are hashed again to create the block hash.

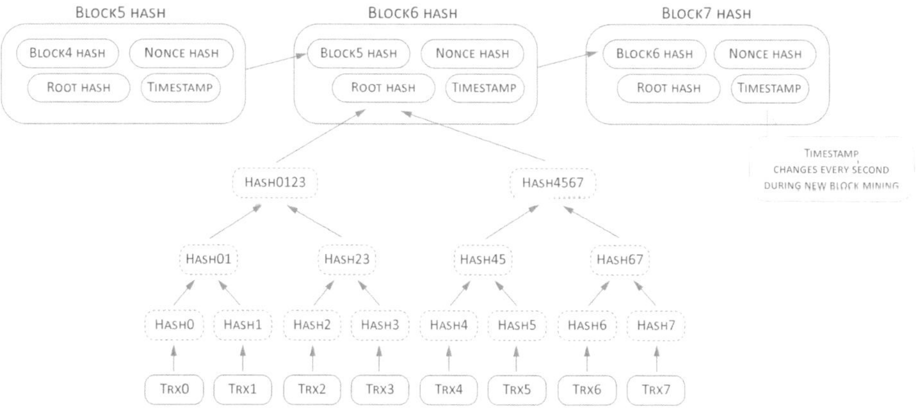

Source: Banking Concepts.

Figure 7. A Merkle tree.

As mentioned in Chapter 2.1, the slightest change in the input of a hash function results in an entirely new and unpredictable hash value. Any change in these three or four input parameters would lead to a new block hash and break the chain. Therefore, the change of a transaction in a block would lead to a new root and block hash, even if the time stamp is manipulated. This change becomes immediately apparent as the next block hash would turn out to be wrong, and the chain would be identified as corrupted. So, changing a transaction in a validated block linked in a chain would require the block hashes of all subsequent blocks to be recalculated. Through this property, blockchains are considered immutable.

However, what if someone had a powerful computer and recalculated the chain? How would anyone know? In other words, where do the network and the distribution of the ledger come into play in this scenario? With the replication of the blockchain data on multiple independent computers, any node could detect if someone tampers with the blockchain as their set of block hashes do not fit into the hashes of the tampering node. In a democratic system supported by a software protocol, this failed comparison would immediately result in the exclusion of the malicious node and would no longer receive transactions. This type of behaviour of a blockchain requires the following conditions:

1. No single node can force other nodes to accept its changes. Otherwise, this would be considered a hierarchy of nodes that breaks a fundamental concept of a blockchain. In this case, a classical distributed database that runs as a master-slave architecture is more efficient and appropriate.
2. Most of the nodes do not co-operate with malicious intend to enforce the acceptance of an altered transaction in a recalculated chain. If a majority of nodes co-operate on a blockchain, the condition of the independence of the computers would no longer be met. Such a scenario is referred to as a 51% attack.

3.2.8. Reaching consensus

As the blockchain is distributed over many independent nodes, there must be a mechanism to synchronise the blockchain across the network and for the participants to agree on the next valid block in the chain. The consensus protocol is the part of the blockchain software that ensures this synchronisation of the blocks.

Consensus protocols can be separated into two categories:

- Competitive protocols, such as proof-of-work (PoW) or proof-of-stake (PoS).

- Cooperative protocols, such as proof-of-authority (PoA) or Practical Byzantine Fault Tolerant (PBFT).

Competitive protocols establish a race between the validating nodes on which block is added next to the chain. Competitive protocols usually feature attractive block rewards for the validators, which is the primary reason to become a validator and enter the race. Because new coins are minted with every block, the participants in the race for validating a block are also called miners. Competitive protocols are more energy intensive compared to cooperative protocols because the more participants who enter the system, the more difficulty it becomes to mine the next block to keep the block times constant.

Cooperative protocols are used in permissioned chains and assign the validation of the next block to a specific node of the network. If there is more than one node in the network, then the protocol ensures that no node can validate two blocks in a row. Because of this condition, a recalculation of the chain by one node is not possible. Cooperative protocols do not prevent nodes from behaving maliciously, especially if malicious nodes cooperate, but, because the identity of the nodes is typically known, this scenario is improbable.

Today, competitive protocols are widely considered to be safer than non-competitive protocols, but this remains debatable. The security of the blockchain is eventually derived from the fact that no miner can alter the blockchain after the chain is well developed.

In competitive protocols, two miners might create a valid block that simultaneously meets the winning criteria. These blocks are called parallel or uncle blocks. Both are linked to the previous block, and in this case this is considered a temporary fork. When this happens, the miners must decide which block to link to their new block. The competitive mechanism does not guide which of the two to select. Instead, it is possible that the fork lasts for several more blocks. As miners receive only their reward after a certain time, and if the block is part of the final chain, then miners always decide for the longer chain to link their blocks. The likelihood that one chain soon becomes longer is rather high, as the block times are not fixed but averaged, and the next block might be mined after a third of the block time. Therefore, after a couple of blocks, the valid chain is determined and the transactions that have not been incorporated in the main chain go back into the pool of non-validated transactions.

3.3. Who can participate?

To start a new blockchain, the first two questions to be answered include: What is the purpose of the blockchain and who can or should participate? Alternatively, in blockchain terminology, who is allowed to run a node? Additional questions to be considered include who can validate the blocks? What should be the incentive? How are the governance mechanisms put into place? Who is allowed to vote on incentive changes, software, and protocol updates and with which quorums? There are two fundamentally different views on how a blockchain should be operated, and how democratic or controlled the blockchain should be. The leading choice is selecting a permissionless or permissioned chain.

3.3.1. Permissionless chains

In a permissionless chain, any person or institution with enough computer resources (primarily, hard-disk capacity) can download the blockchain database and run a node. Permissionless means that the operator of a node is unknown to the rest of the community, and the same person could run multiple nodes. A node is typically set up by downloading and installing node software, which automatically connects to the network (via a boot node server) and synchronises to the database.

As soon as the database is synced, the operator of the node can further decide if they would like to participate in the mining or maintain a copy of the data. The latter option can be valuable if someone wants to retrieve transaction data and perform analytics or to monitor the system, e.g., by a regulator.

In the past, permissionless chains were introduced with the launch of a new cryptocurrency. Also, this type is often called a *public chain* as there is no control over who can run a node and, hence, have read access to the entire blockchain. The core ideas behind a permissionless chain are that no one can control the network, there are no contractual obligations between the participants, and the only law is the software protocol. As it is at the discretion of every node operator to implement an offered protocol update or not, changes in the 'ruling law' are subject to a 'democratic vote' by the network participants. In the next chapter, we elaborate on the software governance and its implications in more detail.

The drawback of permissionless chains is they operate without any legal framework, and no one can be held responsible for damages that may occur. It is also not guaranteed that block times or transaction costs remain within a certain range. Another implication of permissionless chains is that the time for relaying transactions increases with every node. This leads to the situation where miners can start mining on top of an old or invalid block. Therefore, projects have surfaced that aim to help speed up the relaying of transactions[32].

In addition to mining and monitoring, the operation of a new node is useful if someone wants to create a client or wallet application.[33] The developer must decide on the nodes with which the app should communicate. Because node operators may not operate 24/7 or restrict ports or specific function calls on the database, wallet providers typically prefer to run nodes to avoid service disruptions, at least for backup purposes.

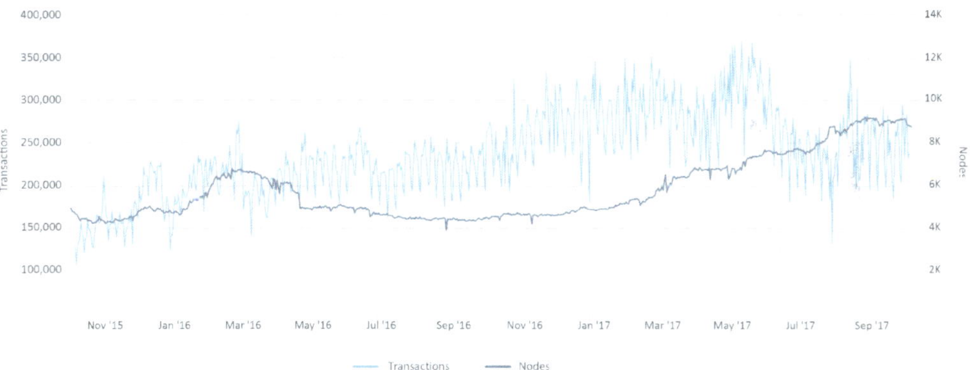

Source: banking concepts based on blockchain.com and coin.dance data.

Figure 8. The correlation between the number of nodes and the number of transactions.

[32] Further reading on solutions for speeding block relaying times is available in (Wirdum, 2016).

[33] A wallet application is supposed to bring new users to the blockchain. It can be assumed that the number of nodes also correlates with the number of transactions. However, as shows, there is no strong evidence for this hypothesis.

3.3.2. Permissioned chains

Permissioned chains are intended to control access to the network of nodes. Access is granted by a central authority based on criteria stipulated by the initiator of the chain. A central authority does not necessarily refer to a single person or legal entity, as it can represent an association or consortium with established governance mechanisms, which may even foresee democratic decisions for granting access to the network with a simple or qualified majority. Likewise, nodes can be excluded with democratic decisions if they did not behave maliciously.

Trust in a permissioned chain is generated by the diversity of the participants in the chain, the governance of the software protocol, the checks and balances, and the law under which the blockchain operates. This integration into a known legal framework is an incentive for businesses to engage with blockchain technology.

As with permissionless chains, the broader the range of participants and the more transparent and stable the governance mechanisms, the more trust a chain receives. Permissioned chains also allow for better control over transaction costs and block times as participants are requested to follow the 'constitution' of the blockchain. An often-heard argument is that permissioned chains are not democratic as there are authorities that control what happens on the chain. This is not necessarily true and depends on the setup of the blockchain, its 'constitution', and its governance. In permissioned chains, nodes can be still independent and can democratically decide on protocol updates.

Some permissioned chains are instead designed to support business groups with common interests, while others might be set up more broadly, and the number of participants may approach those of permissionless chains. There is no mandatory link between the consensus protocol and a permissioned chain. So, a permissioned chain might equally run with competitive as well as cooperative protocols. Generally, competitive protocols are used for permissionless chains, whereas cooperative protocols are used with permissioned chains.

Applications sometimes use the cryptographical linking of blocks without distributing the ledger. In this case, the blockchain has only one participant. Since a single participant undermines the trust and does not have an economic advantage over a centralised database, we do not consider such an application as a blockchain application. The same is true for a specialised architecture where one node takes a 'leading' role within the network. [34] If the permissions are configured in such a way that participants can be forced out of the network or do not decide democratically on protocol updates, then the concept of blockchain technology is also undermined.

Permissioned chains can be used by governments to maintain official registries (e.g., land or company registries), for electronic voting applications, by members of an industry, such as logistics, to track containers on transports or by energy companies to trade electrical power. As illustrated, trust in blockchain technology depends on the technology, the design of the blockchain community, and software governance mechanisms.

3.3.3. Software protocol governance

A blockchain derives its trust from the protocol and the independence of the nodes. Each change in the protocol must be agreed on by most of the nodes or even all of the nodes. Otherwise, the blockchain will fork. It is a prerequisite for the validators to understand the protocol and the consequences of a change. In public blockchains, there is often a series of improvement proposals (e.g., BIPs for Bitcoins and EIPs for Ethereum), which are widely discussed before being adopted by the blockchain community.

New improvements can be implemented using a soft or hard fork. Through either approach, the nodes are required to upgrade to the changes, but, depending on the implementation, the rules for non-upgraded nodes are different. A hard fork means that transactions or blocks submitted under the old rules are no longer valid, and nodes must switch to the new version of the blockchain to continue mining. When more nodes switch to the new version, the old version of the chain no longer exists, so no mining is performed. Hard forks are normally used for changes to the hard-coded limits (e.g., an agreement to increase the Bitcoin block size to 2MB would cause a hard fork), changes to the consensus protocols (e.g., Ethereum Metropolis following

[34] In this case, we consider it a form of a master-slave architecture.

proof-of-stake instead of proof-of-work), changes to the transaction behaviour, and major bug fixes.

The disadvantage of a hard fork is that it can lead to chain splitting, so that, with enough support, the old and new versions of the blockchain could continue to exist in parallel. An example is the hard fork of Ethereum after the exploitation of a software bug of the so-called DAO[35] project and led to Ethereum Classic appearing on the market as the cryptocurrency of the Ethereum blockchain before the hard fork.

Soft forks are forward compatible such that non-upgraded nodes see the transactions and blocks under the new rules as valid, but the upgraded nodes reject the blocks they mine as non-valid. With a soft fork, if at least 51% of the miners switch to the new rules, then the old chain is overtaken by the new one, and eventually all miners switch. If 51% or more decide to stick to the old rules, then the soft fork is more likely to be abandoned. Examples of soft forks include BIP 66, changes to the Bitcoin transaction validity rules, and P2SH, which altered Bitcoin's address formatting.

The blockchain community develops the software protocols, and not all blockchain applications develop a software protocol. Because most of the protocols are funded by foundations with the purpose of promoting open source under copy-left licences, most protocols are available online and can be downloaded and altered. If necessary, they can be used to create new permissionless or permissioned chains. The challenge with adapting existing protocols to a specific use and blockchain is that implementing valuable changes from the original protocol requires substantial effort. Therefore, specific chains may opt to stick to the standard protocol as much as possible. This difficulty is why most blockchain software protocols are today maintained within the Hyperledger framework. Also, this implies that, from our definition, all systems that impose a hierarchical structure on the nodes or orchestrate tasks to certain nodes do

---

[35] The DAO was a digital decentralized autonomous organization and a form of investor-directed venture capital fund that raised more than USD 150 million from the Ethereum community. Due to a software bug, USD 50 million were 'stolen' from the owners, which led to the fork mentioned above.
https://en.wikipedia.org/wiki/The_DAO_(organization)
https://www.coindesk.com/understanding-dao-hack-journalists/

not meet the criteria for a blockchain, as the governance of the blockchain protocol is non-democratic.

Permissioned as well as permissionless chains are in line with the main characteristic of blockchain technology having a database with cryptographically linked blocks of transactions and distribution across independent nodes. The term 'permissioned chain' is often associated with a single point of control for a blockchain, which, however, depends on the setup and architecture of the chain. On the other hand, the independence of nodes requires deep and sophisticated software and IT skills to determine upgrades for the blockchain protocol. Yet these skills are limited for both permissionless and permissioned chains. For a chain to be trustworthy, it is important to provide transparency of the independence of its participants. In this respect, a permissioned chain may offer advantages over a permissionless chain, as the participants are known.

3.4. Incentives

Participating in a blockchain and operating a node requires computing resources of network bandwidth, hard disks, and CPU capacity as well as human effort for software governance. Other than blockchains like Bitcoin and Ethereum, where the type of consensus protocol requires enormous computing power, the hardware and human resource costs for operating a blockchain are low. Still, the miners, validators, or sealers[36] expect a reward for their activities.

The rewards for the validators are of two types:

- Transaction fees collected from each transaction and paid by the signer of the transaction;
- Block rewards granted for every validated block as defined when the blockchain is created.

---

[36] In the following chapters, we use the neutral term validators.

Block rewards are given to encourage enough participants to operate nodes 24/7 continuously, and transaction fees are intended to control the priority of the validation of transactions. These rewards are paid in the cryptocurrency that comes along with most of the blockchain. In addition, speculation on the increase of the value of the cryptocurrency may offer a strong incentive; this was observed in the last two years when the prices of cryptocurrencies skyrocketed. While this phenomenon may be temporary, the primary rewards in the future will result from transaction fees and block rewards.

Blockchain architects must carefully design the incentive mechanisms initially as a later change, which is not incorporated into the consensus protocol (i.e., the genesis block), might be subject to the software governance procedures as outlined previously. The design of the incentive system impacts the security and availability of a blockchain as malicious participants might exploit a loophole in the system to block the chain. The incentive structure also depends on the consensus protocol. For example, in PoS chains, if there is no incentive for the stakeholders to maintain the value of their balances, then they can manipulate the chains without losing anything (Barinov, 2017/2018; Greenfield, 2017).

Some blockchains and consensus protocols operate without incentives, but such applications of blockchains are bound to very specific purposes or to a specific group who have a collective benefit to participate in such a chain.[37]

3.4.1. Transactions fees

Transaction fees are usually paid by the person submitting a transaction to the blockchain.[38] Systems with someone other than the signer paying for the transaction are still under development. The formats for how transaction fees are paid differ between the blockchains. For Bitcoin, the transaction fee is determined as a difference between the sum of the Bitcoin value of the output transactions and the sum of the value of the Bitcoin input transactions.[39]

---

[37] See the Hyperledger fabric as an example.

[38] Advanced versions allow (or will allow) receivers or third parties to pay for the transaction.

[39] See Appendix: Unspent transactions versus accounts.

Ethereum introduced a special transaction currency or energy unit called 'gas' that people can buy against Ether. The block size or gas limit restricts the number of transactions per block, and as more transactions are executed, the transactions to be mined in the next blocks start competing, which leads to growing transaction fees or gas prices. There are different transaction prices for different mining times, i.e., the number of blocks after which a transaction should be mined.

Bitcoin and Ethereum experienced volatility and a dramatic surge in transaction costs during 2017, as seen in Figure 9. In August 2017, the average transaction fee for Bitcoin reached USD 5.35 compared to USD 0.39 at the beginning of the year. The peak price was USD 8.94 on the 25 August 2017.

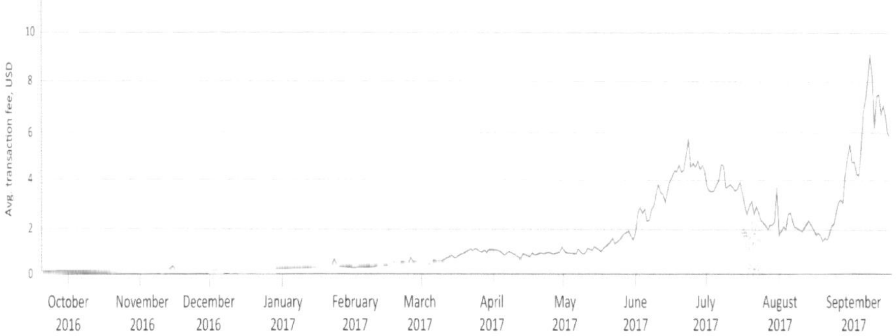

Source: Banking Concepts based on data from BitInfoCharts (n.d.).

Figure 9. Average Bitcoin transaction fee in USD per day from October 2016 through September 2017.

From Figure 10, this surge is partly related to the increase in the price of Bitcoin, but also due to BTC. The dramatic price increase of Bitcoin also spurred speculative transactions on the chain and, hence, also lead to higher transaction fees.

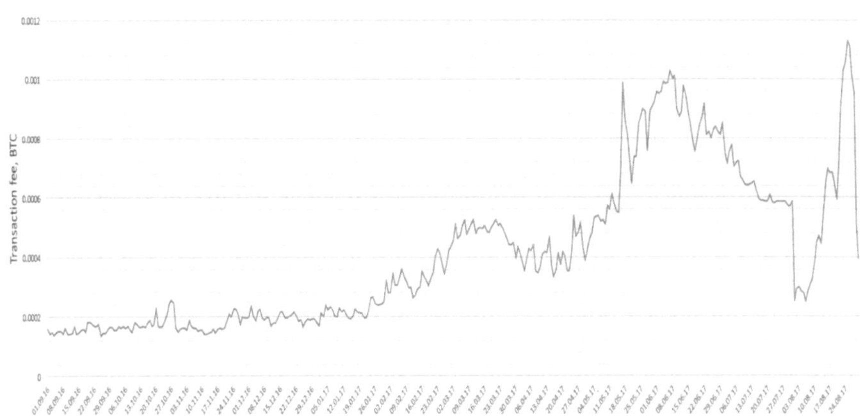

Source: Banking Concepts based on data from BitInfoCharts (n.d.).

Figure 10. Average Bitcoin transaction fee in BTC per day from October 2016 through September 2017.

In August 2017, the average transaction fee on Ethereum reached USD 0.34 compared to USD 0.0074 at the beginning of the year. On 21 June 2017, the peak price was USD 1.37 (see Figure 11).

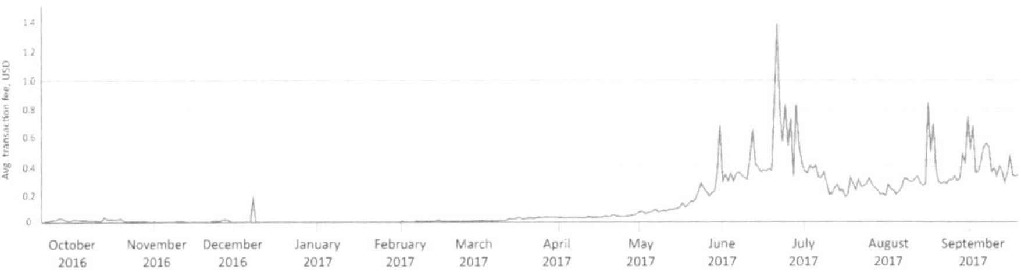

Source: Banking Concepts based on data from BitInfoCharts (n.d.).

Figure 11. Average Ethereum transaction fee in USD per day from October 2016 through September 2017.

As mentioned above, Ethereum uses the energy unit 'gas' to determine the price of a transaction, which itself has a price set in Ether that depends on the 'load' of the blockchain. Figure 12 shows the volatility of the gas price for 12 months.

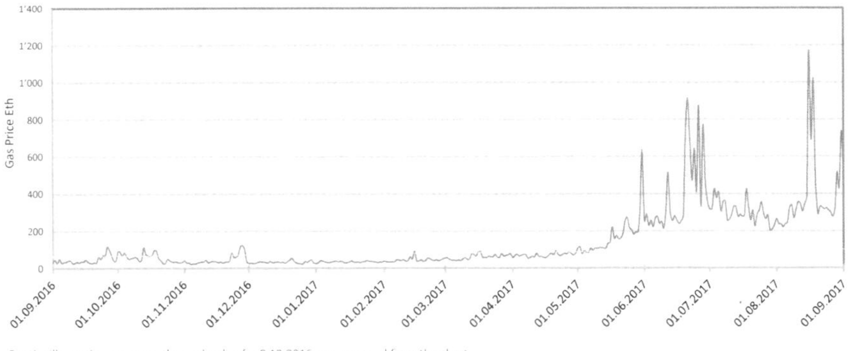

Source: Banking Concepts based on data from (Etherscan.io, n.d.-b).

Figure 12. Average gas price per day over a 12-month period.

Table 4 lists the transaction fees as they depend on the mining time for different currencies considering the exchange rates as of 29 August 2017. For example, a simple transaction to transfer Ether consumes 21,000 gas.

Table 4. Transaction fees and mining time for Ether.

Mining time	ETH	USD	EUR	CHF
< 37 seconds	0.000483	0.17839	0.14910	0.16939
40 seconds	0.000084	0.03102	0.02593	0.02946
151 seconds	0.000007	0.00259	0.00216	0.00245

Source: Banking Concepts based on ETH transaction fee data from ethgasstation.info, USD and EUR to ETH rates from coinhills.com, ETH to CHF rate from fx-rate.net. All data accessed on 29 August 2017.

For a similar transaction, as of 29 August 2017, the fees for Bitcoin are listed in Table 5.

Table 5. Transaction fees and mining time for Bitcoin.

Mining time	BTC	USD	EUR	CHF
< 30 min	0.0004746	2.17599	1.81672	2.05820
60 min	0.0008814	4.04113	3.37391	3.82237
420 min	0.0010848	4.97370	4.15251	4.70445

Source: Banking Concepts based on ETH transaction fee data from bitcoinfees.info, USD, EUR and CHF to ETH rates from investing.com. All data accessed on 29 August 2017.

3.4.2. Block rewards

Another source of income is the rewards given for mining the next block. The rewards are usually paid out in the native[40] cryptocurrency that comes along with a blockchain. These incentives are strong if there is speculation on price increases of the cryptocurrency or if there is widespread use of the cryptocurrency, i.e., the cryptocurrency is widely accepted for payments or there is high liquidity in the market and the cryptocurrencies can easily be exchanged for fiat currency. Table 6 shows the incentives set by block mining rewards and transaction fees for Bitcoin and Ethereum as of September 2017.

Table 6. Block rewards.

	Bitcoin	Ethereum
Block mining	12.5 BTC (halves every 4 years)	5 ETH
Uncle blocks mining	no rewards	4.375 ETH (max 2 Uncles per block)
Transaction fees	not fixed and not big enough to incentivise miners	

Source: Banking Concepts.

[40] As opposed to any kind of tokens which are issued if form of smart contracts.

For public blockchains, the block rewards largely outweigh what can be collected through transaction fees. The high block rewards together with dramatic price increases explain the substantial investment in 'mining farms', especially in locations where energy prices are low.

3.5. Consensus protocols

Together with the genesis block, consensus protocols are considered the 'constitution' of a blockchain. Consensus protocols define who can validate blocks and how likely it is that one participant or a group of participants acting in concert can take control over the blockchain and manipulate data. Such an attempt, also known as a 51% or Sybil attack,[41] could reverse transactions, double spend funds of the attackers, and recalculate the chain by forcing the remaining participants to accept these changes.

As the finality of a transaction is essential for any blockchain, we further elaborate on these protocols while addressing the issue of significant energy consumption for which blockchains are heavily criticised. We suggest that this criticism is valid only for competitive protocols and only under favourable economic conditions. Previously, we distinguished between *competitive* and *cooperative* protocols. In this chapter, we describe the most-used protocols for each of the categories, with a broader overview at the end of this chapter.

3.5.1. Proof-of-work (PoW)

The first and the most popular consensus protocol is 'proof-of-work' originally introduced by Bitcoin.[42] This approach is a highly *competitive* consensus protocol with algorithms requiring validators to solve a 'complex cryptographic puzzle' before they can enter their block of transactions. The effort to solve

[41] The term 51% attack refers to the hashing power needed to manipulate and recalculate a PoW blockchain. A Sybil attack refer to the possibility that malicious cooperating nodes would remain undetected due to forged identities (Bitcoin Stack Exchange, 2017).

[42] Bitcoin and Ethereum blockchains currently use different PoW implementations.

this puzzle is referred to as the *difficulty*, as it might change with the block time, the number of miners, and the mining power in the network. Although the often-used wording 'complex cryptographic puzzle' suggests that miners can compete on strategies to solve the puzzle, proof-of-work is fundamentally a simple trial-and-error process that requires the repetition of millions, billions, or even trillions of calculations with slightly different input until the solution is found.

The difficulty in Bitcoin, i.e., the solution of the 'complex cryptographical puzzle', is to find a hash value that starts with a defined number of leading zeros or, to be technically precise, the number of leading zeros in a hexadecimal representation of a 256-bit binary string.[43] In the first half of 2017, the number of leading zeros fluctuated between 17 and 18 in a hexadecimal format or between 68 and 72 digits in the binary format (see Figure 13). Because we know that a hash value cannot be predicted, and that even the slightest change leads to a completely different value, finding a hash value with a certain number of leading zeros is a trial-and-error process.

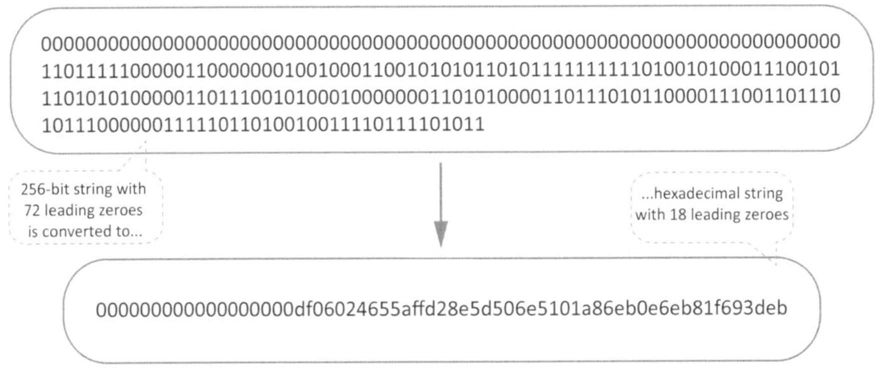

Source: Banking Concepts and based on data from Bitcoin block #486913 (Blockchain.com, n.d.-b).

Figure 13. A 256-bit string in a hexadecimal format for Bitcoin block #486913.

---

[43] A hexadecimal representation of a 256-bit string equals 64 digits (with values 0-9, a-f), so the difficulty equals approximately 72 leading zeros in the 2^{256} binary string.

In Bitcoin, the hash input of a new block consists of four elements (illustration see Figure 7):

- the hash of the previous block (publicly available),
- the root hash of the transactions the miners want to add,
- the hash of a random number (the nonce), which is an integer between 0 and 4,294,967,296, and
- the current timestamp on a second granularity.

To win the competition for a block, the miner takes the hash of the previous block, adds the root hash value of a set of transactions freely chosen from the pool of unvalidated transactions, changes the time stamp every second, and makes up to 4.3 billion attempts to identify a hash with the number of leading zeros defined by the difficulty. If the miner is lucky, they find the valid hash after a few calculations. Otherwise, they continue the calculation for 10 or more minutes until another miner from the pool discovers the valid hash. The first to solve the 'puzzle' is eligible to add the block to the blockchain and receive the block reward. However, the block reward is not paid immediately but only after 72 hours.

The Bitcoin protocol defines a *block time of 10 minutes*, which means that, *on average,* a new valid block should be mined and added to the blockchain every 10 minutes. To achieve this average, the number of leading zeroes, which defines the difficulty of finding a new block, is recalculated every 2016 blocks, i.e., approximately every 14 days. The difficulty is adapted by an algorithm built into the Bitcoin protocol and takes into account the recent hashing power of the network (Bitcoin Wiki, n.d.). The number of leading zeros is set in a way that the block time average of 10 minutes can most likely be achieved. If the average block time falls substantially below 10 minutes, then the number of leading zeros is increased (by one) and decreased if the block time exceeds 10 minutes.[44]

---

[44] An example of reduction in the difficulty was block #460319 on 4 April 2017 with 17 leading zeroes and a predecessor with 18 (Blockchain.com, n.d.-b).

On average, finding a hash value with 17 leading zeros in a HEX representation or 68 leading zeros in a binary representation takes 2^{68} or approximately 3×10^{20} trials.[45] Figure 14 shows the increase of the difficulty and Figure 15 the increase of the hash rate in the Bitcoin network from October 2016 until September 2017. A comparison reveals that the more people who enter the race, the greater the difficulty becomes to keep the block times constant.

As suggested before, there may be scenarios when two miners solve the puzzle with different transactions at the same time. Then, the blockchain forks into two valid chains, and for a short period it includes two valid final blocks. In the Bitcoin blockchain, these blocks are called *orphan blocks*[46] because one of the two parallel blocks eventually are not continued. It is the choice of the next miner to decide which of the two orphaned blocks are used to build on the next trials. Even if different miners chose different orphaned blocks, since the effective block time varies, it is likely that one orphaned chain soon becomes longer than the other. As the miner of an orphaned block loses the block mining reward, if the orphaned chain is discontinued, then new miners always choose the longer chain as the predecessor for the next block. In other words, the longer chain is assumed to be 'correct' and is then backed by the network 'consensus' as it has the highest amount of accumulated work invested.

Transactions of orphaned blocks not incorporated into blocks of the longer chain are considered unverified. On the Bitcoin main, net transactions from orphaned blocks not added to the other blocks fall back to the pool of unverified transactions as soon as the block is identified as orphaned. Typically, after two blocks are mined on top of the other block, it becomes clear which block is orphaned (r/Bitcoin, 2014).

---

[45] Provided that the hash values are uniformly distributed, the probability of finding a number with this property is a Bernoulli distribution of p = 1/2^68 with the expectation value for the number of trials of 1/p == 2^68.

[46] In Ethereum, parallel blocks are called *uncle blocks.*

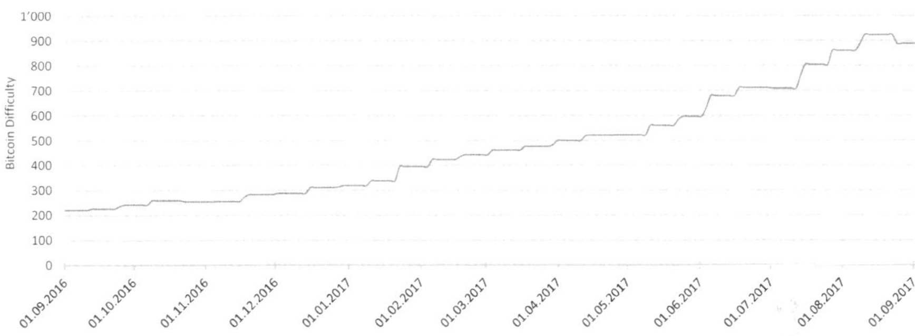

Source: Banking Concepts.

Figure 14. The increase in the Bitcoin difficulty over 12 months.

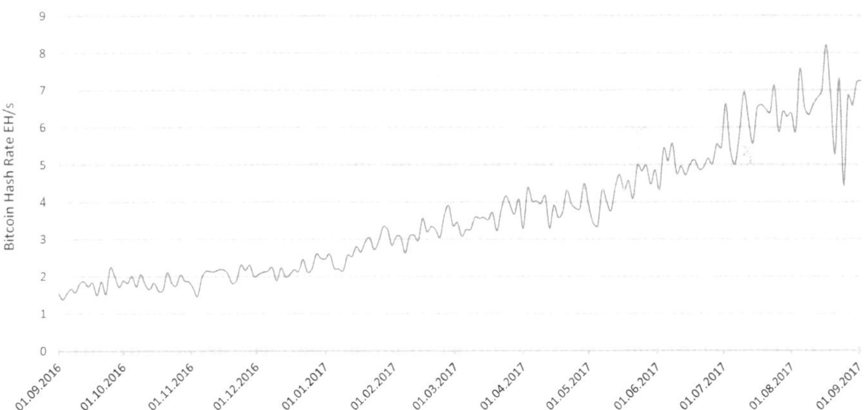

Source: Banking Concepts.

Figure 15. The Bitcoin hash rate in exa-hashes per second (millions of tera hashes).

Ethereum

Ethereum also uses a proof-of-work algorithm consensus protocol called Ethash (previously known as the Dagger-Hashimoto algorithm). As in Bitcoin, Ethash involves finding a nonce input to the algorithm so that the result is below a certain threshold based on the difficulty. The difficulty dynamically adjusts so that on average one block is produced *every 15 seconds*. An essential difference to the Bitcoin algorithm is that the Ethash is memory hard and thus ASIC resistant, which means that it cannot be encoded in dedicated hardware chips (ASICS). Its performance correlates with the available memory, which is why it performs very well with computer card incorporating graphical processing units (GPUs).

Memory hardness is achieved through an algorithm that requires choosing subsets of a fixed resource dependent on the nonce and block header. This resource is called a DAG (directed acyclic graph), which is entirely different every 30,000 blocks (or 100 hours, which is called an epoch) and takes a significant time to generate. The objective of this concept is to discourage the centralisation of mining power and give miners with smaller budgets an improved chance to participate successfully in the network.[47]

Source: Banking Concepts.

Figure 16. Ethereum difficulty over 12 months.

---

[47] The large memory requirements mean that large-scale miners obtain a comparatively small super-linear benefit. The high bandwidth requirement means that a speed-up from piling on many super-fast processing units while sharing the same memory offers little benefit over a single unit. This is important because pool mining has no benefit for nodes doing verification, thus discouraging centralisation.

Figure 16 and Figure 17 show the substantial increase in the Ethereum difficulty and hash rate of the network from September 2016 until September 2017.

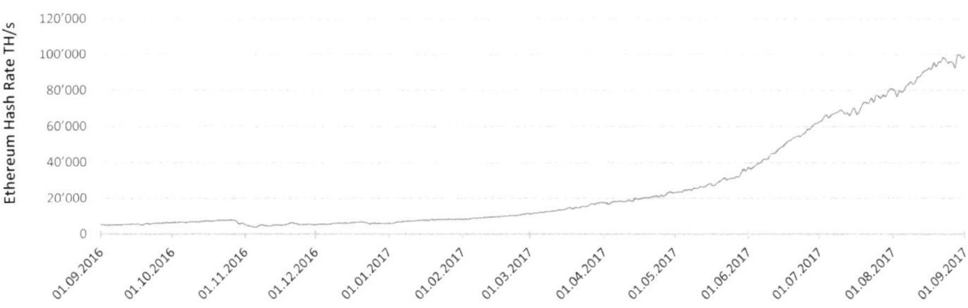

Source: Banking Concepts.

Figure 17. Ethereum hash rate over 12 months.

Digression

Directed acyclic graph (DAG) is designed to hash a fast verifiability time within a slow CPU-only environment while providing vast speed-ups for mining when a large amount of memory and high-bandwidth are available. The DAG algorithm takes the following approach:

- A seed exists that can be computed for each block by scanning through the block headers up until that point.
- From the seed, a 16 MB pseudorandom cache is computable, and light clients store the cache.
- From the cache, a 1 GB dataset is generated with the property that each item in the dataset depends on a small number of items from the cache. Full clients and miners store the dataset. The dataset grows linearly with time.
- Mining involves selecting random slices of the dataset and hashing them together. Verification can be done with low memory by using the cache to regenerate the specific pieces of the dataset needed, so only the cache must be stored.

Another difference with Bitcoin is that the main chain in Ethereum is not the 'longest' but the 'heaviest', which means that uncle blocks are included as part of the block. 'Uncles' are considered correct blocks that, due to reasons of network propagation, were simply not included in the longest chain. Ethereum's GHOST protocol solution assigns these uncle blocks an economic value on the network. The GHOST protocol pays for uncles, which incentivises miners to include uncles in a mined block by referencing uncles in a new field in the header of each block. A reference to these uncles makes the chain heavier and creating a heavier chain with valid proof-of-work blocks increases the security of the chain.

3.5.2. Proof-of-stake (PoS)

Proof-of-stake is a competitive consensus protocol that correlates the chances of winning a block with the amount of money a miner is willing to put at stake. The amount of money represents the amount of the cryptocurrency a miner is willing to lose under certain conditions. Each participant who would like to become a validator deposits some of their coins to have a chance of being selected to create the next block.

There are various approaches for correlating the amount at stake and the chances of winning a block. One approach is to extend the number of trials a miner can perform within a given time frame. The more money a participant stakes, the more trials can be performed. In this scenario, the PoS protocol gives an advantage to participants with deeper pockets. The first suggestions for an Ethereum implementation of PoS varied widely between 10 to more than 1000 ETH,[48] which leads to small participants being excluded as validators.

The PoS protocol also requires substantially less energy than PoW, as the number of participants is limited by the minimum amount to be put at stake and miners with lower stakes continuously drop out of the competition for a block. Hence, the difficulty for a winning a block is substantially lower.

---

[48] In 2016, Vitalik Buterin, co-founder of Ethereum, suggested a minimum deposit of 1250 ETH, which would grow as the number of validators increases. Since then the prices of Ether have grown substantially, but this lower limit is still in discussion (Buterin, 2016).

Implementations of PoS can vary, but the general algorithm consists of the following steps.[49]

1. *Become a validator.* After a coin holder places any amount into a 'depository', they become a potential validator forming a so-called 'validator pool'.
2. *Choose a validator.* The algorithm randomly selects one member of the 'validator pool' and gives them the right to try to create the next block. As mentioned before, the chance of being selected is proportional to the amount at stake.
3. *Create a block.* The validator is given a limited amount of time to solve the difficulty and create a new block. If they fail, then the right is given to the next validator.[50] As in PoW, the longest chain is the canonical one.
4. *Commit the block.* After a block is created, it still needs to be approved to make it to the blockchain. To approve a block, validators must vote on it, and when the block earns the majority, it becomes part of the blockchain. All voters who do not validate legitimate blocks lose their stake.

The validators primarily earn transaction fees or block rewards for creating a block (Blockgeek, n.d.), depending on the implementation. Because participants lose their stake if they do not vote to validate a legitimate block, validators have an incentive to operate their node continuously.

Two issues must be considered when implementing PoS: (1) The 'nothing at stake problem' is when participants have nothing to lose, then nothing prevents them from acting unfair. Applying penalties for unfair players could be a solution, such as through invalidating coins they have placed as a deposit. (2) The chance to be selected as the validator is pseudorandom and proportional to the amount deposited. Therefore, wealthy participants who can stake more coins win more block validations over time. This in turn makes them richer, allowing them to stake more coins to further increase earnings from additional

[49] We refer to the discussion surrounding the proposals for the implementation of Caspar, the next release of Ethereum, which is expected to introduce PoS.

[50] A suggestion for the design is that participants obtain higher nonce ranges to try within a given timeframe.

validations, which effectively drives toward a more centralised validation. Defining a maximum stake in the consensus protocol could solve this issue.

Currently, several coins have implemented a pure PoS method on their blockchains, such as DASH, NXT, NEO, and PEERCOIN. Public interest for these coins remains lower than for Ethereum or Bitcoin, although NXT gained some popularity in 2017. Ethereum is developing an implementation of PoS, called Casper, and is expected to switch to it in 2018. Ethereum's PoS Casper aims to create a more decentralised model than PoW. If a person wants to validate Ethereum transactions, then they can become a validator by depositing a defined amount of Ether to the Casper contract, and this amount remains locked for the entire time the validator participates in the block creation activities.

An essential feature of Casper are penalties for the validators who act maliciously. The size of the penalty is equal to the deposit of the validator so that the perpetrator loses all deposited coins.

The protocol defines anyone as a perpetrator who breaks at least one of the following rules:

1. *Get 2/3 in prepare phase*. In order for the candidate block to get 2/3 of votes in prepare phase, voters must reference the same previous block as the candidate in prepare phase.
2. *Commit*. A block that was suggested for a commit phase should have a minimum of 2/3 of the votes at the prepare phase.
3. *Prepare and Commit consistency*. To prepare a new block, validators must reference their previous prepare and commit blocks, where the hashes of the previous prepare and commit are the same, i.e., indicating that this is the same block as illustrated below.
4. *No double prepares*. Validators cannot vote for more than one prepare block per round.

If a validator wants to stop participating in blockchain building, then they can withdraw the deposit. Withdrawal takes around 24 hours to ensure they did not participate in fraudulent activities. Although the full implementation details of PoS are still under discussion, a trade-off to be solved is how to create appropriate incentives for stakeholders to operate correctly while eliminating concentrations of power.

3.5.3. Proof-of-authority (PoA)

Proof-of-authority is a new consensus mechanism that is considered a cooperative protocol, i.e., is eco-friendly, which was an intended purpose along with scalability when it was introduced in late 2015 by Gavin Wood, co-founder of Ethereum and founder of Parity Technologies. Originally implemented in turboethereum, a C++ Ethereum client, it is now implemented in the Parity client for Ethereum, called AURA, which stands for Authority Round.[51]

PoA requires a permissioned chain as the validating participants must be approved through a vote and should be known to the rest of the network. From this approval, validators derive their authority, and the protocol assumes they can be trusted and act with good intentions. The quorums for approving a validator can be set by the initiator of a blockchain in the genesis block. As a standard, it is suggested that, if a new validator wants to join the network, they should receive confirmations from at least two-thirds of existing validators, who are also called sealers in PoA blockchains.

The sealer of the next block is determined by a pre-defined order (the Authority round), and each sealer who joins the network through approval is added to the list. The PoA consensus protocol usually is accompanied by various functions to detect improper or malicious behaviour, such as sealing two blocks in one step, producing a block out of turn, or simply not sealing a block during a sealer's turn. When such behaviour is detected, sealers can be suspended or removed from the network.

PoA protocols are also suited for side chains with a small number of sealers. Due to the small size of such networks, the relatively small number of replications, and low relay times, PoA blockchains can easily be scaled up by increasing block sizes and reducing block times. It is often argued that by having a small number of sealers, no one can be 100% confident the validators will not act unfair, e.g., forge transactions or include double spends into the block. While this appears convincing at first, not knowing the miners and their concentration may offer even higher risk.

---

[51] For more details, see (Parity Documentation, n.d.).

A good blockchain architecture depends on how good the checks and balances are implemented, i.e., under which law the blockchain is operating, how heterogeneously the interests of the participants are spread, how international the participants are distributed, and how the voting mechanisms are established. The PoA protocol allows for a fine-grained composition of a blockchain that is balanced in governance, control, and eco-friendliness.

3.5.4. Practical Byzantine Fault Tolerance (PBFT)

The Practical Byzantine Fault Tolerance approach also belongs to the cooperative consensus protocols and relies on the assumption that, at any point in time, two-thirds of the network participants are honest and trustworthy. Some blockchains use this algorithm as a baseline to reach consensus in their network, including Ripple and Hyperledger Fabric, whose algorithms are explained below.

Ripple

Ripple uses a proprietary protocol that relies on a quorum of approximately 80% of trustworthy participants. This represents a version of the PBFT algorithm, which requires a supermajority of votes to reach a consensus instead of two-thirds.[52] It relies on a distributed database, called a ledger, to store information about all Ripple accounts. A new ledger is created every few seconds, and the most recent ledger is called the Last Closed Ledger (LCL). The consensus process begins when a transaction, created and signed by an account owner, is submitted to a server and subsequently distributed to all other servers in the network. Each server then performs the following actions:

1. The server forms a so-called candidate set from the transactions it receives using the first-in/first-out principle.
2. Servers receive proposals of the transactions that should and should not be included in the next LCL. They compare these proposals with the

[52] A recent analysis showed that as much as 90% agreement of the participants is necessary to operate the network safely (Chase & MacBrough, 2018).

transactions in their candidate set. This process continues until a timer expires.

3. Upon expiration of the allotted time, the server takes the transactions with at least 50% of votes (both positive and negative), combines them into a proposal set, and sends them to the other servers.
4. Step 2 repeats with transactions now needing to obtain at least 60% of the votes to be added into the proposal set. The next iteration will have the number of necessary votes increased to 70%. With each repetition, the proposal sets become more similar.
5. When a transaction receives at least 80% of the votes, the network reaches a consensus, and a server validates the proposals and closes the consensus process.
6. These validated proposals now form a new LCL, and invalid transactions (which obtained at least 80% of the negative votes) are discarded. Transactions that did not receive any or enough votes remain in the candidate set for new transactions to be again received during the consensus process.

Digression

Practical Byzantine Fault Tolerance (PBFT) is an algorithm designed to solve the problem described by the following allegory:

Several divisions of the Byzantine army are planning to attack the city of the enemy. Each division is commanded by a general who must agree on a common plan. The only means of communication is through messages. It is also possible there are traitors among the generals who would like to confuse the loyalists. The task of the loyal generals is to develop an algorithm where the traitors cannot thwart the loyal generals' agreement of a common plan for attack.

In 1982, Leslie Lamport proposed an algorithm as a solution. Assume the total number of generals is n = 4 and total number of traitors is m = 1. In this case, the algorithm will have four steps (Paralell.ru, n.d.):

1. Each general sends to all other generals a message containing the size of his army. Loyal generals send the real number and traitors can provide

different numbers in different messages. The first general sends the number 1 (1000 soldiers), the second sends the number 2, the third (the traitor) sends x, y, z to the others, respectively, and the fourth sends the number 4.

2. Each general forms a set of information represented in the list below.

   General A: 1, 2, x, 4

   General B: 1, 2, y, 4

   General C: 1, 2, 3, 4

   General D: 1, 2, z, 4

3. Each sends the results to the others, and the third general can again send incorrect values. So, the list of sets they get from this step may look like those in the table below.

	General A	General B	General C	General D
General A		1,2,x,4	1,2,x,4	1,2,x,4
General B	1,2,y,4		1,2,y,4	1,2,y,4
General C	a,b,c,d	e,f,g,h		i,j,k,l
General D	1,2,z,4	1,2,z,4	1,2,z,4	

4. Each general checks each element of all received sets. If a value matches in at least in two sets, then it is added to the 'final' set. Otherwise, it is marked as 'unknown'. In this case, all the loyal generals get one set {1, 2, unknown, 4}, which means that the consensus is reached.

Lamport proved that, in a system where *m* elements are not working properly, consensus could only be reached when at least two-thirds of the other elements work correctly.

Hyperledger Fabric

Fabric is a modular and extensible open-source system for deploying and operating permissioned blockchains. It is one of the Hyperledger projects hosted by the Linux Foundation (Androulaki et al., 2018), which is driven by IBM Hyperledger Fabric supported by more than 240 organisations.[53]

Hyperledger Fabric is a permissioned chain used in business applications where there is a need for high transaction throughput within a group of participants having a common goal, but do not fully trust each other. Hence, this is a scenario very much suited for a PBFT protocol.

To implement this architecture, Fabric contains modular building blocks for each of the following components:

- An ordering service that atomically broadcasts state updates to peers and establishes consensus on the order of transactions.
- A membership service provider is responsible for associating peers with cryptographic identities. It maintains the permissioned nature of Fabric.
- An optional peer-to-peer gossip service disseminates the blocks output by ordering service to all peers.
- Smart contracts in Fabric run within a container environment for isolation, which can be written in standard programming languages but do not have direct access to the ledger state.
- Each peer locally maintains the ledger in the form of an append-only blockchain and as a snapshot of the most recent state in a key-value store.

As stated, both Ripple and Hyperledger rely on most validators acting with good intentions and who do not include fraudulent transactions into the blocks. Also, neither Ripple nor Hyperledger Fabric discloses their incentive mechanisms for the validators. Yet the Hyperledger approach assumes the rewards[54] can go to the validation peer who first publishes the hash that receives two-thirds of confirmations.

---

[53] See https://www.hyperledger.org/

[54] Rewards come in the form of transaction fees or block rewards, if the Hyperledger has a cryptocurrency.

3.6. Smart contracts

The first blockchains like Bitcoin were designed as a payment system or, in broader terms, for the transfer of digital assets. Together with the introduction of Ethereum, more blockchains appeared that allow for the deployment of software code, called smart contracts.[55] A smart contract is, at its core, a *conditional payment* or token transfer instruction. If the established conditions are met, then upon invocation of the contract the transfer of the token is executed. The events against which these conditions are checked must be recorded on a blockchain. For instance, if there is an insurance contract that states party A gets 1 ETH from party B if the average daily temperatures in a specific location and for a certain month are three consecutive days below zero,[56] the average daily temperature of that location must be stored on the blockchain every day. Then, upon invocation by one of the parties involved, the smart contract validates whether the conditions for the payment have been met. Figure 18 illustrates the example given above.

Several aspects need to be highlighted here:

- The transfer from B can happen only if the smart contract has full control over the funds, which, in this case, is 1 ETH. A smart contract can never have control over the funds of the party B. The 1 ETH of party B is sent to an escrow account for the time of the contract and is not accessible. This is an important property of the smart contract and is why smart contracts on the blockchain need not trust the counterpart. The contract also incorporates an instruction that, if the conditions are not met, and the contract expires, then the funds will return to B. Therefore, B can be sure they can retrieve the original funds if the conditions are not met.
- Smart contracts can execute a payment or fire an event. The latter action is represented by an entry made in the blockchain log file, which is readable by other applications. To check a contract, it must be called with a

---

[55] The founder of Ethereum, Vitalik Buterin, compares smart contract technology to a vending machine where you drop a coin into the machine and automatically receive a drink or snacks in return.

[56] Such a condition could be meaningful for harvest insurance.

signed transaction that performs the check function and, in our example, follows three options: do nothing, if the conditions are not met and the contract is still valid; pay to A, if the conditions are met and A is eligible for the payment; or return the funds to B if the conditions are not met and the contract expires. If no other rules are included, then everyone on the blockchain can execute this check contract function at any time, including party A, party B, or a third party.

- Smart contracts assume that the person, function, or device that (in our example) writes the temperature data to the blockchain provides the correct data. To avoid tampering with the data by a single source, multiple verifications and signatures might be used to write a valid average daily temperature to the chain.
- Due to the size limitations of a blockchain, the data needed to check the conditions of smart contracts should be small or, if this is not possible, held in a separate (side) chain (see Chapter 3.7 on scalability and 3.8 on interoperability of blockchains).

Smart contracts can call other smart contracts, and token transfers are not limited to valuable assets, although membership or voting tokens could be conditionally transferred. If, for instance, a member of a group does not fulfil certain membership conditions or misbehaves, then they might be excluded from the group. Another example of a smart contract could be that voting tokens for a shareholders meeting are automatically transferred to a proxy if participation in the meeting is not claimed after a set period provided that the shareholders previously agree to such a clause in the by-laws.

Smart contracts have a myriad of use cases across all industries. They are used to define payment tokens or financial instruments, manage memberships and authorised signatures, monitor token transfers, and grant or withdraw access permissions to systems.

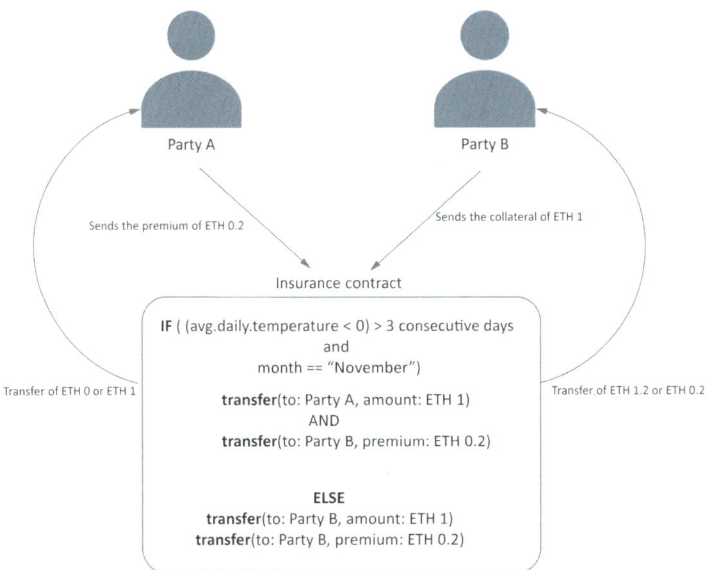

Source: Banking Concepts.

Figure 18. Illustration of a simple insurance contract.[57]

Smart contracts combined with IoT (Internet of Things)

Another use case for smart contracts is IoT, which is the combination of physical items (e.g., locks, vehicles, or microwaves), and sensors with software with network connectivity that allows these devices to exchange data. Smart contracts, with automatic contract-enforcement functions, are considered the missing component for IoT because trust is not required between parties. For example, Figure 19 shows how a smart lock for a rented apartment can work with blockchain. A smart lock contract contains the price per night of ETH 1 and a guest deposit of ETH 3, and the lock calculates the number of nights this

[57] The conditions in the illustration are written as pseudo-code. It is further assumed that for this bet (or insurance) from Party A will pay party B a premium of 0.2 ETH at the expiration of the contract.

guest can have access to the apartment. After the time is expired, the contract fires an event that locks the apartment.

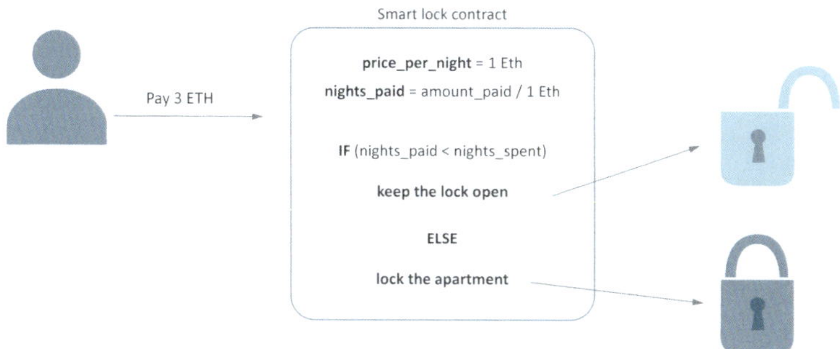

Source: Banking Concepts.

Figure 19. Smart lock model.

By mid-2017, three main players in the blockchain world[58] offered smart contracts, including Ethereum, Hyperledger Fabric, and R3Corda. Although all three aim to enhance paper-based contracts as the core features are the same, they offer the following minor differences.

1. *Programming languages*. Ethereum features a language for writing smart contracts called Solidity, Hyperledger Fabric uses Go and Java, and Corda smart contracts are written in Java or Kotlin.
2. *Chaincode*. Smart contracts in Hyperledger is called 'chaincode'.
3. *Legal prose*. As Corda was primarily designed for the financial services industry, they wanted to fit into this highly regulated industry. So, unlike Ethereum and Hyperledger, Corda's smart contracts can contain legal prose in addition to code.
4. Today, the leader in smart contract development is Ethereum. For this reason, the following sections describing the types of smart contracts, how to deploy them as well as how they interact are based on experience with Ethereum code.

[58] Then R3CEV consortium and Corda is often mentioned in the context of blockchain technology, although in its whitepaper it clearly states that it is not a blockchain.

Updating smart contracts and smart contract interaction

As mentioned above, once published smart contracts are impossible to change without the consent of all parties. As with any other software program, smart contracts can have bugs and programs must be updated. In principle, there are a few approaches on how to update a smart contract after being deployed.

1. *Create a new contract.* After fixing bugs or adding new features, a new contract is deployed which is not connected to the previous version. This approach is the most natural solution, though often not applicable to real applications as data recorded by the old contract may not be usable by the new one.
2. *Create upgradable contracts.* Contracts can be upgraded through consent from all participants.
3. *Break the contract into parts.* Instead of deploying one complete contract with all functionality, separate it into smaller interacting components. Contracts calling one another performs the interaction. This approach solves two issues: (i) smaller parts are less likely to have bugs, and (ii) if there are bugs, then only that portion must be re-deployed. In addition, this approach allows for separation of the part of the contract that stores the data from the logic, which could then be changed without the loss of previous records.

As the third approach above requires contract interaction, Solidity provides the following two methods for how the contract can interact.

1. *call()*: calls another contract to read its data from the blockchain recorder of the called contract;
2. *delegatecall()*: calls another contract to execute one of its functions, which may result in writing data to the blockchain.

These functions are recommended only if there is no other approach because the *delegatecall* method can also influence the data stored in the calling contract, which might cause security risks.

3.7. Scalability

Blockchains are not very well suited for high-volume transaction processing. The reasons are twofold: On the one hand, blockchains set limits for the block size and hence for the number of transactions that can be processed per second.[59] On the other hand, the relay time of a transaction throughout the network increases with the number of nodes.

For Bitcoin, with the current block size limit of 1MB, there is a theoretical maximum of around seven transactions per second, whereas the effective peak performance lies around 3.8 transactions per second.[60] On the Ethereum main chain, the block size is limited by a so-called gas limit, which varies per block. As per September 2017, the daily average gas limit was about 6,700,000 gas[61], which results in a maximum of 15 transactions per second.[62] The daily transaction statistic chart shows that this limit was reached in January 2018 and has since then dropped back to approximately 7 transactions per second.[63] Compared to transactions on commercial payment systems, such as Visa (with an average of roughly 2,000 and a peak capability of 56,000 transactions per second)[64] or airline reservations systems, these performance values are substantially smaller.

The feature of decentralisation in a blockchain brings a vast and potentially unlimited number of replications of the data across the network on independ-

---

59 As described in Chapter 3.3, blockchains that allow the execution of smart contracts also need more computing power.

60 A basic bitcoin transaction with one input and two outputs amounts to approximately 250 Byte. However, due to more complex transactions, the average bitcoin transaction size is around 500 Byte. https://tradeblock.com/blog/analysis-of-bitcoin-transaction-size-trends, accessed 27 August 2018.

61 https://etherscan.io/chart/gaslimit

62 https://www.coindesk.com/information/will-ethereum-scale/

63 https://etherscan.io/chart/tx

64 https://usa.visa.com/run-your-business/small-business-tools/retail.html http://www.digitaltransactions.net/visas-test-results-record-peak-volume-and-expected-smooth-sailing-for-tokens/

ent nodes. Although, with decreasing benefit, each additional node adds more trust to the blockchain. On the other hand, from an economic point of view, each redundant node consumes additional disk space and adds delays due to the required synchronisation of the blocks.

These trade-offs are reflected in what is known as the blockchain trilemma (Jordan, 2018; Raju, 2014/2018), which is the widespread notion that blockchains can maintain only two of the following three properties:

- decentralisation,
- scalability,
- security.

Assuming blockchain solutions should not compromise on decentralisation, the only two conclusions may be offered:

- A blockchain application cannot be scaled up to high-volume commercial applications without losing the trust derived from its replication on independent nodes.
- Transactions fees will increase with the usage of a blockchain as it becomes a scarce resource where transactions compete to be processed in the next block.

There are potential measures available to ease the pressure, and research on new conceptual solutions is ongoing. These approaches are categorised as the following:

- **Increase block sizes and reduce block times.**

  An increase of the block size results in a bigger and faster-growing database, which could lead to a concentration of power where only those nodes that can afford the larger database participate in the chain. The same argument holds for a reduction in the block times.

- **Side chains**.

  Side chains are incorporated to off-load high-volume transaction processing, such as micropayments or high-frequency trading from the main chain. They are designed for a specific purpose and often work with a cooperative consensus mechanism, where the number of participants is limited and know and trust each other (Lee, 2018). Side chains are also used for netting high-volume transactions. For example, in the case of high-frequency trading, the participants can transfer their positions in assets in the morning to the side chain, trade during the day, and settle the balances on the main chain in the evening.

- **Omit parts of the blockchain history and introducing trusted states.**

  This concept aims at reducing the size of the database by 'archiving' transactions from addresses that no longer have active balances or contracts.

- **Sharding.**

  Sharding is a concept of a database architecture where a database is split between different servers to balance the database load and improve performance (Wikipedia, 2018b). The data are separated in a way that the most frequently used data from a group of users (e.g., European vs American users) is maintained together on the same server. Sharding in blockchains requires that the transactions between homogeneous groups be identified and the blockchain be divided into subchains where only transactions between different homogenous groups would be processed across the subchains (Jordan, 2018; Raju, 2014/2018). This concept is closely related to the interoperability of blockchains, which is addressed later.

With these ideas in mind, additional questions should be considered. Why should blockchains be scaled up for high-volume transactions? Do we need the trust derived from blockchains for high-volume applications?

The following are several consequences:

- As stated above, blockchains are not very well suited for high-frequency, real-time transaction processing. In the future, this will continue to be the case beyond blockchain systems, such as in side chains.
- Blockchains are suited for infrequent but important transactions, such as registries for real-world property (land or car registers[65] and shares of non-frequently traded companies).

---

[65] See our use case 1.1.1 Public register (land and commercial registers).

- Many blockchain systems exist in parallel.
- There is a need for the interoperability of blockchains.

So, the important question is for which use cases do we need high-frequency transaction processing systems, where it is not sufficient to split such high-performance systems into a set of independent chains?

3.8. Interoperability of blockchains

Because of the limited scalability and different business purposes, multiple blockchains operate in parallel with the need for intercommunication. This communication between blockchains is necessary for two reasons:

- Data needed for the validation of a smart contract reside on another chain.
- Assets or tokens are swapped across chains, i.e., when someone wants to exchange a token on one chain against tokens on another chain. To ensure that both parties fulfil the exchange contract, both transactions must be validated and confirmed simultaneously. Without this principle, known as Delivery Versus Payment (DVP), cross-chain transactions again require a trusted intermediary, which eliminates the core benefit of blockchain technology.

Hence, the requirements for the interoperability of blockchains can be considered through two questions.

- How can a transaction be securely transmitted to another chain and how can data on another chain be securely read?
- How can both legs of a cross-chain transaction be safely executed?

As of today, there are not many initiatives to address the interoperability of blockchains. Secure communication is addressed by a project called POLKADOT, which was launched in 2017 by Gavin Wood, an Ethereum co-founder and former CTO. According to a talk from March 2017 in Zurich, the first implementation could be expected in late 2018 or early 2019. The main aim of the initiative is to provide an infrastructure for the secure delivery of one transaction to another chain. The proposed concepts include *relay chains*, *parachains*, and *bridges*. The first two are intended to facilitate the setup of a private chain without building a new community to overcome the scalability and transaction cost issues. Bridges are designed to communicate with independent chains.[66]

Recently, the concept of atomic swaps emerged for the synchronisation of cross-chain transactions. This approach uses hash-time-locked smart contracts (HTLC) to ensure that both parties of a token exchange fulfil their obligations. The recipient of a payment must confirm the receipt of the tokens with some confidential information before a specified deadline. Otherwise, the tokens are returned. Although this concept looks promising, there remain hurdles, including the secure communication of the confidential information (Madeira, 2018).

As of May 2018, none of the technologies for blockchain interoperability have reached maturity. Since the blockchain community now acknowledges the importance of the topic, a variety of solutions will likely be tested in the near-term.

3.9. Privacy versus transparency

Blockchains are simultaneously anonymous and transparent and are sometimes called pseudo-anonymous. They can be the source of total control or provide an environment for the perfect crime. Both views are accurate depending on if and how the users of a blockchain are identified and which measures are taken to ensure privacy.

To understand the trade-off, we recapitulate how transactions are stored on the blockchain. When a user creates a wallet, public and private keys are generated. All transactions with this user's wallet are stored with the public key on the chain. So, the public can see what tokens have been received and transferred from this public address or which contracts have been signed or document hashes stored. In principle, if we know the address of a user, say, because we sent tokens to them, then we can see all other transfers to and

[66] More information is available at https://polkadot.io

from their wallet and all other transactions signed. We cannot see the details of the transactions or the content of documents, but we can see the position and the behaviour of the public address.

If the identity of the person behind a public address remains hidden and the amount of the holdings or the behaviour of the public key does not provide an indication of the owner, then others can only speculate on the ownership. A user may also create multiple wallets, i.e., multiple key pairs, to distribute assets across. While creating multiple wallets might be a meaningful instrument to dilute the size of holdings and behavioural patterns, this approach is not well suited for business applications where continuity and transparency are desired, where tokens are used for voting, or investment limits must be monitored.

There are also so-called deterministic wallets, such as the hierarchical deterministic wallet (HD wallet) that can generate an infinite number of public keys from one private key pair, called the master key pair. The public keys of an HD wallet are stored in a tree, and the wallet only needs to know the position of the child in the tree to link the public key of the child to the master key. HD wallets were first suggested to the Bitcoin protocol in 2013 but have not become popular on other blockchains.

In the past, the privacy issue has been very well addressed on public blockchains. This attitude appears to be changing slowly, especially as the General Data Protection Regulation (GDPR) of the EU comes into effect.[67] Concerns are emerging that new privacy regulations could even prevent blockchain projects from being rolled out. The GDPR gives EU citizens the right for all data that could identify a person to be deleted upon request, which is a law that contrasts sharply with blockchain technology benefits. However, how these concerns can be overcome or what it exactly means for blockchain applications is not yet clear.

---

[67] As an example, see a discussion on reddit on data privacy (r/ethereum, 2018).

3.10. Patents

Blockchain innovators are seeking ways to protect their algorithms and unique ideas, and one method is through a patent application. It is difficult to estimate the real number of patents in the blockchain field as sources provide different numbers. For example, the US Patent and Trademark Office (USPTO) received around 390 applications up to July 2017. Figure 20 shows how the number of patent applications at USPTO grew over the past seven years.

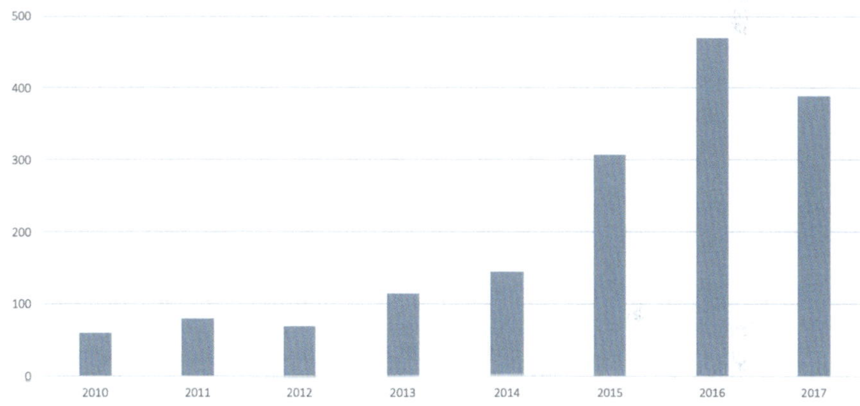

Source: Tuan (2017).

Figure 20. The number of patent applications submitted to the USPTO.

The likely leader in filing patents in the U.S., Bank of America Corporation, has filed 43 patents since 2014 concerning the security of user data, access rights, and payment systems.

On the other hand, according to Espacenet,[68] the number of published patents and their distribution among different patent offices for 2017 is shown in Table 7.

---

[68] Espacenet is a worldwide database of published applications and patents developed by the European Patent Office (https://worldwide.espacenet.com).

Table 7: The number of published patents worldwide.

Patent office	No. published applications
Canadian Intellectual Property Office	2
European Patent Office	1
IP Australia	7
Korean Intellectual Property Office	8
State Intellectual Property Office of China	27
Taiwan Intellectual Property Office	2
UK Intellectual Property Office	2
US Patent and Trademark Office	43
World Intellectual Property Organization	38
Total number of patents	*130*

Source: Banking Concepts based on patent searches using the following keywords: 'blockchain', 'bitcoin', 'ethereum', and 'distributed ledger'.

These patents aim to enhance existing systems with blockchain technology with the most popular category among the published patents of payment architectures. The distribution among the top ten most popular categories in 2017 is provided in Table 8.

Table 8. Top 10 topics of published patents worldwide.

Patent category	No. published applications
Authentication, i.e., establishing identity	7
Authorisation and identity management	5
Banking & finance	2
Commerce	3
Data management	11
Data processing	15
Data protection	13
Investment and trading	4
Payment architectures, schemes, or protocols	49
Security	9
Total number of patents	*118*

Source: Banking Concepts.

According to the data from Espacenet, the top five companies whose applications were published include nChain Holdings, Mastercard Inc., Netspective Communications, Accenture Global Solutions Ltd, and IBM Corp. The number of published patent applications as distributed between these companies is included in Table 9.

Table 9. Top 5 companies of published patents worldwide.

Company	Country	Industry	No. applications
Accenture Global Solutions Ltd	Ireland	IT consulting	4
IBM Corp	USA	IT & Services	4
Mastercard Inc	USA	Financial Services	5
nChain Holdings	UK	Software development	18
Netspective Communications	USA	Healthcare IT	5
Total number of patents			*36*

Source: Banking Concepts.

As with many other industries, blockchain is very attractive to patent trolls. To fight these trolls, the Chamber of Digital Commerce created the Blockchain Intellectual Property Council (BIPC) in March 2017. The BIPC aims to develop a strategy to identify the trolls and interfere with their activities as well as to attract new members. Nevertheless, despite being a young technology, the potential of the blockchain technology attracts more companies from different industries to explore the possibilities.

4. Potential Benefits

The potential benefits and challenges of the application of blockchain technology in the economy go far beyond the creation of cryptocurrencies, which has taken over most of the media coverage today. To identify beneficial fields of application and the likelihood of a successful implementation, the following questions must be answered:

1. Where does blockchain technology replace or add more trust in a business process and, thus, reduce transaction costs?
2. Who benefits from it and who stands to lose?
3. What are the challenges associated with it?

In this chapter, we conceptually analyse the benefits and dissect the transaction costs associated with blockchain technology.

4.1. Where blockchains can generate trust in business processes

4.1.1. Replacing intermediaries

In today's economy, if two business partners are new or unknown to each other and exchange high-value goods, then neutral intermediaries both parties agreed to guarantee the step-by-step execution of their transaction. The process works simply as one party sends money and the other the goods to the intermediary, who then receives both assets and forwards them to both parties. Prominent examples of trusted intermediaries include clearing houses for financial transactions and banks in trade finance. Deposits for rental agreements and software escrow agreements are additional examples where a neutral intermediary creates trust.

Many of these intermediaries could be replaced by blockchain technology, provided that the assets to be exchanged can be safely and securely tokenised. In the financial industry and transactions with securities, the concept of step-by-step execution is also known as *delivery versus payment* (DVP).

4.1.2. Automating the verification processes

Another generator of trust are verification authorities, which are persons or institutions mandated to verify the authenticity of a signature (e.g., notaries) or goods (e.g., independent appraisers) or to verify production processes, such as food quality labels, safety standards and emissions. Together with IoT, these processes can be further automated. Blockchain technology does not replace these authorities but can help reduce the cost of the processes in two important ways. First, supporting documents and data can be safely and transparently stored on the blockchain. Second, the blockchain eliminates the single point of failure risk that any automated centralised solution entails. Blockchain technology could also reduce the cost of regulations as the risks of fraud and monitoring costs decrease.

4.2. How relationships are typically affected

As blockchains are best suited for the exchange of high-value assets, a business model view of trust is used to highlight blockchain's potential.

4.2.1. Business to business relationships (B2B)

In B2B processes, especially in industrial supply chains, high-value goods are exchanged. Business partners in industrial processes typically know one another and have good quality assurance methods in place. The same applies for larger retail supply chains where suppliers are known and quality standards are defined. Although for such supply chains the value-added from blockchain technology may appear limited, high-value goods might be prone to fraud, and hence tracing transfers in a blockchain could provide substantial benefits. In addition, blockchain technology can help reduce the cost of managing inventory across companies as material inflow and outflow do not need to be recorded in separate systems. Blockchains can also add trust in volatile B2B relationships with continually changing partners. Provided that the quality of the goods can be verified easily, or the verification can be automated, especially by sensors, blockchains could play an important role.

4.2.2. Business to consumer relationships (B2C)

Today, B2C processes are based on trust in the brand of the products or in the evaluation of the producer or product by the retailer. This is especially true for repeating purchases, and, in these cases, trust can minimally be improved by blockchain technology. However, it may help for one-time purchases from producers who are unknown to the buyer. A typical example of such a business is the individual travel industry. Here, buyers heavily rely on reviews from other buyers, although studies show that many of the reviews are bought by the suppliers or organisers of the marketplace. Blockchain technology could help to identify the sources and to validate facts. Of course, a recording of a review on a blockchain might discourage some reviewers, but the foundation of product and service reviews based on facts could be improved.

Another aspect of a B2C relationship is the financing of a business. Traditionally, this role has been fulfilled by banks or through banks on the capital markets, which became highly regulated to improve investor protection. Due to the immateriality of financial instruments, blockchains could play a prominent role in replacing a substantial part of this business by allowing direct investments without the involvement of financial intermediaries. The prerequisites include a broad community with adequately written and community tested smart contracts. However, the majority of consumers neither have the capability nor the time to make individual assessments of smart contracts. So, the smart contracts become the object of trust, which opens new possibilities for newcomers as well as for incumbents.

4.2.3. Consumer to consumer relationships (C2C)

In the past, C2C relationships occurred in secondary markets. Used goods were offered for sale through ads in newspapers and, more recently, online sales and auction platforms. C2C relationships now extend into financial markets with crowd-financing, crowd-lending, and collective investments in real estate as some examples. Blockchains and smart contracts could add trust to this process provided that the smart contracts, as mentioned above, can be trusted.

4.2.4. Government to Citizen relationships (G2C)

Governments and public administrations are supposed to organise and regulate how people live together. Governmental tasks include citizen services for registries, levying taxes, public procurements, and the regulation of the use of shared resources, especially as population density increases. These administrative bodies are typically trusted, at least in democratic countries, with their high degree of transparency.

As every citizen contributes taxes to the functioning of the public services, transparency is of utmost importance. In addition, easy-to-apply incentives and monitoring systems for the fair use of public resources are needed to overcome the 'tragedy of the commons problem'.[69] Even if centralised systems can achieve these goals, a blockchain implementation controlled by the citizens could add trust to their implementation. Also, common registry changes, including those with a transfer of assets (i.e., land registries), could become more acceptable as no single authority would maintain the central database.

Blockchain technology could also be used to improve the efficiency of interactions between citizens and the administration. Although equally implementable with centralised systems, a blockchain implementation could improve many reconciliation and validation procedures between administrative departments resulting in decreased costs.

4.3. Transaction cost theory

The focus on transaction costs is rooted in the understanding that the blockchain technology's main benefit is the facilitation of trade. Williamson (1979) describes transaction costs by the three characteristics:[70]

---

[69] See https://en.wikipedia.org/wiki/Tragedy_of_the_commons

[70] Although subsequent scholars refined these characteristics and added new layers, the three presented here are sufficient to provide the general idea.

- *Asset specificity,* i.e., the degree to which the asset in question could be used in a different transaction (ranging from mass products to custom made),
- *Uncertainty,* i.e., both the risk associated with the context of the trade, such as political stability (environmental uncertainty) as well as the conduct of the contractual partner (behavioural uncertainty), and
- *Frequency,* i.e., the likelihood of the transaction reoccurring.

These characteristics impact the trade ex-ante and ex-post. Some ex-ante transaction costs were lowered substantially due to the Internet, such as initiation costs in terms of search costs, for a trade partner, and information search costs, about a trade partner. Other ex-ante transaction costs were reduced by online platforms that facilitate trade by limiting the contract content.

However, the Internet did not meaningfully alter ex-post transaction costs, including handling costs (transportation, matchmaking fees), control costs (surveillance), contract enforcement costs, and costs of adjustment (when the content of the contract is renegotiated).

Lowering transaction costs affect businesses in the following three ways:

- *Cost cutting potential.* Companies can opt to gain a competitive edge (or stay in business by following competitors) by simply offering lower prices resulting in an expanded demand.
- *Business opportunities.* The current transaction costs may be prohibitively high to engage in business. In these cases, lowering transaction costs catalyses new business models.
- *Governance improvements.* When the costs of governance are lowered, new forms of collective ownership with higher active participation thrive.

We next distinguish three types of transactions costs as part of the analytical framework of financial costs, costs of legal certainty, and time costs, which are applied to the use cases in Chapter 1.

4.3.1. Financial transaction costs

The primary mechanism to drive down financial costs is to eliminate intermediaries.

Business perspective: financing cost

Blockchain technology allows companies to address their investors directly without intermediaries. Companies can communicate directly with investors to raise money. If the laws allow, then subscriptions for new investments could be made directly on the blockchain and converted into equity. The impressive surge in ICOs during 2017 documents the vast interest in new forms of financing.[71]

Platforms for raising equity typically cost between 5% and 12% of the capital raised, which does not include the administrative efforts for issuing shares. Although a large part of this margin is used for marketing the investment opportunity, blockchain technology could more efficiently apply capital increases as well as any corporate actions, such as dividend payments, capital split, and conversions.[72]

Individual's perspective: cheaper financing, investment, and insurance costs

For an individual, blockchain technology will very likely reduce financing, investment, insurance and administrative transaction costs. By engaging into blockchain secured peer-to-peer contracts instead of using financial intermediaries, costs could be substantially reduced.

Provided that the regulation of financial intermediaries (banking laws, trading) adapt to take advantage of the lower risk and better compliance associated

[71] For many projects, it is not clear what the money is used for and what rights are associated with the issuing of tokens. As regulators step in, it is likely that this will be a temporary phenomenon.

[72] From an analysis of the costs of dividend payments and the fees banks charge for these activities, in the past, these costs have been up to 1% of the dividend amount.

with blockchain solutions, the 1–2% margin[73] that financial intermediaries typically request from borrowers and investors could be saved or substantially reduced. These margins might be even higher for private equity investments or complex transactions. Also, the process of establishing or refinancing mortgages could become cheaper as liens on title deeds could be easily created and exchanged with tokens used as collateral.

Likewise, insurance premiums could be substantially reduced if insured objects and insurance contracts are registered on a blockchain so that damage claims could be automatically verified. The loss ratio of international insurance varies today between 40% and 90% with the variation depending on the type of insurance or insured object. For life insurance, the loss ratio is at the upper end, whereas property insurance is lower, which suggests that 10% to 60% of the premium is needed for customer acquisition, damage claims, and profit. Similar to the banking industry, the insurance industry is also heavily regulated to ensure that damage claims for any event can be paid. With blockchain-secured collateral and blockchain-verified damage claims, a substantial part of insurance premium could be saved.

Business perspective: corporate governance

Another aspect of investor interaction is the facilitation of corporate governance. Shareholder meeting costs for large international companies can easily add up to millions of dollars as the shareholder registry is maintained through financial intermediaries, which are often the in-betweens for communication with the shareholders and organising proxy voting. Blockchain technology could facilitate shareholder communication and replace physical meetings, provided that corporate laws allow it.

Financial advantages in corporate governance can also be achieved by smaller companies with international and heterogenous shareholders. In addition, international regulation increases the pressure on companies to accurately maintain their shareholder's registry and to identify the ultimate beneficial owners of shares. Blockchain share registries can more easily achieve this process. The financial advantages of blockchain-secured corporate governance might be substantially

---

[73] This assumption is based on a P/L analysis from domestic and international banks, and these are net margins, i.e., without credit risk surcharges.

less for board meetings, but the advantages of an immutable audit trail of board decisions may be a good reason for using blockchain technology. Along with legal considerations, a key hurdle for the introduction of blockchain technology to corporate governance is confidentiality.

Individual's perspective: collective and shared ownership

When purchasing shares, bonds, and mutual funds, individuals engage in collective ownership. Buyers are entitled to financial rights, such as dividends, interest payments, or, in the case of shares, voting rights. The execution of shareholders' rights is cumbersome due to required physical participation, requirements for the transfer of voting rights to proxies, the form and validity of signatures for resolutions, and because entrance tickets to shareholder meetings must be requested through intermediaries. Blockchain solutions could substantially facilitate these processes and allow for more direct participation in the governance of collective ownership, provided that a country's legal framework supports the execution of participation rights via a blockchain solution. Blockchain governance could also be used for communities of owners in real estate or bonds in default.

In addition, blockchains and smart contracts enable more flexible, contractual forms of collective or shared ownership. For example, cars or real estate could be shared or rented, income automatically distributed to the participants, and service and maintenance contributions of individual participants automatically integrated. Participants could agree to the sale or repair of existing objects or new purchases. Such collective agreements are possible today but require manual administration and control, all with the absence of trust. Hence, blockchain and smart contract technologies can enhance the trust between the participants and the efficiency of implementing the interaction.

As all details of such agreements would be encoded into smart contracts, the participants must be able to read the code or rely on a provider of smart contracts or smart contract templates. If smart contract templates are used, the participants would simply fill out forms with the necessary parameters. So, smart contract writing is likely to become a new business opportunity. This scenario also demonstrates that blockchains and smart contracts cannot operate trustless, i.e., in the absence of trust. Trust is merely shifted from the contract parties to the provider of smart contract templates, which is less risky as the smart contracts providers maintain no active stake in the contract.

Payment systems

Universal payment systems, such as credit and debit cards, are advanced, easy to use, and ubiquitous. However, these types of payments are expensive, especially for internationally payments. Also, many companies and institutions create unique payment systems as loyalty programs for returning customers to earn benefits or volume discounts. Although very popular, with the inflation of royalty programs, consumers may lose track, resulting in an increase of claims. Due to continuous enhancements to privacy concerns and regulations, the advantages of loyalty programs for companies will likely decrease.

Blockchain technology can improve this situation in two ways. First, it can help to create anonymous, universal, and cheaper payment systems. Second, it can help to create payment systems where no system currently exists with many different stakeholders. An example of such a payment system is citizen coins, where governmental bodies can set incentives for an intended behaviour and citizens receive rewards if they comply. Blockchain technology could also add trust, in this case, as no single stakeholder could manipulate the data as well as decrease the cost of implementation.

4.3.2. Costs of legal certainty

The primary mechanism for driving down the costs of legal certainty is to increase transparency.

Product Certificates

Issuing product certificates and making the production process transparent and easily verifiable for all consumers generates trust, and this trust can convert into value. Customers are willing to pay for better quality and, thus, companies can ask for higher prices. Companies that provide a more transparent proof-of-provenance may also increase market share. Compared to a centralised solution, blockchain-based labels and certificates, where every step of the label creation is immutably documented, can generate a higher level of trust.

Blockchain-based solutions can also help to reduce counterfeiting as consumers and authorities, such as customs and health authorities, can more easily check if products are forged or the chain of provenance was broken.

Supply chain

Together with IoT and smart contracts, blockchain technology can improve quality assurance and reduce counterparty risks. In international trading and logistics, where there are many participants in the supply chain and parties are unknown to one another, blockchains can create substantially more trust compared to a centralised solution. The use of IoT, e.g., for recording sensor data, can link payments directly with the fulfilment of quality criteria. Malicious actors may be more likely to refrain from tampering with sensors or its data as the fraudulent activity might be detected with cross-checks and pattern monitoring. As a key difference to a centralised solution, the sender of the data could be held responsible as they initiated the transaction with a digital signature.

Blockchains could also help manage cross-company inventories. In trading, where outcoming and incoming goods are often accounted for by each participant in the trading chain, blockchains could track the movement of goods more effectively.

Quality of products

There is a growing need for quality certificates of products, which testify to the product properties, such as the biological production of goods, ingredients, animal protection, fair trade, child work, and environmental-friendly production. As a consumer, we must trust the labels and the organisations behind them. Still, doubts remain as commercial interests could influence the certification process or certificates could be issued without justification. The high cost for systematic production and supply chain monitoring along with the reliance on random, but potentially influenceable, samples add to these doubts of quality labels. Full traceability of products with production properties based on a blockchain implementation could add a substantially higher level of trust and avoid counterfeiting.

4.3.3. Time costs

The primary mechanism driving down time costs is lowering contract enforcement costs.

Conditioned payments

Many contracts contain obligations of payments if certain conditions are met. Typical examples of such contracts are insurances, where payments for damages are defined. By systematically collecting and writing contract relevant information to a blockchain, the validation of damage claims can be sped up. If contract relevant, the data are automatically collected from trusted databases or sensors, e.g., from crash sensors in cars or weather databases, the damage can be automatically calculated and reimbursed by just calling the smart contract on the blockchain. Hence, smart contracts reduce time costs if all data for a contractual clause can be captured and recorded on the blockchain.

5. Technical Challenges

For all the benefits of blockchain technology to come into effect, and apart from resolving fundamental legal issues, a series of technical challenges must be mastered.

5.1. Tokenisation of assets

The process of creating a cryptographical representation of real-world assets is called tokenisation. Cryptographically represented assets are also called digital assets. The legal entity that takes responsibility for the tokenisation is referred to as the issuer of tokens.

5.1.1. Tokenisation for different asset types

Digital assets can be categorised by comparing 'intangible versus tangible' and 'fungible versus non-fungible'. Each category includes unique properties in the corresponding tokenisation process.

Intangible assets

Intangible assets have no underlying physical object, and they exist due to the application of law (e.g., patents, copyrights, and trademarks). These kinds of assets are comparatively easy to tokenise because there is no physical object attached. The main challenge for intangible assets is the creation of smart contracts that represent entirely the legal model of rights. For example, if someone 'buys' a song from iTunes, then the buyer does not gain ownership over the song, but only purchases the right to listen to the music under certain conditions. These rights may be transferable or not, or the duration or number of times a song can be played may be limited. Such restrictions create another challenge, as each time a song is played a transaction must be recorded on the blockchain, which means that each device on which the song is played needs access to the private key of the buyer to sign the transaction. This would be cumbersome as multiple devices require the same key or the buyer might facilitate the process by using a private key service, which imposes a security risk. In addition, depending on the underlying blockchain technology, each transaction could require a transaction fee.

Another challenge might arise from the high number of transactions written to the blockchain, which is a scalability issue of the blockchain the user would encounter.

Tangible assets

As opposed to intangible assets, tangible assets have a physical manifestation. The key challenge for any issuer of a cryptographical representation of such assets is to ensure that the number of tokens issued always represents the quantity or value of the physical goods they represent. The physical goods might be stored at one or more locations or might be transported between them. In addition, the issuer must make sure that the holder of the tokens can have access to the physical goods or can request delivery.

Access and delivery might be more accessible, and associated delivery costs might be lower for fungible assets, where one unit of the asset can be replaced by another identical unit of the same asset (e.g., oil, water, money, or ores). Here, the term 'the same' does not only refer to the same type, but also to the same quality of the asset. The issuer must hence ensure that the mechanisms and instruments used to check the quality of an asset are broadly accessible, to not undermine the additional level of trust the blockchain technology provides. Fungible assets are also easier to break down into smaller units or be grouped at any time, e.g., into millilitres of water or barrels of oil. Digital assets that represent fungible assets are easy to transfer as only the number, or the value, of the corresponding token must be transferred.

The challenges for non-fungible assets are that each unit of the asset is unique, is not replaceable, and has unique identifiers. This uniqueness of items means that a significant number of identifiers must be recorded on the chain during tokenisation, such as with diamonds, DNA, or pills. Concerning scalability, when the ownership of a non-fungible asset token is transferred, the transfer of the unique ID must be recorded on the chain. Another challenge lies in the crypto-anchors that must be assigned to each item of the physical goods. Crypto anchors can be either unique properties derived from physical or biological properties of the corresponding object, e.g., the casting characteristic of gold bars, the spectral characteristics of diamonds or the

DNA of animated beings, or incorporated as markers into undividable units of the nun-fungible item, e.g., for pills or spare engine parts. Similar to the quality measuring for fungible items, the issuer of such tokens must ensure that the instruments to identify the non-fungible unit are available at all checkpoints.

5.1.2. Tokenisation processes

Along with the creation of a new blockchain with a native token, there are two methods for tokenisation. The first is best described as *pegging a digital asset to an existing cryptocurrency*, and the second is the *issuing of a smart contract* on an existing permissioned or permissionless chain.

Pegging

For example, on the Bitcoin blockchain, issuing a token means that some small amount of Bitcoin (counted in units of Satoshi, which equals 1/100,000,000 Bitcoin) is sent to a Bitcoin address. In a metadata field, available with every Bitcoin transaction, it is stated that one unit of Bitcoin on this address represents another asset or usage right, e.g., a ticket for a concert. When a unit of Bitcoin from this address is sent to another address, the metadata and, hence, the usage right (e.g., for the ticket) are also transferred. So, the transfer of a small amount of Bitcoin is pegged to the usage right. Tokens on the Bitcoin blockchain, representing a real-world asset or usage right, are also called coloured coins.[74] Tokenisation with pegged assets also implies that the value of the Bitcoin amount transferred is negligible compared to the value of the pegged asset as the initial Bitcoin amount cannot be necessarily recovered.[75] Pegging tokens to cryptocurrencies must also take into account the transaction fees, which compete with higher value transactions.[76]

---

[74] Term 'coloured coins' loosely describes a class of methods for representing and managing real-world assets on the blockchain and is often used in the context of Bitcoin.

[75] Currently, the only way to recover the Bitcoins and 'decolour' the coin is to spend such coins in an uncoloured transaction, i.e., with standard Bitcoin parameters.

[76] Another possibility to peg assets is through sidechains.

Smart contract tokens

Tokens on the Ethereum blockchain are issued as smart contracts. The Ethereum foundation offers a standard template that handles all aspects of a token, such as a name and symbol, the total supply, and the minimum transferable unit.[77] A token contract also handles the transfer functions and maintains the balances of the token holders. When a token contract is issued, the total supply is assigned to the issuer's account from which the tokens can be subsequently distributed or traded. Smart contract tokens on Ethereum, as opposed to Bitcoin, are not pegged to a unit of Ether.

When issuing tokens, it must be considered that the supply of tokens may change over time. For instance, when shares of a company are tokenised, and the company wants to increase or decrease capital, the supply of tokens changes. Within this context, we consider 'mintable' tokens, and standards for such a dynamic token supply are still under development.[78]

Although technically the process of issuing tokens is simple, linking real-world assets or usage rights to digital assets imposes challenges that are not fully resolved. To better understand these challenges, we first look at the tokens represented as cryptocurrencies.

5.1.3. Cryptocurrencies

Cryptocurrency tokens are created when a blockchain is started. In the first block, the so-called *genesis block*, initiators of a blockchain have the option to mint an arbitrary number of cryptocurrency tokens, which may range from one to billions. The number of tokens minted with the genesis block depends on their purpose. For example, they may fund a project with initial coin offerings or compensate blockchain participants for services provided, such as referrals or maintenance functions of real-world assets.

---

[77] ERC 20 is the standard contract.

[78] This refers to the suggested Ethereum ERC 621 token contract.

In addition, the consensus protocol of the blockchain defines the block mining rewards in the cryptocurrency, which can be freely chosen by the initiator and can vary over time. The block mining rewards are referred to as the inflation of the cryptocurrency. For example, in Bitcoin, there were no initial tokens, and the block mining rewards were set to 50 Bitcoins per block, halving every four years. As of August 2016, the block mining rewards were 12.5 Bitcoins per block with a block cycle of 10 minutes, and by 2140 the limit of 21 million Bitcoins set by the consensus protocol should be reached (Bitcoin Wiki, n.d.). In Ethereum, no coins were created at inception, and the block mining rewards were set constant at five Ether per block with a block cycle of 15 seconds on average.[79] Ripple, in contrast, issued 100 billion coins at inception with half for circulation and half for the company (Ripple Wiki, n.d.).

Cryptocurrency tokens are either created initially or continuously by the mining process and, hence, do not require linkage with real-world assets. Like fiat currencies, cryptocurrencies are based on the principle that people assign a value to them. Holders of the tokens assume they can be exchanged eventually against real-world assets. Unlike fiat currencies, there is no central authority to control and manage the number of tokens, as the number of tokens minted is defined by the genesis block and the software protocol. All participants of the blockchain govern the latter. Therefore, many holders of cryptocurrencies argue that cryptocurrencies are safer than fiat money, as the number of minted tokens and monetary authorities or governments cannot manipulate the inflation.

In Chapter 6.1.2, we elaborate further on cryptocurrencies. For now, it is only important to understand that cryptocurrency tokens are money-like units that can be transferred between parties like standard currency. The individual who owns the token can pay with them for any real-world service as there are no further rights or obligations associated with them.

---

[79] The block mining rewards may decrease to three Ether with the introduction of the next Ethereum release (Metropolis).

5.1.4. Fiat currencies and lifecycle-less assets

As most real-world assets are valuated in fiat currencies, there might be a strong need to create tokens that present fiat money to pay for another digital asset in the same transaction. Currently, there are not many examples of fiat currencies being tokenised.[80] Tokenising a fiat currency that is backed by a real-world asset could be achieved by putting money into an escrow account, while simultaneously minting the corresponding number of fiat currency tokens on a blockchain.[81] The owner of the escrow account must ensure that the fiat currency token supply always corresponds to the balance of the fiat currency in the escrow account. Once the fiat currency tokens have been minted, they can be used to pay for other digital assets on the same blockchain.[82] From a legal perspective, the owner of fiat currency tokens in such a blockchain would become a partial owner of the escrow account to the extent of the fraction of the total supply.

An additional challenge of the escrow account owner is mirroring the fiat currency transaction on the blockchain. Especially if someone sends fiat money to the escrow account to get fiat currencies tokens, the additional tokens must be minted and sent to the corresponding blockchain address. This process might turn out to be error-prone as the blockchain address must be submitted together with the bank transfer of the fiat currency. Currently, there is no standard reference field for submitting the blockchain address. If the currency tokens for an incoming payment on an escrow account are not to be transferred manually, then some additional functionality, such as bank account number checks, name, or reference fields, must be implemented to ensure

80 In 2018, a series of so-called stable coins was issued. However, most are not backed-up by real-world assets but are algorithmically composed. Hence, there is no legal guarantee that the money will be paid back.

81 This would, in most cases, require a token contract with a dynamic token supply as the liquidity needs for a blockchain might grow with the number of transactions.

82 See Chapter 5.2 Delivery versus payment.

that the person who sent the fiat money also receives the corresponding tokens. In the opposite direction, paying out fiat money, i.e., exchanging corresponding tokens against money from the escrow account, is easier. If fiat currency tokens are exchanged against fiat money in the escrow account, then the tokens must be disposed of or the total supply reduced. In such a transaction, the tokens would be sent to a function that reduces the total corresponding fiat currency token supply while sending a payment instruction to pay for the corresponding money from the escrow account to the owner. As opposed to incoming transactions, these instructions are standardised.

The same process for fiat-related currency tokens can be applied to any asset that is standardised, divisible, and exchangeable, i.e., where the tokens represent a fraction of a real-world asset. This may include metals, such as gold or silver, and any standardised commodity. The common characteristic of these assets is that they can be used as a value store and do not have a lifecycle, i.e., they do not perish or mature. Instead of an escrow account holder, there must be one or more depositaries who jointly control the token supply of the lifecycle-less tokenised real-world asset. Another requirement for the tokenisation of physical assets is that the depositary resides in a trusted jurisdiction or location and the shipping cost for physical delivery not be prohibitively high.

Although blockchain applications promise an intermediary-free exchange of digital assets without the need for trust, the trust in depositaries cannot be removed if fiat currencies or real-world assets are included. For fiat currencies, it would be beneficial if central banks would offer escrow accounts and ensure the total token supply for any blockchain wanting to trade digital assets. Alternatively, the central banks could offer a fraction of the fiat money supply on a blockchain, which is then used for payments on other blockchains. For real-world assets, the necessity of trust in the depositary cannot be eliminated.

5.1.5. Assets with a lifecycle

Other types of assets do have a lifecycle, which means that the asset or usage right expires, lapses, or have alternate rights associated. Many such lifecycle-bearing assets are financial instruments.[83] For example, a bond normally bears interest payments until maturity, and shares of a company may hold dividend and voting rights. Another example is a call option, where the buyer of the option pays a premium and the writer agrees to deliver the underlying if the spot price on a date or during a period is higher than the strike price.

All these assets have in common lifecycle events that might lead to an update of the contract including an invalidation at the end of the lifecycle. The challenge for such smart contracts is how the owner or group of owners can execute a contract update or invalidation. The conditions under which a contract update is allowed must be carefully designed to avoid centralisation of power.

5.2. Delivery versus payment

As opposed to single-leg asset transfers, such as gift donations, an economic transaction is defined as the exchange of goods and services. In nearly all transactions, money is used as a means of exchange.[84] Hence, an economic transaction always includes two legs, the delivery of the good or service and the corresponding payment. Taken from the financial world, we use the expression 'delivery versus payment', or DVP, to describe the exchange process.

---

[83] A financial instrument is defined as an agreement to exchange a series of cash flows. The most straightforward example for a financial instrument is a loan where the lender sends the credit amount to the borrower and the other party agrees to pay interest on a regular basis while paying the loan back before maturity.

[84] For the sake of simplicity, we exclude the exchange of two physical goods or goods against services, although this is an interesting use case for blockchain technology.

When purchasing goods or services, one side of the transaction takes the first step. For example, a payment or delivery is made, and the opposite party is trusted to fulfil the contract. Executing only one leg and trusting the opposite party to fulfil the second leg depends strongly on the value of the transaction and the effectiveness and cost of contract enforcement in a jurisdiction. Otherwise, a trusted intermediary is involved who waits until both legs of a transaction have been received, i.e., the goods or title and the payment. Once confirmed, then the contractual obligations are met, and the intermediary passes each leg to the corresponding party.

The novelty of blockchain technology is that it allows the exchange of two tokens for the same transaction, thereby eliminating the need to trust the opposite party or involve an intermediary.[85] Most blockchain applications today[86] use cryptocurrencies for the money leg.[87] As long as fiat currencies remain the primary currencies for economic transactions, we need a mechanism to bring fiat money onto the blockchain. In principle, the DVP can be achieved by tokenising a token for payments (other than cryptocurrencies) with, most likely, a fiat currency on the same chain or synchronising the mining of transactions between chains.

5.3. Voting

Blockchain technology is closely associated with the promise of fostering democratic decision-making. As seen in the previous chapters, the governance of the blockchain protocol, often called the law, is democratic by nature. Voting is not limited to the software protocol but is ubiquitous as part of public or corporate decision-making.[88]

---

[85] Delivery versus payment systems exist today in the financial world to settle financial contracts or ensure payments (e.g., PayPal). However, all are owned by an intermediary.

[86] Not including Bitcoin, which was not designed to exchange both legs. If Bitcoin is used for the exchange of two tokens, then metadata are used.

[87] Verification and examples needed.

[88] Under the term *corporate decision making*, we subsume any kind of governance of collective ownership.

Today, the majority of blockchains use tokens to define eligible voters. Although any cryptocurrency blockchain can use pegged tokens for voting, blockchains with smart contracts are much better suited to handle the various aspects of voting, such as the submission of voting proposals, weighted votes, and anonymous voting.[89] Smart contracts may also allow for submitting proposals 'on the fly' or executing decisions (e.g., a money transfer) once the minimum threshold for a proposal is passed. Smart contracts can also use existing tokens for defining the eligibility, e.g., a membership token of a loyalty program, everyone who holds a certain share class of a company at a certain point in time or an active board member token. Figure 21 depicts the principle, and Figure 22 provides a detailed structure of a voting contract.

When creating a general voting contract, basic rules can be specified, such as margin of votes for majority and voting deadlines for the proposals. Smart contracts can be customised for the needs of every type of voting. Some voting contracts may allow for changing these rules after contract deployment if needed by the owner of a contract,[90] which might be meaningful for issues such as the prolongation of a deadline. On the other hand, some rules must not be changed, and so it is important to analyse the voting contract with respect to the allowed changes. For each proposal, the voting contract allows seeing how many people voted if the proposal passed the threshold, and other details such as the content of the proposal entered by the proposal creator (e.g., topic, proposal text, if proposal concerns token transfers and amounts).[91] For confidential proposals, the text should be held off-chain or be encrypted for each eligible voter.

---

[89] For blockchains without smart contract support, the logic and the interpretation of the votes must be built outside the blockchain.

[90] The owner of a contract is not necessarily a person but could also be another contract for which multiple signatures would be required for modifications.

[91] The code for a basic voting contract is available at https://ethereum.org/dao

5.3.1. Voting tokens

The right to vote can be defined explicitly in a list with their public addresses or based on the ownership of a specific token contract address, such that anyone who claims ownership in a token address (e.g., a share or a membership token), irrespective of the number of units held, is eligible to vote. The weighting of the votes, done through the number of shares for which a vote has been submitted, is a function of the voting contract and is calculated after the vote closes. For the voting in a shareholder's meeting, the address of the shares can be used. However, if proxy voting is allowed, which exists in many corporate laws, then a new voting token must be issued because the voting rights cannot be transferred without transferring the assets. So, proxy voting is executed by transferring the voting tokens to another person or voting representative.

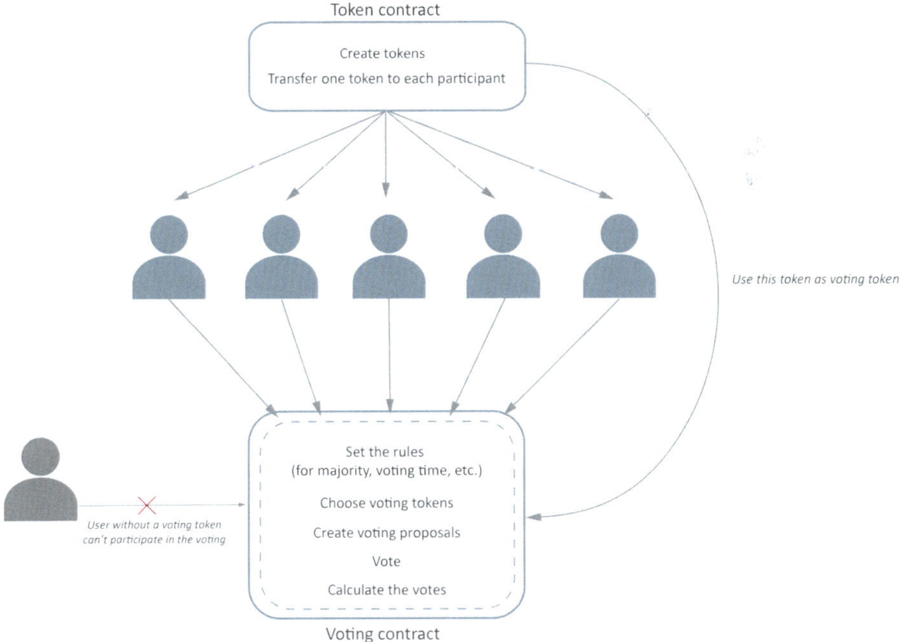

Source: Banking Concepts.

Figure 21. A voting contract.

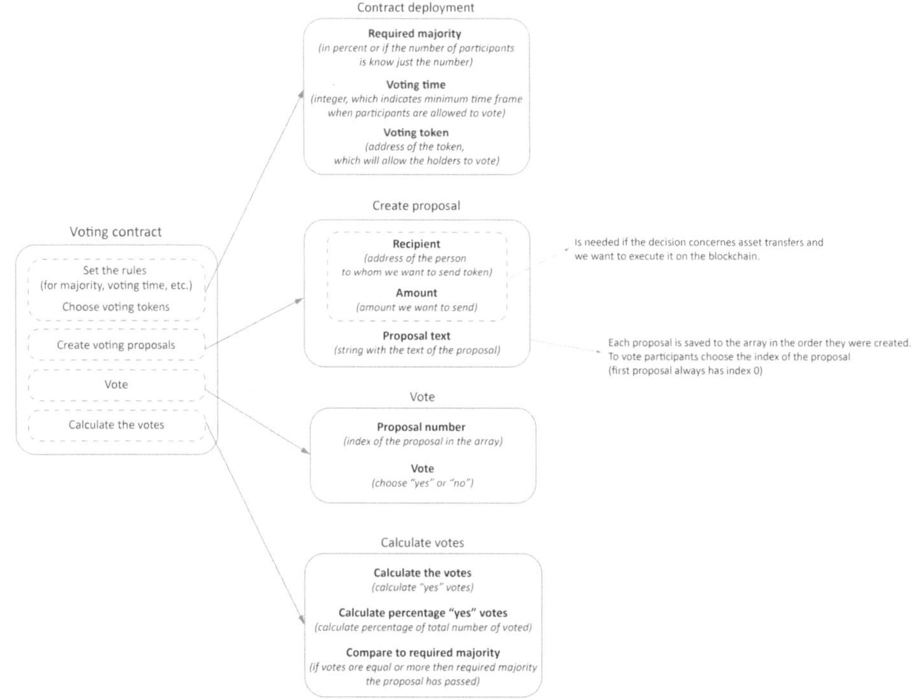

Figure 22. Details of a voting contract.

5.3.2. Open voting

A core element of a blockchain is its transparency, which means that the initiator and all details of any transaction are available to the blockchain users (and the public in the case of public blockchains). For example, anyone can see how much Ether was transferred from an account to another (Etherscan.io, n.d.-e).

Transactions representing a vote are not an exception to transparency. Although the details of such a transaction may not be as evident as an Ether transfer, anyone who knows the public address of a voter and the contents of the voting contract can see how a person voted. Every transaction on a blockchain contains some metadata, also called input data, where the function and other details of the transaction are encoded. With simple 'yes/no' voting, it is straightforward to see the result of the vote by simply looking at the last digit of the input data, which is 1 if the vote is 'yes' and 0 if the vote is 'no'. For example, Figure 23 shows a voting transaction with input data indicating the vote was 'yes'. In addition, within the first eight digits of the input data (after the '0x', which stands for a hexadecimal representation), the smart contract function (a vote) and the voting proposal are encoded. For an outsider, some effort is required to analyse and decode this data, but the information is otherwise transparent. An interested voter likely knows the address of other voters, and from the timestamp and their voting record, the voter intent of others can be derived.

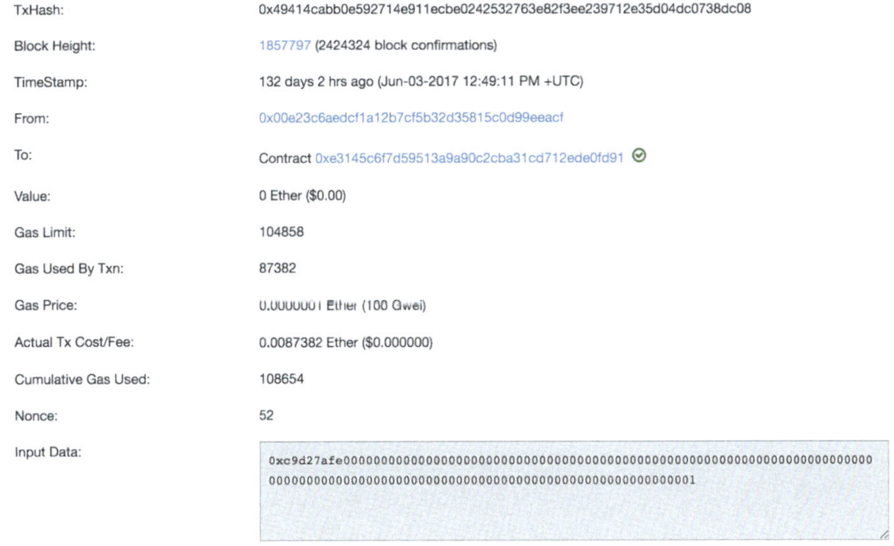

TxHash:	0x49414cabb0e592714e911ecbe0242532763e82f3ee239712e35d04dc0738dc08
Block Height:	1857797 (2424324 block confirmations)
TimeStamp:	132 days 2 hrs ago (Jun-03-2017 12:49:11 PM +UTC)
From:	0x00e23c6aedcf1a12b7cf5b32d35815c0d99eeacf
To:	Contract 0xe3145c6f7d59513a9a90c2cba31cd712ede0fd91
Value:	0 Ether ($0.00)
Gas Limit:	104858
Gas Used By Txn:	87382
Gas Price:	0.0000001 Ether (100 Gwei)
Actual Tx Cost/Fee:	0.0087382 Ether ($0.000000)
Cumulative Gas Used:	108654
Nonce:	52
Input Data:	0xc9d27afe00000000000000000000000000000000000000000000000000000000000000000000000 00000000000000000000000000000000000000000000000000000001

Source: Etherscan.io (2017) for transaction performed on the Kovan testnet.

Figure 23. Voting transaction details.

5.3.3. Confidential voting

Confidential voting imposes a substantial challenge on blockchains as the transactions are public, so voting on blockchains remains controversial. While transparency might be desired from a stakeholder's point of view, some decisions are highly confidential and could create substantial damage if public, e.g., a corporate merger or take-over decision. In addition, the same vote should be transparent for the decision-makers (e.g., the board members) and a selective audience while remaining confidential from the public. Some blockchain initiatives, such as Hyperledger Fabric and Corda, address these concerns.

5.3.4. Anonymous voting

Many types of votes, such as political elections, require the vote to remain secret. This means that it must be known that someone voted but not *how* they voted. Creation of an anonymous voting system is not trivial and requires a cryptographer to participate in the system creation to ensure anonymity of the vote is preserved (see the use case in Chapter 6.2.4).

There are exiting projects aimed at implementing anonymous voting. A well-known proprietary project is the TIVI voting system by Smartmatic and Cybernetica, which focus on voting solutions for governments. Several open source projects, such as Follow My Vote and the Open Vote Network, offer two substantially different characteristics. Unlike Follow My Vote, the Open Vote Network does not rely on a central authority (e.g., a centralised database checking voter eligibility). The advantage of Follow My Vote is that it is suited for a large number of participants (e.g., voting at the country-wide level), whereas the Open Vote Network applies to scenarios like boardroom voting.

6. Use Cases

The previous chapters set the foundation for understanding blockchain technology. Potentially different intermediaries and new types of decentralised interactions make it difficult to assess the abstract impacts. Therefore, we discuss 12 current use cases in varying stages of implementation along with three maturity levels of interaction with different technologies.

The first four use cases use pure blockchain in the sense that they rely only on the technology's main characteristics. The first is a public registry in its simplest form which only covers one leg of the transaction while the financial details are settled elsewhere. The other three cases (cryptocurrencies, crowdfunding/ICO, private payment systems) focus heavily on the financial aspects of the transaction.

The next five cases are presented by the degree of complexity and the benefit from the interaction with smart contracts (see Chapter 3.6). The simplest two forms are gambling and parameterised insurances, where money is paid into an escrow account and the smart contract decides who receives which payouts. The e-ID use case explores a decentralised self-sovereign enabled by blockchain, while the topic of decentralised democracy is further analysed in Chapter 6.2.4. With an even higher complexity, due to the number of different stakeholders involved, is trade financing, where great hope is associated with an impulse to digitise processes. The final blockchain-based smart contract use case looks at efforts to cope with multiple chains simultaneously by providing cross-chain exchange services.

The final two use cases unleash their full potential when combined with IoT. While the energy use case (6.3.2) could be seen as a special case of the proof-of-provenance use case (6.3.1), it is distinctively different as the blockchain is also used as a trading platform.

Impact on transaction costs

It is essential to use a methodology that allows for the isolation of the benefit of the blockchain, so we focus on transaction costs and compare the blockchain solution to the current process or a hypothetical process that would be feasible, such as if IoT was widely in use.

With respect to the use cases, the handling costs (eliminating intermediaries) and costs of legal certainty (bookkeeping) are the primary drivers for bringing down the total transaction cost. In combination with smart contracts, the contract enforcement costs are more relevant for consideration. Figure 24 illustrates that the use cases cover nearly all possible combinations of transaction cost reductions. While the insurance case is not the most complex use case, it nonetheless affects all three types of transaction costs analysed.

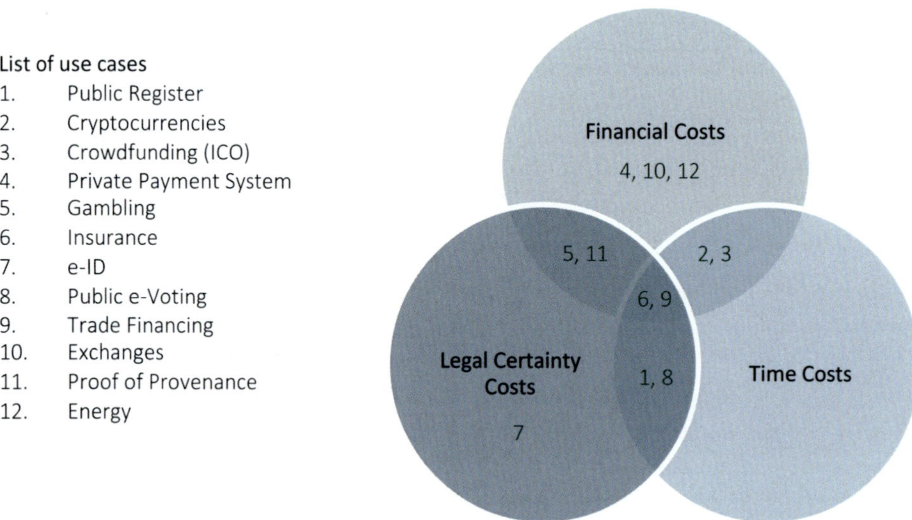

Source: IWSB.

Figure 24. Use cases grouped by transaction costs.

It is often not feasible to quantify the (potential) transaction cost savings with a blockchain implementation, as many use cases exist only on paper or remain in a proof-of-concept stage where the effective operational costs are yet to be determined.

6.1. Pure blockchain use cases

6.1.1. Public register (land and commercial registers)

Modern civil service involves a multitude of different registers, such as a land title (cadastre), commercial, civil status, and patent register. As a bookkeeping instrument, blockchains are well suited as registers, especially those involving the transfer of ownership. Additionally, their decentralised nature suggests they are a natural fit for decentralised countries like Switzerland.

Based on the transaction cost theory, the main benefit varies between countries with strong institutions under the rule of law and those with weaker institutions without legal certainty. For countries without legal certainty, the main benefit of using a blockchain is that it allows people to trust the public register without having to trust or bribe the registrar or registry office. In countries with strong institutions, the trust in the public registers is both understood and warranted. Here, the blockchain offers the expectation of lower financial costs due to lower fees and reduced time costs through improved public access or faster registration. These benefits also apply to countries without strong institutions. However, they are less important in this context.

In this use case, we focus on the public registers of a land register and commercial register to illustrate the current state and future possibilities of blockchain technology. Since early 2017, a land register using blockchain technology is in use in the Republic of Georgia. The Canton and Republic of Geneva are currently in trials with the use of blockchain in its commercial register. While the two applications use the blockchain in a register context, the goal for each is different. Georgia wants to build a secure and immutable land registry that people can trust, so the drive is to reduce the cost of legal certainty with respect to land titles.[92] Geneva uses the blockchain to certify the authenticity of the register excerpts, which could reduce the time cost associated

[92] Financial costs in Georgia cannot be reduced from a consumer perspective, as the fees for registration are zero. Time costs should also be negligible as registration currently takes one day.

with waiting for legally binding register excerpts and reduce legal certainty costs from uncertified excerpts.

Conventional process: land register

In Switzerland, all public registers are maintained digitally and at a cantonal level (the patent register is kept a federal level), while often under the superintendence of the federal administration. The land register is one such register, which provides information on the ownership of a plot of land, the rights of other people relating to the plot (e.g., joint use of paths and access roads), and the plots mortgage burden. The data in the land register are open to the public, so anyone who can demonstrate an interest in the plot of land is entitled to detailed information from the land registry. Today, access to the register is available online and free of charge. However, inquiries on the ownership of all properties by certain individuals are generally not possible as the right of public access must be weighed against the right for individual privacy.

Currently, the cantonal land registers use a centralised database infrastructure to store information. The registrar makes the entries into the register. For some entries, such as a sale or an encumbrance of property, a request by a notary and proof of certification are required. These claims in rem are valid only if they are recorded in the land register. Registration costs a fee that can be fixed or proportional to the value of the transaction to be registered. In the canton of Basel-City, minor entries, such as easements, cost CHF 100, while the transfer of ownership costs one-tenth of a percent of the property value.[93]

The land register is the highest legal authority regarding all property claims, and its integrity is paramount. The authenticity of the entries is guaranteed by the registry and relies on the conventional security measures in place to ensure the confidentiality, integrity, and availability of the data. Essentially, the government is entrusted to keep the data safe and, for a country with good and strong institutions, this is a sensible approach.

[93] The minimum fee is CHF 200 and the maximum is CHF 50,000.

Conventional process: commercial register

The commercial register contains information on the companies in the jurisdiction (canton) in which they operate, including who controls the firm and who is accountable. As in the case of the land register, the data are stored in a centralised cantonal database and entries are updated upon submission of the required documents by a registrar. Once entered, the data are publicly available and can be accessed freely online. However, in certain cases, officially certified excerpts from the register are required, which can be obtained at a counter or ordered and delivered by mail. The fee for such an excerpt is CHF 50 in the case of the canton of Geneva.

Blockchain-based process

Blockchain-based registers guarantee the immutability of the data and remove the necessity of trust into a central record keeping authority. However, for the land register, the law restricts access to the records (data privacy), and only a private permissioned chain is conceivable without changing the law. In countries with weak institutions, the benefit of an immutable public decentralised ledger might be valued higher than the individual privacy of landowners.

The two implementations of blockchain technology in registers in Georgia and Geneva circumvent the issue of public access vs privacy as is described below.

Georgian National Agency of Public Registry

Together with BitFury, a full-service blockchain company, the Georgian National Agency of Public Registry introduced blockchain secured land titles to its register in February 2017 (Shin, 2017). The process consists of the following steps:

1. The registrar creates a PDF of the land title to be registered.
2. A hardware security module digitally signs the PDF, which is validated by a certificate authority.
3. The PDF is stored in a database.
4. A Bitcoin transaction object that contains the hash of the PDF is created. The transaction is sent to the Bitcoin network, where it is validated. The hash of the PDF is then publicly and immutably stored.
5. A local database stores the metadata and the hash of the PDF.

No registry data are stored on the blockchain, so the issue of privacy of the land title owner is eliminated. The advantage is that, by leveraging the immutability property of the Bitcoin blockchain, the legal certainty of the land titles is significantly increased. In a country such as Georgia, with a moderate level of corruption (ranks 44 of 176 countries in the Transparency International's Corruption Perception Index 2016), this feature is valuable. Securing land titles worth thousands of Swiss francs still justifies paying the currently very high transaction fees of the Bitcoin Network (in December 2017, the maximum average daily transaction fee was USD 55).

Geneva commercial register

Since August 2017, Geneva has been conducting trials of blockchain technology to secure its digital commercial register excerpts. When an excerpt is created, a PDF is encrypted, and the hash value is sent to the Ethereum main chain as a transaction. The registry client receives the digital excerpt by email together with a PDF receipt. They then upload to a validator service that shows if the excerpt was issued by the State of Geneva denoting it as valid and unchanged. Currently, these excerpts are not legally binding, but legislation is expected to be adjusted accordingly.

However, the question arises whether using the blockchain to make digital excerpts verifiable is an efficient solution. The Swiss Federal Law on electronic signatures (ZertES) allows the digital signing of legal documents using a trusted service provider for certification of the signature. This path is available to Geneva and does not require changes in legislation. Financially, Ethereum-based transactions are currently expensive with costs of nearly CHF 3 as of January 2018, while a SuisseID[94] that allows digital signing documents in a ZertES-conforming way only costs CHF 197 for unlimited uses over three years. Therefore, only 66 Ethereum-based excerpts represent a break-even with the SuisseID approach. Additionally, the validity of ZertES-PDFs is easier to verify for a typical user.

[94] The pricing scheme of the replacement service, called SwissID, remains unknown.

Conclusion on current implementations

As initially stated, a blockchain appears to be a natural choice for a public register. However, we know of no public registers fully implemented with a blockchain. The use cases described here only peripherally use the blockchain to guarantee the integrity of or certify an official document. The main reason for this limited use is that it conflicts with the rights to privacy and public access, which can only be solved by using a private and permissioned chain. The advantage of not needing to trust a central authority with data integrity is then replaced by trust in a selected group of validating entities (e.g., the 73 districts in Georgia), which would still be sufficient, as long as they act independently. In summary, while the Georgian use case adds value by guaranteeing the integrity of the land titles stored, the Geneva commercial registry's use of the blockchain seems more like a proof-of-concept with no long-term inherent value.

Potential and conclusion

The potential of blockchain-based public registers is greater when combined with smart contracts. ChromaWay, a Swedish blockchain start-up, together with the Swedish land registry (Lantmäteriet) and other partners piloted a blockchain application for real-estate transactions in Sweden. They use a private permissioned blockchain (Postchain) to improve the speed and security of real-estate transactions. The system includes multiple actors, such as sellers, real-estate agents, buyers, banks, and the land registry. Trusted parties other than the land registry are also responsible for validating transactions on the chain. The blockchain is used to store the sales contract and the hashes of off-chain documents. By using digital signatures (Telia e-identification) and making the status of the property (as recorded in the off-chain land register) transparent to all parties, the processing time of a real-estate transaction has been reduced. ChromaWay claims the transaction time was improved from four months to a few days. However, the World Banks regulation-measuring project, 'Doing Business', states the median time for a property transaction in Sweden is only seven days. Therefore, for the median property transaction, the time cost savings are not significant. Even for real-estate transactions, which currently take longer, the benefit of reduced time costs may be limited, since the time between signing the sales contract and taking ownership of the property can be utilised for planning, selling previous property, and making moving arrangements.

A next step could be to have the ownership of the real estate represented by tokens on a blockchain, i.e., smart contracts that link the owner to a specific property. People could then transfer their property using smart contracts that do not trigger until conditions are met, such as acknowledgement of in rem rights tied to the land plot or payment. They could also use this token as collateral to receive mortgages from banks or other parties to initially buy the house. However, several current prerequisites of real-estate transactions would need to be changed in Switzerland for this to be possible.

First, the right to freely access the land register and the right to privacy conflict. This has led some cantons to restrict the number of online queries a specified IP address can submit per day. However, any computer enthusiast can put together a script to automatically and systematically query and recover the entire land register using proxy IPs. Therefore, in the case of the land register, the right to privacy is de facto null and void. Accepting this inherent property would allow the use of a public blockchain on which the transactions could take place.

Second, because of the large sums involved and the long-term consequences people face when transacting with real estate, today notarisation of the contracts is required. The notary ensures that all parties understand the contract, that all legal provisions are met, and that the contract is entered of their own free will. To prevent fraud, even without notarisation of the contracts, multiple solutions are possible. Standardized sales contracts could be designed to allow the parties to forego the notarisation of the contracts, which would also include automatic checks of certain legal prerequisites, such as if the legal residence of the buyer is in the country, requiring digital identities that provide these attributes. Additionally, within the token, a time-limited right of withdrawal for any ownership transfer could be embedded, which would make accidental or fraudulent transfers reversible. Alternatively, multisig accounts could be required for property transactions, where two parties from any account could be a public court along with the land registry. A simple transfer would automatically receive the approval of the land registry. However, in case of fraud or pressure through a court order, the keys of the court and the land registry could jointly be used to repossess the property in question.

Third, the entire current land register must be moved to the blockchain, which requires a proxy wallet be created for every landowner. From this, the properties would be transferred to the personal wallet of the owner. If the owner sells the property (without creating a personal wallet first), then it is directly transferred to the new owner's wallet (personal or proxy).

Fourth, the wallets must allow ZertES conforming transaction or the requirement of the contracts to be in writing must be relaxed.

6.1.2. Cryptocurrencies

Economic relevance

On December 17, 2017, Bitcoin's market value reached USD 321.7 billion, and Ether reached a maximum market value of USD 131.8 billion on January 14, 2018. These market values are often compared to the gross domestic product (GDP) of nations to demonstrate how important the cryptocurrencies market has become (Haig, 2018). Other sources compare the market capitalisation of cryptocurrencies to the market capitalisation of companies. The former comparison is not appropriate as a flow variable such as GDP cannot be compared to a stock variable such as market valuation. The latter is also flawed as the market capitalisation of a company is the valuation of all expected future profits. Bitcoin is not a business and has no profits (Back, 2017). The correct comparison for Bitcoin (and Ether) depends on whether it is perceived as a currency, a payment system, a speculative asset, or a store of value, which is considered below.

If cryptocurrency is considered a currency, then its market value could be compared to the currency circulation of other currencies. So, compared to the currency circulation of the U.S. dollar and the euro of each approximately USD 1.5 trillion, the market capitalisation of Bitcoin and Ether of USD 219 billion and USD 106 billion, respectively, are considerably smaller. However, the use of a currency as a medium of exchange is not limited to the banknotes and coins in circulation. Therefore, the slightly broader monetary aggregate M1 that includes funds that are readily accessible for spending might be a better comparison figure. In January 2018, M1 for the U.S. dollar was USD 3.6 trillion and USD 9.5 trillion for the euro. Even the Swiss franc had an M1 of 666 billion USD in January 2018. These numbers make clear that as a medium of exchange, even the main cryptocurrencies are relatively small compared to major currencies. Additionally, there is evidence provided by Chainanalysis, a digital forensics firm, that large parts of Bitcoin are not tradeable because they are lost, with an estimate of as much as 3.79 million Bitcoins (nearly a quarter of all currently existing Bitcoin) that are no longer accessible due to loss of private keys (Roberts & Rapp, 2017). Given these numbers, it may be assumed that some Ether are also lost, which reduces the market capitalisation of both cryptocurrencies.

If we consider a cryptocurrency to be a payment system, then the correct unit of comparison is the number of transactions per day. Established payment systems, such as Visa's VisaNet electronic payments network, process on average 150 million transactions per day. The theoretical maximum is close to 5 billion transactions per day (Visa, n.d.). Bitcoin and Ether have achieved a maximum of 0.49 and 1.35 million transactions per day.

Alternatively, we could look at transaction value. Bitcoin's transaction value peaked at nearly USD 5.78 billion in December 2017, while the daily average for 2017 was only USD 1.03 billion. The interbank payments in the eurozone and the U.S. had daily transaction values of EUR 1,632.55 billion (USD 1,991.63 billion) and USD 3,090.96 billion on average in 2016, respectively. Again, traditional currencies transact sums several magnitudes larger than cryptocurrencies. Table 10 gives an overview of these figures for comparison.

Table 10. Comparing Bitcoin and Ether to mainstream currencies.

	BTC	ETH	USD	EUR	CHF
Market Capitalisation	219,478	105,866			
Currency Circulation			1,611,339	1,399,395	83,070
Monetary Aggregate M1			3,632,000	9,512,739	665,523
Average daily transaction value	1,029		3,090,964	1,991,629	131,809

Notes: All numbers are in million USD. Currency conversion is done using average January 2018 rates. Sources: FRED St. Louis, SNB, ECB, etherscan.io and blockchain.info

In 2017, the prices of cryptocurrencies increased exponentially, especially in the last quarter. The price of Bitcoin increased more than 1,800%, while that of Ether increased by more than 8,400%, as seen in Figure 25 and Figure 26. The high volatility of the Bitcoin and Ether prices is apparent, and, as shown by the high standard deviations in Table 11, the volatility of Bitcoin increased by a factor of 35 from the first to last quarter in 2017 and a factor of 12 for Ether. This high and increasing volatility together with the exponential increase in prices indicate that cryptocurrencies could be considered speculative assets, which was confirmed by a statement on December 13, 2017, by Janet Yellen, the then Chair of the Board of Governors of the Federal Reserve System, calling Bitcoin a 'highly speculative asset' (Torres, 2017). Recent research supports this view (see Kasper, 2017, for an overview), and other research on the volatility of Bitcoin found that the volatility is higher than that of the least developed currencies (Kasper, 2017) and higher than that of the S&P 500, an American stock market index based on the market capitalisations of 500 large companies having common stock listed on the NYSE or NASDAQ (Wieczner, 2018). This observed high volatility is one reason why cryptocurrencies may not be considered good assets for a store of value.

In later chapters, we discuss the possible functions of cryptocurrencies, including medium of exchange, store of value, and payment system, in detail.

Source: IWSB. Based on calculations on data from etherscan.io and kraken.io.

Figure 25. Bitcoin price development in USD during 2017.

Source: IWSB. Based on calculations on data from etherscan.io and kraken.io

Figure 26. Ether price development in USD during 2017.

Table 11. Mean values and standard deviation of Bitcoin and Ether prices.

	Bitcoin		Ether	
	Mean	Std. Deviation	Mean	Std. Deviation
2017 Q1	1032.94	123.74	19.23	13.66
2017 Q2	1898.22	593.97	158.96	113.45
2017 Q3	3495.76	827.22	272.60	51.86
2017 Q4	9376.65	4369.46	430.07	169.24

Notes: All numbers in USD. Calculations based on data from etherscan.io and kraken.io

Geography of the cryptocurrency industry

While cryptocurrencies are a global phenomenon, different countries remain relevant in various areas of the cryptocurrency industry. The four key sectors of the industry include exchanges, wallets, payments, and mining. Because the two major cryptocurrencies use proof-of-work consensus protocols, mining is a primary physical manifestation of the cryptocurrency industry. Mining requires an enormous amount of computing power supplied by millions of processing units located in servers or mining farms. These farms require low-cost electricity, a reliable Internet connection, and a cold climate, which reduces the cost of cooling hardware. Currently, China is the number one place for cryptocurrency mining with 60% of the Bitcoin mining capacity as of January 2018. Many mining farms are in Szechuan province, which has excess capacities in electricity supply making it inexpensive. Other major mining locations are in Canada, Island, Georgia, and Russia (Kennedy, 2018).

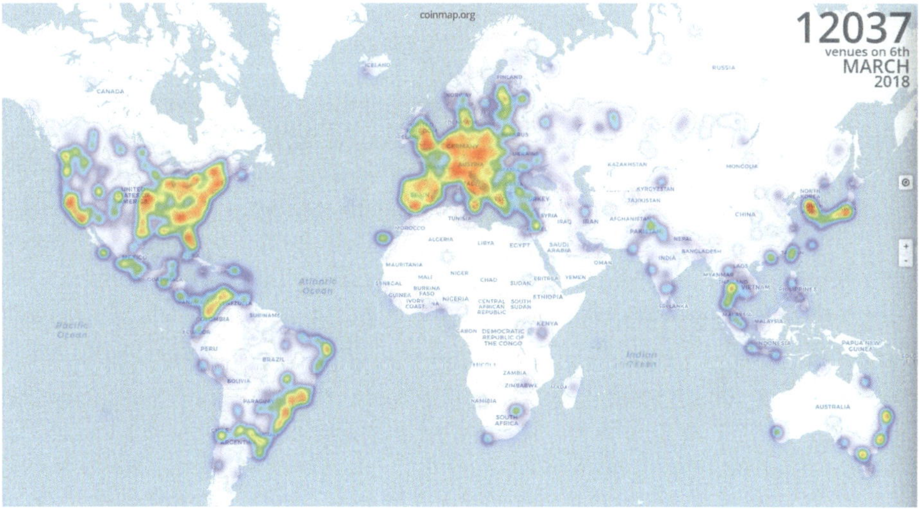

Source: coinmap.org

Figure 27. Coinmap.org Screenshot of the Bitcoin-accepting venue heat map on 6 March 2018.

Exchanges are situated around the world. According to a study by Hileman and Rauchs (2017), in early 2017, most exchanges were situated in Europe (37%) followed by Asia-Pacific (27%). The largest exchange was a Hong Kong-based exchange called BitFenix. However, the price increases in cryptocurrencies and changing regulations mean that this study may already be outdated. Looking at newer data from coinmarketcap.com, BitMEX, an exchange based in the Republic of Seychelles, appears to now be the largest.

An indication of the adoption of cryptocurrencies for payments is provided by coinmap.org, which lists all the venues that have self-declared to accept Bitcoin as a method of payment. A screenshot from the website from March 6, 2018 (Figure 27) shows the global distribution of Bitcoin acceptance. However, 12,037 venues accepting Bitcoin pales in comparison to the tens of millions of locations where credit cards are accepted. According to popular news coverage, the country where cryptocurrencies are most accepted for payment is Japan, where thousands of stores and retail chains are said to accept Bitcoin and other cryptocurrencies to pay for services and goods (Helms, 2017a, 2017b).

Political support for and opposition to cryptocurrencies

Political interest in cryptocurrencies largely depends on the perceived dangers and opportunities of cryptocurrencies for the country. The perception difference between opportunity and danger features time and geographical dimensions. In the developed Western world, politics mostly ignored cryptocurrencies until their exponential growth in prices in late 2017. In emerging markets and especially in countries with strong financial controls and currency restrictions, governments have taken a more active approach in dealing with cryptocurrencies.

For instance, in mid-September 2017, China closed many cryptocurrency exchanges, making it hard for Chinese cryptocurrency owners to convert their funds to fiat money. Only weeks before, ICOs were banned. These events caused Chinese citizens to circumvent China's capital control policy (Kuo, 2017), although making possession of cryptocurrencies illegal was likely intended to better enforce capital controls. In March 2018, China began to shut down cryptocurrency mining throughout its territories (Wildau, 2018).

Other countries that see cryptocurrencies as part of the Fin-Tech industry have issued rules and laws to govern the marketplace. For instance, in addition to regulating and licensing exchanges, tech-friendly Japan has established Bitcoin as a legal currency (Terazono, 2018).

Another indication of the growing role of cryptocurrencies in politics is the fact that they are being used for campaign financing in the U.S. Already in its Advisory Opinion 2014-02, the U.S. Federal Election Commission decided that Bitcoins may be accepted as campaign contributions. In the past four years, the significance of Bitcoin campaign contributions rose with more candidates accepting them (Keneally, 2018). In Switzerland, politicians started taking an interest in cryptocurrencies at the end of 2017 when cryptocurrency prices were at an all-time high, and more people began investing. Initial calls were made to implement a regulation that protects small private investors from these types of high-risk investments. Concerns were also raised about the potential economic risk, taxation of cryptocurrencies and its usage in criminal activity (Leo Müller, 2017). In reaction to growing political and administrative awareness, the federal government commissioned a Blockchain/ICO working group with the aim of increasing legal certainty, maintaining the integrity of the financial centre, and ensuring technology-neutral regulation. The group will report to the Federal Council by the end of 2018.

Overall, an increased public awareness around cryptocurrencies, driven by the price rally in late 2017, led to more political support. However, the resulting political actions are diverse.

Cryptocurrencies as money

Currency can be broadly defined as a medium of exchange that is used and generally accepted. In addition to government-issued fiat money, many different forms of currency exist or have existed, such as in prisons where cigarettes may be used as currency. Frequent-flyer miles issued by airlines are also considered a currency as they are generally accepted as a medium of exchange for services and products provided by airlines. Cryptocurrencies are generally accepted in limited spheres. For instance, in the darknet, cryptocurrencies are the generally accepted medium of exchange. However, this limit in acceptance of a currency is not specific to cryptocurrencies. While the U.S. dollar is generally accepted in the United States, it cannot be used to buy groceries at a supermarket in Switzerland.

While cryptocurrencies should be considered currencies, the question remains contested whether they are money[95], as currency must fulfil three functions to be considered money:[96]

[95] Questions on whether a cryptocurrency can be legal tender have arisen in the cryptocurrency community. Legal tender are coins of banknotes that must be accepted in payment of debt. It is the only accepted vehicle of payment for government taxes. In countries with a stable currency, it seems highly unlikely that a government would accept a foreign currency to settle tax debt and

- *Medium of exchange:* Exchanges without money require a double coincidence of wants. By serving as a medium of exchange that is accepted by all parties, money facilitates the exchange of goods and services. It avoids the inefficiency of a barter system and improves the allocation of resources in an economy.
- *Unit of account*: As a nominal monetary unit of measurement of the market value of goods and services, this feature enables their direct comparison. By functioning as a unit of account, money removes the need to know rates of exchange for all goods and services. Instead, only the rate of exchange between the good and money needs to be known, i.e., the price.
- *Store of value:* Money must be savable, retrievable, and exchangeable (or predictably useful) to act as a store of value. Additionally, money must maintain its value over time.

Some currencies do not fulfil all these functions, especially the store of value aspect, which is often undermined by substantial inflation. Other cases take the unit of account aspect, as illustrated by the digital currency WIR Franc, which is used exclusively by the customers of the WIR Bank as a medium of exchange within the small circle of WIR Bank customers. This currency is not a unit of account as prices are quoted in Swiss francs to which the WIR Franc is tied. Because no interest is paid on WIR Franc holdings (to encourage spending), inflation is not compensated for, which makes it (intentionally) a poor store of value. Another example is the ECU, the predecessor to the euro, which was primarily a unit of account used within the European Exchange Rate Mechanism. Similarly, since frequent-flyer miles typically expire, they are also poor stores of value.

---

thereby weaken the importance of its own currency. However, even without being legal tender in a country, a cryptocurrency could become an accepted medium of exchange. For instance, U.S. dollars are used as the main currency in many industries (e.g., oil industry), even though they are legal tender only in the United States.

[96] A fourth function that remains contested is 'a standard of deferred payment'.

To achieve these three functions, money must meet the following seven characteristics:

1. *Acceptability:* Money must be widely accepted as a settlement of debt or as a discharge of an obligation.
2. *Durability:* Money should withstand repeated use without deteriorating in value or quality.
3. *Portability:* Easy transport and transfer means that money can act as a medium of exchange and store of value.
4. *Divisibility:* Dividing a unit of the currency in half should represent two equally valuable parts. Therefore, artwork and diamonds make for poor currency.
5. *Fungibility:* The individual units must be mutually substitutable, such that two 5 Swiss franc coins are entirely interchangeable.
6. *Uniformity:* To function as a unit of account, the individual denomination must be completely uniform in that it has the same purchasing power. For example, one 10 Swiss franc bill has the same purchasing power as another 10 Swiss franc bill.
7. *Scarcity:* Limits in the supply of money ensure that it retains its function as a medium of exchange and store of value.

We can now evaluate cryptocurrencies based on these characteristics to determine whether they satisfy the functions of money. We discuss Bitcoin as an example.

- *Acceptability:* Bitcoin has increased in acceptance over the years. However, it is far from generally accepted in any country, the only exception being the criminal underworld.
- *Durability:* Because Bitcoins are digital, they do not deteriorate with use. They can only be destroyed if all copies of the Bitcoin blockchain are deleted.
- *Portability:* Because Bitcoins are digital, they can be easily transported on mobile devices. During times of high transactions fees and long confirmation times, transfer of Bitcoins is not as easy as using a credit card or cash.

- *Divisibility*: Bitcoins can be divided into 100 million units.
- *Fungibility:* The digital nature of Bitcoin means that every Bitcoin is substitutable by another Bitcoin.
- *Uniformity:* Because they are fungible each Bitcoin has the same purchasing power at a certain point in time.
- *Scarcity:* The supply of Bitcoin is absolutely limited with only 21 million Bitcoins to ever be created.

While Bitcoin features many characteristics of money, the remaining issues are acceptability and, to a lesser extent, portability. Two conditions preventing Bitcoin from having these characteristics are the high transaction fees and the long confirmation times. These limit the transferability of Bitcoins and, therefore, portability as well as making the acceptance of Bitcoin as means of payment less attractive. Further issues include the high volatility and the uncertainty regarding regulation of cryptocurrencies, which both hamper the acceptability of Bitcoin. These shortcomings affect Bitcoin's functions as a medium of exchange and a store of value; the latter is thoroughly discussed in the following subsection.

A feature not reflected in the above characteristics above but one that makes Bitcoin an unlikely unit of account is the final supply of 21 million Bitcoins fixing the money supply. However, long before the final Bitcoins are mined, inflation will be close to zero since when demand for Bitcoin increases deflation initiates. As prices quoted in Bitcoin start to fall, it becomes more attractive to hoard Bitcoin, which further increases the deflationary pressure. If Bitcoin were a unit of account of an economy, then deflation would lead to unemployment because the wages of workers cannot be adjusted fast enough. Deflation decreases the liquidity in the currency market, making Bitcoin an unattractive medium of exchange.

In summary, Bitcoin is presently not well suited to be a replacement for traditional fiat money.

Cryptocurrencies as a store of value

With the exponential increase in 2017 in the value of many of the main cryptocurrencies, proponents began declaring cryptocurrencies 'digital gold', suggesting they are in fact a store of value. The support for this statement is based mainly on the idea that cryptocurrency, like gold, has a finite supply, and that price increases have coincided with geopolitical tensions (Kharpal, 2017). However, a store of value is not defined by a few basic similarities with gold.

A good store of value can be saved, retrieved, and exchanged at a later point in time. Once retrieved, it is predictably useful, which implies that a store of value is an asset that retains purchasing power in the future. Using Bitcoin as an example, above we found that not all these properties are met by cryptocurrencies. While Bitcoin can be bought and kept in a wallet (saved), retrieval and exchange depend on whether the infrastructure supporting Bitcoin remains in use. Miners and exchanges may someday be regulated in ways that make it hard or impossible to retrieve and exchange funds. This case occurred in China where exchanges were recently closed, and the government continues to restrict mining activity. Furthermore, the usefulness of the Bitcoin is far from guaranteed as they have no inherent value. Gold, on the other hand, is used in many industries, including electronics, jewellery, and art. Moreover, Bitcoin exhibits tremendous volatility of more than seven times that of gold (Kharpal, 2017), which suggests it might not meet the condition of retaining purchasing power over time.

Nevertheless, a large number of cryptocurrencies are bought and held. According to one analysis, more than 3.38 million Bitcoin lie on addresses that have not been touched since January 2013 (Ripple, 2017). The Chainanalysis study of the lost Bitcoin lists as many as 5.11 million Bitcoins as 'out of circulation' or 'holders'.

A related consideration is how cryptocurrency wealth is concentrated. An analysis by blocklink.info finds that 1% of the users own more than 50% and the top 10% have more than 87% of the Bitcoin (Blocklink.info, n.d.). Other analyses based on the Blockchain Rich List find even more skewed wealth distributions, e.g., 10% own more than 99% of the Bitcoins (BitInfoCharts, n.d.-b). In other cryptocurrencies, the distribution is no more equal. A Bloomberg article states that in some cryptocurrencies the top 100 addresses control more than 90% of the currency (Kharif, 2017).

If cryptocurrencies are used as a store of value, then the issue of taxation arises. Because of their pseudo-anonymous nature, funds in cryptocurrencies are easy to hide. As soon as they are exchanged for a fiat currency using a centralised exchange, they become linked to an identity and can be observed by tax agencies. In either case, cryptocurrency holdings are taxable and must be declared to the relevant tax administration. In Switzerland, cryptocurrencies are treated like cash as moveable assessable assets, i.e., they are subject to the wealth tax. In Germany, cryptocurrencies are taxed as intangible assets and are subject to a capital gains tax. As stated earlier, in the United States, cryptocurrencies are considered property and are taxed as such.

In summary, while cryptocurrencies do not constitute a good store of value they are still used as such and, hence, are subject to taxation.

Cryptocurrencies as a payment system

A system used to settle financial transactions through the transfer of monetary value are payment systems, and cryptocurrencies were initially designed for this purpose as indicated by the title of Nakamoto's original whitepaper, 'Bitcoin: A Peer-to-Peer Electronic Cash System'. This initial intention is also true for those cryptocurrencies that forked, such as Bitcoin Cash and Litecoin. Ethereum, on the other hand, was designed as a distributed computing platform. Its native token Ether is used to pay transaction fees and as a unit of account for its smart contracts.

As noted in the previous section, cryptocurrencies can only be used in relatively few venues around the world. In Tunisia, Bolivia, Ecuador, Kyrgyzstan, Bangladesh, Nepal, Cambodia, Indonesia, Vietnam, and Macedonia, cryptocurrencies are entirely illegal, or at least payment using cryptocurrencies is illegal. Still, millions of Bitcoin and Ether transaction are processed daily. But statistics on what the transactions are for are not available. However, given the volumes of trade in cryptocurrency exchanges, it can be assumed that a large part is in exchange for fiat currencies and not as a means of payment for goods and services. Using a cryptocurrency as a payment system has advantages and disadvantages that weigh differently for its use cases. The following reviews the key comparisons.

Advantages

- *Relatively fast transaction speed:* In 2017, the median confirmation time of a transaction was around 12 minutes. A traditional wire transfer from a bank account to another takes one to several business days.
- *Relatively low transaction fees:* Bitcoin and Ether transaction fees can be relatively low, with fees of a few cents to a few dollars for transactions of any amount, which is inexpensive compared to wire transfers in the U.S.

with fees of up to 30 U.S. dollars. For larger transactions, cryptocurrencies are also inexpensive compared to credit card payments that cost businesses around 2–2.5% (Dwyer, 2011). As transaction fees depend on the value of the cryptocurrency itself, the typically low transaction fees can suddenly become very expensive (see Disadvantages).

- *High transaction certainty:* As the transactions are written to an immutable ledger, by waiting for several confirmations, funds are guaranteed. In contrast, cash payments might include forged bills, and credit card payments might be revoked.
- *(Pseudo)anonymity:* As cryptocurrency addresses (accounts) are not tied to the identity of a user, transactions can be considered anonymous, although this anonymity can be defeated (see Chapter 3.9).
- *Smart contracts:* By allowing the automatic execution of payments based on conditions set, the contract increases legal certainty and reduces time costs for the involved parties (see use cases in Chapters 6.2).

Disadvantages

- *High volatility:* Cryptocurrencies exhibit incredibly high volatility, which makes it dangerous to quote fixed prices in Bitcoin. The cost for most products and services still accrue in fiat currencies. Therefore, daily changes can be significant enough to erode profit margins completely.
- *High transaction fees:* Transaction fees can sometimes be very high. In December 2017, Bitcoin transaction prices exploded reaching a maximum daily average of 55 U.S. dollars. A fee this high makes Bitcoin payments prohibitively expensive for payments below 2000 U.S. dollars. Even with the lower transaction fees of around 2 U.S. dollars seen in March 2018, micropayments are still not economical.
- *Slow transaction speed:* Because the space for transactions is limited by the block size, not only can transaction fees explode but transactions with transaction fees below the current market rate might not be validated for many blocks. On January 23, 2018, the average confirmation time for a transaction peaked at 11,453 minutes (7 days, 23 hours and 53 minutes). Even if the lower median confirmation time of around 15 minutes is obtained, then this is still much slower than alternative electronic payment

systems, such as PayPal offering near-instant transaction of funds. Additionally, for increased security with high-value transactions, a single confirmation is not considered sufficient. The number of confirmations required to achieve a certain level of certainty that a transaction is valid depends on the hashing power of the potential attacker. To achieve a certainty level of at least 99.9% (given the attacker has 10% of the hashing power), six confirmations are required. Therefore, for higher value transactions, transaction times increase from minutes to hours.

- *Capital gains tax:* In the United States, the IRS treats cryptocurrencies as property for tax purposes, which means that any transaction of a cryptocurrency, even if merely paying for a pizza, is technically treated as a sale of property and potentially subject to the capital gains tax.

Solutions exist or are being developed for some of the drawbacks of cryptocurrencies as a payment system. For instance, the high volatility of cryptocurrencies can be managed by quoting prices in fiat currency and converting them on the fly to the cryptocurrency chosen using real-time exchange rates. This reduces the exposure to volatility. However, the seller still needs to manage their cryptocurrency funds by converting to fiat currency to reduce the exposure to a minimum. Cryptocurrency payment providers will take on this risk by immediately crediting confirmed transactions to the seller's fiat currency denoted account. Examples of such providers are Bitpay, Coingate, and Coinbase.

Transaction fees and speed are related issues. Due to the limited block size, the supply of transaction space is always limited. As soon as the demand for transactions exceeds supply, prices begin to rise. The longer the list of outstanding transactions, the tighter the price competition is for the limited space on the next block. In late 2017 through the beginning of 2018, prices of Bitcoin and Ether skyrocketed, leading to excess demand and the increase in transaction fees. Transaction speed or confirmation time depends on whether the user is prepared to pay the market price for a transaction. For Bitcoin, the relatively constant median confirmation time of around 12 minutes indicates that most users were prepared to pay the high fee at the time. Transaction fees can be reduced by increasing the supply or by reducing demand, as reviewed in Chapter 3.7.

In summary, on the supply side, the block size can increase, use additional alternative chains, or implement distributed transactions among multiple groups of validators (sharding). As an example, Bitcoin Cash has a block size that is eight times larger than Bitcoin. Historically, demand has never been large enough to exceed this increased block size. Consequently, transaction fees have remained low. On the demand side, implementing methods for off-chain transactions, such as the p2p payment channels proposed by Bitcoins Lightning Network, would reduce the demand for block space while increasing the number of transactions and reducing fees.

While cryptocurrencies have advantages as payment systems, the disadvantages might be solvable in the future. Current payment systems do not stop innovation. For instance, the slow transaction speed of current bank transfers is being addressed by new payment standards. The European Payment Council has launched the SEPA Instant Credit Transfer to allow bank clients to transfer funds of up to 15,000 euro within 10 seconds.

Currently, smart contracts are a unique feature of certain cryptocurrencies. However, they require funds used in the contracts be locked into an escrow account until the contract is fulfilled. It is conceivable that traditional financial service providers will develop tools to allow smart contracts to be directly connected to bank accounts that are backed by a letter of credit to ensure contract fulfilment. This would free up funds that are otherwise stuck in escrow.

Privacy-focused cryptocurrencies

As noted above, traditional cryptocurrencies are pseudo-anonymous. Once a public address is linked to a real identity, all transactions linked to that identity are revealed. Several methods exist that allow cryptocurrency users to increase anonymity. First, the user can create a new address for every transaction to avoid the transactions being linked to a common owner, and modern software wallets have this feature. However, when transactions require pulling Bitcoins from multiple addresses, it becomes public knowledge that these addresses belong to the same wallet. Linking just one of these addresses to a user's identity removes anonymity. Second, multi-wallets can be used such that multiple separate identities are maintained. Last, a user could use a mixing service that allows for the exchange of Bitcoins for Bitcoins with a different transaction history that is not related to the user. Mixing is comparable to moving funds through banks located in countries with strict bank secrecy laws in the traditional financial system. While the idea of mixing services is compelling, they require trust in the mixing service provider that no protocol of the mixing is kept, and that funds sent for mixing are returned. Additionally, using mixing services for large amounts may violate anti-money-laundering laws.

Because of these drawbacks of traditional cryptocurrencies, multiple privacy-focused cryptocurrencies have emerged. We focus here on Monero, a cryptocurrency launched in 2014 that features four important characteristics for a so-called 'privacy coin' of being private, untraceable/unlinkable, fungible, and decentralised:

- *Private:* The number of coins owned, sent, and received by users is not observable on the blockchain.
- *Untraceable/unlinkable:* Transactions cannot be traced or linked to an identity.
- *Fungible:* All coins are mutually interchangeable, and no coin is devalued or blacklisted due to deprecating transaction history.
- *Decentralised:* No one person, company, or institution is in control of currency creation, maintenance, and representation.

Monero uses different techniques to achieve these characteristics. Stealth addresses and random one-time addresses are automatically created for all transactions, which are used to prevent linkability. These stealth addresses are known only by the sender and the recipient of the payment. While this prevents linking transactions by uninvolved third parties, the sender could still trace the coins sent when they are transferred away from the recipient's address. To break traceability, Monero uses ring signatures where the transactions being sent are grouped with other transactions from the blockchain to obfuscate the outputs being spent and allowing for plausible deniability. Only the recipient can see their corresponding transaction. To achieve privacy, Monero uses ring confidential transactions (RingCT), which is a cryptographic tool that conceals the amount being transacted while allowing the network to verify the amount without having to reveal details.[97] Monero is also working on

[97] The basic idea is to check within a ring transaction that the inputs equal output, i.e., if a ring transaction contains inputs 1 + 2 + 3 + 4, then the outputs need to be 10, e.g., 3 + 5 + 2. As these transaction values are hidden, all amounts are multiplied by a random number, A. We then

Kovri, an implementation of the invisible internet project (I2P) network protocol, which allows for users to make transactions without revealing their geographical location or IP address. Therefore, Kovri further improves untraceability and unlinkability of transactions.

Monero is private by default, such that the privacy features implemented must be actively disabled by the user if transparency is required for a transaction. Due to this default privacy setting, most transactions made in Monero are private. Therefore, private transactions do not stand out as they do when using a mixer service with Bitcoin.

Fungibility is achieved via Monero's cryptographic privacy, untraceability, and unlinkability features. Coins avoid the potential of being tainted by deprecating transaction history. Thereby, the risk of Monero coins being blacklisted or devalued is mitigated, and all coins are worth the same value and are mutually interchangeable. Monero is considered decentralised as it is led by volunteer workers and is funded by user contributions. Additionally, all discussions regarding development are public, and the code is open source.

While Monero has impressive privacy features, there are still weaknesses and critiques. First, the transaction size is much larger than Bitcoin, causing the Monero blockchain to grow quickly. Second, Monero is not integrated with multi-coin wallets, making widespread adoption harder. Third, integrating Monero for merchant payments is difficult, which also limits the use of Monero as a payment system.

Because of the excellent privacy features incorporated in Monero, it is very interesting for illicit activities. For instance, transactions on the darkweb may be paid using Monero. As with other cryptocurrencies, Monero can be used to evade taxes as funds stored on Monero are extremely difficult to link to a real identity. Income and wealth can be hidden from tax authorities. However, as Monero is not very widespread, the use of Monero funds is limited. As soon as funds are exchanged for other cryptocurrencies or fiat money, the privacy protection offered by Monero is lost. Additionally, the price volatility of Monero

---

get (1A) + (2A) + (3A) + (4A) = (3A) + (5A) + (2A), which can be written as A * (1 + 2 + 3 + 4) = A * (3 + 5 + 2), so we can be sure that 1 + 2 + 3 + 4 = 3 + 5 + 2 still holds true. With RingCT, only the sender and receiver know the value of A. RingCT does not use a random coefficient, as in this example, but a hash function with the same distributive property.

makes it suboptimal as a store of wealth. Therefore, we see only limited potential for using Monero for large-scale tax evasion.

6.1.3. Crowdfunding (Initial Coin Offering)

An Initial Coin Offering (ICO) is primarily used by start-ups to raise capital via crowdfunding. Synonyms for ICOs are 'token sale' or 'token-generating event'. Similar to an Initial Public Offering (IPO) on the stock market, an ICO describes the event in which a company sells a predefined number of digital tokens to the public or an exclusive group of investors. The sold cryptocurrency tokens are usually paid with other established cryptocurrencies (e.g., Bitcoin or Ether) or conventional money. ICOs were made possible by blockchain technology with the first ICOs occurring in 2013. In contrast to IPOs, ICOs are still largely unregulated, and the structure of an ICO can greatly vary.

Figure 28 depicts the number of ICOs since January 2014, with the peak occurring at the end of 2017. Shortly thereafter, in February 2018, total market capitalisation reached USD 2.4 billion. Since most of the ICOs are valued through Bitcoin or Ether, market capitalisation broke down with the plunge of Bitcoin and Ether prices. Still, with the lower prices, the number of ICOs remained high, with 64 ICOs in May 2018 alone.[98]

Currently, ICOs provide a possibility for companies to raise money without the cost and time of a classic IPO. Even more, ICOs provide alternative financing to debt or capital funding from classic risk-capital providers, such as venture capitalists or banks. In many cases, an ICO is not covered by regulation. Therefore, they also include risk on the investors' side. In the wake of the blockchain and Bitcoin hype in 2017, there have been many scams and failed ICOs that tried to take advantage of their 'investors'. So, regulatory bodies have moved ahead to establish basic guidelines concerning ICOs, as the Swiss Financial Market Supervisory Authority (FINMA) issued guidelines concerning the regulatory framework for ICOs.

---

[98] The number of ICOs varies between sources. For instance, (PwC, 2017) counted 438 ICOs from January to November 2017. In contrast, (CoinDesk, n.d.) only includes 341 ICOs in its database while tokendata.io has over 900 in its database for 2017.

The intention of the discussion of this use case is to provide a general idea of how an ICO works and highlight the main differences of process, cost, and regulation compared to an IPO.

Source: www.coindesk.com

Figure 28. The market capitalisation and quantity of ICOs since 2014.

Conventional process

There are many ways for companies to raise capital. Traditionally, financing occurred through private investment, venture capitalists, or debt. Newer forms of start-up financing come in the form of crowdfunding initiatives (e.g., Kickstarter). The majority of the ICOs were also financed via crowdfunding in contrast to closed group funding. As the word ICO is already inspired by IPO, they share many similarities, and especially large and professionally guided ICOs can be compared to IPOs. Smaller ICOs can be better perceived as some form of crowdfunding.

The conventional process of an IPO in Switzerland takes about five months (Keller, 2016). Since it goes beyond the scope of this paper, the conventional IPO process is only described in terms of listing-prerequisites and costs. To obtain a listing at SIX, the Swiss stock exchange, a company must have a minimum track record of three complete financial years. The issuer must have reported equity of at least CHF 2.5 million with at least 20% of the issuer's outstanding equity securities in the hands of the public, which must amount to at least CHF 25 million. Financial reporting standards must follow Swiss GAAP, IFRS, or US GAAP as well as specific admission standards for investment and real estate companies (SIX Swiss Exchange, n.d.).

As there are more details and requirements for going public with an IPO, a successful IPO is possible only with the consultation of at least one bank and a variety of consulting firms (audit, marketing, and legal).

Expected costs

The cost of an IPO depends on the amount to be raised, since most fees are expressed as a percentage of the raised amount. According to Tomasz Tunguz, a venture capitalist, the typical technology venture raised around USD 107 million and paid fees of roughly 8.8% or USD 9.4 million in total fees (Tunguz, 2017). PwC, a consulting company, estimates the going-public costs to be around USD 10.1 million (for raising USD 107 million), which consists of an underwriting fee averaging between 4% and 7% of the gross proceeds and another USD 4.2 million of various fees (PwC, 2017). Concluding from this source, the U.S. IPO cost is between 9% and 10% of the raised capital. Not included in these figures are the organisational costs, which are around USD 1 million (PwC, 2017).

In Switzerland, costs are similar to the U.S., albeit a bit lower with underwriting fees of around 4% to 7% of the issuing money, and lawyers' and accountants' fees are approximately 1% to 1.5% (Glasl & Maag, 2013). For an issuing volume around 100 million, Swiss IPO costs are between 6.5% and 8% on average.

Blockchain process

It often is reasonable to distinguish tokens into three categories of utility tokens, asset tokens, and cryptocurrency tokens. In practice, tokens are also often a mix of these three categories. A utility token provides usage rights of the product and is the most common form of coin used in an ICO. For instance, Filecoin, one of the largest ICOs, aims to build a decentralised storage platform. Their tokens will give its buyers the right to use a certain amount of storage of their decentralised network. To raise capital, Filecoin issued a certain amount of their coins before the service was initiated. Once the storage network is fully functional, it is possible to mine Filecoins by offering storage and bandwidth. Filecoin investors anticipate that the demand for Filecoins will increase, as will the price of a token to profit from their investment.

According to a study from PwC and Crypto Valley (2017), ICOs are disrupting the traditional venture capital funding, where business angels and venture capitalists fund the seed money and funding rounds until the company goes public through an IPO. With ICOs, a hybrid model has appeared in which only seed money for a potential first series is funded before the ICO. Pure ICO funding does not require any venture capital funding, so the company begins with the ICO developing their product.

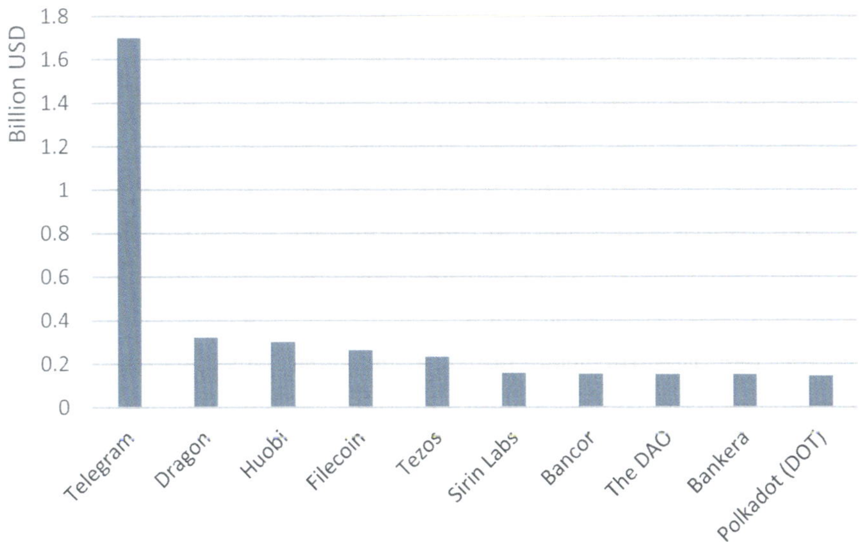

Source: www.coindesk.com

Figure 29. Largest ICOs by market capitalisation.

Figure 29 shows ten of the largest ICOs to date. Telegram was organised as a closed group ICO in contrast to public ICOs, and five of the top ten ICOs by market capitalisation are based in Switzerland (Tezos, Sirin Labs, Bancor, The Dao, and Polkadot).

Expected cost

Calculating the cost of an ICO is difficult. A rough estimation, based on the average cost over various source from January 2018, put the cost for a proper ICO at a total of USD 145,000. This results from the sum expenses for expected requirements i.e., a website (USD 10,000), marketing expenses (USD 15,000), legal services (USD 40,000), token smart contract (USD 16,000), ICO smart contract (USD 24,000), and a smart contract audit (USD 50,000).

The listing of the token for the ICO on a cryptocurrency exchange platform is typically free of charge since the exchange earns money via the transaction fees charged to its users. However, most exchange platforms require an audit of the tokens. If the issuer cannot provide enough information, then some exchanges charge increased auditing costs (around USD 5,000). However, some exchanges are beginning to change their policy of free listings. According to a report by Business Insider (Williams-Grut, 2018), prominent exchanges have started to charge between 50,000 to 1 million U.S. dollar for the listing of tokens.

Regulation

FINMA recently introduced guidelines for ICOs (FINMA, 2018) with broad definitions of three categories for tokens (utility, payment, and asset), its legal implications as a security, and potential anti-money laundering (AML) regulations. Utility tokens are designed to give access to the issuing platform and to provide the right to use a specific service (see the above Filecoin example). Payment tokens are understood to be classic cryptocurrencies, with the goal to facilitate transactions or store value. Asset tokens are understood to be a security, according to FINMA, and represent debt or equity from the issuing company. Chapter 7.1 highlights the legal aspects and frameworks for ICOs in detail. Currently, most ICOs contain utility tokens, which can change in the future as soon as legal uncertainties of asset tokens become clearer.

In general, the FINMA guidance paper has been a light regulation allowing this new field of investment to contain its dynamic.

Conclusion

ICOs give companies a new financing possibility via crowdfunding. Especially in Switzerland, where risk capital is not abundant, ICOs offered a large boost to new start-ups in Fin-Tech. Switzerland became one of the main hubs for ICOs largely due its favourable tax and legal systems, its significant background in FinTech, and a large talent pool from several universities researching in this area.

6.1.4. Private payment systems (World Food Programme)

The World Food Programme (WFP) is a branch of the United Nations Development Group committed to addressing hunger and promoting food security (UN Sustainable Development Goal number 2 'Zero Hunger'). It provides food assistance to approximately 80 million people worldwide, particularly in conflict-torn areas.

Delivering aid in underdeveloped countries is often costly as it requires the help of intermediaries. In addition, it is a challenging task susceptible to fraud because of the wealth gap and the dependency on local partners having less control over their behaviours. The decentralised nature of aid delivery corresponds well with blockchain technology's decentralised database. However, due to privacy concerns, this decentralisation of data is also seen as a liability.

The main motivation of the WFP to consider blockchain technology was the elimination of the financial service providers as intermediaries in cash-based food schemes, which included various disadvantages for the WFP. Most important were the banking fees for all transactions, banking accounts, and exchange of money as well as the financial risks due to unstable banks in developing countries and upfront payments of money. Other challenges, according to information provided by the WFP, include the reliance on vendor data to release a transfer as it might be the case that WFP disagrees with the number of transactions or what a refugee purchased.

Conventional process

The way food relief is distributed has changed over time and will always depend on specific conditions. When first starting in the 1960s, it took the form of food staples bought in developed countries and distributed directly to the poor. Today, aid programs have increasingly switched to offering Cash Based Transfers (CBT) and sourcing food locally. CBT exerts a multiplier effect on the local economy by strengthening the existing food market, building national capacities, and empowering the beneficiaries. Recent research further suggests that food vouchers and cash benefits are a cheaper method of relieving poverty compared to food aid, while simultaneously improving nutrition health. Food vouchers and CBT have clear benefits with regard to distribution costs, food waste, and dietary diversity (Cohen, 2017; Economist, 2011; Hidrobo, Hoddinott, Peterman, Margolies, & Moreira, 2014).

Indeed, cash and voucher-based policies may not work smoothly in remote or disaster-hit areas where food markets no longer function properly. They depend on well-functioning infrastructure requirements (electricity, internet ...), but where markets are stable, they are more advantageous. WFP often distributes vouchers that are redeemable in local shops for food and other staple items. In 2017, 14 million out of 80 million people fed by the WFP received cash disbursements.

A study conducted by the WFP in 2013 concluded that electronic pre-paid cards linked to financial institutions are the most appropriate and cost-efficient transfer modalities in the Lebanese context (Herzog, 2014) for an urban setting in a middle-income country where financial infrastructure is widespread. In practice, the e-voucher approach means that WFP contracted a local bank to produce the e-cards in partnership with MasterCard. WFP contracted partner shops that opened accounts at the local bank and installed their own sale machines.[99] In 2013, more than 400 shops throughout Lebanon had been contracted, and the program reached nearly 900,000 Syrian refugees.

The global partnership announced by MasterCard and WFP in 2012 goes well beyond e-cards. It also includes an 'Integrated Giving' platform, which allows brands and retailers to integrate donation mechanisms into their products. MasterCard cardholders then fund micro-donations in aid of the WFP by using their card.

Blockchain-based process

In early May 2017, the WFP launched its pilot project 'Building Blocks' in an Azraq refugee camp in Jordan. Cash-based transfers to 10,000 Syrian refugees were relocated using blockchain technology, and the implementation of the new technology went unnoticed by the beneficiaries. WFP does not use existing cryptocurrencies, only blockchain technology (via a private Ethereum fork) as a back-end. The beneficiaries go to the supermarket, identify themselves through an iris scan, and with a valid identification, the transaction is transferred on the blockchain and later settled using the standard bank infra-

[99] In other cases, e-vouchers via mobile phones have been tested and implemented (GSMA, 2017).

structure by transferring the money from WFP's main bank account to the vendor (Cohen, 2017; Paynter, 2017; Wong, 2017).

A prototype of the project was tested in the Sindh province of Pakistan in a small-scale version with about 100 people. (This trial did not involve iris scanners but relied on text-based mobile voucher codes.) Based on these results, the pilot for the Syrian refugees in Jordan was approved. Originally scheduled to end on 31 May 2017, the pilot was extended indefinitely and by November of the same year had already transferred USD 1.4 million in food vouchers. By January 2018, it expanded from one to four camps, covering 100,000 people, later becoming available in other countries (Wong, 2017).

The WFP Building Blocks project's major differences to a conventional process include the abolition of the financial intermediary and the data encryption technology used to forward the transactions. The blockchain used here is a fork of the Ethereum codebase as modified by the engineering firm, Parity, to be private, so transactions are not exposed. The network has only one full node and, therefore, does not meet our definition of a blockchain.[100] The WFP operates the chain, although it simulates a scenario where four parties work together for future expansion. Today, there is no decentralised database, and important advantages of the technology are not yet utilised. It also does not benefit from the security of a blockchain as there is only one central authority that can change the chain at any time; system crashes and data failures can and do occur. The project so far remains a database using blocks for data encryption.

WFP processes the payments, the accounting, and the identity checks. Miners are not required to validate these transactions, which removes a bottleneck to transaction capacity as well as transaction fees. Trust in this permissioned network depends on WFP as the central authority. The data stored on the chain include the date, beneficiary, vendor, transaction ID, category, credits, and the complete transaction history.

The financial motivation and saving costs, which were drivers for the project, seem to be the major advantage of the project so far. Fees from local bank

[100] However, we chose to include this use case nonetheless, since it is a very prominent example of using blockchain technology.

accounts have been reduced by 98% (Cohen, 2017) from 1.5% to nearly 0 (Pisa & Juden, 2017). Once the pilot is fully scaled, the WFP estimates to pay only USD 150 in monthly financial service fees, compared to USD 150,000 before. The usual intermediaries for transactions became unnecessary with the blockchain connection between WFP and vendors (Pisa and Juden, 2017). According to Paynter (2017), organisations working in international relief can lose up to 3.5% of each aid transaction to various fees and costs.

Time and speed are additional advantages, as the direct transaction between the vendor and the WFP has the added benefit of quicker reconciliation of accounts, no need to front funds to financial service providers, which also reduces problems with exchange rate fluctuation and inflation or deflation, and lower risk of instability or inoperability of the system.

Privacy for beneficiaries and protection of respective data are additional advantages. Security and trust seem to be less important issues for the WFP because the conventional process, in this case, is developed in a way that it is quite safe, and the WFP operates as a central authority in the aid process and will continue to do so.[101]

However, the challenges addressed and the improvements achieved are not due to the blockchain technology. The WFP has integrated the intermediary and manages the virtual wallets. While the cost savings are remarkable, they come entirely from the fact they run the system alone. They happen to use a blockchain as their database (Gerard, 2017), and WFP is aware of this fact.

Potential and conclusion

Various alterations are planned to use the full power of blockchains. Decentralisation of the information (other full nodes) is one element to offer refugees the possibility to review their balances and itemised lists of purchases as well as providing them with personal cryptographic keys. The ultimate goal, as stated by Houman Haddad, the WFP executive leading the project, is to give

---

[101] Across the industry, up to 30% of all development funds are considered to not reach their intended recipients, as UN Secretary-General Ban Ki-moon stated in 2012 (Pisa and Juden, 2017). Recent attempts by the World Bank to measure corruption on aid indicate that the funds lost to corruption are much lower (Myrna & Fletcher, 2012).

the beneficiaries as much control as possible and to link existing information from different aid agencies, including medical records (WHO), educational certificates (UNICEF), and nutritional data (WFP) (Wong, 2017).

Expanding the technology into the supply chain is another project that could help the WFP and all participating suppliers and local partner organisations to follow the resource allocation. Blockchain technology could give assurance to donors that their money reaches the people for whom it is intended. In their whitepaper on blockchain technology in the context of economic development, Pisa & Juden (2017) affirm that blockchain can contribute to improve outcomes and overcome the challenges above. They emphasise that in many cases the key constraints addressing these challenges lie outside the scope of blockchain technology. As in the case of the WFP, other pilots involved only one single donor or agency. So, the real promise would be the potential for coordination across multiple donors and agencies. According to Pisa & Juden (2017), this could prevent unnecessary duplication of efforts, promote greater harmonisation of the procedures, and allow partner governments to integrate aid into their budget decisions better. However, unlocking this potential had less to do with technology than with political will.

6.2. Blockchain with smart contracts

6.2.1. Gambling (vDice)

The gambling industry is generally fast at adopting new technologies. When the public use of the Internet gained traction in the early 1990s, entrepreneurs soon seized on the new opportunities for the gambling industry. Each of the traditional forms of gambling, widely available in land-based venues, soon appeared in electronic format over the Internet and have since been readily accessible to any person with an Internet connection and means of electronically transferring money (Wood & Williams, 2011). In 2015, the estimated global market size for online gambling reached approximately 40 billion U.S. dollars, and it is expected by 2020 that the market will reach up to 60 billion U.S. dollars (Statista, 2017). Nevertheless, the traditional land-based venues are still by far the predominant players in the market, as an estimate of the global revenue of land-based casinos in 2016 was still around seven times larger than the market for online gambling (Statista, 2017).

When online gambling took off in the late 1990s, it also started to attract the scrutiny of regulators. Switzerland legalised gambling for land-based casinos in 1998 with a new law called 'Spielbankengesetz'. From the beginning, the new law explicitly forbid telecommunication-supported gambling services, whereas simply participating in an online-gambling game was not illegal (Eidgenössische Spielbankenkommission ESBK, 2014).

The gross gaming revenue[102] of all 21 Swiss casinos in 2016 reached 689 Million CHF (Schweizer Casino Verband, 2017), which was down from a high of 1 billion CHF in 2007. The Swiss casinos mostly blame foreign online-gaming platforms for the decline. Opponents of blockchain-based gambling believe that it will accentuate this trend as it is nearly impossible to block access to blockchain-based casinos, while proponents believe it will make gambling fairer because of the increased transparency.

Conventional process

There is currently no conventional process for online gambling in Switzerland since it remains illegal. However, in 2009 the ESBK started to think about legalising online-gambling in Switzerland, and a new law passed both chambers in 2017 for a popular vote in 2018. It would legalise online gambling under similar restrictions as land-based casinos.

The casinos are required to be transparent, fair, and prevent money laundering as well as socially harmful effects. To guarantee these requirements, the operational processes are highly regulated and will be audited by the ESBK on a regular basis. Derived from Article 106 in the Swiss constitutions, numerous laws and decrees were put into effect concerning the regulation of land-based casinos (and soon online casinos) in Switzerland.[103] For online gambling, the most essential regulations include:

---

[102] The gross gaming revenue is similar to the gross revenue, pay-outs to players are retracted but operating expenses are not.

[103] Bundesgesetz vom 18. Dezember 1998 über Glücksspiele und Spielbanken (Spielbankengesetz) (SBG, SR 935.52), Verordnung vom 24. September 2004 über Glücksspiele und Spiel-

- The legal form must be a public limited company according to Swiss law.
- Players must be unambiguously identified to prevent addictive behaviour and money laundering.
- Processes must be well documented, and the automated processes must be recorded.
- The ESBK must be granted access for inspection.
- Required to pay progressive taxes and amounts on average to under 50% of the gross gaming revenue.

Foreign online casinos have, therefore, a substantial competitive advantage in less regulated countries. It is nearly impossible to prosecute online casinos based in a foreign judiciary even though their services are widely available to the public in Switzerland. The current formulation of the law provides the possibility for an Internet block by the ISP (internet service provider), and the ESBK will provide the list of blocked IPs. But this block will have a limited effect. First, there are many online casinos or similar services, so updating the IP list is tedious. Second, for the average tech-savvy person, it is trivial to circumvent these blocks using IP proxies that are readily available. Third, if foreign online casinos want to gain access to the Swiss market, then they could change their URL or IP address regularly. Finally, it is not illegal to play online from within Switzerland, so there is no deterrence for players from accessing foreign-based casinos.

banken (Spielbankenverordnung) (VSBG, SR 935.521), Verordnung des EJPD vom 24. September 2004 über Überwachungssysteme und Glücksspiele (GSV, SR 935.521.21), Verordnung der Eidgenössischen Spielbankenkommission vom 24. Juni 2015 über die Sorgfaltspflichten der Spielbanken zur Bekämpfung der Geldwäscherei (Geldwäschereiverordnung ESBK) (GwV-ESBK, SR 955.021), Bundesgesetz vom 10. Oktober 1997 über die Bekämpfung der Geldwäscherei und der Terrorismusfinanzierung im Finanzsektor (Geldwäschereigesetz) (GwG, SR 955.0), Schweizerisches Strafgesetzbuch vom 21. Dezember 1937 (StGB, SR 311.0), Bundesgesetz vom 22. März 1974 über das Verwaltungsstrafrecht (VStrR, SR 313.0) Bundesgesetz vom 20. Dezember 1968 über das Verwaltungsverfahren (VwVG, SR 172.021), Bundesgesetz vom 8. Juni 1923 betreffend die Lotterien und die gewerbsmässigen Wetten (LG, SR 935.51), Verordnung vom 27. Mai 1924 zum Bundesgesetz betreffend die Lotterien und die gewerbsmässigen Wetten (LV, SR 935.511).

Blockchain-based process: vDice

The simplest form of blockchain online gambling may be found on the site http://www.vdice.io, and its game mechanics work as follows: Several games offer different winning odds and payouts, but all games work the same. The gambler bets on a range of lucky numbers (e.g., 1 to 500), and if the number drawn (out of 1 through 10,000) is one of the lucky numbers, they win. For example, one could play the game with 5% winning odds and a payout multiplier of 19.62. In a fair game, the multiplier would be 20, but the operator takes 1.9% points, called the house edge, to cover operating costs (i.e., also all transaction fees). In this game, the player wins if the randomly drawn number is equal to or below 500. When a player wins, they are paid automatically, and if they lose, then they get back 1 Wei (10^{-18} Ether) as a confirmation that the game occurred. Due to the transaction costs of the Ethereum blockchain, the minimum bet is 180,000 gas ('vDice', 2018), which is currently valued at 228 CHF[104]. The game vDice is not peer-to-peer in the sense that two gamblers play against each other, but is a classic casino scenario where participants play against the bank where in this example the bank is the Ethereum wallet from which the smart contracts draw the pay-outs and deposits the bets of the players.

The games are simple and would not be a serious competition to traditional games in casinos (online and land-based) as they lack the 'excitement' factor. However, as a proof of concept, it shows how smart contracts can be used for online gambling. The games are anonymous (neither the players nor the owners know each other), transparent (the code of the smart contract is public), and accessible from anywhere with an Internet connection.

Gambling platform and decentralised ownership

Many start-ups are developing blockchain-based casino and gambling protocols.[105] Most plan to act as a gambling platform, which brings casinos, game-developers, and players together. A predominant advantage of the blockchain is its *transparency*, and games based on smart contracts cannot be changed

---

[104] Ether price of 1,264.90 (9 January 2018) (CoinDesk, Inc., 2018).

[105] Such as funfair.io, dao.casino, and edgeless.io

and are therefore easy to audit (by experts). This increased transparency is only theoretically a clear advance vis-à-vis the black box of current online casinos. The average user is unable to understand smart contract code (and how the oracle involved works, see below), while the user must 'only' trust the authorities in the relevant jurisdiction.

Decentralised infrastructure is another advantage of the blockchain with possible use in the gambling industry. Opening an online casino with traditional technology involves significant investment in centralised servers. Decentralised blockchain-casinos use the processing power of the miners, and most existing blockchain-casinos are Ethereum-based. This approach allows for reducing overhead cost, and its effect on the marginal cost ultimately depends on the specific blockchain technology used. Funfair.io, a blockchain casino start-up, developed a method for scaling transactions on the Ethereum blockchain, which is supposed to lower the cost of transactions. Because third parties, like credit-card companies, can be excluded from the process, a reduction of marginal costs is expected.

Platform tokens used as in-game currency and developer rewards. The use of secure tokens makes the transaction slightly more secure for players because there is no need to deposit credit in the online casino. Rather, players can use their blockchain wallets and only use the money they wager, contrary to the conventional process where they place a deposit with their credit card (say, with a minimum of USD 10). Tokens are also used as a reward for game developers if the blockchain casino serves as a platform for gamblers and developers.

With the blockchain technology, it is possible to develop casino platforms that are 'owned' by the token owners. This can be achieved through two scenarios: One is to pay out a dividend (casino-edge) proportional to the tokens held by every participant in the platform. Another is to make it possible for everyone to open an online casino on the platform. This approach would be the foundation for crowdsourced casinos and gambling websites.

Blockchain technology in its current state has a major disadvantage of extremely high transaction fees.[106] Additionally, blockchain transaction verification is too slow to be implemented for each round played (especially in fast games, such as slot-machines-like games). Some start-ups claim to have solved this problem by scaling the transactions (e.g., limiting transactions on the blockchain to a minimum), which cuts down the cost per transaction and allows a viable business case with smaller bets, contrary to the first example of vDice with a minimum bet of over USD 100.

Another problem with blockchain concerns required information from outside the blockchain. For online casinos, this would be in the form of a random-number generator, which cannot be part of the blockchain. The current workaround involves so-called oracles, which are services that write external information onto the blockchain. These services cannot confirm whether the information they retrieve is correct but rather only confirm the origin of the information. This means the potential player now must trust the specific source of the random-number generator, which dilutes the gained transparency of the smart contracts because the source codes of these third-party services are not always public.

Potential and conclusion

The blockchain technology offers the possibility to increase transparency, security, and efficiency for online casinos. This direction will also help regulators audit online casinos since the blockchain records are untampered and could theoretically be constantly monitored.

The most farfetched hopes lie on decentralisation of the casino industry through decentralised casino ownership, which would drive down the house edge to the operating cost, which would be the mining costs for the transactions. This evolution would be a transformative development for the online casino industry and could have a similar impact that P2P-Sharing had on the music and film industries.

[106] The blockchain transaction fees depend on the protocol used (PoS or PoA are more efficient than PoW).

6.2.2. Insurance (Etherisc)

Insurance is an essential part of our modern society; it allows us to share the risk of financial losses due to health, age, labour status, and natural disasters. Insurance works by pooling the risk for unforeseen and infrequent adverse events from many insured entities.

Like any financial service, insurance requires trust between the customer and the service provider. When an insured incident occurs, there must be certainty that the insurance can and will pay. This trust that claims are paid is based on the reputation of the company, the soundness of the legal system, and insurance market regulations. This trust also means that the insurer is not required to place the premiums in an escrow account out of which claims can be paid. Instead, insurers are required to hold reserves as a percentage of the yearly insurance premium. A private individual cannot participate in this market as they cannot pool the risks from different individuals and, thereby, achieve risk diversification. Moreover, buying insurance from a private individual would require trusting that the insuring individual can and will play should a claim be made.

As a trust machine, a blockchain enables people to engage in the insurance market without the need to trust one another. Instead, their trust in the chain and the smart contracts that can be deployed are what make peer-to-peer insurance possible. An alternative is a blockchain-based insurance platform where individuals buy insurance from smart contracts where many investors cover the risk of these insurance policies for a fee. This scenario essentially represents risk pooling on a blockchain.

Similar to other blockchain applications, it is argued that transaction costs are reduced. Financial transaction costs could be lowered compared to traditional insurance due to the standardised contracts and automatic claims management, which could also improve legal certainty and save time for the insured and insurers. The possibility to buy insurances online within minutes is an additional transaction cost lowering advantage of blockchain-based insurances.

In this use case, we look at the difference between new Fin-Tech and InsurTech type insurances as offered by the Lemonade Insurance Company and blockchain-based insurances as those proposed by Etherisc.

Conventional process: centralised insurances

Classical indemnity insurances are designed to make the insured whole again after the occurrence of a specific event. Risk is transferred from the insured to the insurer through an insurance contract or policy, which includes information on the parties involved, the premium, the coverage (period, amount, and event), and exclusions. The premium needs to cover the expected value of the risk transferred, long-term risks, and overhead costs of the insurance company. The expected value of the risk is a probability-weighted value of the instance covered. For example, 0.1% of the buildings in a country may burn down per year based on a long-term average. The expected value of the risk, then, is 0.1% times the value of the building insured. In some years, more buildings might burn down and increase the risk the insurance must cover. This so-called long-term, or long-tail, risk is captured by the probability of these rare events.

Insurance companies exist because they reduce the cost of the pooling risk and can practice better risk diversification. The more people insured for a specific event, the more likely the expected value of the risk will be equal to the claims paid. However, the coordination the insurance companies provide comes at a price as the overhead cost of the insurance company. They must sign new customers, manage claims, and earn a profit while doing so. Claim management and acquisition in traditional insurances are very labour-intense. For instance, when household insurance is sold, the insurance agent might visit the household to better estimate the value of the contents to be insured before offering a tailor-made insurance solution for the client. When a claim for the same insurance policy is filed, the agent might inspect the damage, request extensive documentation from the insured, process the claim, and, finally, release the payment of the claim.

As in other competitive markets, insurance companies look for ways to reduce these overhead costs to improve profits and increase the customer base. This is achieved by automating policy generation and claims management. One company that has taken this to the extreme is the Lemonade Insurance Company based in New York. Lemonade is a Fin-Tech company that uses chatbots and machine-learning algorithms to provide renters and home insurance policies. The algorithms and bots allow policies to be created automatically and claims to be processed in seconds instead of days.

Lemonade also builds on insights from behavioural economics. Customers digitally sign their name on a pledge of honesty before submitting the claim. They speak the claim into a camera instead of filling out claim forms. Honesty is further encouraged by the practice of 'social good'. From the premiums, Lemonade takes 20%, and the rest is used to pay claims and buy reinsurance to cover the tail risks. Each year, the unclaimed premiums are donated to non-profits of the insureds' choosing. The decoupling of the profits from the claims is said to realign the interests of the insurer and insured, so that rejecting claims does not increase profits for the insurance.

Blockchain-based process

Blockchain-based insurances present themselves to make insurance transparent, inexpensive, and open to investment for everyone. The Zug-based start-up, Etherisc, is developing a decentralised insurance platform with Ethereum using smart contracts. On this platform, anyone can design and offer an insurance product, which will be built on risk models and data sources provided either by the issuer or third parties that earn a fee for the usage of their property. The insurance policies require a risk pool to hold collateral used to settle the claims and a reinsurance pool that insures the risk pool against catastrophic long-tail events. The former pool is filled by the part of the premiums intended to cover the expected value of the risk. Tokenisation and the sale of the tokens fill the latter pool. These tokens entitle the holders to dividends from the revenue stream of the risk pools.

The first application built as a proof of concept is Etherisc Flight Delay, which allows people to buy insurance for flight delays. The premium for the insurance policy is calculated based on chosen parameters, such as pay-out and minimum delay, and on the prediction from the risk model for the specific flight. The insurance is bought online, and if the flight is delayed by at least the amount specified in the policy, then the payment to the insured is automatically executed. This process is completely automated and defined in a smart contract.

A crucial element to this process is the data source. The smart contracts cannot access external data directly, so they require an oracle to act as a data carrier between the smart contract and the data source. In the case of the flight-delay insurance, the data source is FlightStats, a global flight tracking service.[107]

Another proof of concept is a decentralised social-security model, which is essentially a microinsurance for disastrous life events, such as death or grave illness. Participants join a small local group of peers, e.g., a family, close friends, or co-workers, and pay small monthly premiums of, say, one U.S. dollar. The local groups then join together in higher-level groups that are again connected at a higher level. A tree-like structure is created that corresponds to the existing social structures. The higher-level groups could be the extended family, neighbourhood, or city. At each group level, a spokesperson is selected who checks and approves the claims. If a claim is approved, funds travel up and down the branches of the tree to reach the claimant.

Although Etherisc's aim is to provide decentralised insurance, by providing a platform they are centralising the insurances. With smart contracts, it is possible for anyone to offer insurance. The private insurer would set up a smart contract, send money to the smart contract to collateralise the potential risk pool, and then sell the insurance to anyone interested. If no claims materialise, then they are rewarded with the premiums paid and the collateral posted. Of course, unless the private insurer developed a working risk model for the event they are offering to insure, then this type of private insurance is more of a gamble than an investment. Additionally, because the private insurer cannot easily reinsure the risk pool against long-tail risks, they would have to post collateral in the sum of all potential claims to be trusted by potential clients. This scenario illustrates the case for a platform solution, such as what is being implemented by Etherisc.

Potential & conclusion

Etherisc sees four issues with the traditional insurance markets.

1. *High overhead costs.* Traditional insurances require large coordination costs in big firms.

---

[107] AXA fizzy is another example of blockchain-based flight-delay insurance. It is currently limited to flights from Paris Charles de Gaulle to North America. While the insurance runs on a smart contract on Ethereum, the payment of the premium as well as any potential pay-out are off-chain.

2. *Disadvantageous policies and biased claims management.* Insurers have an incentive to devise policies that are disadvantageous to its clients and to reject claims.

3. *Asymmetric information.* Insurance companies have an information advantage over their clients due to the massive amounts of claims data accumulated over the years.

4. *No investment into risk pools.* Access to investment into risk or reinsurance pools is limited to few investors.

Etherisc offers a solution for each of these perceived issues. By automating policy issuance and claims management, it can reduce overhead costs in the insurance business. However, this is not a blockchain-specific advantage, as standardised policies and parametrisation provide this benefit. Similarly, Lemonade can lower overhead costs by automating large parts of its daily business. Traditional insurances operate in a highly competitive market. A plethora of products are offered with different coverages, and a potential customer needs to compare the options available by reading the fine print. If this is what makes insurances disadvantageous, then smart contracts have similar issues. While anyone might review them, this is not a trivial task and requires considerable programming skills. In Etherisc, claims management is seemingly decoupled from insurance profits. If the insurance is not parametric, then independent experts are used to appraise the damage. However, investors are not willing to invest in risk pools with bad returns due to negligent claims management.

Asymmetric information is a problem in the insurance business. However, it is usually seen as a problem for the insurance companies as they face the double issues of moral hazard and adverse selection. Moral hazard means that the insured might change their behaviour to be more risk averse once insured. Adverse selection implies that bad risks are more likely to buy insurance as they know they are more likely to require it. Insurance companies use their data to counter these issues and offer premiums that also reflect the individual risk of the customer. For instance, they design policies that include a deductible to counter moral hazard, or they subsidise gym memberships to counter asymmetric information. They might also have to exclude from coverage events where the risk is too high and would make premiums unaffordable or the potential for insurance fraud too great.

Investing in risk pools is already possible today. Most big insurance companies are publicly listed, and buying stock from these companies represents an investment into their risk pool. Similarly, you can invest in the reinsurance pools by buying stock in reinsurance companies. However, Etherisc's proposed tokenisation of the risk pool would allow for direct investment into a specific pool, for instance, the risk pool of flight-delay insurance.

Etherisc offers interesting new features by creating an open market for insurance policies, risk models, data sources, and risk pool investments. However, the advantage over centralised insurance appears to remain marginal.

- While blockchain-based insurances can have lower overhead costs, the advantage seems to be based more on the choice of insurance policies they offer than the technology they use. Parametric insurances, such as flight-delay insurance, is cheaper by design as it does not require a claims management due to the automatic execution.
- Creating risk models requires large amounts of data to calibrate the model. Brick-and-mortar insurances have this data and the human resources to build good risk models, and it is unclear whether blockchain-based insurances have a comparative advantage in building these models.
- Data sources can be sold for use in applications and can easily be accessed through the data provider's application programming interface (API). On the blockchain, oracles are needed to integrate these data sources, and as an intermediary, these create additional costs.
- Direct risk pool investment might be interesting for some investors. However, on average, investors profit from the diversification over risk pools offered by investing into insurance or reinsurance companies.

These points aside, Etherisc provides the potential for the creation of insurance policies for fringe events as it lowers the barrier of entry to the market. For example, you might want to insure the flowers in your garden against draught or your summer house against pest invasion. Traditional insurances might not be able to offer such policies. The decentralised social-security microinsurance is another instance where a blockchain solution offers some additional potential over centralised insurances as it allows the inclusion of a payment system. This is advantageous in developing countries where functioning payment systems might be missing but where microinsurances are usually deployed.

In summary, blockchain-based insurance offers some advantages but not nearly as strong as suggested by the developers. The main transaction cost reducing factor is found in the use of technology to reduce manual inputs, to speed up policy issuance, and claims management. However, the technologies used to achieve this are not exclusive to the blockchain.

6.2.3. e-ID (City of Zug)

An electronic identity (e-ID) allows an entity to prove their identity electronically and thereby gain access to services. A state-of-the-art e-ID can take different forms depending on the user requirements. In a business context, a user might want to prove they are an official representative of a company. When shopping online for wine, this same information is not relevant but instead needs to prove they are above the legal drinking age. This ability is known as self-sovereign identity, i.e., all access to the information connected to an identity is controlled by the user, and the release of information can be granular. The self-sovereign identity is what provides the e-ID with the potential to replace all the service-specific digital identities we use to login to our email account, social media, online shops, and e-banking services.

Confidentiality, integrity, and availability of the data are paramount for e-IDs. Unauthorized parties should not have access to personal data belonging to an e-ID. The data stored should be consistent, accurate, and trustworthy at any time, and the e-ID needs to be accessible at any time to be useful. A blockchain-based e-ID can fulfil these requirements but so can centralise solutions. In this use case, we look at an example of a centralised (SwissID) and blockchain-based (uPort) e-IDs. Because they are both in the early stages of implementation, it is hard to differentiate the two solutions from a transaction cost perspective. The financial costs are still mostly uncertain, time costs seem to be comparable, and neither appear to have an advantage in legal certainty. The main cost advantage is compared to existing authentication schemes. Additionally, both solutions offer specific advantages discuss below.

Conventional process

E-IDs are currently issued in many countries around the world, often in the form of a credit card-sized smartcard. These devices store the identity information that is printed on the cards plus (optionally) biometric information in the embedded RFID chip. In most countries, the government issues these e-IDs. In Norway, Sweden, and Finland, the bank issues e-IDs that are accepted by the government, and the e-IDs are used for online authentication for government services and age verification. In some countries, private companies can provide an electronic signature that is also stored on the chip. However, these e-IDs do not include a self-sovereign identity.

In Switzerland, no officially recognised e-ID has been introduced. However, the federal administration is currently preparing legislation for privately provided government authorised e-IDs. In late 2017, SwissSign, a joint venture of Swiss Post and the Swiss federal railway (SBB) together with SIX Group, Swiss banks, and the insurance company, Mobiliar, launched SwissID as a privately provided e-ID aimed at offering easy and secure access to many online services from shopping to banking to e-government. In the spirit of a self-sovereign identity, it promises its customers control over what data they share with a service provider. With the growing concern about data collection by private firms, the ability to govern who receives what personal data is a valuable feature.

The system includes five actors of the e-ID owner, ID provider, ID broker, service provider, and the official administrative registers.

- The e-ID owner requests an e-ID from an ID supplier. Once received, they own the e-ID and all data connected to it. They can use e-ID to authenticate to service providers.
- The ID supplier provides the e-ID to the owner who first physically identifies the owner using official identification documents provided by the owner. They request further authentication of data from an official register through a broker.
- The broker is responsible for the transfer of authentication requests between the service provider and the ID supplier. They are a necessary actor to achieve double blindness, i.e., the service provider does not know the ID supplier and vice versa.
- The official administrative registers are needed to cross-check and verify the identity data of the e-ID.
- The service provider can be an online service that requires user authentication. Examples include online shops, financial services, and e-government services.

Figure 30 illustrates the interactions between the five actors in a conventional e-ID system using the example of SwissID.

The system is still in its early days, and as of January 2018, only a limited amount of Swiss Post services are accessible via SwissID.

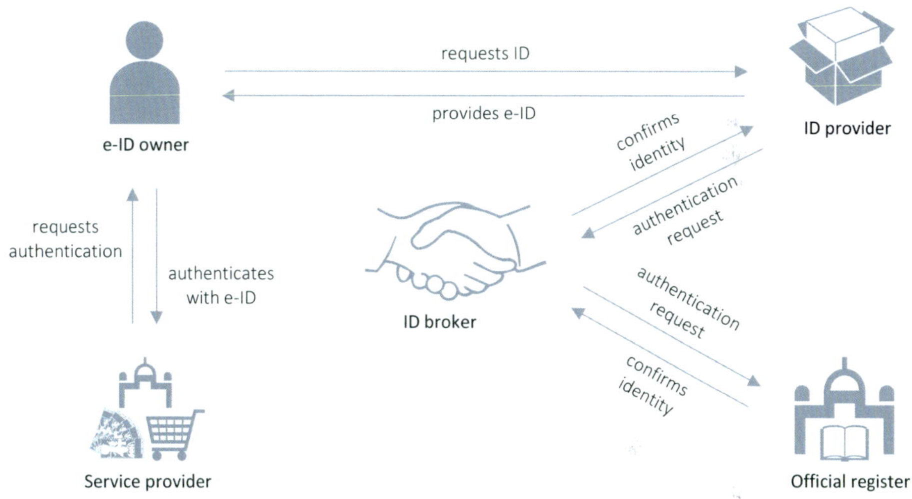

Source: IWSB.

Figure 30. Overview of the process with a conventional e-ID.

However, even without e-IDs available, the online services in use today work through existing user-authentication systems. In practice, this type of verification is enough for most online services and can be enhanced using video calls or photos to verify the identity of a user as do online banks or Airbnb. The potential for cost savings on the consumer side is limited. However, the time costs for some applications could be significantly reduced as these use cases are also infrequent, such as opening a bank account. E-IDs could improve legal certainty for retailers as an online wine shop could be sure they sell product to an e-ID holder that is older than the legal drinking age. This would lower the risk of fines and other legal procedures. Other financial processing costs are already zero for consumers in the current system. The e-ID promoted by SwissSign would be free for consumers.

On the side of the companies, a unified solution, like the SwissID, is potentially cost saving. Instead of developing and maintaining a user-authentication system, they simply pay a fee per customer login. Additionally, an e-ID could save costs for vetting customers and better handle anti-money laundering regulation in financial services. Consumers could use different financial service providers without being vetted every time.

Blockchain-based process

As an immutable and distributed ledger, a blockchain is a secure place to store e-IDs. The Swiss company, Consensys, created an e-ID called uPort as a self-sovereign identity system built on Ethereum. To build this decentralised identity system, uPort creates four smart contracts and a mobile App.

- The *uPort App* on the smartphone of the user stores the private key, which is used to control the e-ID.
- The *Proxy Contract* is the persistent identifier of an uPort identity. It is a minimal contract that forwards transactions from the Controller Contract to the (distributed) application.
- The *Controller Contract* allows users to interact with the Proxy contract and allows for additional functionalities, such as specifying a Recovery Quorum Contract.
- The *Recovery Quorum Contract* stipulates how users can recover their identity when the device storing the private key is lost.
- The *Registry Contract* maintains cryptographic links between all uPort identities and the off-chain data attributes associated with them.

The interaction between the different contracts and actors is illustrated in Figure 31 and explained in more detail in the following paragraphs.

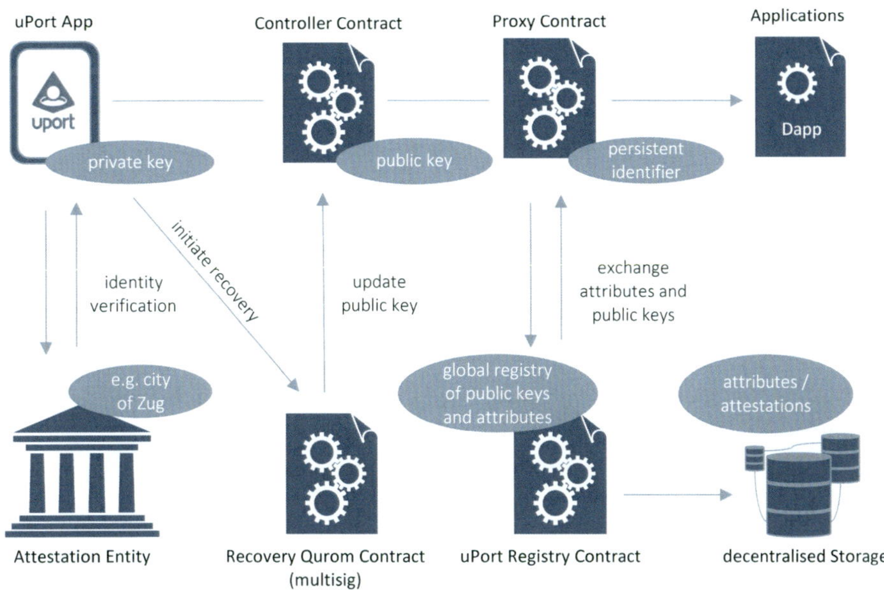

Source: IWSB.

Figure 31. The uPort processes.

The central feature of the uPort e-ID is the ability to recover an identity even when the device storing the private key of the identity is lost. So, a user does not lose the reputation, assets, and history tied to the uPort identifier. This is possible due to the Recovery Quorum Contract, which is a multisig contract controlled by the user's friends and other trusted entities (e.g., banks and public authorities) that together form the recovery network. They can specify a new public key that controls the Controller Contract. When the user replaces the lost device, they communicate the device's public key to the recovery network. As soon as most of the network confirms the key change, the Controller Contract updates the public key, and the user regains control over their uPort e-ID.

The Registry Contract is a global registry for looking up public keys and attributes of uPort identities. It maps every uPort identity to the user's attributes and attestations stored off-chain in decentralised storage solutions (IPFS). The attestations are what make the uPort e-ID comparable to existing centralised e-ID solutions, and it allows for third parties to attest to the correctness of attributes connected to a uPort identity. An example of such attestation by an official public entity is the pilot for e-ID for the City of Zug's residence project using uPort. This pilot was publicly launched in November 2017 by the IT company ti&m together with ConsenSys and the City of Zug. Identities created with uPort are verified by the city officials and signed using its uPort identity. Therefore, in this pilot, Zug takes on the role of the 'trusted service provider' replacing the traditional intermediaries in the public key infrastructure (e.g., Verisign or QuoVadis). Other entities or users that trust Zug can trust the identity of any user attested by the City of Zug without knowing the user.

The financial costs of the uPort e-ID are small. As with all use cases that rely on public blockchains, costs accrue when transactions are committed to the blockchain. In the case of uPort, these are the smart contracts created for every identity. ConsenSys calculated it would cost about CHF 700 to create identities for all 30,000 Zug residents. The financial and legal certainty cost advantages are the same as with non-blockchain-based e-IDs described above. The question then is if a blockchain-based solution is cheaper or the additional features offered are valued more by the users.

Potential & conclusion

The federal government states that an e-ID is important for the future development of e-government and e-commerce applications. Today, official identification on the Internet is possible only through the help of video calls and photos of an ID. An e-ID offers a more secure and possibly cheaper way to verify identities.

However, even in cases where identification is assumed essential, such as the sale of alcohol, it still is not performed. For instance, online wine shops do not verify the age as they only ask the customer to state their age. In the past, some shops required identification using the SuisseID (the predecessor of SwissID), but as the usage of SuisseID did not spread, shops requiring this type of identification were at a disadvantage to other online-shops and stopped the practice. Moreover, pseudo-ID verification is not limited to the Internet. In Swiss conveniences stores (Coop Pronto), the self-checkout may be used when buying alcohol with age verification performed by swiping your

ID. Of course, this only checks that you are in possession of an ID for a person who is 18 years or older, and does validate if it is the purchaser's ID.

A key feature of the e-IDs discussed here is the self-sovereign identity system. The ability to let the user decide explicitly what data to share when identifying oneself is a valuable asset for a time when general awareness about the data being shared is increasing. Although the concept of a self-sovereign identity is compelling in theory, problems remain. First, big tech (Amazon, Google, Apple, and Facebook) offer such compelling services they could still require you to give up all your data to use their (free) services, and most consumers would probably do so. Second, people today have some control over what rights they give new apps when installing onto smartphones. Still, the average user probably confirms all rights without giving it too much thought. The value of a self-sovereign identity system then lies mainly in making it more transparent what data are being shared. This, in turn, could better educate people in the long term in the handling of personal data.

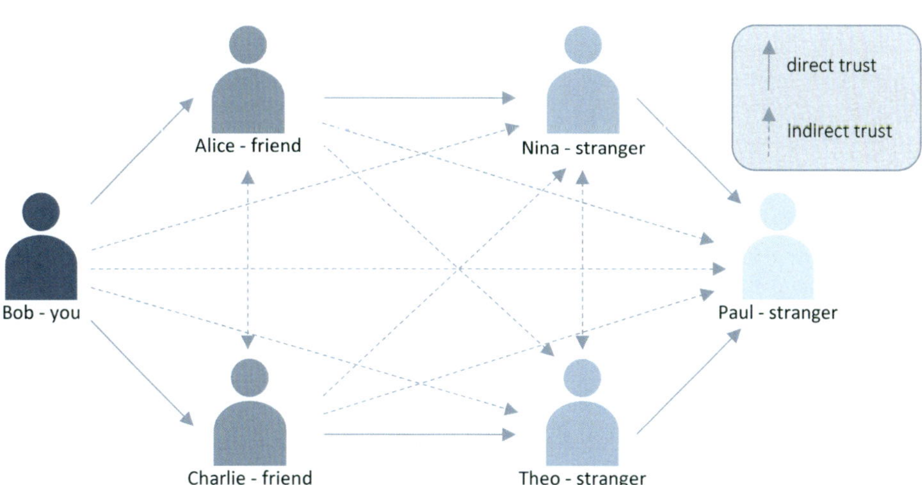

Source: IWSB.

Figure 32. Example of a Web of Trust.

A feature not yet implemented in uPort, but one that would set it apart from the SwissID, is a decentralised non-hierarchical model of trust. An attribute belonging to an identity no longer needs to be attested by an official third party, but other uPort users can attest to the attributes. If enough users have attested an attribute, then others can also trust the information. This generates what is called a Web of Trust, where trust is no longer based on a hierarchy (see Figure 32 for an example of a web of trust). A non-hierarchical attestation of attributes allows users to add and have attested a broader range of attributes that no official body would (e.g., favourite food, personal traits, best friend, and dog's name). uPort then becomes a compelling solution for social networks. Together with the self-sovereign identity, people could share personal information that would be relatively trustworthy while still being in control of the data.

The web of trust is the baseline to attest attributes. For example, your tennis club can attest that you are a member, your friends can attest to your having two kids, and your boss and co-workers could confirm your excellent project management skills. We could imagine different use cases that require different thresholds for full attestation within the Web of Trust. For instance, the uPort identity could be used to apply as a medical doctor. The potential employer would probably have different thresholds for trusting whether the applicant plays the violin in free time, attended the University of Hyderabad, and whether they are a fully certified medical specialist accredited to practice in Switzerland. For the first, they might consider any form of attestation sufficient. For the second, they would require the university to attest the attribute, and that at least two of the trusted people directly attest that it is the University of Hyderabad that attested to the validity of the university studies. For the certification as a medical specialist, an attestation through the Web of Trust may no longer be sufficient. Here, the employer might require (by law) an attestation by an official authority whose identity they know to be valid. In the case of the medical doctor, this is the Federal Office of Public Health. Figure 33 illustrates this example.

The solution could potentially include current trusted services providers who could attest and verify identities that need a more official attestation, such as firms. If you trust the trusted service providers, then you also trust all accounts they trust.

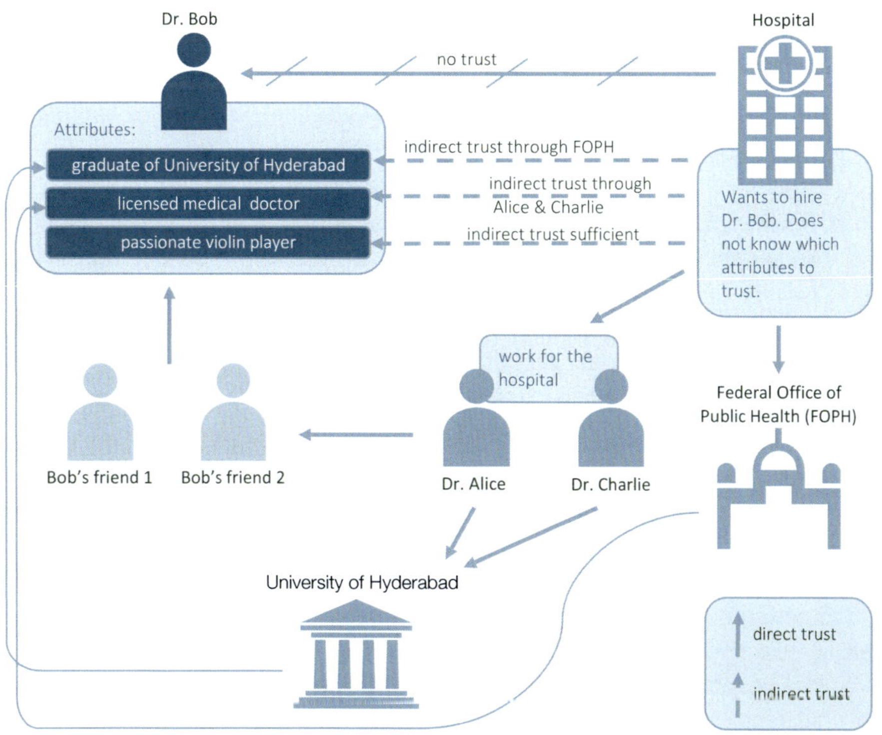

Source: IWSB.

Figure 33. An example of applying a Web of Trust.

Without decentralised non-hierarchical attestation of identity attributes, the differences between the two e-ID solutions come down to technological differences and the users they target. Technologically, uPort profits from improved availability of good data thanks to the decentralised nature of the blockchain and distributed storage. Data integrity can also be assured due to the immutability property of the blockchain. However, the use of the blockchain is currently also likely to hamper the spread of the solution. Most potential users do not know what it is and how it works, so they may be reluctant to entrust their identity to the blockchain. Furthermore, ConsenSys is a company unknown to the broader public.

In contrast, the companies behind SwissID are known to nearly the entire population of Switzerland: Nearly every inhabitant is a customer of at least one of the companies, which likely results in advance trust from the potential users but, more importantly, from the companies that must pay to use the service. Therefore, SwissID has the potential to realize network effects, i.e., more users lead to more companies and more companies lead to more users. On the downside, the SwissID is a very national e-ID that is tailored specifically to Switzerland. This might hinder its spread beyond the borders such that a future global ID supported by a larger network might then supplant it. uPort's flexible low-cost solution for e-ID means it could become a global player in the niche of Ethereum identities. With growing faith and knowledge in blockchains, smart contracts, and decentralised applications, uPort might then be the global ID that supplants the SwissID.

6.2.4. Public e-voting (Follow my Vote)

Voting allows people to express their opinion and make community decisions. In Switzerland, citizens regularly vote on referenda and popular initiatives as well as electing representatives at communal, cantonal, and federal levels. Over the decades, trust has been built that votes are counted as cast, and that the secrecy of the vote is guaranteed, which has not been mitigated by the introduction of voting by mail. In Switzerland, e-voting has only been introduced on a trial basis and is currently being used in nine cantons.[108] Furthermore, it is restricted to certain parts of the electorate, namely, Swiss voters living abroad and the physically disabled.

As it is paramount to ensure that trust in the voting process is preserved, every technological solution should be thoroughly reviewed. Furthermore, technology also has the potential to reduce some of the transaction costs related to voting. First, secure e-voting might reduce legal certainty costs if it is less prone to voter fraud and foreign intervention, making challenges in court less

[108] The cantons of Aargau, Basel-City, Berne, Geneva, Luzern, and St Gall use the system CHvote. The cantons of Fribourg, Neuchâtel, and Thurgau use the system by Swiss Post. The cantons of Vaud and Glarus plan to reintroduce e-voting in 2018 and 2019, respectively (Der Bundesrat, n.d.).

frequent. Second, the financial costs of voting in Switzerland are small yet not insignificant. Numbers from the commune of Zurich estimate the cost at around CHF 2.4 per person per ballot. Given that e-voting will remain optional for the foreseeable future, the potential financial savings are not very important in the short run. Third, we could expect e-voting to lower the time cost of voting due to the possibility of voting from any place at any time.

Conventional process

Conventional voting processes require people to either vote personally at the ballot box or use early postal voting. The voting documents are sent by mail to every eligible voter with no prior registration necessary (even for postal voting). If they decide to vote by mail, they fill out their ballot papers, place them into a plain envelope, and send it together with their voter legitimation to the voting authorities before the deadline. The process is relatively easy to perform by anybody.

Proponents argue that e-voting reduces the financial transaction cost of voting and, thereby, increases voter turnout. This argument for e-voting in Switzerland from a voter's viewpoint is weak both analytically and empirically. While the postage costs for postal voting (returning through the mail) are not covered in all cantons, the cost of a stamp is only CHF 0.85 and a low financial barrier. Further, even in these cantons, it is possible to personally deliver your postal votes to a communal mailbox ahead of the official election or ballot day for free.

The time costs for postal voting and e-voting are comparable. In both cases, the ballot papers must be filled out and sent. The voting process for e-voting also requires some time to run through the ballot, and, on average, is probably not significantly faster than voting by mail. Empirically, studies of the cantonal e-voting trial in Geneva found no increased mobilisation of voters (Germann & Serdült, 2014; Sciarini, Cappelletti, Goldberg, Nai, & Tawfik, 2013). The increased convenience of e-voting relative to voting by mail is not high enough for new voter groups to participate. Therefore, while the federal government and cantons aim to introduce e-voting nationwide, the argument is not based on financial or time transaction costs. Benefits are seen in preventing invalid votes, improving the speed of determining results of polls and elections, and enabling physically disabled voters to vote autonomously (Der Bundesrat, n.d.).

Currently, systems by two e-voting providers are in use in Switzerland. One was developed by the canton of Geneva (CHvote) and another distributed by Swiss Post but developed by the Spanish electronic voting company, Scylt. The voting processes of both providers are similar and consist of multiple steps, so the process for the Swiss Post's e-voting is provided below.

1. *Identification:* The voter is identified and legitimised to vote by inputting the authentication code printed on the voting card.
2. *Voting:* The voter fills out the electronic ballots.
3. *Vote sending:* Using end-to-end encryption, votes are sent to a server where they are stored.
4. *Verification:* The voter receives a verification code for each vote cast that they compare to the verification codes included with the voting card. They can check whether the votes were cast as intended and recorded as cast. In case of discrepancies, they can then correct and resend the vote.
5. *Vote casting:* Using a ballot key, the voter can confirm the vote, which is then recorded in the electronic ballot box.
6. *Confirmation:* The voter receives a vote cast code that is compared with the vote cast code on the voting card.

Before the confirmation step, the voter can at any point decide not to vote electronically but by mail or personally. In both cases, a bar code is scanned to check whether the voter has already voted electronically.

Leaving aside the transaction cost argument,[109] the e-voting channel currently implemented in Switzerland has three advantages over postal and personal voting. First, it allows the voter to verify that the votes were cast as intended, i.e., the votes cast represent the true voter intent. Hence, an error in filling out the ballot can be corrected. Second, the voter can check if the vote was recorded as cast, i.e., the vote is properly recorded in the ballot box. Third, all

[109] With respect to the financial transaction costs, of the CHF 2.40, approximately CHF 0.80 are for counting the vote. This cost could be saved with e-voting solutions that automatically count the vote. For comparison, the e-voting solution used in Basel-City costs CHF 5.9 million for all 55 votes and elections over 10 years. This results in costs of CHF 107,272 or about CHF 1 per eligible voter.

votes are recorded on a bulletin board (a log file), so the voting process is fully auditable without sacrificing voter privacy. To achieve immutability of the log file, the bulletin board is hashed in regular intervals, and the hash value is sent to the Bitcoin blockchain using pegged coins. Therefore, modern e-voting systems in place in Switzerland today already use blockchain technology, although not for the voting process.[110]

While the security standards are high, the centralised infrastructures are a weak point, as it gives hackers a clear target to attack. However, because the blockchain-secured bulletin board guarantees the integrity of the vote, any attempt to manipulate the results would be noticed. If the results could not be recovered, a revote might be necessary. However, certain detection and recovery would lower the incentive for an attack considerably.

Blockchain-based process

In general, blockchain-based e-voting is seen to have three advantages. First, *transparency*, as voters can trace their ballots in the system and ensure they are counted correctly. Second, *immutability*, since once a vote is entered into a blockchain it cannot be (easily) modified. Third, *non-equivocation*, since a blockchain cannot show different information to different people. However, the centralised e-voting system described above also has advantages as it also partially includes blockchain technology. The question becomes whether a pure blockchain voting can be a cheaper, more convenient, and more secure solution. To answer this, we first need to understand how a blockchain-based implementation of e-voting could look.

A blockchain-based e-voting system needs to solve the problem of allowing only eligible voters to cast votes without compromising the secrecy of their vote. To receive a voting token on a blockchain, a voter must reveal their identity so an electoral authority can check eligibility. The challenge is to break the connection between the voting token and the voter. Any organisation that wants to implement blockchain-based voting for public elections and polls must solve this issue as the Universal Declaration of Human Rights

[110] This is only the case in the system distributed by the Swiss Post.

guarantees the secrecy of the vote. 'Follow My Vote' is an example of a project with a solution.

Follow My Vote is an open-source, end-to-end verifiable blockchain-based voting system that runs on BitShares, a public blockchain with a distributed ledger that uses a proof-of-stake consensus protocol. The blockchain processes three types of transactions: voter eligibility verification, voting account creation (anonymous and unique), and vote broadcast. The voter verification process uses a 'blinded token' to separate voter identity from the vote after verification. A blinded token is obscured in a manner that is akin to putting a token into a carbon copy envelope.[111] A signature of the envelope would then be printed on the token inside. The verification process to obtain a voting account works as follows and is illustrated in Figure 34:

1. The voter's real-world identity is verified, and their public key is certified on the blockchain as belonging to that identity (voter eligibility verification).
2. The voter submits a unique and verified ID to the registrar. Upon submission, a blinded token is created by the voter.
3. The registrar checks that the ID has not already been registered to vote and signs the blinded token.
4. The blinded token is returned to the voter, which can then be unblinded. However, in order to break the immediate connection to the registrar by receiving the blinded token, they wait for multiple other voters to receive the signed blinded token before unblinding it.
5. The voter creates a new voter identity, which is sent to the registrar together with the unblinded token.
6. The registrar checks whether this token has ever been used and certifies the voter identity, i.e., a certificate stating that this public voting key has been checked by the registrar and is added to the blockchain. The voter may now vote through the system.

---

[111] The blinded token is known as a blinded signature in cryptography. Follow My Vote uses a blinded RSA signature.

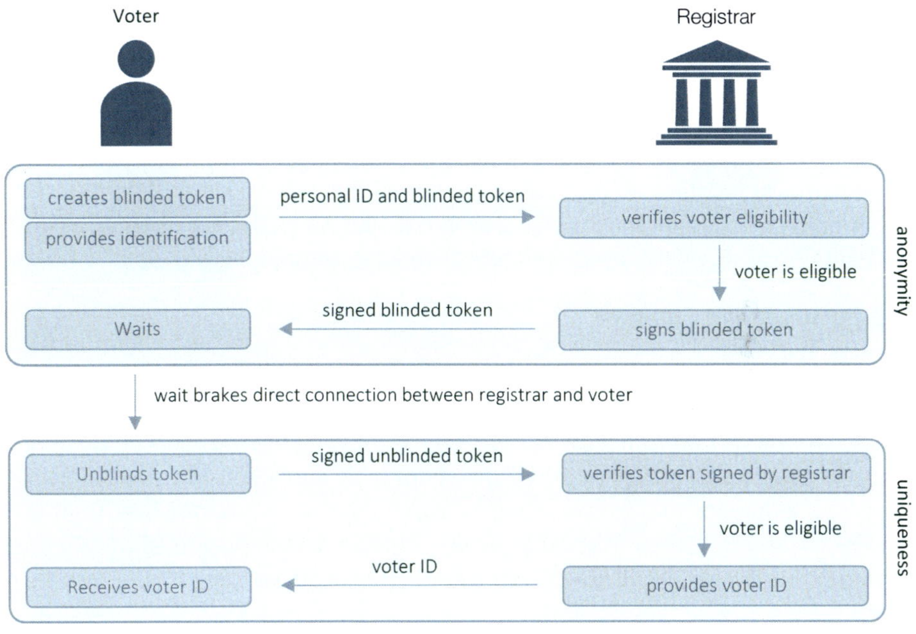

Source: IWSB.

Figure 34. A unique and anonymous voter registration process.

The voter can now use a private voting key to sign votes (voting transactions), and the tally is adjusted accordingly. Everyone on the chain can verify that the vote was cast by an authorised voter by checking the certificate using the public key on the blockchain. Additionally, anyone can recount the votes as they are all registered on the blockchain. This makes the result of the vote completely transparent.

Challenges

Blockchain voting faces several challenges. First, usability challenges are not limited to e-voting and could have enormous effects on democracies. People are bad at securely storing and managing private keys. Once a voting account is verified, the private voting key allows the owner of that key to vote without further verification of identity. Voters would need to be taught to make backups to a safe location, so the key is recoverable. Considering that many people fail to back up their personal computer sufficiently, it seems difficult to ensure that this would be achieved. Second, there is the potential for voter fraud. As in any voting system, fraud is always possible. In the case of blockchain voting described above, it would, however, only require obtaining the private key of the voters. These could either be bought from voters or cybercriminals could steal them from voters.[112] If the voters whose keys are stolen do not vote regularly and do not check that their vote was counted as cast, then it would be easy for third parties to cast fraudulent votes without ever being detected.

Potential and conclusion

Comparing centralised e-voting used in Switzerland to the solution proposed by Follow My Vote, the differences are technical. Both systems increase the transparency of the vote and make it completely auditable while maintaining the secrecy of the vote. As no information is available on the cost of Follow My Vote, it is also hard to say whether blockchain voting is cheaper than centralised e-voting. Given that centralised e-voting solutions are already implemented and tested in live elections, the cost advantage would have to be significant for a blockchain system to replace the centralised e-voting systems.

6.2.5. Trade financing (Batavia)

Trade finance is the financing of both international and domestic trade transactions. These transactions between a seller and a purchaser of goods involve several commercial risks, as delivery and payment are not simultaneous. Therefore, the seller and the purchaser might look for a way to reduce their risk exposure. The seller would prefer not to send the goods until payment is received and the seller does not want to pay until receiving the goods. This dilemma can be somewhat mitigated by splitting payments into different installments, such as one-third up front, one-third after shipment, and one-third at the reception of the goods. However, the trade still requires trust as part of the risk remains, such as non-payment of an installment, poor quality of the goods, or non-delivery. When trust is lacking, banks and other financial

[112] However, the second option would require considerable effort since access to the devices of the voters is necessary to steal the private key.

institutions can act as trusted intermediaries between the parties. Using bank guarantees and letters of credit, they provide financing conditional on the presentation of certain documents that prove the goods have reached a certain point in the deal. For instance, a bill of lading can prove that the goods have been shipped, and subsequently the bank releases the second installment of the payment.

Trade finance is a 10 trillion U.S. dollar business (WTO, n.d.), and even small changes on the cost side could, therefore, have huge impacts globally. Additionally, trade finance still experiences a gap between the amount of financing requested and the amount provided. This trade finance gap was estimated to be around 1.6 trillion U.S. dollars in 2016 (ADB, 2016). Reducing transaction costs by introducing new technologies into trade finance might help reduce this gap. First, blockchain-based solutions could help simplify, streamline, and digitise trade finance, which today remains largely paper-based. Second, legal certainty costs could be lowered by reducing the necessity of trust between the parties involved and the reliance on third parties. Last, blockchain solutions offer to dramatically reduce the time required to achieve trade financing, thereby further reducing time costs.

Conventional process

Trade financing is a highly complex process involving many entities, such as banks, customs agencies, freight companies, importers, and exporters. Figure 35 below and corresponding explanations provide an overview of a simple trade finance process.[113]

1. An importer places an order with an exporter. They agree on a price and a date for delivery, and the exporter provides an invoice.
2. A financial agreement is drawn specifying the details of the deal.
3. The importer approaches the exporter bank with a request for the financing of the trade and provides the bank with a copy of the financial agreement.

[113] This section and the following build on the World Economic Forum's report, 'The future of financial infrastructure' (McWaters, Galaski, & Chatterjee, 2016).

4. The import bank provides financials to the export bank. In case the import and export banks have no established relationship, then additional correspondent banks might be introduced.
5. The export bank forwards financing details to the exporter, which can now initiate the shipment.
6. A trusted, third-party checks that the goods match the invoice.
7. Customs checks goods based on export country codes.
8. The goods are transported by freight to the importing country and checked by customs at entry.
9. The importer inspects goods at reception and provides the import bank with a receipt.
10. Payment is executed by the import bank to the export bank.

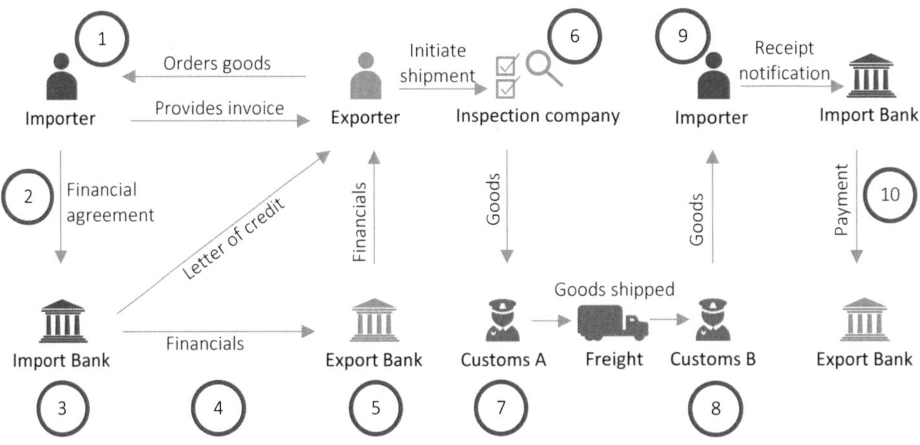

Source: IWSB based on McWaters, Galaski, & Chatterjee (2016).

Figure 35. A conventionally secured trade finance process.

The current process includes many vulnerable points. Acquiring trade finance is still primarily a paper-based process that involves manual review of the financial agreement and manual anti-money laundering (AML) checks by the exporter bank using the financials provided by the importer bank. Documents, such as bills of lading, are financed multiple times because the banks cannot confirm their authenticity. As financials are sent from one entity to the other, they are amended manually. This leads to version control challenges, i.e., there is no single version of the truth. Additionally, the numerous parties involved operate on different platforms. Therefore, miscommunication is common, and the likelihood of fraud and errors are high. Combining all this leads to a process that is slow and error-prone. For instance, the average time to process a letter of credit can be as high as 30 days (Deloitte, n.d.).

Blockchain-based process

Blockchain offers the potential to standardise and digitise the processes in trade finance on a platform that is transparent, allows for real-time reviews, and, therefore, builds trust. A blockchain-based process would include the following features and is illustrated in Figure 36:

1. The importer and exporter share their financial agreement with the import bank via a smart contract.
2. The import bank reviews the agreement, drafts a letter of credit, and sends it to the export bank for review.
3. The export bank reviews the letter of credit, approves it, and creates a smart contract from the letter of credit.
4. The export initiates shipment by digitally signing the letter of credit.
5. Goods are inspected and digitally signed by a third-party organisation and the customs agent in the country of origin.
6. The goods are shipped to the importer and checked by local customs agents before being handed over to the importer.
7. The importer acknowledges the receipt by signing the smart contract. This initiates payment from the import bank to the export bank.

Source: IWSB based on McWaters, Galaski, & Chatterjee (2016).

Figure 36. A blockchain-secured trade finance process.

The processes as described above include some advantages over the current ones. First, they allow all parties to review all documents linked to the smart contract in real-time, which reduces the time costs considerably. Second, thanks to the trust created by the blockchain, the import and export banks can directly assume risk without requiring a trusted correspondents bank. This form of disintermediation reduces the financial costs of trade finance. Third, because the bill of lading is tracked on the blockchain, the counterparty risk is reduced, i.e., legal certainty costs are lowered. Fourth, the settlement is automated via the smart contract, which also reduces the financial transaction costs. Last, the entire process is more transparent and makes adherence to regulatory standards, such as AML, easier and cheaper.

Potential and conclusion

Today's trade finance process is highly fractured, complex, and time-consuming for the reasons highlighted above. It is not surprising that numerous initiatives have been created in recent years with the aim to improve trade financing using blockchain or distributed ledger technology. These initiatives contain banks, transport and logistics companies, customs authorities, and large trade finance customers.

The Batavia trade finance platform, initiated by UBS and IBM, is one such initiative that works together with Bank of Montreal, Caixabank, Erste Bank, and Commerzbank. It is based on IBM's Hyperledger Fabric framework and aims to further automate payments by incorporating IoT device trigger payments. Apart from technological challenges, there are two core issues. First, current initiatives have not managed to bring shipment companies on board. Instead, major companies, like Maersk, are building a separate platform. Second, due to the sheer number of different solutions being developed, the market might fragment, and clients might be reluctant to participate.

The digitalisation of trade finance could potentially also be achieved with a centralised infrastructure. However, trade finance is also a business that involves many different parties who do not necessarily know or trust each other. By using a decentralised infrastructure, mutual trust is no longer necessary. Hence, trusted intermediaries, like correspondent banks, can be removed from the process.

The industry sees potential in blockchain-based trade finance, and this is not surprising given that it can reduce financial costs by disintermediation and automated settlement. It improves legal certainty by being real-time reviewable and providing a single source of truth. Blockchain-based trade finance platforms could make current trade cheaper while the digitalisation of the process significantly reduces the time costs. By reducing the costs of trade finance, it could help close the trade finance gap seen today and thereby let the market grow significantly. While the potential for blockchain-based trade finance is apparent, it remains in the early stages of development, and it is unclear which of the many endeavours will bear fruit.

6.2.6. Exchanges (Lykke)

An exchange is an organised market where the participants trade financial assets. Within the blockchain context, the assets traded are cryptocurrencies and other tokens. Exchanges are crucial as they allow for the efficient dissemination of price information for the assets traded and, thereby, the efficient allocation of funds. The use of exchanges entails transaction costs. First, there are the financial costs, such as fees per trade or the spread (i.e., the difference between the bid and the ask price of an asset). Second, the safety of assets depends on the design of the exchange, which impacts the legal certainty costs. Last, the execution of trades can take different amounts of time, which entails a cost.

Exchanges have two key features: order matching and settlement. Order matching is done by a matching engine, a software that matches buy and sell trades based on the price and other criteria. The settlement is the process of delivering the assets to the new owner and taking payment. The settlement can either be physical or electronic, i.e., assets are immobile, and the change of ownership is recorded in a register. Both order matching and settlement can be centralised or decentralised. The decision on how these processes are organised impacts the speed of trading and the security of the assets traded.

In this use case, we look at centralised and decentralised exchanges and how the Zug-based start-up, Lykke, tries to combine the advantages of both organisation types in the semi-centralised exchange.

Conventional process: centralised exchanges

Centralised exchanges are the standard in non-blockchain-related applications like a stock exchange as well as in cryptocurrency exchanges. They are the traditional means to change fiat currency into cryptocurrency and back. These exchanges centralise both the matching of trades and the settlement. Centralised matching engines run on dedicated high-performance servers, with the data held in fast databases. Therefore, they are capable of matching thousands of trades per second. This allows for high-frequency trading, which can help improve market liquidity.

Settlement of trades requires delivery versus payment. If the payment and delivery are not simultaneous, trust (or a trusted intermediary) is required, which is especially important when cryptocurrencies are involved as the anonymity offered means that legal recourse is not feasible. Centralised exchanges solve this issue by acting as a trusted intermediary. However, because the exchange faces the same trust issues towards its customers, it requires full control of the assets of the parties involved in the trade. Therefore, a centralised exchange requires the participants to deposit their assets in the wallet of the exchange, i.e., it holds the private keys of the assets deposited. As the exchange holds the private keys, they can be sure that the participants cannot double spend while the transactions for a trade are being validated. This is especially important in cross-chain transactions (e.g., 1 Bitcoin for 10 Ether), where validation takes different amounts of time.

Centralised settlement by an exchange also means that settlement can be instant if the liquidity in the market is sufficiently high. A centralised exchange does not need to wait for validation of transactions on the chain. However, this also means that the exchange becomes the proprietor of the account and could potentially do improper things, so it is not a recommended approach.

The drawback of centralised exchanges stems from assets having to be deposited in the wallet of the exchange. Participants need to trust the exchange to keep their assets safe. In the past, this trust was not always warranted. Because assets worth millions of Swiss francs can be stolen by hacking an exchange, they are premier targets for criminals. For instance, the 2014 Mt Gox and 2016 BitFinex attacks led to the loss of 436 and 116 million U.S. dollars of assets (Bitcoins).

Because centralised exchanges are run by legal entities, they are subject to regulatory oversight. For the customer, this offers the benefit of additional insurance that the exchange is operated properly, and that it can be held liable for their actions. However, the regulatory oversight comes at the cost of lost anonymity of the traders. Centralised exchanges are required to identify and verify their customers in a know-your-customer (KYC) process. Removing anonymity is not an option for all exchange users.

Blockchain-based process: decentralised exchanges

Decentralised or peer-to-peer (P2P) exchanges use decentralised order matching and decentralised settlement. Decentralised exchanges require the participants to run a software client that connects to other participants. The participants place their orders (buy or sell), and the network of independent computers handles the order matching. Once a matching pair of orders is found, the settlement is delegated to the participants of the trade. Different types of decentralised settlements are possible with two secure and trustless options being the processes used by the P2P exchange Bitsquare and Atomic Swap.

The Bitsquare P2P exchange allows trading Bitcoin for fiat money, cryptocurrencies or other tokens. However, to trade, participants need to own a small amount of Bitcoin, as security deposits in Bitcoin must be made to enter a trade. The settlement works by locking up the funds from the Bitcoin side of the trade plus the security deposits in a 2-of-3 multisig address. The funds are only released when the receipt of the non-Bitcoin funds is confirmed by the recipient. In case of a dispute between the two parties, a randomly chosen arbiter settles the deal. The security deposit of the losing party is transferred to the arbiter, and the winning party receives the Bitcoin funds traded and the security deposit.

The above solution requires both a security deposit (in Bitcoin) plus a random arbiter to ensure that trades are followed through. Atomic Swaps, or atomic cross-chain trading, require neither and also allow direct trade between different cryptocurrencies without a centralised settlement. Atomic refers to the fact that, if the currency swap or trade is not successful, neither party loses out. This is achieved by using hashed-time-locked contracts (HTLC) where the 'hashed-lock' ensures that neither party can take the offered funds without first offering their funds. The 'time-lock' ensures that if one party steps back from the trade, then the funds are returned to the original owners. For example, assume Alice and Bob want to exchange Bitcoin for Ether. Both send their respective funds to an HTLC. They declare receipt of their new coins by confirming a cryptographic code issued by the HTLC. If either fails to confirm the code within a set timeframe, then both sets of coins return to the original owners, and the exchange is cancelled.

Decentralised exchanges have multiple advantages. First, *privacy*, as the traders can remain anonymous as the settlement does not involve a regulated third party. Second, *transaction censorship resistance*, due to the decentralised nature, it is not possible for governments or regulators to impose any restriction without blocking access to all communications channels completely. Third, *security*, as decentralised exchanges do not hold the assets that are traded on them, so they are not a point of attack for hackers.

The disadvantages of decentralised exchanges are chiefly *slow trading* and *lacking liquidity*. The trading is slow because an ad hoc network of computers has high latencies, which results in *slow order matching*. Second, the *lack of liquidity* in these exchanges also makes order matching time-consuming. Third, the *settlement phase can be long* as the receipt of funds needs to be manually confirmed. These disadvantages also mean that high-frequency trading is not possible, which is a further reason for low liquidity. Another disadvantage is that decentralised exchanges require participants to safeguard their private keys and, as suggested before, people are bad at this responsibility. For all the above reasons, these decentralised exchanges are unattractive to many cryptocurrency users.

Lykke: a semi-centralised exchange

Lykke aims to combine the advantages of both centralised and decentralised exchanges to become a global marketplace for all asset classes and instruments.[114] It uses a centralised matching engine but a decentralised settlement. The former allows it to match trades efficiently using dedicated systems. Furthermore, Lykke ensures the different asset markets are liquid by providing liquidity where necessary. The settlement is decentralised to make the exchange a less interesting target for hackers. Lykke users do not entrust their assets to the exchange, they merely deposit there, which is achieved by using 2-of-2 multisig wallets, i.e., any transaction requires the private key of both the user and Lykke. This way if Lykke is hacked and the private keys are stolen, then assets cannot be moved out of the user wallets by perpetrators. The advantage for Lykke is that they have control over the flow of assets on its exchange, which is important for regulatory reasons. As a registered company, operating in the financial sector is subject to KYC and anti-money laundering regulations. The actual settlement of trades is done using atomic swaps, i.e., directly between the two participants involved in the trade.[115]

Financial costs of exchanges

The financial costs of the exchanges are a mixture of a conversion fee, the spread in the exchange rate, and possible blockchain transaction fees. Many (centralised) exchanges charge a fee for their conversion service (e.g., converting Bitcoins to U.S. dollars), and this conversion fee is usually a percentage of the transaction value. For exchanges targeted at retail consumers, like Coinbase, the fees are 1.49% or 3.99% depending on if deposited funds or credit cards are used to fund the transaction. In exchanges that target profes-

[114] As a marketplace for tokenized assets, Lykke issues foreign exchange coins, tokenized precious metals, crypto-equity and derivatives. These digital assets are created using Bitcoin's coloured coins.

[115] Since December 23, 2017, due to the extremely high transaction costs of both Bitcoin and Ether, Lykke operates as a centralized exchange. This is to be a temporary measure until an efficient and sustainable solution is found.

sional traders, like GDAX or Kraken, fees are around 0.25% or lower.[116] Decentralised exchanges have fees that can be comparable to their centralised counterparts, and some exchanges, like Bisq, have implemented incentives to encourage market clearing. On Bisq, the fees depend on how far from the current market price an order is. Orders exactly at the market price incur no conversion fees. Lykke does not charge any conversion fees.

The second financial cost faced by exchange participants are the spreads, which is the compensation for the market-maker for their exposure to unanticipated price moves. Spreads are wider in illiquid markets as the market-maker needs to hold the asset for a longer time and is exposed to greater risk. The major centralised exchanges have high liquidity for the main cryptocurrencies with spreads lower than 0.0001% for BTC/USD. Retail consumer-targeted exchanges charge high spreads of up to 2%. For Lykke, on March 2, 2018, the spread for BTC/USD was around 0.7%.

Blockchain transaction fees have become a huge cost factor for exchanges. Centralised exchanges are affected only when participants move money out of the exchange into private wallets. Decentralised exchanges suffer multiple times for every trade. Security deposits, conversion fees, and the asset transfer all require transactions on the blockchain and, therefore, lead to transaction fees. Decentralised exchanges are either waiting for off-chain transactions to be implemented in the blockchains they use (e.g., Bitcoin Lightning Network and Ethereum Raiden Network) or they have developed proprietary solutions for their exchanges (Lykke off-chain settlement).

Potential and conclusion

Exchanges are essential for the blockchain economy. Only when cryptocurrencies and other tokens can be swapped seamlessly will adoption be improved. The decision between centralised and decentralised essentially depends on the user's preferences for regulation, transaction speed, privacy, security, and financial costs.

---

[116] The fees depend on if you are a market-maker or taker. A market-taker's trade is immediately matched to an existing order, thereby removing liquidity from the market. A market-maker improves liquidity on the market by adding and a trade to the order book.

Today centralised exchanges are financially the most attractive. They have daily trading volumes worth billions of U.S. dollars versus only millions of U.S. dollars on decentralised exchanges (CoinMarketCap, n.d.). Centralised exchanges also offer fast transaction speeds and regulatory protection. Together this makes these exchanges ideal for both high-frequency traders, traders requiring AML regulated environments, and casual retail customers.

Decentralised exchanges are in their current state only out of interest for traders who require anonymity and can ensure the security of their private keys. If improvements in scalability of blockchains are achieved, and transaction costs can be kept constantly low, then decentralised exchanges might see increased usage.

6.3. Blockchain with smart contracts and IOT

6.3.1. Proof of provenance (Provenance, Ambrosus, Chronicled)

Provenance can be defined as assuring the quality, safety, ethics, and environmental impact of goods at all levels of the supply chain. The importance of provenance as part of supply-chain management has increased over recent years. Consumers now demand to know more about the origin of the products they buy. Events like the horsemeat scandal, the Rana Plaza collapse in Bangladesh in 2013, and the 2017 Fipronil eggs contamination have highlighted the need for better information. Increasingly, it has also become a regulatory issue. Companies are required to report on their policies about environmental protection, social responsibility, and treatment of employees.[117] Similarly, the United States' Federal Drug Administration is introducing the Drug Supply Chain Security Act to eliminate counterfeit pharmaceuticals by requiring the industry to adopt an interoperable system to track and trace prescription drugs securely.

[117] Directive 2014/95/EU of the European Parliament and of the Council of 22 October 2014 amending Directive 2013/34/EU as regards to disclosure of non-financial and diversity information by certain large undertakings and groups (2014), OJ L 330.

As with other blockchain use cases, the introduction of blockchain technology changes transaction costs in supply-chain management. Financially, blockchain solutions might be more efficient as the decentralised structure is a good match to the way supply chains are built, as the different contractors and sub-contractors can easily be integrated. This makes tracking goods along the supply chain cheaper and, therefore, open to a broader range of products. A blockchain will also lower the cost of legal certainty for the firm and, potentially, for the consumer. Audit processes are easier if the entire supply of a certain good is registered on the blockchain, and double-selling certified goods becomes much harder. Trust in the dominant player in the supply chain that usually controls the current centralised software solutions is no longer required. Additionally, blockchain helps eliminate counterfeit goods from entering the supply chain and reaching consumers when combined with IoT. However, we do not see how the time cost could be affected differently by a blockchain solution rather than a centralised supply-chain management solution.

In this use case, we look at three examples of blockchain supply management. Provenance by the London-based Project Provenance Ltd, Ambrosus, an EPFL spinoff based in Lausanne and Zug, and San Francisco-based Chronicled. The first utilises blockchain for easier supply-chain management from the first mile to the consumer. The latter two enhance their solution with IoT sensors that allow for monitoring the quality of the goods and detecting tampering. This enables the creation of more secure supply chains.

Current process

Today, supply chains are managed using software modules in the enterprise resource planning (ERP) systems of a company. ERPs are large-scale centralised business management software solutions. For every product, they document production and shipment dates, customs and tax declarations, producers, and raw input information. Ideally, the supply-chain management system gives firms all information on the origins of their products back to the producers of the raw materials.

Next, we illustrate how a supply chain might look like today using the sustainability-certified Indonesian Skipjack tuna caught using the traditional pole and line method. The amount of fish that can be sustainably caught in a specific fishery is defined by a certification body, usually an NGO, and an external environmental auditing firm audits the supply chain.

1. The fishermen sell their catch to a merchant who pay in cash.
2. The merchant sells the Skipjack to restaurants and local tuna cannery. Both pay in cash but the tuna cannery hands out a paper receipt. It maintains a digital record of all fish it purchases.
3. The tuna is processed, canned, labelled, dated, batched, and prepared for export. Batch and production date of the cans are digitally stored.
4. A European wholesaler buys the cans. They receive the batch numbers and production dates for the purchase by email. The data are input into the wholesalers SCM system.
5. A freight company is responsible for the shipment of the tuna to Europe. It guarantees that the cans are kept at temperatures below 40 °C during shipment. It sends the shipping information it receives to the wholesaler in real-time via email. Because it is not entirely compatible with the wholesaler's SCM system, it must be edited before it can be input into the system.
6. The wholesaler checks the products on reception and forwards them to retailers. The retailers SCM system is compatible with the wholesaler's and can import the provenance data into his system.
7. The retailers sell the poll and line-fished tuna to consumers. Basic information on the place of origin is provided to the consumer on the can.

This simplified fictional example illustrates issues with current systems. The supply chain involves many players with different technical systems that are not connected nor fully compatible with each other. Further, even today, parts of the supply chain are not documented at all (fishermen) or are still paper based, rely on fax machines or similar technologies (merchant). This makes integrating the entire supply chain difficult, costly, and error-prone. The information on who caught the fish, when and where, is essentially lost. Additionally, the undocumented parts of the supply chain are especially susceptible to fraud (KPMG, 2017). Because of the lack of systematic tracking and accounting from beginning to end, there is a significant potential for double-dealing with certified fish. In other words, more 'certified' fish is sold than allowed under the sustainability agreement by bringing additional non-sustainably-fished fish into the supply chain. Effectively, the current system is largely based on trust between the players, especially between fisherman and merchant as well as merchant and cannery. It also depends heavily on auditing firms to ensure no double-dealing is conducted or related practices.

The system could be improved by implementing compatible IT systems throughout the entire supply chain. However, industry experts point out that this is extremely challenging to do in an established chain (Earls, 2016) – and even more so if the suppliers are part of multiple supply chains with different IT systems.

Blockchain-based process (Provenance)

A blockchain-based solution is thought to help alleviate some of the problems of current supply-chain management systems. Provenance is one start-up with a blockchain solution for supply-chain management with a system that uses the Ethereum blockchain to track food from producers to consumer. They have proposed use cases for fair-trade coffee, coconuts, clothing, and organic meat. More importantly, they have run a pilot for tracking Indonesian Skipjack tuna from origin to the point of sale.

Applying the Provenance solution to the process for tuna described above might look like the following process:

1. A local NGO registers the fishermen on the blockchain (they receive private and public keys).
2. The fisherman registers their catch via SMS, which creates a new token on the blockchain that uniquely identifies the catch and contains information, such as the fisherman, the location of catch, attributes (e.g., type of fish), and certification and audit information. When the fisherman sells the catch of tuna to the merchant, they also transfer the token to the merchant. The merchant now physically and digitally owns the fish.
3. When the merchant sells the fish to the cannery, they transfer the token to the factory.
4. The processing of the fish is mirrored on the blockchain using smart contracts. These contracts contain information on how much tuna and other ingredients are required for a can of tuna. So, even if a specific tuna is spread over multiple cans, the sum of all cans produced cannot be larger than the input of the raw tuna required. On the blockchain, each tuna can

be linked to the fish catch that it contains via fractions of the tokens from these catches.

5. With the sale of the cans, the fish tokens are transferred to the wholesaler, who connects this supply-chain management system with the Provenances blockchain solution to gain access to the information stored there. When the cans are sold to the retailer, the system automatically initiates the transfer of the tokens to the retailer.
6. The retailer makes the provenance of the goods accessible to the consumer via QR codes or RFID tags. This allows the consumer to check any part of the information stored on the blockchain from the can of tuna and the journey the fish took from fishermen to the retailer.
7. When the can is sold to the customer, the tokens for the fish need to be removed from the retailer's ownership to prevent double selling. Otherwise, there is the possibility that malicious retailers relabel non-certified cans and link them to tokens belonging to cans already sold. Therefore, the consumer must either take ownership of the token at purchase, tokens must have an expiration date, or the purchase must be defined as a termination event.

In summary, by using blockchain technology, it is possible to track goods from the point of origin to the point of sale transparently. The solution offers an audit layer that can be integrated with existing systems.

Ambrosus and Chronicled

Ambrosus and Chronicled take the proof of provenance using blockchain one step further by integrating IoT devices into the process. The two differ in their initial focus of using IoT in the supply chain. Ambrosus aims to develop a blockchain supported supply-chain management system that can support highly sophisticated sensors that monitor the entire production and transportation process. These include analytical systems for pH levels, allergens or DNA and protein assays as well as sensors for environmental attributes, such as temperature, light, exposure, humidity, movement, and oxygen. Because of a large amount of data generated by the sensors, all transactions are recorded on a private Ambrosus blockchain,[118] which is periodically copied to the Ethereum main chain for further validation. The Ambrosus protocol is based on three smart contracts.

- *Measurements Smart Contract* stores the readings from the sensors for a specified batch of the product. It is also responsible for authenticating and cryptographically verifying the sensor data.
- *Requirement Smart Contract* contains the quality requirements that are to be compared with the Measurements Smart Contract. It also gives the ability to define instant financial rewards or penalties if requirements are not met.
- *Amber tokens* are data-bonded ERC-20 compliant tokens. They are both a method of payment within the Ambrosus network and means of tracing a product through the supply chain. Amber tokens are assigned to a batch of the item (e.g., tuna) being traced. When an item is transformed in a manufacturing process, the Amber tokens can be split (or merged) into multiple Measurements contracts. The tokens are locked into the Measurements Smart Contract for as long as the batch moves through the supply chain. End consumers can claim the tokens and return them to the producer for some type of reward in a customer-loyalty scheme.

In contrast to Provenance, the Ambrosus is less focused on ensuring a sustainability standard but focuses on quality assurance along the entire supply chain. In the tuna fish example, the Ambrosus sensors could monitor the quality of the tuna during production in the cannery or ensure the temperature that during shipment lies within the agreed-upon limits.

Chronicled is a blockchain solution for supply-chain management, and like Ambrosus and Provenance, it is Ethereum-based. However, Chronicled plans to roll-out its solution to use other public or private blockchains. While Chronicled also offers simple sensors that measure environmental conditions, they actively promote their IoT device called CryptoSeal, which is a tamper-evident packaging solution registered on the blockchain that allows securing the chain

---

[118] New measurements of data is stored off-chain such that a Merkle tree of all measurement data is created and the root of the Merkle is periodically transmitted to the Measurements Smart Contract.

of custody. If the CryptoSealed container is opened, then the antenna of the NFC chip is broken and can no longer be accessed. The recipient of the container can then no longer verify that the container on the blockchain suggesting the container was tampered with. Chronicled is promoting this for pharmaceuticals, where assuring the chain of custody is becoming ever more important with the rise in counterfeited legal drugs entering the market.

Potential and conclusion

Blockchain solutions in supply-chain management offer some advantages. In the Provenance case, the main advantage lies in the possibilities for auditing adherence to certified standards. When the entire quota of sustainably fished tuna is registered on the blockchain, double-dealing certified tuna becomes impossible as tuna in excess of the quota cannot be registered. This alleviates the reliance on audits to uncover fraud at this level. The inclusion of the first mile of the supply chain by using SMS to register the catch is not blockchain exclusive. Such a solution could also be designed in a centralised system. The question then is whether we trust the party operating the system enough to run this platform and which solution is less expensive to operate. Today, we only trust a retailer that includes products that live up to the standards they promote. However, for some consumers, this might not be good enough. Additionally, small producers or retailers might not be able to elicit the same amount of trust as their bigger competitors. The consequences of small producers cheating a small buyer are arguably less severe as the producer easily finding new buyers for the product. Both Provenance and Ambrosus explicitly promote their solution for small producers and retailers as a way of building trust with the consumers. For consumers, blockchain-supported supply chains would then reduce the uncertainty and the time costs associated with it. For producers, the financial costs of running and building a traceable and trusted supply chain are reduced.

While even the blockchain solution is not trustless, double-dealing is still possible as fish above the quotas could still be sold outside the chain. NGOs could do a poor job of checking that sustainability criteria for the fishermen are met. Therefore, even a blockchain solution requires trust in the guarantor of the system (auditors and NGOs).

The additional potential of blockchain in supply-chain management unfolds when IoT is integrated. Together, they have the potential to reduce financial and legal certainty costs of assuring product quality and preventing counterfeits in the supply chain. While product quality can also be monitored without blockchain-registered sensors, the blockchain increases the trust in the data produced and, together with smart contracts, allows for automatic actions based on this data. The main cost advantage, therefore, lies in the reduced costs of legal certainty.

The financial advantages are less clear, as they depend on the cost of a centralised solution managing vast amounts of sensor data versus the cost of storing the data decentralised and ensuring the integrity of the data using the blockchain. In the battle against counterfeit goods, a blockchain secured chain of custody together with innovations like the CryptoSeal by Chronicled will likely lower financial costs. Today, to achieve similar security, containers would need to be regularly visually monitored. Analysing this data for every container is prohibitively expensive.

Securing the chain of custody also improves legal certainty and thereby lowers costs. If a pharmaceutical company can prove that its products are not altered, then they cannot be held liable for damages done by counterfeit drugs. For the future, it seems possible that blockchains are needed for both supply-chain management and financial transactions. We could envision people selling their capacity or raw materials directly on a blockchain. However, this would require lower transaction fees and greater scalability compared to current blockchain solutions. We explore this in the use case on trade financing.

6.3.2. Energy (Brooklyn Microgrid and Tal.Markt/Elblox)

The energy industry is expected to soon experience radical changes. The transition from unrenewable energy sources to a sustainable energy supply through renewable energy is a declared political goal in Switzerland. This development overlaps with the second trend of large-scale digitalisation. Both megatrends have been gaining in importance in the industry for some time, adding new participants, increasing the dynamics in the electricity market, and probably supporting each other to the next breakthrough.

The integration of new forms of energy generation by heterogeneous Distributed Energy Resources (DERs) into the existing electricity grid bears new challenges and requires increased flexibility of the electrical grid since the power generation tends to be more volatile (due to weather dependency) and decentralised. Microgrids, a delimited group of electricity sources and loads capable of operating either connected to the traditional centralised electrical grid or in an islanded mode as well as virtual power plants and cloud-based distributed power plants that aggregate the capacities of DERs, can facilitate the integration of renewable energy generation without requiring a redesign of the national distribution system. Smart metering technology maintains and manages the network's stability, allowing for the creation of smart grids that integrate all actors in the electricity market through the interaction of generation, storage, network management, and consumption into the overall system, no matter how small the energy suppliers and storage locations.

Smart metering technology and the development of IoT enables these objects to connect and exchange data. Together, they help to optimise household energy consumption and can potentially increase energy efficiency. However, a study by the International Energy Agency (IEA, 2014) concluded that IoT devices also waste energy and in the end may consume the energy they had originally saved through intelligent energy management.

Renewable electricity offers are still under criticism while they gain attraction from consumers. About one-third of Swiss households actively choose electricity from renewable energies (Verein für umweltgerechte Energie VUE, 2018). However, it is provided via the electricity grid where it is physically impossible to distinguish between renewable and non-renewable electricity. The electricity providers can only guarantee that the renewable electricity the consumer pays for is fed into the grid by reporting the requested amounts of guarantees of origin. Consumption of locally produced renewable electricity is possible only in self-sustaining microgrids.

In this context, various applications arise for blockchain technology in the energy sector.[119] Decentralised energy transaction and supply systems, decentralised data storage in the metering and billing of electricity consumption, proof of provenance, and the possibilities of smart contracts in automatically

[119] See PWC (2016) and Luke, Lee, Zdenek, and Dimitrova (2018) for an overview on blockchain technology in the energy sector.

balancing the grid are the most cited. Many companies are currently developing and testing applications, and blockchain projects exist in peer-to-peer platforms, energy trading, invoicing, proof of origin, asset management, security, network management, and mobility. Overviews of current projects and companies and their blockchain projects in the energy sector can be found in PWC (2016), Carle (2018) and Luke, Lee, Zdenek, and Dimitrova (2018).

Energy suppliers are partnering with and developing blockchain applications, even though they are unlikely to be greatly interested in a rapid change and emancipation of consumers who actively market their energy. Digitisation and the announced energy transition will force them to rethink business models. Some argue that the management of exchange platforms, mensuration, and the certification of origin could become their new activity. Amongst the other actors involved are blockchain developers, start-ups, and industrial companies.

In the following, we focus on peer-to-peer models, also called neighbourhood models because these models allow for a localised peer-to-peer trading of renewable electricity and exploit the possibilities of blockchain technology in its entirety. Peer-to-peer trading projects include the Brooklyn Microgrid (BMG), which is the most noticed and pioneering effort today. On June 29, 2016, they realised a first peer-to-peer energy exchange between two people living across the street. A recent European peer-to-peer platform project is the German Tal.Markt (www.wsw-talmarkt.de), a joint project by Elblox (an Axpo Group trademark) and WSW (Wuppertaler Stadtwerke). Also, there are initiatives to implement pilot projects in Switzerland, one of which is 'quartierstrom' (www.quartier-strom.ch), a local electricity market in Walenstadt/SG.

The motivation of neighbourhood models like BMG and Tal.Markt is to enable small-scale local trading of environmentally friendly electricity. These platforms enable power consumers to establish themselves as equal energy partners with power producers and suppliers, to customise their product, and to act as prosumers.[120] The energy transfer can be handled directly between

[120] A prosumer is a person who consumes and produces a product. Households can act as prosumers when they produce their own electricity to cover demand but sell their energy surplus. Typically, private households would use PV panels and battery storage to enable this process.

producer and consumer. Intermediaries, such as energy companies, metering operators, or payment services providers, could become completely obsolete.

The central motivation recurring with blockchain technology is the transaction costs, financial motivations, and advantages of securing data transfer and storage. The participants at EventHorizon 2017, a global conference on blockchain in the energy sector held in Vienna, expected that blockchain technology could reduce process costs by between 20% and 60% (ESMT Berlin & Grid Singularity, 2017). A majority also imagined reduced grid costs through blockchain technology. However, they expected the share of peer-to-peer trading to be less than 20%.

Proof of provenance is not the prime motivation; a closer look reveals it is a key differentiator over traditional databases. However, we do not elaborate further on proof of provenance in this use case but instead refer to our supply-chain management use case for inspiration where a blockchain enables proof of provenance. Also, the proximity and regionality of the market is a clear advantage in all peer-to-peer energy trading projects known to us.

For BMG, security of supply and the possibility of maintaining an islanded grid in case of crisis are additional facilitators. Severe weather events (e.g., hurricane Sandy in 2012 and annual heat waves) raised operation issues of the outdated electrical infrastructure in Brooklyn. The region has also been vulnerable to grid failures as electric capacity utilisation is already approaching its limits. This problem is not relevant for Switzerland, where the security of supply is very high and the grid redundant.

Conventional process

Today's value chain generally involves several business and process steps between the power producer and the consumer (see Figure 37). Energy is produced in centralised generation facilities or decentralised production sites, bundled to be allowed to participate in the balancing energy market, and then delivered to final consumers via the networks (separated by transmission and distribution networks) operated by energy companies. Energy traders are involved, and banks act as payment service providers. Meter operators may be in between.

Quelle: PWC (2016a), p. 18.

Figure 37. Market structures with traditional and blockchain-based processes.

Blockchain-based process: outlook

In the extreme case, blockchain-based energy processes would no longer require energy companies, traders, and even banks. Also, meter operators would not be necessary. This simplification involves the considerable potential for process cost reduction. Full implementation of blockchain technology in all these elements, i.e., a real decentralised peer-to-peer trade with a decentralised database, is not possible with current energy industry regulations, which provide considerable obstacles. Energy suppliers need to have a concession and ensure the security of energy supplies. Also, there are rules on reporting to transmission system operators and on registration as meter operators. The electricity market in Switzerland is not fully open, and small consumers are not allowed to participate in the market. The electricity produced by a company's installations can be bought and sold exclusively to other members of a so-called 'self-consumption community'[121] or to the local grid operator. These requirements make real peer-to-peer deals and transfers

[121] Self-consumption communities are groupings of final consumers who share one production site.

impossible through the traditional public grid. They can only be established in microgrids, which are considered as a single entity by the grid operator. Pilot projects can be implemented in Switzerland only with the cooperation of the grid operators, who place the public grid at disposal for the experience.

Peer-to-peer platforms with intermediation of central authorities are an alternative. In these cases, the platform operator generally acts similarly to a traditional energy supplier. There are some projects on peer-to-peer trading in Europe and worldwide, with a review in Zhang et al. (2017) that compares several. They conclude that, although these platforms might share some similarities, they have different focusses. Some might consider stable tariffs by including storage facilities, and others focus on direct connections between consumers and producers, which means passing on oscillating energy prices to consumers. Others look toward the development of information and communication technologies (ICT) or the proof of origin.

In the following two subsections, we look at two examples of peer-to-peer platforms using blockchain technology which have a different focus: the Brooklyn Microgrid and the non-microgrid Tal.Markt/Elblox project.

Blockchain-based: Brooklyn Microgrid

The Brooklyn Microgrid (BMG) is an energy market in Brooklyn, New York, with the objective of being a communal energy network composed entirely of local, clean energy. The project consists of the virtual community energy market platform and a physical microgrid.

The microgrid is built in addition to the existing distribution grid and currently comprises 10-by-10 housing blocks. Siemens Digital Grid Division installed the hardware-network control systems, converters, smart meters, and storage in the form of lithium-ion batteries (Mearian & Maier, 2017). LO3 Energy (lo3energy.com) is responsible for the realisation of the transaction platform, the TransActive Grid, and currently runs the BMG. The BMG and its TransActive Grid is LO3 Energy's most prestigious project due to the significant attention evoked by the realisation of the first blockchain-based P2P electricity transaction. BMG's first community activity took place in April 2016, enabling three residents on President Street in Park Slope to participate in the first peer-to-peer energy transaction.

The transaction platform started using a private Ethereum fork but then switched to a proprietary chain (Besnainou, 2018). Today, it is based on a private blockchain using the Tendermint (tendermint.com) protocol (see Mengelkamp et al., 2018), which claims to be more effective than Bitcoin and Ethereum because it does not require mining (see Kwon, 2014; Faggart, 2016).

In addition to the TransActive Grid blockchain architecture, a TransActive Grid smart meter is necessary. Consumption and generation data are transferred from the participants' Transactive Grid smart meters to their blockchain accounts. Thereby, it is documented at all times. Orders are created according to this information and sustained by smart contracts. Consumers set their maximum price limit for their preferred energy sources. Prosumers bid the minimum price limit that they request for selling their generation. Trading is mostly done automatically, and traditional energy sources supply consumers with bids below the clearing price. Once a match is completed, a transaction is carried out via users' accounts and a new block is added on the blockchain. The payment is carried out according to predefined payment rules that are also part of the market mechanism (Mengelkamp et al., 2018).

The proprietary blockchain of BMG stores kilowatt-hours as well as volts, vars, phase angle, reactive power, and real grid telemetry. All these data are needed to run a grid, and this is what the blockchain serves. It is a prototype of Exergy (exergy.energy), a blockchain-based energy marketplace that LO3 Energy is planning to launch in Q3 or Q4 2018 (Besnainou, 2018).

Blockchain-based: Tal.Markt/Elblox

A similar peer-to-peer trading project is the German Tal.Markt (www.wsw-talmarkt.de), a joint project by Elblox (www.elblox.org), an Axpo Group trademark, and WSW Wuppertaler Stadtwerke (see AXPO, 2017; Energate, 2017). Elblox operates a blockchain-based peer-to-peer platform that enables the personalised distribution of electricity locally between distributed renewable energy producers and potential consumers. The project has been active since November 2017 after two years of development and is initially limited until December 2018.

Tal.Markt participants sign an energy supply contract with WSW, who ensures supply security by delivering CO_2-neutral electricity from the waste incineration plant of AWG Abfallwirtschaftsgesellschaft GmbH Wuppertal. WSW provides all customers with a digital measuring system free of charge. Each participant can choose individual energy sources (electricity mix) based on preferences regarding energy sources and willingness to pay. The actual amounts of electricity purchased from the individual sources are billed, and the total costs are calculated monthly and include the product price as well as network charges, taxes, and levies, including a surcharge to WSW for the security of supply and for legally intermediating the transaction between the producer and consumer as well as compensation to Elblox for licencing the platform.

The project experience is particularly interesting because the present national fixed feed-in tariff for renewable electricity will probably disappear in the future. Decentralised producers will then need to search for potential buyers and be forced to sell into the national wholesale power market.

The platform stores all the information concerning production, consumption, and the contractual relationships between the platform participants. The platform is divided into a blockchain and a conventional database. While most of the information (e.g., buy and sell offers and participants characteristics) is stored in traditional databases, the blockchain stores the transactions and guarantees that every kWh produced is assigned, and the provenance of the electricity is guaranteed. It is a private network based on the Ethereum blockchain. The energy exchange is verified based on a proof of stake mechanism by all full nodes. Elblox offers the platform as a white-label product to electricity suppliers and retailers that want to establish a local marketplace for renewable energy. Each marketplace operator runs blockchain nodes. Currently in the pilot phase, the system has three full nodes. In parallel with the expansion and licensing of additional regional markets, the number of nodes should increase in the future and establish a distributed database and transaction layer for renewable energy across Europe. The incentive to run a node is the availability of the real-time and high-resolution proof of provenance information, which no traditional register could credibly assure so far.

The prototype of the Elblox platform featured a full integration of blockchain technology with each peer running a full node and transactions handled by smart contracts on the blockchain. The Tal.Markt uses the blockchain technology with reduced scope to test user feedback, reduce cost, and achieve better scalability. Based on the insights gained from the operation of the Tal.Markt, the future implementations of the Elblox platform will feature a deeper integration of blockchain technology for specific elements of the value chain, where the technology can provide significant advantages over conventional technology both in terms of system properties and economics (Schönenberger, 2018).

Potential and conclusion

Blockchain technology has many uses in the energy sector with similar hurdles as previously discussed (e.g., ID loss). Also, there are industry-specific challenges with respect to peer-to-peer trading. On the one hand, the question of the security of the energy supply, which must be solved, on large-scale implementation, which presumably will not be handed over to market forces alone. On the other hand, the question arises as to the extent to which consumers are interested in flexible prices. Although they ensure higher market efficiency and trigger innovation that might help curb energy demand peaks, they also create uncertainty. However, if the political will exists, it seems inevitable that the blockchain technology will play a key role in implementing a solution. Otherwise, proof of provenance-type solutions (see Chapter 6.3.1) will likely remain the main use case in the energy sector.

7. Legal, Social, Political, and Ecological Aspects

7.1. Legal aspects

With the increasing prevalence of blockchain applications and tokenised assets, one realises that existing laws no longer meet the requirements of this new technology in all fields. Thus, calls to create a legal and regulatory basis for this emerging technology have been increasing, requiring legislation to shift from paper to digital paradigms.

The claim is not primarily about creating new laws. The existing legal framework (Civil Code ZGB, Code of Obligations OR, Federal Law against Unfair Competition UWG, and tax laws) applies to both traditional and blockchain-based worlds. Also, blockchain-based projects conducted analogously to regulated activities (e.g., in banking) cannot simply circumvent the existing framework. The ambiguity is more about how to classify blockchain tokens, or crypto-assets, in the existing legal framework. Who has which rights associated with tokenised assets? Are the civil law concepts of ownership applicable to non-tangible items as crypto-tokens? What is needed to transfer the rights? What responsibilities does the issuer have?

Of course, depending on the sector in which blockchain technology is used, different regulatory questions may arise, which also may necessitate adjustments on the part of the regulator. In certain cases, or for certain applications, an adaptation of the regulatory framework might even be necessary in order to enable distributed ledger technology (see the use cases in Chapter 6). However, in general, it is more about creating predictability within the existing framework.

Independent from its practical application, blockchain technology allows the creation of a variety of new assets or asset-like elements in the form of digital representations of goods, which, from a functional perspective, contain elements of property rights. Through these digital information units, a tokenised ecosystem is emerging. However, these new asset types raise a series of questions in different areas of law, such as codes of obligation, tax law, and corporate law.

Categorisation or classification of the diverse applications of blockchain technology can help clarify the expectations of the market participants. Various experts addressed this topic, and MME, a leading Swiss consultancy firm for law, tax, and compliance in blockchain applications, proposes a functional approach based on a classification of the types of tokens used in a legal and risk assessment (Luk Müller et al., 2018).

Recently, the Swiss Financial Market Supervisory Authority FINMA, in guidelines for enquiries regarding the regulatory framework of ICOs (FINMA, 2018), issued a categorisation model outlining the principles it uses to assess the applicability of financial market regulations. While the FINMA classification simplifies the available token landscape to meet its regulatory purpose, both classification models are based on the underlying economic purpose and the functionality. Experts propose this path, as it is applicable regardless of national legal and regulatory frameworks and may facilitate multijurisdictional understanding even though different practical implications may arise in each jurisdiction (Luk Müller et al., 2018). Today, there is no internationally recognised token classification model. The two Swiss initiatives pioneered this field, while the Swiss tax authorities are advanced with regard to blockchain-based technologies (see Glarner et al., 2018). The Swiss Federal Tax Administration (SFTA) already clarified that it would treat Bitcoin as a means of payment in the same way as any other fiat currency, which means that it is not subject to Swiss VAT. Since December 2015, the SFTA has published an 'official' exchange rate for Bitcoin that serves as a recommendation to the cantonal tax authorities for wealth tax purposes. In 2017, the SFTA added nine additional cryptocurrencies to their exchange list, including Ether, Ripple, Bitcoin Cash, Litecoin, Cardano, NEM, Stellar, IOTA, and TRON, which is unprecedented in the rest of Europe or the U.S.

Chapter 7.1.1 summarises the classifications of the types of tokens proposed by MME; Chapter 7.1.2 includes the FINMA guidelines and the underlying categorisation of the tokens they apply; Chapter 7.1.3 deals with the special case where the transfer of assets must be confirmed in writing according to existing law and proposed solutions for adaptation of tokenised assets; Chapter 7.1.4 provides economic reflections on the legal implications of the use of blockchain technology in transactions as well as on the role of human judgement in this context.

7.1.1. MME: Framework for legal and risk assessment

The purpose of the MME classification model is to guide legal and risk assessment of tokens that can be applied to civil law or tax law issues. As it serves as a general guidance, the classification model proposed by MME (Luk Müller et al., 2018) is based on technical functionalities and, consequently, is more complex than others, e.g., by FINMA (see Chapter 7.1.2).

The MME classification distinguishes three token categories, also referred to as 'Blockchain Crypto Property' (BCP), thereby pointing at the functional similarities between crypto-assets and property rights. Each is subdivided into three to five sub-categories. Three functionality layers are distinguished to capture the stage of development, which may also have effects on the regulatory assessment of a token. Next to the classification model, a catalogue of risk assessment criteria is proposed. The model serves as a basis for establishing governance and diligence standards for all aspects of creating, offering, transferring, and holding crypto-assets.

The three token categories are:

- *Native Utility Tokens* can be transferred on a decentralised ledger from user 1 to user 2, but do not grant any rights to a counterparty. The owner of a Native Utility Token does not have any relative or absolute right, except for the right relating to the token. Native tokens subdivide into *basic tokens* (examples are Bitcoin, Bitcoin Cash, Litecoin, Monero, ZCash, Ripple, and IOTA), *infrastructure access tokens* (Ether, Ether Classic, IOTA, Ripple, and Tezos), *application access tokens* (Wings), and *application settlement tokens* (Siacoins, Filecoins, and Mysterium).
- *Counterparty Tokens* include any form of a relative right either against the token generator or a third-party. Based on the characteristics of these rights, they classify as *IOU tokens*, *derivative tokens*, *fund tokens*, *equity tokens*, and *membership tokens*. *IOU tokens* represent any underlying claim for the payment of a specific amount, participation on future income or delivery of a material or immaterial asset. Typically, the details of the claim are part of a separate contract. Examples include tokens on the Lykke Marketplace. *Derivative tokens* are counterparty tokens whose value derives from an underlying base value, for example, gold and Swiss francs. *Fund tokens* represent centrally managed shares of a collective investment fund. *Equity tokens* relate to tokenised shares and share-

holders' rights. In Switzerland, daura AG, a joint venture of Swisscom and MME, is currently developing an *equity token* infrastructure for small- and medium-sized enterprises. Finally, membership tokens represent a simple personal membership right, for example, in an association or club.

- *Ownership Tokens* include tokens that provide smart contract-based ownership rights on assets other than the tokens. Depending on the specific ownership model, it is referred to as a *joint-ownership token*, *co-ownership token* or *sole-ownership token*.

The three functionality layers (Ledger Functionality 'LEF' Layers) distinguish *Pre-BCP*, situations in which contributions are recorded without allowing a contributor to make a transaction, *Pre-Operational BCP*, where tokens are transferable but cannot yet offer its intended utility on the network and usually are traded on a secondary market exchange, and *Operational BCP*, that can be classified into the above-mentioned categories.

The risk assessment includes the following criteria:

- *Functionality and Protocol-Related Risks* consist of (1) risk of security weaknesses of the underlying technology, (2) risk of weaknesses or exploitable breakthroughs in the field of cryptography, (3) risk of the underlying technology, and (4) risk of blockchain consensus attacks.
- *Storage and Access of Private Key-Related Risks* consist of (1) wallet system risk, (2) cybersecurity risk, (3) risk of insufficient user wallet encryption, (4) risk of insufficient user wallet backups, and (5) risk of insufficient contingency tools.
- *Regulation and Money Laundering-Related Risks.*
- *Market-Related and Counterparty Risks*, including (1) general market risks, (2) risk of value decrease of BCP, (3) operator counterparty risk, and (4) risk of alternative (hard-sforked) underlying technologies.

The assessment suggested by the MME framework combines the token categories, which considers technical aspects, value, and the presence of counterparties with the risk category, based on security, legal, and market considerations (see Figure 38). The resulting rating aims to provide visibility to regulators and protection to investors. Of particular interest is the list of relevant data to answer these questions (as outlined in the introduction of Müller et al., 2018), i.e., the underlying protocol data, market and distribution data, and functional data. The list discloses which information is relevant from a legal point of view and, therefore, should also be taken into consideration by the market participants.

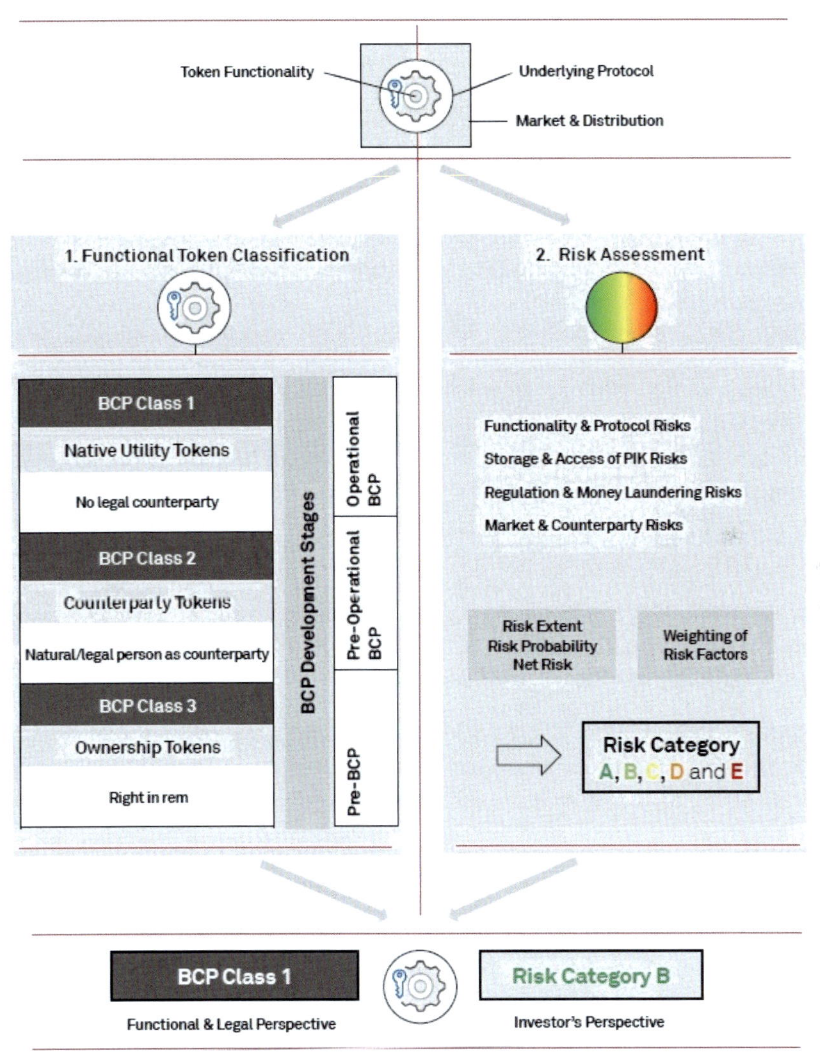

Source: Müller et al. (2018), p. 2.

Figure 38. BCP Classification and Risk Assessment Method.

Müller et al. (2018) conducted the assessment for the example of Bitcoin and generated a BCP 1-A rating, which means that Bitcoin is a native utility token, and, more precisely, a basic token with relatively low risks for investors.

7.1.2. FINMA: Applicability of financial regulation for ICOs

By publishing its guidelines on the applicability of financial market regulations for ICOs (FINMA, 2018), FINMA became the first global regulator to provide detailed and principle-based rules on how it intends to treat inquiries from ICO organisers and analyse the applicability of industry regulation. The FINMA guidelines complement its Guidance 04/2017 (FINMA, 2017), published on 29 September 2017.

At the core is the question of whether the tokens issued by an ICO fall under the securities trading regime, and whether their trade and exchange are subject to the Swiss anti-money laundering regulation (AMLA). These guidelines refer only to issuing of tokens on the primary market (ICOs). Furthermore, the classification of a token as security has, in particular regarding the secondary market, considerable legal consequences due to the financial market regulations that apply to securities. The applicability of these laws is discussed.

The key element of the guidelines is the classification of the tokens based on their function and transferability. The FINMA token classification distinguishes Payment Token, Utility Token, and Asset Token:

- *Payment Tokens* are synonymous with cryptocurrencies and have no other intention than to be used as a means of payment. According to FINMA, they give rise to no claims on the issuer.
- *Utility Tokens* are intended to access an application or service digitally.
- *Asset Tokens* represent assets such as a debt or equity claims on the issuer (e.g., participation in companies and future capital flows). Participations in real physical assets traded on the blockchain also fall into this category.

The token categories are not mutually exclusive, and asset and utility tokens can also be classified as payment tokens (referred to as hybrid tokens). Of these three token categories, only asset tokens are treated as securities and consequently fall under securities regulation. Once payment tokens become functional (i.e., transferable and tradable), their trade and exchange qualify as a financial intermediary service and, therefore, fall under the Swiss anti-money laundering regulation (AMLA). As mentioned previously, however, the guidelines do not address the secondary market, where under certain circumstances utility and asset tokens may also be subject to AML regulations.

Overall, the guidelines create a positive and lightly regulated environment for a highly dynamic market (see Glarner et al., 2018). It is commendable that FINMA acknowledges the innovative potential of blockchain technologies. As with every high-level guidance, they leave some unanswered questions and ambiguity. In particular, practitioners have commented that FINMA's qualification of Asset Token as an (uncertified) security may not be sustainable. The authors argue that, under the applicable laws, securities must be suitable for mass trading. However, if the rights created under the ICO until the transfer of the tokens are not transferable under the terms of the agreement, then they are unsuitable for mass trading, and the token cannot be qualified as secure (Essebier & Bourgeois, 2018).

Furthermore, the position paper on the legal classification of ICO's of the Blockchain Taskforce points out that not every issuance of a payment token also qualifies as a financial intermediary activity. They conclude, contrary to the opinion expressed by FINMA in the Guidelines, that the issuance of a Payment Token does not necessarily trigger the application of AML regulations. Therefore, it remains to be seen how case law and further regulations fill in the gaps as the market matures.

7.1.3. Transfer of tokens on the blockchain

A special issue is the transferability of crypto-property or tokens in the case of uncertificated securities. The potential of digital, blockchain-based, book-entry securities cannot be realised in Switzerland today because the law requires confirmation in writing. When transferring a claim (assignment), the Swiss Code of Obligations (CO) requires the written form for a legally valid transfer (Article 165 CO).

The already approved, qualified electronic signatures are, as of today, not compatible with the signatures used on the blockchain. Therefore, we recommend examining whether the Swiss electronic signature (ZertES) can be adapted so that it becomes blockchain-compatible (e.g., by including specific hash algorithms of blockchains in the list of algorithms approved for the Zert-ES-signatures). Adjustments are therefore necessary, and with the aim of facilitating the search for the best solution to enable blockchain-based value rights, Meisser (2018) summarises various suggestions to overcome this problem.

Meisser proposed three possible solutions:

- The version 'subsidiary arrangement' (original: *dezentral*) suggests leaving the decision and responsibility to the issuer, i.e., the issuer decides on the offering, definition, and design of an electronic signature to transfer book-entry securities. If the issuer fails to set the prerequisites for the transfer of the securities, then the existing regulation applies, i.e., confirmation in writing is required, and a transfer of tokens on the blockchain is not possible.
- The version 'assignment' (original: *Abtretung auf der Blockchain*) stipulates that debtors can update their register upon proof of a corresponding assignment. Both the written form and the advanced electronic signature can be considered as proof.
- The version 'token' suggests explicitly introducing the recognition of issuance and book-keeping on the blockchain if the company statutes or conditions of issue provide for this possibility.

These propositions have strengths and weaknesses. While the version 'token' is the most elaborated, 'subsidiary arrangement' does not provide any technical restrictions regarding implementation. The 'assignment' version is interesting as it relies on the 'advanced electronic signature', which is already a defined legal concept. The major disadvantage of this approach is the mixture of electronic and written signatures and transfers.

The above propositions are complemented by two recommendations to address the issues of written form requirements for the transfer of uncertificated securities by the Blockchain Taskforce (Eggen et al., 2018), a comparatively broad initiative by academics and practitioners include the following:

- In its first recommendation, based on various doctrines, the Blockchain Taskforce concludes that the applicable law does not necessarily oppose a purely digital transmission of tokens, provided that they be designed as electronic securities qualifying as 'certificated securities' (*Wertpapiere*) and denominated in a decentralised trade repository. To achieve this result, Art. 922 of the Civil Code must be widely interpreted: In addition to a physical transmission, a digital transmission should also be possible and lead to the transfer of title to a deed. However, as there is yet no case law, this solution is subject to great legal uncertainty, and an amendment to the law would probably be the more legally secure solution.

- The second recommendation of the Blockchain Taskforce is to change the current law in two ways: Art. 165 CO could be amended so the written form requirement would no longer be required for the assignment of a claim. Such an adjustment would, however, be associated with major political difficulties, as the written form requirement of assignment still appears necessary in many areas (e.g., assignment of claims after collection). Alternatively, the requirement of the written form from Art. 973c CO. could be removed. With this solution, all uncertificated securities, even those that are not maintained in a decentralised trade repository, could be transmitted formlessly. The disadvantage of this change in the law is that not all tokens issued in practice qualify as uncertified securities.

7.1.4. Economic reflections

Blockchain technology automates data, transactions, and contract processing. It is generally presumed that this machine or code-based handling increases efficiency and leaves less room for interpretation because the code specifies the actions and only allows 0 or 1. In certain aspects this might be true, but not in others.

Role of lawyers: It must be considered that only the contracting parties know the deal they want to close, and the lawyers know the applicable law, but the software developer does not. The code simply executes what is specified. Lawyers and software developers have to get together and translate the intentions of the parties into the code and smart contracts. Mlynar and Schaefer (2016) see this translation and creation of smart term sheets as a new role of lawyers.

Like model contracts, smart contracts strive to cover the standard problems as well as possible. Also, smart contracts, like any contract, are not able to specify every eventuality. Although the content of the smart contract is stored on the code level and, in many cases, defines and executes the transactional relationship, the contractual relationship continues to take place on a different, interpersonal level. This as smart contracts are at the time being limited to binary logic and can therefore not yet adequately represent the complexity of legal relationships. Therefore, the interpretation of disputes will always remain for human judgement.

While the adoption of smart contract technology will lead to a standardisation of contracts, challenges arise if the coded functionalities are not in line with the expectations of the contractual parties. Consequently, there will likely still be a market for (centralised) trust where smart contract template providers reduce respective risks.

Clear facts: The principal advantage of blockchain technology is that the contract or the information is stored immutably on the chain. As the facts are undeniable, risk of non-compliance is reduced, which is special advantage in cases where, in a traditional setting, the cost of the contract enforcement exceeds the cost of the disputed value because the values at stake are too small and would not be worth activating legal levers or the burden of proof and enforcement costs are too high.

Another advantage is the traceability. Blockchain increases transparency, reduces the possibility for corruption, and creates strong incentives for good governance and social responsibility.

Auto-execution: Smart contracts create a concurrency of transactions or a sequence of actions that are triggered automatically. Consequently, default positions might be changed. For example, the obligor in a smart contract loses the ability to withhold payment as it is automatically charged. This shift in weight to control processes prior to transaction execution leads to a shift of (contract enforcement) costs (the obligor, in this case, must go to court to get the money back). Also, smart contracts automatically initiate the default process (via third parties such as an oracle), which may not always be desired in practice. The contracting parties may be willing to be lenient because they value the relationship more than the strict adherence to the previously agreed terms, and because they expect to have such favour returned, should they ever come into a similar situation.

7.2. Ecological aspects

There are numerous news reports on the immense energy consumption caused by the Bitcoin network, and this is an issue to be discussed in Chapter 7.2.1. In addition, the sheer energy consumption per transaction can be further amplified if the number of blockchains (using PoW) increases. However, the Blockchain technology might benefit nature if it increases accountability in the global supply chain (see Chapter 7.2.2). Furthermore, it might even solve market failures if externalities can be better monitored and attributed.

7.2.1. Main ecological problem: proof-of-work-based mining

The two most popular blockchains, Bitcoin and Ethereum Main Net, use PoW as a consensus mechanism. When they started, they consumed much less energy compared to today. Mining was even possible on a simple PC. Due to the dramatic increase in the prices of both cryptocurrencies and, with it, the value of the block rewards, more and more money was invested into better equipment to increase the chances of mining the next block. With incentives of 12.5 BTC per block and at a price of about USD 10,000, the block reward for Bitcoin is well above USD 100,000 every ten minutes or more than USD 600,000 per hour. For Ethereum, the reward is currently 3 ETH[122], and with a price of more than USD 500 every 15 seconds this amounts to well above USD 300,000 per hour. These financial incentives paired with the competitive nature of PoW explain why mining became so energy intensive.

PoW-based mining uses immense amounts of energy. By May 2018, Bitcoin alone is estimated to consume 65 terawatt hours (TWh) per year (Digiconomist.net, n.d.-a). To put this energy consumption into perspective:

- If Bitcoin were a country, it would rank 42nd in the world, which places it between Switzerland and the Czech Republic with 8.4 million and 10.6 million inhabitants, respectively.

[122] The block rewards were reduced from 5 to 3 as of October 2017.

- Bitcoin's electricity consumption is 0.29% of the total world electricity consumption.
- The electricity consumed per transaction is 850-kilowatt hours (KWh). In 2016, an average Swiss Household could have been powered for more than 59 days with 850 KWh.
- The amount of electricity used for Ether mining is 18.6 GWh (Digiconomist.net, n.d.-b), which is more than the yearly consumption of Croatia or Jordan.
- Electricity consumptions for mining Bitcoin increased from January to May 2018 by more than 75%. Over the same period, Bitcoin prices fell by over 30%. This indicates that the mining rewards still at least cover the marginal cost of mining and new mining power continues to enter the network.

This amount of energy consumption means cryptocurrencies have a massively adverse effect on the environment. However, the exact ecological impact depends on the energy source used. In January 2018, most Bitcoin mining took place in China where the operations are situated either in hydropower-rich provinces of Yunnan and Sichuan or the coal-rich provinces of Xinjiang and Inner Mongolia, which have low electricity prices due to overcapacities (Fickling, 2018). Because the exact location of mining farms is unknown and therefore the type of electricity they consume is unknown[123], accurate estimates of the total environmental impact of PoW are hard to obtain.[124]

While PoW mining uses a lot of electricity, the market incentives at play ensure that the use is as efficient as possible. Mining operations are situated in places that are cool and have low electricity costs. A cool climate helps

[123] Generally speaking, hydropower is climate-friendly and coal power is not. The ecological impact of cryptocurrency mining using electricity from coal power plants in this case is somewhat mitigated by the fact that China has some excess baseload in those regions until the new ultra-high-voltage circuits currently under construction connects them with the coastal areas. Hence, the ecological impact depends a lot on whether excess baseload is actually used or whether additional baseload has to be provided (or if the current baseload is kept as power consumption increases in the medium to long term due to Bitcoin mining).

[124] Some proponents of Bitcoin go as far as to argue that it is financing the green-energy revolution since excess supply is prevalent with renewables, such as solar and wind (Antonopoulos, 2017a).

reduce the cost of cooling which can be as high as 40% of operational costs (Peck, 2017). This is one reason why many mining operations are located in Iceland or Canada, which offer both cool weather and inexpensive (excess) electricity (Pickering & Fraser, 2017).

We should further consider that the energy used is partly the price paid for a decentralised, highly-redundant, immutable database. Redundancy in data storage always involves higher electricity usage. Similarly, the immutability of the cryptocurrencies is guaranteed by the PoW consensus protocol by ensuring there is a cost to validating transactions.

The high energy usage of PoW is one reason[125] why alternative consensus algorithms should be used. In business applications, blockchains use non-competitive consensus algorithms, such as proof-of-authority (PoA) or Practical Byzantine Fault Tolerant (PBFT) instead of PoW. Further, Ethereum, the second largest blockchain using PoW, is preparing to switch to a proof-of-stake (PoS) consensus protocol. In summary, without PoW consensus algorithms, the ecological cost of cryptocurrencies would decrease immensely and would be proportional to the level of redundancy (number of full nodes) offered by the network.

7.2.2. Potential ecological gains through accountability

Benefits for the environment come from improvements in monitoring. For example, a distributed ledger might lower the cost of monitoring the origin of goods in the supply chain, the electricity produced and consumed in a peer to peer (P2P) electrical grid, and the emission of carbon or pollutants, especially when combined with IoT devices. In our use case on proof of provenance (see Chapter 6.3.1), we observed that blockchain is seen to have great potential when it comes to monitoring adherence to standards in sustainability certified goods. The openness of the platform means it can be easier to integrate with existing systems, and it enables smaller producers to build trust with the

[125] Another important reason is that, when buying mining equipment and operating mining farms, the economies of scale lead to greater centralisation of mining power, thereby reducing the redundancy aspect of the network.

consumer. The benefits of supply-chain management could help grow the market for sustainable products by building trust with the consumer.

The registering and monitoring of greenhouse gas emissions on a public blockchain could increase the level of trust of public places in this data. It can also be a first step toward the implementation of a decentralised cap and trade system, such as for greenhouse gases. In a traditional centralised emissions-trading system, emissions are capped at a sustainable level, emission certificates are distributed or sold by a government body to polluters and then traded on a centralised market. In a decentralised system, emission certificates could be offered by anyone with carbon offsetting assets (e.g., a forest or carbon-dioxide extraction technology). The transactions between the supplier and the buyer of the certificates could be written in a smart contract on a blockchain and include conditions of the expiration of a certificate. This could be a date or conditions such as regular confirmation of the state of the offsetting capacity with automatic reimbursement in case of non-compliance. The advantage of such a decentralised scheme would be the lower entry barriers into the carbon trade. This would enable the governments and people in developing countries, where large parts of the today's endangered forests are located, to participate in carbon trade and earn additional income (Hübner, 2017).

Blockchains could also help bring carbon-offsetting schemes to consumers. For instance, the platform Poseidon[126] aims to build a system where the carbon impact of a product can be directly offset at purchase by buying carbon credits. CarbonX,[127] aside from offering a similar carbon offsetting scheme, goes further by envisioning giving consumers tokens when they buy locally sourced or energy-efficient products. These tokens can then be used to buy products from participating stores.

Overall, blockchain technology has the potential to be beneficial for the environment. However, it is too early to quantify *how* significant these ecological gains will be and whether they will more than compensate for the ecological drawbacks of the technology (especially as long as PoW prevails).

---

[126] See https://poseidon.eco/

[127] See https://www.carbonx.ca/

7.3. Social and political aspects

Like any technological advancement, blockchain will affect our society. While it remains too early to tell how deep or profound these changes will be, let us look at possible paths through which society could be impacted.

As we have seen in the use cases presented in this report, blockchains have applications across many industries and thus affect large parts of society. There exist many other projects that aim to do social good by benefiting all of society. A study by the Stanford Graduate School of Business (2018)[128] found 193 projects that use blockchain to achieve social impact. They use the technology to tackle issues such as transparency, fraud, financial transaction costs, and identity. The study attests that 25% have transformative potential, and in 20%, blockchain is the only viable solution to the problem the project addresses. While not all of these projects will bear fruit, it shows that even in these early stages of the application of the technology, blockchain is a force for societal change to reckon with.

To assess social and political changes likely to occur due to the rise of blockchain usage, we return to the basics of blockchains. How is trust generated and how does the public deal with it? What is the impact of increased transparency due to blockchains? What is the backdrop for eliminating intermediaries? How does society change if collective ownership becomes easier to handle? What is the impact of the decentralised and more participation-oriented nature of a blockchain? Finally, combining the latter two questions raises the prospect of blockchains leading to more decentralised democracies.

7.3.1. Change in trust

Three levels of trust are needed: trust in cryptography, trust in probability instead of control, and trust in the community.

[128] https://drive.google.com/file/d/19o2BM81ANS3MC1juFIfAidouXphqh1i5/view

Trust in cryptography

Many people are at unease when it comes to encryption due to a lack of knowledge and much publicity of cases where law enforcement or criminals gain access to accounts. However, this is not a new aspect of the digital economy, and no major change is expected. It might even be the case that blockchains help the public to obtain a better feeling for when encryption is secure. Furthermore, the discussions around lost Bitcoin accounts (private keys) may even more forcefully illustrate why it is of the utmost imperative to securely store personal private keys.

Trust in probability instead of control

Chapter 2.2 illustrated how incredibly unlikely it is that two people generate keys that yield the same hash value, and no such cases have been reported cases where it happened so far. However, it probabilistically *could* happen, so conceptionally, society must cope with the fact that systems may make such errors by design. This is in stark contrast to the current situation where mistakes by machines are the result of poor programming and, consequently, nobody can be blamed. Hence, damage resulting from such a highly unlikely event must be reclaimed from the other account holder, which is very difficult to achieve in anonymous networks.

But it has never happened yet, and it is unclear how significant a financial loss would occur in such an isolated incidence. It is speculative to imagine the effective impact of a high-stake incidence. Cases with small- to medium-size impact would likely lead to (i) people using different accounts to limit the potential losses, (ii) people turning to permissioned blockchains to ensure the capability to reclaim their wealth, and (iii) insurance policies are likely to be offered.

Trust in the community

The strength of a blockchain depends significantly on an active community, as it validates the blocks and identifies problematic changes in the code. As a society, we are used to having a defined entity in charge and is responsible for failing to achieve set goals. Here, the goals are informal, and it is nearly impossible for a layperson to judge whether it is an active, vibrant community with independent actors. This is especially true for smaller blockchains.

One partial solution is that blockchains eventually gravitate to a finite number of medium- to large-sized hubs (such as Ethereum for smart contracts). While this elevates pressure with respect to the validation of blocks, it does not tackle the issue of ensuring that, for example, smart contracts are well written. It is conceivable that some trusted parties (e.g., known law firms) offer some form of guarantee for blockchain solutions they support (e.g., smart contracts). Other options involve private chains, where the actors are (somewhat) known to each other allowing to take legal action. Not solving the trust in community aspect for the laymen is unsustainable for a blockchain as society will likely reject it.

7.3.2. Transparency

Blockchain-based registers, for example, require that society come to an agreement about what information is public and what needs to remain private. This is especially true if multi-wallet solutions are not widely used in all blockchains. In that case, it is sufficient to know one's public key to track all personal transactions. Initially, this information is not very valuable, and the transaction counterparts remain pseudonymous. Many transaction partners (e.g., companies that sell goods or services) may wave their anonymity, so then the analysis becomes easier. Furthermore, the patterns alone may be valuable. Currently, many Internet companies own massive amounts of detailed data on individual users. A public ledger is very different as everyone can analyse them and even link them to other records available. The issue becomes exponentially worrisome if said companies link their data with this public record as they then both know an individual's public key as well as those of many other users. This scenario would accelerate the current discussion on user privacy, especially when it comes to the 'right to be forgotten', which is the opposite of what occurs on a blockchain.

While there are instances where the loss of privacy is a significant worry, the benefits in some areas cannot be overstated. Blockchain applications in the supply chain make the provenance of a good more transparent, making it easier for consumers to adopt sustainable behaviour. That is something many state are willing to do, but have so far lacked the trustworthy information to do so.

7.3.3. Missing intermediaries

Eliminating the need for certain intermediaries is a good goal, as it makes the entire economy more efficient. Naturally, disintermediation, like any structural change, leads to job displacement. If fewer banks are involved in financing a trade due to the use of blockchain and smart contracts, then this will affect the personnel requirements of the finance industry. However, new jobs are then created, for instance, in the drafting of smart contracts and management of blockchain infrastructure. The social impact of this structural change depends on the speed at which blockchain technology disrupts industries.

More challenging for society is that the absence of intermediaries may limit the government's option for regulating certain industries. A case in point would be the idea of blockchain-based, decentralised power grids with decentralised trading and the question of supply guarantees.

Typical goods in a supermarket are available most of the time but not always. The supermarket has a vital market interest in keeping all goods stocked to maintain the image that it is always worth going to the store. Imagine a case with decentralised markets, where there is little to no market pressure to preserve such an image. It must be expected that short-term shortages would occur more frequently. While this might be acceptable for some goods, it would be less so for goods such as electricity.[129]

To incentivise electricity suppliers to keep some excess supply, prices must be free to flow so that peak energy providers earn enough money. This, in turn, in a completely decentralised trading system, means that consumers must accept the fact that prices may fluctuate much more over the course of a day than in a centralised system (increased uncertainty), and that they pay more for the 'same' good compared to their neighbours. If regulators wanted to implement price controls, it would lead to a dysfunctional market where supply shortages are more likely to occur in situations of high (peak-load) demand. If there is a broad demand for more stable prices, then forward transactions are commonplace. This can easily be achieved using smart con-

[129] To reduce the likelihood of undersupply, the decentralised market could include fines for undersupply, a scenario that is easily enforced on the blockchain using smart contracts.

tracts. However, the penalty for non-performance in a blockchain is limited, as it is either limited to the reimbursement of the agreed-upon payment from the buyer or requires a setup of an escrow account by the supplier or both. The escrow account solution is very capital intensive, which limits its scope and solutions without an escrow account, which may not offer the assurance of supply needed. Hence, completely decentralised trade of critical services may not be desired societally.

The fact that someone may have to pay a different price for the 'same' good is not as strange of an idea as it may seem at first. Flight fares depend on the timing of the booking even though the seat is the same. It is also worth noting that, by the time such a decentralised system is implemented, IoT devices may be more common and so devices may switch off or hibernate if prices start to soar.

7.3.4. Collective ownership

Blockchains simplify and expand the realm of possibilities with respect to collective ownership. By itself, collective ownership is not a new phenomenon. Today, this is usually achieved by using a legal entity that owns the assets in question. What is new is that collective ownership may become more widely applied because one can easily own a specific item.

A societal consequence will be that more private law will be present but only where already permitted today. Considering a chain that tokenises real estate on a large scale, real-estate companies can do the same right now so Swiss law still applies here, too (including Lex Koller, which restricts ownership by foreign nationals). Hence, the government's role remains largely unchanged, and the expansion of private law does not alter the social contract agreed upon before.

7.3.5. Decentralisation

With blockchain technology, disintermediation and decentralisation go hand in hand. Removing the middleman can be considered a prerequisite for decentralisation. Abstractly, decentralisation implies that the barriers to entry are lowered, and power is shifted to the original producer of the goods and services. Both aspects are positive effects but are unlikely to cause fundamental changes as coordination platforms are still needed to facilitate P2P transactions, which fulfill part of the role of the middleman again.

7.3.6. Participation

Apart from the transactional benefits of decentralisation, the governance of a core technology of the future can be organised without a central hub. It is this democratisation in the governance of software protocol that is novel. Changes to the protocol are proposed, amended, discussed, and voted on, and these changes to the protocol (and its potential side effects) can be challenging to understand even for professionals as they are very technical. This makes opinion leaders very powerful. For instance, in Ethereum the co-founder, Vitalik Buterin, has great influence, and he can rally support even for far-reaching changes, such as the 'DAO hard fork'. In this forced split of the Ethereum blockchain, funds lost in the hacking of an Ethereum-based crowd fund 'Decentralised Autonomous Organisation' (DAO) were returned to the owners. This shows that some opinion leaders have enough influence even to overturn fundamental properties of a blockchain, such as immutability of the transactions.

The DAO in the DAO hard-fork was the first of its kind. In the future, we might see more decentralised autonomous organisations, that is, organisations run through rules encoded in smart contracts, which aim to reduce coordination costs of large (decentralised) organisations and remove classical hierarchy. It could be argued that the removal of hierarchy in organisations and its replacement with rules-based participation could lead to less hierarchical social structures.

Conclusions

A blockchain is a decentralised database replicated on many servers or computers owned or governed by independent legal entities. As the name suggests, it is a chain of blocks, each of which stores newly added data (a transaction) as well as a link to the previous block. Hence, it is a chronological chain. Its decentralised nature means that there is never only a single version of the ledger but various asynchronised replications. Therefore, every blockchain also needs a consensus protocol so that all participants converge to one, synchronised version of the blockchain.

The biggest strength of a blockchain is its immutability. First, every transaction is cryptographically signed and every block is sealed. The property of the utilised hash function means that even the slightest mutations yield vastly different hash values and make changes readily detectable. Second, a distributed ledger does not have a single point of failure. Even if many participants in the network collude, the blockchain remains accessible and intact.

Conceptionally, appreciating a blockchain requires a different mindset for various aspects. Often governments and businesses look for someone who is responsible and who can be held accountable. Furthermore, people usually instinctively trust a system more where someone actively controls the processes rather than a probabilistic control, even though the latter is ultimately more secure due to the removal of human error. The main security risks associated with the probabilistic approach are a collision (the same combination of private and public keys) and a pre-image attack (finding the input that generates a given hash value). Both scenarios are highly unlikely to occur, and businesses will presumably be able to buy insurance against it at a reasonable price (due to its very low probability).

Through the lens of the transaction cost theory, there are three reasons why the blockchain technology may substantially alter current businesses: reduction of financial costs by eliminating intermediaries, reduction of costs associated with legal certainty (increased transparency and immutability of the stored information), and time costs in connection with increased automation of contract enforcement.

If we look at the current use cases of blockchains in existence today, we see the usage of the technology is still in its infancy. The current processes are often reproduced on the blockchain instead of rethinking the entire process. Disruptive changes are likely to occur first in the area of financial services, where the link to the real world is easily achievable (many electronic representations of assets already exist). However, the elimination of intermediaries has the potential to alter service industries radically, and the increase in legal certainty helps countries and companies combat corruption (illustrated in the use case of Georgia's land-title register). The latter is more impactful in developing countries and might prove to be one of the most successful means of transforming corrupt states. Here, the 'export' of the Swiss legal framework in smart contracts with exclusive jurisdiction in Switzerland or a Swiss private arbitrator may further help companies in those countries to avoid corrupt legal systems.

For developed countries, the cost of legal certainty is lowered in areas of proof of provenance (tracking the origin of goods) and the corresponding supply chains. This applies to carbon credits (as the P2P trading of those credits can also be done on a blockchain) as well as goods that meet certain conditions set out by labelling organisations. In the long run, when improved and less expensive solutions for the individualised tagging of physical good exist, blockchains are likely to aid in fighting counterfeits. In general, blockchain's potential is vastly greater in developed countries if combined with smart contracts. They expand the possibilities to eliminate intermediaries and to expand the business opportunities in areas where currently potential contract enforcement costs are prohibitively high. As soon as more interconnected sensors acting as IoT devices are available, the prices will become cheaper and the IoT networks will expand the potential increases to use blockchain with smart contracts and IoT.

The most prominent application of blockchain – cryptocurrencies like Bitcoin – are in our estimation not the most promising in the long run. Generally, those pure cryptocurrencies struggle with the issue of deflation (if they are 'successful') and inflation (if they are a fringe product). In addition, with a fixed money supply and an unregulated marketplace, prices are likely to have increased volatility, regardless of their upward or downward trends. Price stability, however, is a key component of a strong currency that is used both as a means of payment as well as wealth storage. Deflation solidifies the strength of a cryptocurrency as wealth storage at the expense of the means of payment, as seen in the surge of prices of many cryptocurrencies in late 2017. Unless new mechanisms are invented to mitigate the issue of deflation and inflation, cryptocurrencies will not become the main currencies for a broad range of goods and services.

In addition, cryptocurrencies based on permissionless blockchains are incompatible with current interpretations of anti-money laundering laws (AMLA). More broadly, it is likely that AMLA will also hinder even the use of permissionless utility tokens in the future. Permissioned blockchains do not necessarily mean that everyone must be publicly known to everyone else through their blockchain transactions.

While blockchain technology is a trust machine or engine, the required trust mainly shifts to other areas (e.g., to the smart contract creator or the respective blockchain community). Services that provide the link to the real world are likely to grow and may compensate for jobs lost due to blockchain-driven automation. The automization will likely accelerate the trend towards more high-value human contributions. For instance, smart contracts may lead to less trivial legal cases but also lead to work in establishing well-structured smart contracts or proving consultancy services for contract evaluation.

Societally, blockchains allow people to possess collective goods more efficiently. They even democratise current shared ownership (including companies) by lowering the cost of private e-voting. While it is unclear which goods and services will be more often owned collectively, it will include things where the cost of coordination (where to store it, where to use it, and how and when to lend it) are currently too high. With respect to public e-voting, society does not benefit from higher voter participation due to direct use of blockchain technology but rather by an increase in trust of the e-voting process.

All these points aside, at its core a blockchain is a decentralised ledger, so that it is highly likely that it will be another influential backbone technology everyone uses without realising it. A case in point is the e-voting system operated by Swiss Post. While it is not a purely blockchain-based system, it uses the Bitcoin blockchain to securely store the hash values of the voting log file.

Specific challenges

Despite the generally positive outlook for blockchain technology, there are still additional technological, economic, legal, ecological, and societal challenges as well as risks and limitations to mitigate. The four key *technological challenges* are limited scalability, privacy, the tokenisation of lifecycles, and the absence of a globally accepted and utilised e-ID.

1. The scalability problem concerns the fact that every new block increases the size of the blockchain. The decentralised nature of the blockchain means this increasing size must be saved by each node, which limits the number of transactions per minute. With current consensus protocols, it is not possible to increase the scale of a blockchain without either compromising its decentralisation or its security properties. Consequently, blockchains are suited for infrequent but important transactions, such as registries for real-world property. Hence, many blockchain systems will exist in parallel which will require better interoperability of blockchains.

2. Blockchains are pseudonymous, meaning that every transaction is immutably recorded in the blockchain under a pseudonym and therefore cannot be deleted. Once the identity behind the pseudonym is known, all actions of a natural person can be traced back, which collides fundamentally with the latest privacy regulations, such as the GDPR and especially with the 'right to be forgotten'. This is especially true as public records of transactions may be linked with privately owned data by companies such as Google and Facebook. Technologies that could help guarantee more privacy, such as zero-knowledge proof or permissioned side chains, are not yet well explored. However, whatever technological solution prevails, privacy contrasts with the fundamental idea in blockchain technology of transparency. This is a fundamental political question that needs to be addressed.

3. Many items in the world have lifecycle events (e.g., rights expire, lapse, or generate further rights). For example, financial derivatives such as a put option that expires or food that becomes unedible. Smart contracts mimicking this behaviour face the issue of granting someone or a group of people the right to update a contract without creating unwanted hierarchies.

4. The inexistence of universally accepted, secure e-IDs pose a challenge, as they are a prerequisite for permissioned blockchains to spread. This is especially worrisome as bigger blockchains cannot use workaround solutions for physically identifying people.

Economically, there are also three obstacles, all of which revolve around payment. First, as already touched upon, existing payment tokens struggle with price stability. This can be expanded to utility or asset tokens because there is no way to prevent people from using them as wealth storage or means of payment. Second, to combat this volatility, it might be necessary that fiat money get tokenised in sufficient quantities. Third, a broadly applicable delivery versus payment mechanism is still missing. It would be important to be able to pay on a chain while transferring the rights to a good or service, too. While this can be achieved natively with utility tokens, it would be far more ideal to use a broadly accepted cryptocurrency so that one does not always have to change one's asset before a trade happens.

Formal written requirements and AML regulations are the two most pressing issues on the *legal* front. It is currently not possible to sign transactions on a blockchain in a way that is equal to a signature according to Swiss law (ZertES). With respect to the AML regulation, it is helpful to have the FINMA categorisation of the three classes of digital tokens for the primary market (i.e., the issuance of new coins). It remains unclear, however, whether this classification can be upheld in instances where, for example, utility tokens turn into broadly accepted payment tokens in the secondary market.

The immense energy consumption of the PoW consensus protocol is the only significant *ecological challenge* facing blockchain technology. The impact depends on the energy type used to produce the electricity for mining. At the end of 2018 large parts came from coal-fired powerplants in China, but also from renewable energy sources in regions with an abundance of hydro- or geothermal energy. In any case, a shift to different consensus protocols will be necessary in the long run. While all major blockchain communities discuss switching to other consensus mechanisms, it remains a balancing act to ensure the same level of security as well as to provide the current miners with enough incentive to support such a change.

Societally, the role of tech-savvy opinion leaders should not be underestimated. The founders of a blockchain are relied upon in the community to such an extent that even hard-forks (i.e., altering the rules ex-post) are relatively easily accepted. This group behaviour undermines the decentralised structure upon which the blockchains are built. Another area of concern is the degree of opaqueness in these theoretically incredibly transparent pieces of software. However, smart contracts require a great deal of programming knowledge to be read, and the community must be trusted to flag and challenge problematic smart contracts. While new translation tools of software code to normal languages might solve this problem in the future, they currently present a substantial obstacle.

All of these challenges do not put the core of blockchain technology in question. Quantum computing, however, has this potential. It uses quantum physics, which allows multiple calculations on one bit per time in an exponential curve. By doing so, the current security methods can become obsolete, which is at the core of blockchain's ownership claims. Although quantum computing is still in its infancy, in its current form, it requires specific software for every type of encryption, which makes it less scalable. Furthermore, the encryption used in blockchains is the same as in all other Internet-related transactions as well as database protection mechanisms. Hence, it is not a blockchain-specific issue and would lead to massive consequences in the digital world everywhere. Therefore, parallel to the development of quantum computing, scientists are developing quantum-computing-resistant encryption.

Potentials for Switzerland

Aside from these general potentials and challenges, Switzerland's position in the blockchain world is formidable. This might be surprising as one of this country's main strength is its role as a trust provider, which could be replaced by blockchain. However, as seen before, the requirement for trust does not entirely vanish but instead shifts. Providing trusted links to the real world and safely depositing real-world objects is a known business practice in Switzerland (e.g., with duty-free warehouses).

The long-standing liberal practice of private arbitration increases the comparative advantage in depositories. It is likely that many blockchain-based smart contracts will opt for private arbitration, which itself is a business model of Switzerland. Having depositories in the same jurisdiction streamlines the process and increases legal certainty. Having the court of jurisdiction in Switzerland and, therefore, somewhat exporting the Swiss law would also grant the Swiss companies and people a small comparative advantage in the sense that they already have a familiarity with the overarching legal framework.

Switzerland's current strength in blockchain stems from a lean regulation approach (and a bit of luck) that created a vibrant community in the region of Zug and Zurich. Despite the Federal Council's slogan 'Crypto Nation Switzerland', the brand 'Crypto Valley Zug' better describes the status quo. The steps by FINMA to slowly provide a legal framework for ICOs is beneficial, too, and in line with the lean regulation approach.

The banking industry is the most endangered sector in the short run. Here, it is imperative that the banks invest in and experiment with FinTech start-up companies and do not shy away from 'cannibalising their businesses'. The federal council's decision to foster FinTech companies by allowing certain activities without obtaining a full banking licence will likely be a great help.

In the long run, IoT integration into blockchain-based smart contracts will offer further business opportunities. With a strong industrial sector in Switzerland, the opportunities will indeed also exist there. However, it would be too speculative to proclaim an expected impact on Switzerland.

Finally, the Swiss electoral system already benefits from blockchain technology in the current iterations of public e-voting. While improving the security of e-voting strengthens our direct democracy, it is unlikely to change democracy significantly.

Appendices

Unspent transactions versus accounts

There are two fundamentally different concepts of how balances are kept on blockchains. The traditional approach is through accounts or unspent transactions. While Ethereum implemented the concept of accounts and balances, Bitcoin works with the concept of spent and unspent transaction outputs (UTXO).

As Figure 39 shows, if Alice would like to transfer BTC 0.15 to Bob, her wallet does not select BTC 0.15 from the total balance of the wallet of BTC 4.22. Instead, the wallet selects the closest spend candidate from the existing 'outputs' in the wallet (in this case, it is BTC 0.2).[130] This spend candidate is sent to the blockchain where it is broken down into three parts of (i) the amount to send, (ii) the transaction fee, and (iii) the 'change'. The amount to send goes to the recipient, Bob, in this case, forming a new output for his account, the transaction fee is paid to the miners, and, finally, the change is returned to Alice, creating a new output on her account.

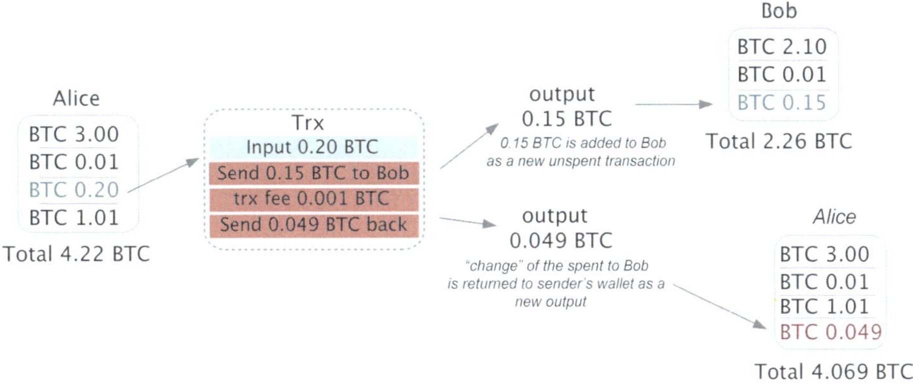

Source: Banking Concepts.

Figure 39. Bitcoin balance maintenance using UTXOs.

[130] Based on the example by CCN (2014).

One of the arguments in favour of the UTXO approach is scalability. Because the balance is stored as a set of outputs, the user can create two or more independent transactions. Each transaction can use different outputs, and the order in which they are processed does not matter. On the other hand, storing the unspent transactions in the database consumes a lot of space, as each output stores the owner's address, the transaction ID where it was created, and the value. Taking Alice's account from the example above, we see four UTXOs. Each consumes 20 bytes for the owner address, 32 bytes for the transaction ID, and 8 bytes to store the value. Finally, for the four UTXOs, we end up with 240 bytes to store the balance of Alice's account. Compared to the Ethereum accounts, which store just one value per account with a 20-byte address, 8-byte value, and 2-byte nonce,[131] we end up just with 30 bytes per account.

From decentralised applications (dApps) or scripts implemented on the blockchain, which require interaction with the account, UTXOs are not the easiest choice. As Figure 40 shows, the database of Bitcoin UTXOs almost doubled since the beginning of 2017 and equals 57 million UTXOs, which is more than 3GB.[132]

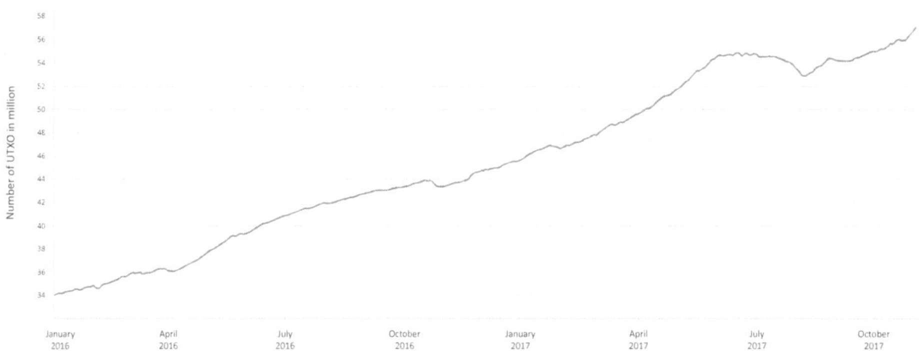

Source: https://charts.bitcoin.com/chart/utxo-set-size; accessed November 6, 2017.

Figure 40. The number of UTXOs over nearly two years.

[131] Every account on Ethereum keeps track of the nonces used in transactions and only accepts a transaction if its nonce is the next one after the last one used.

[132] Since one UTXO has the size of 60 bytes (20 bytes for the owner address, 32 bytes for the transaction ID and 8 bytes to store the value), 57 million UTXOs have the size of ~3.2GB.

Finally, the choice of how to maintain the balances depends on the purpose of created system. In case of Ethereum, unspent transactions have no advantage compared to accounts. Ethereum aimed to create a blockchain with much more complex transactions than Bitcoin has the unspent transactions, and the UTX-Os would unnecessarily complicate the architecture of the system.

Blockchain: A New Socio-Technical Environment

The Computer Science Centre, Institute of Information Service Science, University of Geneva

Cintcom Foundation

Antoine Burret
Simon Perdrisat

Summary

This report forms part of a study on blockchain technology conducted by the Foundation for Technology Assessment (TA-SWISS). Its intention is to supplement other technical descriptions and case studies by providing background information. In it, we take a close look at blockchain from both social and historical perspectives. We analyse the circumstances in which it appeared and how it came to be institutionalised, then pose questions regarding the sociological challenges it engenders and the new circumstances it has prompted.

We have taken the approach that blockchain is still in its experimental phase, and that it would therefore be premature to look at any specific repercussions of its development at this stage. We advocate an exploratory investigation of the field. We conducted an extensive analysis of other academic studies and reports published by consulting firms such as McKinsey, Deloitte, KPMG, and PwC as well as studies conducted at the government level in the US, France, the UK, and the EU as well as by international organisations such as the UN. We explored aspects relating to national legal systems and the recommendations made by financial institutions such as the Bank of England and other supervisory authorities such as FINMA. We investigated social behaviours and the cultural aspects of communities as well as internet resources including press archives, email lists, blogs, code repositories such as GitHub, social networks like Reddit and Medium, Wikipedia, and messaging apps such as Telegram. We studied the profiles of leading figures and contributors as well as communication and financing methods and the economic models involved.

We carried out various types of transactions on the public blockchains of Bitcoin and Ethereum in order to gain practical experience. In other cases, such as Libra, we studied the technical systems through existing documentation (i.e., whitepapers, developer documentation, product presentations).

Finally, we spoke to about 20 people[133] involved in the field, both in Switzerland and abroad. These interviews lasted between one and three hours. Some interviews took place over the phone or by videoconference, while others were

---

[133] See list of contributors, p. 333.

conducted in person. Interviews were decidedly unstructured in order to maintain a situational overview within this dynamic approach. Therefore, interviews with subject-matter experts did not utilize pre-defined questions; instead, the interviewees were provided a list of topics we wished to address. Specific challenges included adopting a balanced outlook while staying up to date on a subject that is rapidly and continuously changing.

This report is divided into five sections. The first introduces blockchain as a historical construct, a concept that gradually developed through the course of computing history. We describe the evolution of the reasoning behind it and the achievements that gradually led to the consolidation of blockchain, with a special focus on cryptography and distributed systems.

In the second section we examine the creation and proliferation of Bitcoin as the first large-scale application of blockchain technology. In this exercise we not only trace the biography of bitcoin, but also present the constituent elements of blockchain in order to consolidate our analytical framework.

The third section introduces the way in which the technical concept enabling the operation and administration of Bitcoin – the blockchain – has become an object of study in itself. We describe how the Bitcoin protocol represents other assets, and how the concept of a distributed ledger was developed to meet the requirements of major industrial and financial players.

In the fourth section, we describe how blockchain has been socialized, i.e., how it interacts with social structures. We study two types of socialisation models: an exogenous model, which considers how terminology developed and normalisation strategies; and an endogenous model, based on blockchain's technological capabilities, such as financing methods, distribution rules, fork possibilities[134], and incentive mechanisms that enables blockchain to be assimilated into social structures.

In the last section, we describe how blockchain has found a niche in the collective imagination and how it has changed the ways in which certain problems are approached. We call this movement 'designing through blockchain.' We

---

[134] A fork happens when developers take a copy of source code from one software and start independent development on it, creating a new and separate project.

explain this phenomenon by analysing the emergence of an entirely new industrial sector centred around blockchain technology. We look at the ways in which regulation and identity recognition techniques have undergone both concrete and conceptual upheavals because of blockchain.

The report's conclusions pave the way for further discussion on the growing connections between blockchain and the administration of public affairs. They describe how blockchain has exposed the ways in which national legal systems can and have been bypassed, and address new normalisation regimes enshrined in global law. Lastly, we raise wider questions about the democratic methods for managing information in the public space.

Zusammenfassung

Die Blockchain ist ein noch experimenteller Gegenstand und es ist verfrüht, ihre konkreten Auswirkungen untersuchen zu wollen. Wir haben eine sondierende Untersuchung des Bereichs befürwortet. Die von uns durchgeführte State-of-the-Art-Analyse betrachtete sowohl wissenschaftliche Studien als auch Berichte von Beratungsfirmen (z. B. McKinsey, Deloitte, KPMG, PwC) und Studien, die von Regierungen (z. B. US, Frankreich, UK, EU) und internationalen Organisation (z. B. UNO) durchgeführt wurden. Wir haben den Stand der nationalen Rechtsprechungen und die Empfehlungen der Finanzinstitute (z. B. Bank of England) und Aufsichtsbehörden (z. B. FINMA) untersucht. Danach haben wir das Sozialverhalten, die kulturellen Aspekte der Gemeinschaften und die im Internet veröffentlichten Ressourcen untersucht: Pressearchive, Mailinglisten, Blogs, Code-Ablagen (z. B. Github), soziale Netzwerke (z. B. Reddit, Medium), Wiki, Messaging-Dienste (Telegram-Gruppe). Wir haben die Profile der Leader und Beitragenden, die Kommunikations- und Finanzierungsarten und die Geschäftsmodelle studiert.

Wir haben verschiedene Transaktionsarten auf öffentlichen Blockchains (z. B. Bitcoin, Ethereum) ausgeführt, um eine praktische Erfahrung zu erhalten. In anderen Fällen haben wir einfach die technischen Systeme (z. B. Libra) studiert, indem wir uns auf ihre Dokumentation (Whitepaper, Entwicklerdokumentation, Produktpräsentation) stützten.

Wir haben uns schliesslich mit über zwanzig Personen[135] unterhalten, die in der Schweiz und im Ausland einen Bezug zu diesem Bereich haben, um verschiedene Standpunkte zu untersuchen. Wir haben uns entschlossen, freie Diskussionen zu führen, die zwischen einer und drei Stunden dauerten. Einige Gespräche wurden telefonisch oder in einer Videokonferenz geführt, andere persönlich. Für die Gespräche hatten wir keine zum Voraus festgelegten Fragen, sondern eine Liste mit Themen, die wir ansprechen wollten. Auf diese Weise haben wir versucht, einen Überblick und einen dynamischen Ansatz zu bewahren. Die Herausforderung bestand darin, einen gerechten Standpunkt zu behal-

[135] Siehe «list of contributors», S. 333.

ten und trotz der raschen und laufenden Weiterentwicklungen in diesem Bereich auf dem aktuellen Stand zu bleiben.

Dieser Bericht besteht aus fünf Teilen. Im ersten Teil präsentieren wir die Blockchain mit einem geschichtlichen Aufbau – wie sie während der langen Geschichte der Informatik entstand. Wir beschreiben die Entwicklung der Argumentation und der Realisierungen, die sie schrittweise konsolidierten, indem wir insbesondere auf die Kryptografie und die verteilten Systeme fokussieren.

Im zweiten Teil schildern wir den Lauf der Schaffung und des Wachstums des Bitcoin-Projekts als erste formelle und grossflächige Anwendung der Blockchain. Mit dieser Übung ergründen wir nicht nur die Biografie des Bitcoins, sondern präsentieren auch die grundlegenden Bestandteile der Natur der Blockchain, um den Analyserahmen zu konsolidieren.

Der dritte Teil zeigt auf, wie das technische Konzept, das den Betrieb und die Verwaltung der Bitcoins ermöglicht, zu einem Studienobjekt – die Blockchain – wurde. Wir beschreiben, wie das Bitcoin-Protokoll für die Darstellung von anderen Kapitalanlagen verwendet wurde und wie das Konzept der verteilten Register gebildet wurde, um eine Antwort auf die Zwänge der grossen Industrie- und Finanzakteure zu finden.

Im vierten Teil wird erklärt, wie die Blockchain sozialisiert wird, das heisst, wie sie mit sozialen Strukturen und anderen interagiert. Wir betrachteten zwei Sozialisierungsmodelle. Ein exogenes Modell über terminologische Entwicklungen und Standardisierungsstrategien und ein endogenes Modell, das über Finanzierungsformen, Vertriebsregeln für die Fähigkeit zur Spaltung[136] und Anreizmechanismen in die Technik integriert ist, um ihre Assimilierung in die sozialen Strukturen zu ermöglichen.

Der letzte Teil beschreibt, wie die Blockchain heute im kollektiven Bewusstsein präsent ist und wie sie die Art, wie bestimmte Problematiken angegangen werden, verändert. Wir nennen diese Bewegung «Designing through the Blockchain». Wir erklären dieses Phänomen, indem wir die Bildung eines regel-

---

[136] Eine Abspaltung (Fork) findet statt, wenn Entwickler eine Kopie des Quellcodes einer Software nehmen und damit eine unabhängige Entwicklung beginnen, wodurch ein neues und separates Projekt entsteht.

rechten Industriezweiges um die Blockchain analysieren. Wir untersuchen anschliessend, wie die Regulierungstechniken und die Identitätserkennung einen konzeptuellen und formellen Wandel erleben.

Die Schlussfolgerung dieses Berichts eröffnet die Diskussion zur Beziehung, die zwischen der Blockchain und der öffentlichen Verwaltung entsteht. Sie zeigt auf, wie die Blockchain Situationen beschreibt, in denen die nationalen Rechtsprechungen überfordert werden, und regt zu Überlegungen über die neuen Standardisierungsformen an, die vom globalen Recht verkörpert werden. Abschliessend wird die Frage nach den demokratischen Modalitäten des Umgangs mit der informationellen Dimension des öffentlichen Raums gestellt.

Résumé

La blockchain est un objet encore expérimental et il est prématuré de vouloir étudier ses répercussions concrètes. Nous avons préconisé une enquête exploratoire du domaine. Nous avons procédé à une analyse de l'état de l'art aussi bien au niveau des études académiques que des rapports de consultants (p. ex. McKinsey, Deloitte, KPMG, Pwc) ou encore des études menées au niveau des gouvernements (p. ex. US, France, UK, Union Européenne) et des organisations internationales (p. ex. ONU). Nous avons exploré l'état des juridictions nationales et les préconisations des institutions financières (p. ex. Bank of England) ou des autorités de surveillance (p. ex. FINMA). Nous avons ensuite exploré les comportements sociaux, les aspects culturels des communautés, et les ressources publiées sur internet : archives presse, mailing-lists, blogs, dépôts de code (p. ex. github), réseaux sociaux (p. ex. reddit, medium), wiki, messageries (groupe telegram). Nous avons étudié le profil des leaders et des contributeurs, les modes de communication, de financement et les modèles économiques.

Nous avons effectué différents types de transactions sur les blockchainspublics (p. ex. bitcoin, ethereum) afin d'avoir une expérience pratique. Dans d'autres cas, nous avons simplement étudié les dispositifs techniques (p. ex. Libra) en nous appuyant sur leur documentation (white-paper, documentation développeur, présentation du produit).

Nous nous sommes enfin entretenus avec une vingtaine de personnes impliquées dans le domaine[137], en Suisse et à l'étranger, afin d'examiner différents points de vue. Nous avons pris le parti de procéder à des discussions libres. Les entretiens ont duré entre une et trois heures pour les plus longs. Certains entretiens ont eu lieu par téléphone ou en visioconférence, et les autres en personne. Pour chaque entretien, nous n'avions pas de questions prédéfinies, mais une liste de thèmes que nous souhaitions aborder. Nous avons ainsi tenté de garder une vue d'ensemble et une approche dynamique. L'enjeu était d'adopter un point de vue équitable et de rester à jour en dépit de la succession rapide et constante des évolutions dans ce domaine.

---

[137] Voir «list of contributors», p. 333.

Ce rapport se structure en cinq parties. Dans la première partie, nous présentons la blockchain comme une construction historique, développée dans le temps long de l'histoire de l'informatique. Nous décrivons l'évolution des raisonnements et des réalisations qui l'ont progressivement consolidée en nous concentrant notamment sur la cryptographie et les systèmes distribués.

Dans la seconde partie, nous retraçons le parcours de création et de croissance du projet Bitcoin en tant qu'il constitue la première application formelle à grande échelle de la blockchain. Par cet exercice, nous ne retraçons pas uniquement la biographie du bitcoin, mais nous présentons les éléments constitutifs de la nature de la blockchain afin d'en consolider le cadre d'analyse.

Dans la troisième partie, nous présentons la manière dont le concept technique permettant le fonctionnement et l'administration du bitcoin est devenu un objet d'étude en soi, la blockchain. Nous décrivons comment le protocole bitcoin a été utilisé pour représenter d'autres actifs et comment s'est construit le concept de registres distribués pour répondre aux contraintes des grands acteurs industriels et financiers.

Dans la quatrième partie, nous expliquons la manière dont la blockchain est socialisée, c'est-à-dire comment elle interagit avec les structures sociales et avec autrui. Nous étudions deux catégories de modèles de socialisation. Un modèle exogène, au travers des évolutions terminologiques et des stratégies de normalisation. Et un modèle endogène, qui est intégré à la technique au travers des modes de financement, des règles de distribution des capacités de scission[138] et des mécanismes d'incitation afin de permettre son assimilation dans les structures sociales.

Dans la dernière partie, nous décrivons comment la blockchain est désormais présente dans l'imaginaire collectif et comment elle modifie la manière dont sont approchées certaines problématiques. Nous appelons ce mouvement « designing through the blockchain ». Nous expliquons ce phénomène en analysant la constitution d'un véritable secteur industriel autour de la blockchain.

---

[138] Une scission se produit lorsque les développeurs prennent une copie du code source d'un logiciel et commencent un développement indépendant sur celui-ci, créant ainsi un nouveau projet distinct.

Nous étudions ensuite comment les techniques de régulation et la reconnaissance des identités subissent un bouleversement conceptuel et formel.

La conclusion de ce rapport ouvre la discussion sur la relation qui se construit entre la blockchain et les administrations publiques. Elle décrit la manière dont la blockchain illustre des situations de dépassement des juridictions nationales et renvoie aux réflexions sur les nouveaux régimes de normalisation incarnés par le droit global. Elle pose enfin la question des modalités démocratiques de gestion de la dimension informationnelle de l'espace public.

Sintesi

La blockchain si trova ancora in fase sperimentale ed è quindi troppo presto per indagarne gli effetti concreti. Ci siamo espressi a favore di uno studio esplorativo del settore. L'analisi dello stato dell'arte che abbiamo condotto ha preso in considerazione studi scientifici, rapporti realizzati da società di consulenza (per es. McKinsey, Deloitte, KPMG, PwC) nonché studi condotti da governi (per es. Stati Uniti, Francia, Regno Unito, UE) e organizzazioni internazionali (per es. ONU). Abbiamo esaminato le posizioni della giurisprudenza nei vari Paesi, le raccomandazioni di istituti finanziari (per es. Bank of England) e autorità di vigilanza (per esempio FINMA). Abbiamo quindi analizzato il comportamento sociale, gli aspetti culturali delle comunità e le risorse pubblicate online: archivi stampa, mailing list, blog, repository di codici (per es. Github), social network (per es. Reddit, Medium), Wiki e servizi di messaggistica (gruppo Telegram). Abbiamo studiato i profili dei leader e dei contributori, i metodi di comunicazione e di finanziamento e i modelli di business.

Per acquisire esperienza pratica, abbiamo svolto diversi tipi di transazioni su blockchain pubbliche (per esempio Bitcoin, Ethereum). In altri casi abbiamo semplicemente studiato i sistemi tecnici (per es. Libra) basandoci sulla relativa documentazione (white paper, documentazione dello sviluppatore, presentazione del prodotto).

Infine abbiamo consultato più di una ventina di persone[139] legate a questo ambito, sia in Svizzera che all'estero, per analizzare diversi punti di vista. Abbiamo optato per discussioni libere della durata di una-tre ore. Alcune conversazioni si sono svolte per telefono o in videoconferenza, altre di persona, senza definire a priori delle domande ben precise, bensì un semplice elenco di argomenti da trattare. In questo modo abbiamo cercato di conservare una visione d'insieme e un approccio dinamico alla materia. Particolarmente complesso è stato conservare una prospettiva equa e mantenersi sempre aggiornati nonostante i rapidi e costanti sviluppi nel settore.

Il presente rapporto è suddiviso in cinque parti. Nella prima parte presentiamo la tecnologia blockchain con un approccio storico, ossia spieghiamo com'è nata

[139] Vedi «list of contributors», pag. 333.

nel corso della lunga storia dell'informatica. Descriviamo lo sviluppo delle argomentazioni e realizzazioni che l'hanno progressivamente portata a consolidarsi, concentrandoci in particolare sulla crittografia e sui sistemi distribuiti.

Nella seconda parte descriviamo il percorso di creazione e crescita del progetto bitcoin, ossia della prima applicazione formale e su larga scala della blockchain. Questo excursus ci consente non solo di esplorare la biografia del bitcoin, ma anche di presentare le componenti essenziali della blockchain in quanto tale, al fine di consolidare il quadro analitico.

La terza parte spiega come il concetto tecnico che consente di usare e amministrare i bitcoin sia diventato un oggetto di studio: la blockchain. Illustriamo come il protocollo bitcoin sia stato utilizzato per rappresentare altri investimenti di capitale e come sia stato creato il concetto dei registri distribuiti per rispettare i vincoli dei principali player industriali e finanziari.

La quarta parte descrive le modalità di socializzazione della blockchain, ovvero come interagisce con strutture sociali e altro. Abbiamo preso in considerazione due modelli di socializzazione: un modello esogeno, fondato sugli sviluppi terminologici e le strategie di standardizzazione, e un modello endogeno, che per favorire l'assimilazione nelle strutture sociali si integra nella tecnologia attraverso forme di finanziamento, regole di distribuzione della capacità di scissione[140] e meccanismi di incentivazione.

L'ultima parte spiega in che forma la blockchain è presente oggi nella coscienza collettiva e come sta modificando il modo di affrontare determinati problemi. Definiamo questo movimento «designing through the blockchain». Spieghiamo il fenomeno analizzando la nascita di un vero e proprio ramo industriale intorno alla blockchain. Successivamente passiamo a esaminare come le tecniche di regolamentazione e il riconoscimento dell'identità stiano subendo una trasformazione concettuale e formale.

Le conclusioni del rapporto aprono la discussione sulle relazioni emergenti tra blockchain e pubblica amministrazione. Mostrano come la blockchain descriva situazioni in cui la giurisprudenza nazionale si scontra necessariamente con i

---

[140] Una scissione (fork) avviene quando gli sviluppatori prendono una copia del codice sorgente da un software e iniziano a svilupparlo in modo indipendente, creando un progetto nuovo e separato.

propri limiti e incoraggiano la riflessione sulle nuove forme di standardizzazione rappresentate dal diritto globale. Affrontano infine la questione delle modalità democratiche per gestire le informazioni nello spazio pubblico.

8. Blockchain as a Historical Construct

From the earliest days of computing, questions regarding the sharing, reliability, auditability, and confidentiality of information have been treated as strategic issues by governments, businesses, and universities. Between 1950 and the 2000s, buoyed by military, academic, and industrial research, taking place mostly in the United States, these questions led to major technical advances as well as to the commercialisation of computing. Blockchain forms part of this historical continuum in terms of both technology and culture.

In this chapter we demonstrate that blockchain is a historical construct. Technically speaking, it comprises a series of concepts that were developed over the course of the history of computing. Here, we present the chronological evolution of the reasoning behind blockchain as well as the achievements that led to its consolidation. We explore in particular the ways in which the essential technical underpinnings of blockchain, namely, distributed cryptography and distributed systems, were developed and tested, and how they subsequently matured. We also explain the origins of certain practices, rules, incentives, and behaviours that shaped the field. The challenge we set ourselves is to bring together the initial elements of an analytical framework for the field.

8.1. Cryptography and decentralised networks in the post-war period

Cryptography is the art of protecting communications against disclosure using keys or secrecy. Its use was an important facet of the Enigma project during the Second World War. At the end of the war the armed forces retained secrecy around the project, considering it to be a strategically important asset. Confidential research was conducted for the national intelligence agencies NSA and GCHQ to develop information encryption systems capable of preserving the confidentiality of electronic communications. In 1945, while conducting research at Bell Industrial Laboratories, Claude Shannon wrote a paper entitled *A Mathematical Theory of Cryptography*, which was classified as secret by the US government. He also addressed the issue of signal transmission in his renowned work on the mathematical theory of communication. In 1949, Shannon published another paper entitled *Communication Theory of Secrecy Systems*. There he laid the foundations for modern cryptography, approaching the field from the perspective of information theory for the first time. Also of interest is Horst Feistel's research on encryption algorithms, which he completed while working at IBM.

The problems associated with decentralising computer networks were first addressed during the Cold War, notably with the development of ARPANET in 1968. It is generally understood that, for reasons of security, the US military authorities and their affiliated university researchers designed a large network enabling computers from a large number of universities as well as the research centres with which DARPA worked, to communicate with each other. Technical and economic considerations led them to develop a non-centralised network model consisting of interconnected nodes. In this model, routers served as gateways to transfer information between computers using the telephone network. Some claim that Arpanet's decentralised structure was intended to standardise connection techniques, while others argue that it was designed to maintain the reliability of a network even when part of it was damaged or destroyed.

In the early 1970s, the Network Working Group, an informal university group which was to define ARPANET's peer-to-peer communication protocols, developed the email system and the TCP/IP suite of protocols (Transmission Control Protocol and Internet Protocol), in order to transfer information securely between different computers connected over a network. The increasing availability of personal computers and microcomputing (e.g., the Hewlett-Packard 9100A and the Apple II) for businesses and the general public opened up the possibility of networking on a massive scale, a theme that was explored by the Xerox Palo Alto Research Center.

8.2. Consequences of the growth of electronic communications

The National Bureau of Standards, an agency of the United States Department of Commerce, went on to employ Horst Feistel's research at IBM and to adopt the Data Encryption Standard (DES) as the standard for the corporate world. This is a symmetric-key algorithm in which a single 56-bit key is used to encrypt and decrypt messages. In response to this approach, Whitfield Diffie and Martin Hellman of the University of Berkeley wrote the foundational paper 'New Directions in Cryptography' in conjunction with Ralph Merkel. In this paper, the authors develop the concept of asymmetric cryptography. It is this encryption method, which differentiates between public keys and private keys, that is used to encrypt and decrypt transactions in a blockchain.

The significant success of this article within the scientific community paved the way for many other works to be published in specialised journals such as ACM and IEEE Journals. In 1978, a paper written by Ronald Rivest, Adi Shamir, and Leonard Adleman at MIT modelled an application for asymmetric cryptography using an encryption algorithm called RSA. At around the same time Usenet, the first network of forums organised into discussion groups, was connected to ARPANET. With the rapid expansion of electronic communications, researchers began to commercialise their work and file patents, including Diffie-Hellman for key exchange and RSA encryption.

Conscious of the ever-increasing number of emails being sent across the Arpanet network, researchers Zaw-Sing and Paul Mockapetris of the University of Southern California set out the entire concept for the implementation of a Domain Name System (DNS) in a series of classified reports for DARPA. The architecture they designed involved a database in which information was fragmented into small calculation units and then distributed over several computers connected to each other through the Arpanet network.

At that time, university research in the field of communications focused mainly on issues specific to communications networks. At the University of Berkeley, Leslie Lamport's work on the resilience of networks with failed nodes and ways of addressing problems that arose led him to come up with his much-quoted metaphor of the Byzantine generals[141]. One of the inventors of asymmetric cryptography, Ralph Merkle, was working on a digital signature scheme. He created cryptographic hashing and hash tree functions to digitally fingerprint digital objects so they could be identified. This is the same method that is used to structure information storage in a blockchain.

[141] In computer science, the problem of the Byzantine generals is a metaphor that deals with the questioning of the reliability of transmissions and the integrity of interlocutors.

8.3. Designing privacy

In the wake of the commercialisation of cryptography and the expansion of the ARPANET computer network, cryptology began to be recognised as a scientific domain in its own right. In 1982, the International Association for Cryptologic Research at the University of California, Santa Barbara, organised the Annual International Cryptology Conference, one of the largest international conferences in the field. At the same university, David Chaum was in the process of modelling a network communications system in which messages were anonymised through blind signatures and the links between their sources and destinations obscured (known as mix networks).

Chaum was especially interested in privacy and the accessibility of the personal information used in electronic financial transactions. In an attempt to guarantee the confidentiality of financial transactions, he designed and produced a cryptographic system in which neither banks nor governments would be able to trace personal payments made online. This model led to the creation of the eCash project, one of the first attempts to launch a cryptographic electronic currency on the international markets.

The question of the rights and the level of control that producers of information have over their productions is also at the heart of the creation of free software rights. While working at the Artificial Intelligence Laboratory at MIT in 1983, Richard Stallman launched the GNU project. Its aim was to develop an operating system that could guarantee certain rights for its users. He announced the project on the Usenet forum and invited others to take part in its development.

In order to enable people to make voluntary contributions to GNU, Stallman asked lawyer Eben Moglen to formulate a legal text that would standardise the extension of intellectual property rights. In 1989, he published the first version of the General Public Licence (GPL), which established new legal conditions for the freedom to operate, study, modify, and distribute software. This licence forms the legal basis for the distribution of most blockchains.

8.4. Consequences of public access to the global computer network

As the ARPANET project came to a close at the beginning of the 1990s, it ushered in public access to the global computer network through the internet. At CERN in Geneva, Tim Berners Lee launched the HyperText Transfer Protocol (HTTP) build on top of TCP/IP. This protocol would lead to the development of a user-friendly World Wide Web browser capable of providing access to different types of resources via a single interface. The authentication and encryption protocol used to protect payments made over the internet, Secure Sockets Layer (SSL), was developed by the same company that produced the Netscape Navigator browser. The SSL protocol was based on the RSA encryption algorithm. The Internet Engineering Task Force (IETF) went on to add to the development of SSL by creating the Transport Layer Security (TLS) protocol.

Numerous new projects inspired by DNS architecture, including Seti@home and Folding@home, tested the viability of distributed computing. The results showed that a data analysis process that would require a large amount of computing time for a single computer could be done by distributing or sharing the work between a large community of computers connected to each other through the internet.

'Strong' cryptography was still a classified research area. In a form of 'crypto-war', the US government tried to restrict access to cryptographic methods by both the public and other nations. Concerns about the control of communications systems by state bodies were widespread amongst US academics and computer-industry players such as Intel and Sun. The debate centred around the export of encryption technologies, in particular the RSA algorithm used in SSL, which was heavily regulated at the time.

A form of information activism was beginning to emerge. Philippe Zimmerman designed the PGP ('Pretty Good Privacy') encryption software and distributed it under the GNU GPL licence (General Public Licence) in order to ensure public access. Personalities such as Tim May, Eric Hughes, and John Perry Barlow published texts such as *A Declaration of the Independence of Cyberspace*, which contained strong political messages regarding the need for information independence. Regular meetings were held at Stanford, the cypherpunk collective was established, and global discussion lists were created (cypherpunks-request@toad.com). The Electronic Frontier Foundation was set up as a lobbying force to defend the right to information privacy. Between 1996 and 2000, under the Clinton administration, US regulations on the use of cryptography were relaxed and then virtually abolished.

At Bellcorp's Bell Laboratories, cryptographers Stuart Haber and Scott Stronetta were developing a method for timestamping digital documents. The challenge was to date the creation and modification of documents with complete accuracy. The method was supplemented by a digital signature scheme that could guarantee the integrity of an electronic document and authenticate its author. Haber and Stronetta then set up their own timestamping company, Surety, using the AbsoluteProof software, which continues to provide cryptographic sealing for digital documents. Every week since 1995, Surety has published all of its new seals in a single signature in the 'Notices & Lost and Found' section of the daily issue of *The New York Times*. The same method is used to protect author rights in blockchains by creating proof of precedence.

In 1994, lawyer and computer scientist Nick Szabo began to publish a series of papers about the concept of the Smart Contract. Szabo had worked with David Chaum as a consultant on the eCash cryptographic electronic currency project. His experience in the field led him to develop ways of adapting specific commercial and contractual practices to electronic commerce between individuals over the internet. His premise was that many types of contractual clause, such as privileges, guarantees, and ownership rights, could be converted into code and executed automatically.

Nick Szabo conceptualised the computer protocols that would enable several parties to a contract to observe its execution, check that the agreed conditions had been met, disclose only those details necessary for the execution, and, finally, reduce their costs by automatically implementing the contract once all the criteria had been met. To illustrate his concept, Szabo compared the operation of smart contracts with that of vending machines that dispense a beverage when the exact amount has been fed into the machine. Once the parameters have been initiated, the smart contract runs automatically, regardless of external events such as one of the parties changing their mind.

Cithy Dwork and Moy Naor of the IBM research division in San Jose published a paper in the review of the Annual International Cryptology Conference which presented a method for fighting spam and other undesired electronic communications by asking the sender of the email to provide proof that a certain algorithm had been executed. This is called 'proof-of-work' and is based on the idea that some form of cost should be incurred for the use of free online services such as email. Inspired by their work, Adam Back posted a solution on the Cypherpunk mailing list which could fight spam more effectively – a proof-of-work system he called Hashcash.

In 1989, David Chaum exploited the eCash patent through a company called Digicash. In 1994 he introduced Digicash at the first international World Wide Web conference in Geneva, in a talk entitled 'World's First Electronic Cash Payment Over Computer Networks'. With the aid of financial players such as Credit Suisse, Deutsche Bank, and the Mark Twain Bank, Chaum was able to experiment further with his new centralised cryptographic money system. Digicash filed for bankruptcy in 1998. Chaum put this down to the fact that his system had entered the market before e-commerce had fully taken root on the internet.

Others would go on to design decentralised currency systems without implementing them. These included Nick Szabo's BitGold, which incorporated digital signatures, timestamping, and proof-of-work. We can also cite Wei Dai's B-money, which he described as 'a scheme for a group of untraceable digital pseudonyms to pay each other with money and to enforce contracts amongst themselves without outside help'.

In the early 2000s, against a backdrop of increasing internet speeds and a proliferation of access providers, computers and peripherals, cryptography was fully declassified by Al Gore. Audio file-sharing sites began to emerge, especially for music files. Napster enabled its users to share music files in MP3 format by making a list of files available on a server that could be searched and downloaded by anyone. Only the downloading of files was decentralised. In March 2000, the Gnutella protocol was created to allow objects to be searched and retrieved without a central server.

Napster and Gnutella paved the way for further upheavals in the cultural sector. Audio, video, and literary file-sharing services using completely decentralised peer-to-peer systems, like Soulseek, LimeWire, SETI, Bitorrent, and Tor took off. Media production and distribution companies filed a plethora of copyright violation suits. These early services were important driving forces in the evolution of peer-to-peer systems.

9. The Design and Implementation of the Bitcoin Protocol

In the previous chapter, we examined the historical, social, and cultural contexts of blockchain. In the second section we look at the creation and proliferation of Bitcoin as the first large-scale application of blockchain technology. We also explore how the advent of the Bitcoin project resulted in the development of blockchain technology as a coherent technical system.

The influence of Bitcoin on the blockchain domain was not limited to the technical characteristics of its protocol. Its development methods, distribution policy, and communication channels are the patterns that allowed blockchain technology to begin to enter the collective imagination. By retracing the timeline of the Bitcoin project, by focusing on the ways in which it was developed, implemented, published and transferred to the public domain, we introduce the constituent elements of blockchain and consolidate the framework of its analysis as a social phenomenon.

9.1. The publicising of the Bitcoin project

In August 2008, the bitcoin.org domain name was registered on anonymous-speech.com, a website that allows domain names to be registered anonymously. On 31 October 2008, an unknown entity using the pseudonym Satoshi Nakamoto published a message entitled 'Bitcoin P2P e-cash paper' on the metzdowd.com cryptography-themed mailing list. He announced that he was working on a new, purely peer-to-peer electronic payment protocol without the need for a trusted third party. In presenting the main features of the protocol, he used the key concepts of Hashcash proof-of-work and peer-to-peer networking. His protocol aimed to avoid 'double spending', the simultaneous double use of any information object, in this case money.

The author referred to a document that was available for download at http://www.bitcoin.org/bitcoin.pdf called *Bitcoin: A Peer-to-Peer Electronic Cash System*. The document was precise and concise, and it observed the formal structure and norms of a scientific publication. It posed the question of how to do away with all forms of trusted third party, whether financial and governmental institutions or centralised servers, in the context of electronic financial transactions.

The demonstration covered 9 pages and was divided into 11 sections with alternating text, diagrams, models and formulae outlining the technical details of the proposal. The bibliography was succinct, citing Wei Dai's B-money project, the work of Haber and Stronetta, and Ralph Merkle's Hashing functions. Despite the conventional format of his paper, the author did not mention affiliation with any organisation and only provided a URL and an email address. Other researchers associated with cypherpunk, such as Adam Back in 2002, had presented their research in a similar way.

On 1 November 2008 version 0.1.5 of the Bitcoin software was made available for download on Bitcoin.org.

Two days after the publication of the paper on the prototype Bitcoin software on the Cypherpunk mailing list, initial exchanges began between fewer than a dozen respondents. Some of the names, such as James A. Donald, were probably pseudonyms, but most respondents revealed their real names. They were cryptographers, experts in artificial intelligence and security like Ray Dillinger, PGP developers like Hal Finney, and specialists in messaging infrastructure like John R. Levine.

Some had long been working on the issue of electronic transaction protocols: Hal Finney had published on the so-called reusable proofs-of-work system, RPOW, in 2004. Having studied, prototyped, and tested recent developments in the field such as E-gold, B-money and DigiCash, all remained sceptical as to the technical feasibility of the code. The social feasibility of the project also seemed dubious, since all previous experiments had led either to commercial failure, as in the case of DigiCash, or court action and imprisonment, as in the case of E-gold. The article was researched in the manner of a specialist academic text aimed at advancing knowledge and awareness of the subject.

Members of the list began to send emails to each other. Satoshi Nakamoto answered many questions and asked others. All the possible issues surrounding the protocol were probed: scalability, privacy, legality, information storage methods, bandwidth requirements, potential responses from government institutions, etc. The interlocutors asked for more formal descriptions, proposed improvements and put forward hypotheses. The discussion not only verified the feasibility of the technical protocol, it anticipated the social phenomenon that it would engender (Figure 41).

Bitcoin P2P e-cash paper

Satoshi Nakamoto satoshi at vistomail.com
Thu Nov 6 15:15:40 EST 2008

- Previous message: IBM Zurich Research Laboratory Internet Transaction Security on Your Key Chain
- Next message: ADMIN: no money politics, please
- **Messages sorted by:** [date] [thread] [subject] [author]

```
>[Lengthy exposition of vulnerability of a systm to use-of-force
>monopolies ellided.]
>
>You will not find a solution to political problems in cryptography.

Yes, but we can win a major battle in the arms race and gain a new territory of freedom for
several years.

Governments are good at cutting off the heads of a centrally controlled networks like
Napster, but pure P2P networks like Gnutella and Tor seem to be holding their own.

Satoshi


---------------------------------------------------------------------
The Cryptography Mailing List
Unsubscribe by sending "unsubscribe cryptography" to majordomo at metzdowd.com
```

Figure 41. Screenshot of a message from Satoshi Nakamoto on 6 November 2018.

9.2. The collective design process of the Bitcoin protocol

While these discussions were taking place, the Bitcoin project was registered on SourceForge.net, a collaborative platform for free open-source software development and distribution. Version 0.1.5 served as the basis for further work by the participants. Ray Dillinger checked the code and Hal Finney performed a security audit. The first time-stamped block, today often called 'block 0' or 'Genesis block', was created on 3 January 2009 at 18:15:05 GMT'. It contained 50 Bitcoins awaiting transaction. This was the formal basis for the transaction chain in the Bitcoin protocol.

Next to the usual information present in the first block, Satoshi Nakamoto entered the following text: 'The Times 03/Jan/2009 Chancellor on brink of second bailout for banks'. The text was a headline in the 3 January 2009 issue of the British newspaper *The Times*. The article reported on how the efforts of the British government to stimulate the economy after the 2008 financial crisis had failed. Inscribed into the very backbone of Bitcoin, this message was a statement of intent.

On 9 January 2009, the first alpha version of the Bitcoin code was released on SourceForge (version 0.1.0). The code was distributed under the MIT/X11 licence, which is compatible with the GPL (General Public Licence). This implied that the authors of the protocol agreed that any person receiving the code had unlimited rights to use, copy, modify, merge, publish, distribute, and sell it as well as to change its licence. The only obligation was that the initial conditions of the MIT license had to be included. On 12 January 2009, Hal Finney made an announcement on the metzdowd.com mailing list. He set out the main requirements (e.g., the number of Bitcoins) and addressed the risk that Bitcoin might be of interest to no one as it had no intrinsic value.

On 13 January 2009, a test transaction took place between Satoshi Nakamoto and Hal Finney. The amount transacted was 10 Bitcoins.

After its initial publication, the code became stable and Hal Finney stopped working on the project. Several technical discussions took place on the metzdowd.com mailing list. In one of the messages, John Gilmore of the Electronic Frontier Foundation raised questions about the consequences of such a system for the environment.

On 11 February, Satoshi Nakamoto presented Bitcoin at the Peer to Peer Foundation Forum. Some interlocutors compared it to the OpenCoin project, a free-license version of the electronic money system invented by David Chaum. Satoshi Nakamoto explained how many people viewed electronic money as a lost cause, since all companies involved in the field since the 1980s had gone bankrupt. Using the example of David Chaum's eCash ('the old Chaumian central mint stuff'), he theorised that it was the centralised nature of these systems which had sealed their fate. Nakamoto presented Bitcoin as a distributed global database to which additions could be made with the consent of the majority based on a set of rules to be followed by everyone.

In August 2009, a Finnish developer, Martti Malmi, put forward the first modifications to the code published in SourceForge. In October 2009, Bitcoin's first trading website was registered under the name New Liberty Standard. Using an equation that calculated the cost of the electricity required to run a computer generating Bitcoin, the website established its value at USD 1 = BTC 1309.03. Martti Malmi was the first person to convert Bitcoin into US Dollars. He sent 5050 Bitcoins to New Liberty Standard and received USD 5.02 via PayPal in return.

Thanks to an increasing number of contributions to the Bitcoin project through SourceForge (mainly by Satoshi Nakamoto, Martti Malmi, and Gavin Andresen, a developer based in Massachusetts), version 2.0 was eventually released, followed by version 3.0.

9.3. Community ownership of the Bitcoin project

New chat channels appeared dealing specifically with the subject, including the forum BitcoinTalk and the #bitcoin-dev channel on the Freenode IRC network. Magazine articles were written, and test purchases of actual items were made. The announcement of the release of v3.0 of Bitcoin on the Slashdot news website attracted the attention of a wider audience of developers.

In January 2011, the Electronic Frontier Foundation website introduced Bitcoin in an article entitled *Bitcoin – A Step Toward Censorship-Resistant Digital Currency*. At the end of the article, the Foundation announced that it would henceforth accept donations in Bitcoin. The next month, the SilkRoad website came into existence, selling all manner of illicit products. Items could only be purchased using Bitcoin.

In December 2010, as a result of the controversial revelations it disseminated, the Wikileaks organisation was subjected to a 'financial blockade' by VISA, MasterCard, Bank of America, PayPal, and Western Union. An article was published in PCWorld magazine with the title *Could the Wikileaks Scandal Lead to New Virtual Currency?* On the bitcointalk forum, Satoshi Nakamota was trying to temper the enthusiasm of the participants regarding this issue. According to him, Bitcoin was still only at the beta testing stage and could not be scaled up too quickly. He also expressed concern on chat pages about the close interest government institutions were showing in Bitcoin.

In June 2010, Wikileaks announced in a tweet that it would be accepting anonymous donations in Bitcoin. During the same period, and citing doubts about the legal aspects of Bitcoin, the Electronic Frontier Foundation decided to stop accepting donations in the cryptocurrency. In October 2011, Joshua Davis published a long article in *The New Yorker* describing the thorough investigation he had conducted into who was actually behind the pseudonym of Satoshi Nakamoto.

This publicity generated rapid growth in the number of transactions, and consequently the number of contributors. Citing problems accessing SourceForge from countries sanctioned by the US Office of Foreign Assets Control, such as Cuba and Iran, the community decided to migrate the project to another, similar type of platform: GitHub. As the Bitcoin protocol was licensed under MIT, it could be forked, i.e., be split and a new protocol created from the existing code. As a result, many other electronic currencies based on Bitcoin's protocol began to emerge, such as Netcoin, Litecoin, Ixcoin, Diskcoin, Bandwidth, and Cyclecoin, which were then themselves forked. An example of a fork path would be: Bitcoin → Litecoin → Junkcoin → Lukycoin → Dogecoin. Most of these currencies had a very limited lifespan.

Bitcoin Magazine was created by Vitalik Buterin, of Russian origin, and Mihai Alisie, from Romania. Bitcoin smartphone payment services such as Bitpays appeared, and conferences on the subject were held in locations including New York, Prague, and London. In January 2012, Bitcoin was featured as the main plotline of the third episode of CBS's TV series 'The Good Wife'. The episode was called 'Bitcoin for Dummies'.

The high levels of media attention resulted in an explosion in the number of Bitcoin transactions and the number of people contributing to the project. The value of Bitcoin was rising, and a number of trading platforms began to appear. In 2012, the CoinBase platform enabled people to buy and sell Bitcoin over the Internet by bank transfer. The Bitcoin Foundation was created in September 2012. The challenges it faced were twofold: to restore confidence in the system after its reputation had been tainted by perceived association with fraud and crime; and to accelerate the global growth of Bitcoin through the regulation and protection of cryptocurrencies and by promoting the Bitcoin protocol. Openly based on the models of non-profit organisations such as the Linux Foundation, the Bitcoin Foundation was mainly funded by donations from for-profit corporations like Mt Gox, Bitinstant, and CoinLab, whose business relied on the ongoing stability and maintenance of the Bitcoin code and its publication under a free licence.

10. Blockchain as a Distributed Ledger Technology

We have seen how the field expanded considerably as the Bitcoin project progressed. The emergence of new applications as well as changes and extensions to the code led to the objectification of Bitcoin's conceptual structure. Attention gradually shifted away from the Bitcoin project as a whole and towards one of the technical concepts underpinning it: blockchain.

This chapter explains how the success of Bitcoin actually led to the objectification of blockchain technology, when the technical concept that permitted the operation and administration of Bitcoin became an object of study in itself. We then examine how the concept became relevant to the handling of all types of transactions. Lastly, we look at the ways in which industrial sectors have tried to adapt the concept to their requirements by integrating other conceptual and semantic changes – from blockchain to distributed ledgers.

10.1. Other applications of the Bitcoin protocol

Namecoin was the first project to use the Bitcoin protocol for a type of asset other than money. In 2010, a discussion took place on the #bitcoin-dev IRC channel regarding the possibility of using the Bitcoin protocol to create a DNS system for generating domain names that could circumvent the risk of the Bitcoin domain being censored, as Wikileaks had been. The Namecoin code base consists of the Bitcoin code base with some relatively minor changes and a few additional features. In 2012, the American engineer J.R. Willett was seeking ways of promoting greater acceptance of Bitcoin by the general public. Rejecting the idea of creating a new cryptocurrency to compete with Bitcoin, he designed a new feature within the Bitcoin protocol intended to serve as a base on which everyone could build their own currencies. Mastercoin software (today OmniLayer), which implements this new feature, provides the tools required to design and publish proprietary currencies with their own rules by configuring a new token. The idea of layering other software on top of Bitcoin arose from the custom of stacking protocols (for example, the HTTP protocol is stacked on top of TCP/IP).

The concept of adding new layers to the Bitcoin protocol was then tested for other applications. The challenge was to find ways of using the Bitcoin protocol to represent other assets. These included personalised currencies and financial products like Colourcoin, property ownership (Smartproperty), and even contractual relationships for executing clauses (Smartcontract) and the management of organisations (DAOs). In 2013 the Colourcoin project published its prospectus and described the situation in the following terms:

"The natural question is: is it possible to use the same functionality for other applications as well? The answer, it turns out, is yes. The fundamental innovation behind Bitcoin, that of using cryptographic proof-of-work to maintain a secure distributed database, is good for more than just the single limited-supply currency originally envisioned by Satoshi Nakamoto in 2009; exactly the same technology can be used to maintain ownership of company shares, 'smart property', alternative currencies, bank deposits and much more. Anything which is representable as a digital asset, and a 'rivalrous good', meaning that only one person can own it at a time, is potentially fair game for representation in the Bitcoin blockchain."

10.2. The objectification of blockchain

In 2014, Vitalik Butarin, one of the authors of whitepapers for Colored Coins, finalised the conceptualisation of Ethereum: a new platform that used a more generalised scripting language than Bitcoin and intended to facilitate decentralised application development.

Ethereum borrows most of Bitcoin's design concepts but operates on its own network with its own protocol. It also has its own cryptocurrency, called Ether. Ethereum implements the smart-contract concept invented by Nick Szabo. In this context, however, the term 'smart-contract' is somewhat of a misnomer. It is actually a type of computer programme. Network users can run the programme whenever they want as long as they pay the costs of executing it. It can perform a variety of procedures, such as notarial and financial contracts, equipment rental, or equity sharing. The results, whether movement of Ethers or information storage are held in a type of distributed database: a blockchain.

The blockchain is considered here to be a type of administrative ledger that is not managed from a single point but is distributed over the network. Despite this distributed architecture, the ledger establishes and maintains the uniqueness of an asset, or any piece of information for that matter. It establishes an inviolable link between an object and its identifier. For example, it guarantees that a Bitcoin has not been spent twice (the problem known as double spending), or that a property asset or contract has not been forged or registered twice. It is this technical characteristic that attracted the attention of major industrial and financial players and resulted in services being developed to meet the needs of specific industrial sectors and groups.

For example, Ripple is a settlement infrastructure system that enables payments to be sent and received without an intermediary, regardless of their value or the financial institution. The project relies on a database that records all the information from all Ripple accounts. Financial transactions are verified, validated and compared in a closed network of servers that can belong to anyone, including banks and market players.

Another example is the Hyperledger project, a blockchain development platform created in 2015. Hosted by the Linux Foundation, Hyperledger was founded by major industry players such as IBM, Intel, Cisco Accenture, and J.P. Morgan. Hyperledger aims to improve the performance and reliability of blockchains and distributed ledger techniques to enable them to handle global business transactions for leading technology, finance, and supply-chain companies. The platform combines a number of development structures (frameworks) and tools to explore the capabilities of distributed ledger techniques when faced with a wide variety of problems, such as those of supply chains and digital identities. The goal of Hyperledger is to enable large industrial companies to create blockchains that guarantee the confidentiality of certain types of information. The Fabric project was one of the first Hyperledger projects: a protocol for the deployment and exploitation of permissioned blockchains. Like all Hyperledger projects, Fabric is hosted by the Linux Foundation. Members must abide by a code of conduct, and the protocol is shared under a free open-source licence (an Apache 2 licence, which is GPL-compatible).

10.3. The emergence of permissioned distributed ledger techniques

In the Bitcoin and Ethereum blockchains, anyone can join the network. This means that anyone can read and write transactions and take part in validating them; the blockchain is considered to be public. In 2015, developments began that sought to create distinctions between public, private and consortium blockchains.

In 2015, the family office R3 CEV (Crypto Consulting Exchanges Ventures), chaired by David E. Rutter, a former Wall Street executive, organised a number of roundtables for those working specifically on blockchain projects such as Ripple, the beginnings of the Hyperledger project as well as other major public and private players in the banking industry like the Bank of England and Bank of America. These roundtables were intended to examine the transformation of the finance sector by cryptocurrencies. One of the issues discussed was how banks could trade foreign currencies on community-managed ledgers, as in a blockchain.

Following the roundtable discussions, R3 published an article summarising the lessons learned: *Consensus-as-a-Service: A Brief Report on the Emergence Of Permissioned, Distributed Ledger Systems*. The article raised the issue of permissions, i.e., the ways in which transactions are validated, differentiating between Bitcoin and distributed ledgers. For the author, distributed ledger models like Hyperledger and Ripple solved some of the problems associated with Bitcoin and Ethereum in that the information was managed by an identified community and authenticated using a permission system. The author, Tim Swanson, concluded that this capacity enabled the various distributed ledgers to be interoperable.

The article laid the foundations for differentiating between permissioned and permissionless blockchains, and also examined the use of private blockchains (Table 12). Unlike Ethereum and Bitcoin, so-called closed blockchains are forms of centralised ledgers, the decision-making powers for which are centralised within a single organisation. They can be used to test new techniques and increase expertise in this area. A consortium blockchain is a closed network that is partially decentralised and requires permission from members to join it. The power to audit it can be reserved for members and decisions regarding it are taken by this closed community. This aspect of permissioned blockchains serves to keep certain information confidential. The model is intended to prevent inappropriate sharing of customer information in that not all transactions can be shared with all network participants.

Table 12. Permissioned and permissionless public and private blockchains.

	Permissionless (no restrictions for validators)	Permissioned (transaction validation is limited to specific users)
Public (No restrictions on reading blockchain data)	All users can read transactions All users can validate transactions	All users can read transactions Only certain users can validate transactions
Private (Direct access to blockchain data is limited to specific users)	Transactions can only be read by selected users All users can validate transactions	Transactions can only be read by selected users Among these users, only those with specific permissions can validate transactions

R3 sent this paper to the banks with which it regularly worked, garnering a good deal of attention. In 2015, R3 and nine major financial players (Barclays, Commonwealth Bank of Australia, Credit Suisse, Goldman Sachs, J.P. Morgan, Royal Bank of Scotland, State Street, and UBS) founded an interbank consortium called the Distributed Ledger Group (later to take on the name R3). Between 2015 and 2018, nearly 200 major players in industry and finance joined the consortium. They included Bank of America, Thomsons Reuters, Société Générale, UniCredit, BNP Paribas, Toyota Financial Services, and the Bank of Canada.

The intention of this consortium was to create a framework, based on the Hyperledger model, for the development of distributed consortium ledgers in order to share information between companies in the banking sector. In 2016, the consortium announced the Corda software project, designed to record, execute, and manage the financial arrangements of companies within a community of financial institutions. The platform was also intended to be used to launch financial applications for a number of markets, including foreign exchange and loans.

In 2016, the consortium announced that the source code for the Corda software was to be shared under the same licence as that of the Hyperledger projects: Apache 2.0. The use of this license demonstrated the formal rapprochement between the two projects, with Corda becoming a Hyperledger project, though remaining distinct.

Some members left the consortium to develop their own networks. In 2017, J.P. Morgan left the Hyperledger and Corda consortiums to develop Quorum, which was presented as a 'permissioned implementation of Ethereum supporting data privacy'. Quorum might be called a hybrid blockchain, in that it combines several characteristics of public and private blockchains. Like Ethereum, Quorum is shared on Github and under a free GPL (General Public Licence). Quorum determines which information should remain private and which information can be made public. Instead of transactions being shared privately within a consortium, they could now be displayed in other blockchains, such as Bitcoin. This feature enabled companies to use a number of ledgers and to selectively share information in the course of their business operations.

10.4. Other distributed ledger techniques

A dissection of the issue of distributed ledgers reveals that blockchain is not the only technique that can be used. The majority of distributed ledger implementations, like Bitcoin and Ethereum, are based on a blockchain, whether closed or consortium, such as Hyperledger or Corda, but other techniques have also been explored. The differences can include the ways in which transactions are stored in the ledgers, or the transaction validation rules themselves.

For example, the Internet of Things Application (IOTA) is a distributed ledger that is not based on a blockchain, but on an open-source experimental protocol known as The Tangle. IOTA aims to provide a secure payment method for transactions between different devices connected via the Internet (the Internet of Things). It is designed to process micropayments and payments between devices, creating an entire machine-to-machine micro-economy. The very large number of possible transactions between connected objects in the IOTA project requires a highly scalable architecture, which is difficult for blockchains to achieve.

Other experiments exist, such as the Hashgraph, another patented distributed ledger technique. Hashgraph is based on consensus and information-sharing techniques that differ from blockchain: the so-called 'Gossip about Gossip' technique. Hashgraph uses information-sharing and polling techniques that demand network participants share all their information, meaning that all participants are aware of all the information that has been created since the outset.

11. Blockchain Socialisation Patterns

In the next section we explore how blockchain came to be a social phenomenon. The challenge lies in getting past the deterministic attitude that the trajectory of blockchain was purely one of a technological innovation that was welcomed, grew, and proliferated organically – and then impacted people, collectives, companies, enterprises, and social institutions rather than also being shaped and impacted by them.

We describe how blockchain interacts with people and social structures, using what has been termed the socialisation patterns to determine how blockchain is incorporated into pre-existing structures. We observe and study two versions of this model: an exogenous model, which remains distinct from technology and describes how society attempts to adapt it; and an endogenous model, which is integrated into technology in order to describe its assimilation into social structures.

11.1. Exogenous socialisation patterns

We begin by looking at the exogenous model of the socialisation of blockchain. This refers to motion from outside the blockchain towards the inside. This model can help to explain how people and social structures incorporate blockchain through language and normalisation.

The evolution of terminology

The development of the language used around blockchain is an important aspect of the socialisation process, enabling people to develop an abstract representation of the technology. The Bitcoin protocol and its operation based on blockchain technology resulted in new terms coming into usage, such as crypto-assets and distributed ledgers. The proliferation of cryptographic currencies transacted over decentralised networks led to a differentiation between these types of assets and other state-issued or local currencies. The specific terms cryptocurrencies or cryptoassets were assigned to them. Similarly, the term Distributed Ledger Technology (DLT) was formulated to explain the technical concept of blockchain as well as to take it further.

These terminological changes follow on from the growth and popularisation of scientific knowledge on the subject as well as from the popularisation of the field as a whole. In the original document by Satoshi Nakamoto, the term 'blockchain' does not appear; instead, the author uses the term 'distributed timestamp server'. Hal Finney first used the term blockchain to refer to Bitcoin's timestamping system during initial discussions on the Metzdowd mailing list. In the years that followed, some scientific papers presented blockchain as a distributed database technology, while others referred to it as a general ledger, a decentralised ledger, or a shared ledger. The term distributed ledger took hold in 2015, though it had barely been used before that date (Figure 42).

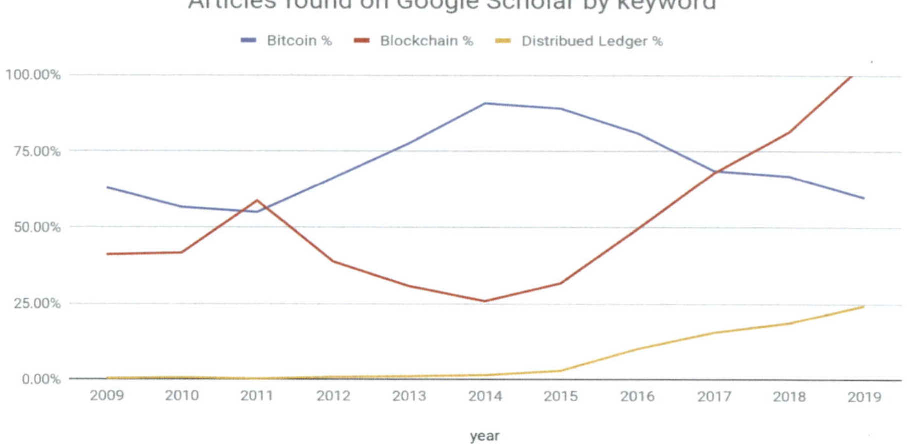

Figure 42. Articles found on Google Scholar by keyword. The total may exceed 100% as multiple keywords can be used in an article.

This increase in usage was prompted in particular by reflections on the use of permissions in the various blockchains. In 2015, a paper on permissioned blockchains by R3 drew a clear distinction between a blockchain and a distributed ledger. It explained that blockchains, such as Bitcoin, are public. To differentiate between consortium blockchains and public blockchains, the author uses the term Distributed Ledger. In 2016, Richard Brown, Head of Technology at R3, published a whitepaper on the Corda software entitled *Corda: A Distributed Ledger for Recording and Managing Financial Agreements.* In this document the author argued that public blockchain architectures such as Bitcoin and Ethereum did not fulfil the information-sharing requirements of various legal agreements used by major industries, nor did they respond adequately to other challenges these players faced. According to the author, a blockchain that was not public was not a blockchain. Expanding on Tim Watson's paper, Consensus-as-a-service, the author presented Corda, and all other private and consortium blockchains, as distributed ledger technologies. Blockchain was to be defined as a public distributed ledger.

As a result of this distinction, intended to address the needs of large corporations, in 2016 the Chief Scientific Adviser to the UK Government, Sir Mark Walport, published a government report entitled *Distributed Ledger Technology: Beyond Blockchain.* In 2017, the World Bank published *Distributed Ledger Technology (DLT) and Blockchain*.

A study of the usage of these terms on the Reddit.com community website, however, reveals that the term 'distributed ledger' is currently only marginally used in comparison with the term blockchain (Figure 43). This is also the case in academic scientific publications (Figure 44). A peak in the usage of both terms occurred in September 2018, in keeping with intense media coverage of the subject during this period. To interpret the subsequent drop as the result of a sense of fatigue around blockchain would seem to be exaggerated. It appears rather that usage of these terms was becoming diluted by the proliferation of other terms. In the remainder of this report we continue to use the term blockchain.

Figure 43. Number of posts on Reddit.com from 2014 to 2019.

Figure 44. Number of scientific articles found on the Web of Science bibliographic databases (https://clarivate.com/products/web-of-science/) for 'Blockchain' and 'Distributed Ledger'.

Normalisation strategies

The exogenous motion towards the socialisation of blockchain can also be observed in the process of normalising the field. Efforts at normalisation extended from the period of disruption following the conceptual upheavals caused by the discovery of the potential applications of blockchain. These upheavals included both the influence blockchain could have on human activities, and the ways in which it could interact with institutions and regulations. The normalisation process was a natural reaction to the potentially paralysing effect of this disruption, intended to adapt blockchain and set out models of behaviour to preserve the coherence and functional sustainability of institutions. Each behavioural model is embodied in a set of social norms intended to regulate and govern a particular set of human activities. In the context of blockchain, the normalisation strategy is comprehensive in that it covers all dimensions of normalisation at the same time:

- The *legalistic dimension*, in which the norm is *de jure*, i.e., binding and obligatory within the framework of legal norms formalised in law.
- The *private-sector dimension*, often applicable to technical standards, in which the norm aims to regulate the behaviour of members of an industry and their relations with third parties on a voluntary basis.
- The *advisory dimension*, in which the norm aims to encourage desirable and timely behaviours.

In the field of blockchain, the legaliste dimension of normalisation involved attempts to impose national regulations on cryptocurrencies. The complexity of the field arises from the fact that cryptocurrencies based on public permissionless distributed ledger protocols (i.e., public blockchains such as Ethereum and Bitcoin) are not associated with any legal entity. They are essentially borderless and operate without the support of institutions. As such, they cannot be subjected directly to national regulations and could be seen as a proper case for global law.

Legal authorities at state, regional, and local level in various countries are currently discussing possible actions to address this or are already taking action. Depending on the prevailing legal culture in each country, some are seeking to regulate individual usages as they arise, while others are creating the conditions required to experiment with the technology in an advisory environment before implementing legislation, then gradually adapting it.

In some countries national regulations have banned the use of cryptocurrencies for financial transactions, while in others their use as money has been prohibited, with the principal aims being to combat the use of funds for illicit purposes, protect consumers and investors, and maintain the integrity of markets and payment mechanisms. In 2018, the Bank for International Settlements (BIS) identified 151 measures and declarations emanating from the authorities and representative bodies of Australia, China, Chinese Taipei, the European Union and its member states, Gibraltar, Hong Kong, India, Indonesia, Israel, Japan,

Korea, the Philippines, Singapore, Switzerland, and the United States as well as from international organisations, groups and regulatory bodies such as Eurozone institutions, BIS, IOSCO, CSF, and the G20. After this study, it advised regulatory authorities to use certain tools. To combat illicit activity, it recommended focussing actions on cryptocurrency infrastructure providers, i.e., the intermediaries who manage cryptocurrency portfolios. In particular, it recommended extending certain existing regulations, such as the laws on anti-money laundering (AML) and combatting the financing of terrorism (CFT) as well as laws intended to protect consumers and investors. It also recommended addressing the interoperability of cryptocurrencies with traditional financial institutions such as banks and credit-card providers by drafting and enforcing regulations regarding the validity of cryptocurrencies in regulated markets as well as by moderating the ways in which banks could trade cryptocurrencies on behalf of their customers. Lastly, the BIS recommended that the legal status of cryptocurrencies be clarified. It invited countries to define whether cryptocurrencies were to be treated as securities and regulated as such, or as generic assets that did not necessarily require special monitoring practices.

The normalisation strategies applied to blockchain also have a private dimension through processes of technical standardisation. According to the various standardisation bodies, whether national (such as SNV in Switzerland, ANSI in the United States, or AFNOR in France) or international (such as ISO), technical standardisation is the process whereby a common, non-binding, and non-coercive technical reference framework is developed consensually by an ad-hoc grouping of private actors, generally from the same sector. We have already seen this kind of strategy used in the private sector with R3, for example. Also noteworthy is the Enterprise Ethereum Alliance (EEA), which brings together nearly 300 organisations of different sizes, including JPMorgan Chase & Co., Microsoft Corp., and British Petroleum as well as startups such as NICO. This alliance aims to normalise the use of the public blockchain Ethereum.

One of the first international organisations to take an interest in the normalisation of blockchain was the World Wide Web Consortium (W3C), which launched the Blockchain Community Group in 2016 to establish message formatting standards and propose guidelines for use cases such as interbank communications. Also, in 2016, on the initiative of Australia, the International Organisation for Standardisation (ISO) established the ISO/TC 307 international technical committee to deal with blockchain standardisation. This committee is made up of delegations from various national standardisation bodies. Each delegation includes 'experts' from the corporate, industrial, and academic sectors. A total of 54 countries take part in the discussions, either as members or observers. The participating countries are mainly from Europe (24 countries, including Russia), North and Central America (6 countries) and the Asia-Pacific region (12 countries). Countries from South America, Africa, and the Middle East are poorly represented. International organisations are also represented through liaison officers, with The Society for Worldwide Interbank Financial Telecommunication (SWIFT), the European Commission, the International Federation of Surveyors, the International Telecommunication Union, and the United Nations Economic Commission for Europe participating in meetings, recommending experts and submitting comments, but having no power to vote on future standards. According to ISO, the majority representation from countries with advanced levels of industry and expertise in the area reflects the highly technical nature of blockchain development.

As far as ISO is concerned, blockchain technology is already widely implemented and has potential applications in all sectors of industry as well as, more specifically, in traceability applications, accounting and regulatory compliance (including financial and payment systems, border control, logistics and medical records). It is also possible that the spread of blockchain will be so prolific that it becomes an invisible part of many of the services we use. In order to be able to address all aspects of blockchain, ISO established eleven working groups to deal with standards relating to terminology, privacy, technical architecture, security and confidentiality, identity management, smart contracts, governance, and interoperability. A strong focus was placed on the 'internormalisation' of the ISO standards and their adequacy regarding changes to legal norms and government requirements in different countries (e.g., compliance with the GDPR). The draft agenda proposed by ISO schedules the public release of the standard for 2020.

The advisory dimension of the normalisation process is embodied in the ways in which organisations are created to formulate legislative proposals, guidelines and reports in order to influence the regulation of blockchains. This dimension is formalised through forums, roundtables, and the publication of reports by consulting firms like KPMG), tech companies such as IBM and thinktanks as well as blockchain working groups and other international organisations. In 2018, the European Commission created the European Blockchain Partnership (EBP), which incorporated the EU Blockchain Observatory and Forum, to map initiatives, monitor developments and inspire joint action. One of the duties of the forum is to publish reports on different aspects of blockchain, such as identity or governance. In the same vein, the European Commission gave strong support to the creation in Belgium in 2019 of the International Association for Trusted Blockchain Applications (INATBA), which brought together 105 organisations based in Europe, North America, and Asia. The purpose of this association is to establish a dialogue between public authorities and regulatory bodies to facilitate convergence of the applicable legal frameworks.

Another important advisory aspect to the blockchain normalisation process comes from the domain of technology applied to financial services ('fintech') and is known as the 'Regulatory Sandbox'. First implemented in the UK in 2015, this approach is now also being used in Switzerland, Australia, Singapore, Malaysia, Hong Kong, Thailand, and the United Arab Emirates. Regulatory Sandboxes are the regulatory frameworks created by financial regulators such as the FCA and FINMA to test new financial services. In Switzerland, for example, the Blockchain/ICO working group – set up by the State Secretariat for International Finance (SIF) with the participation of the Federal Office of Justice (FOJ) and the The Swiss Financial Market Supervisory Authority (FINMA) – proposed that a sandbox be set up to trial blockchain-related business models. Switzerland already has a sandbox for projects in the banking sector. The working group seeks to create a specific sandbox to solve regulatory problems associated with companies engaged in the development of blockchain-related services, particularly by creating new authorisation categories. The challenge involves the implementation of domain-specific regulatory frameworks that can identify and target issues specific to blockchain applications.

The limited scope of this report prevents an exhaustive study of this subject, but it should be noted that the issue of normalisation is one of the most widely discussed topics surrounding blockchain technology. Normalisation strategies appear to be the preferred method for the socialisation of this technology. This has resulted in attempts to create ad-hoc infrastructures in order to control behaviour, such as the European Blockchain Partnership (EBP), which is working towards the establishment of a European Blockchain Services Infrastructure (EBSI) capable of respecting EU legal rights and norms in the areas of privacy, cybersecurity, interoperability, and energy efficiency as well as the idea of governments also having the ability to create sovereign cryptocurrencies.

Blockchain also demonstrates another dimension of normalisation known as regulation by design, whereby a technical system makes use of its own set of rules in order to impose behavioural constraints on people. This dimension will be explored later in this report as an endogenous model of socialisation.

The banalisation of blockchain

Since it first emerged, blockchain has been perceived as an atypical concept and one that is difficult to tackle. The fact that its initial field of application was a currency certainly played an important role in this situation. The interest Bitcoin aroused within circles holding what some might call alternative ideological views, such as Cypherpunk and Wikileaks, as well as the importance of decentralisation to the concept, have generated a degree of scepticism. The fact that it is a distributed system has only added to the confusion. Regulatory systems operate through clearly identifiable central bodies which are accredited as being responsible for a particular sector. The promise of blockchain is 'to do away with intermediaries' – which is what many institutions consider themselves to be.

It is, above all, the uses of the technology which will drive its banalisation. The aim is to create uses that will render blockchain both familiar and ordinary. An example would be making cryptocurrencies available for purchase at special ATMs. The terminology associated with the field has also been chosen in order to contribute to its banalisation. Presenting private blockchains as simple distributed ledgers enables the use of vocabulary that the corporate sector is accustomed to. The concept of the ledger is commonly known; this is just a version of it that uses new technology to provide certain advantages.

In the world of finance, pioneering cryptoasset management companies such as Bitwise Asset Management sought to demonstrate to the US Securities and Exchange Commission (SEC) that the Bitcoin market was sufficiently regulated and stable to support the creation of an exchange-traded fund (ETF). Bitwise argued that Bitcoin was behaving as expected for an asset of this type and wanted to offer conventional financial services in the shape of investment funds, which provided exposure to this asset. Bitwise was the first to create a 'cryptocurrency index fund' providing exposure to the 'top 10 cryptos'. To make it more familiar to people, it introduced the fund as the 'S&P 500' of the crypto-world. These cryptoassets were presented as simultaneously innovative and banal; the inevitable result of changes brought about by the digital transformation.

Blockchains were also described as having uses in humanitarian aid, especially for people without access to conventional financial services (known as 'unbanked' people), as well as in personal identification. Binance Charity and Libra both justified the creation of new systems in this way, while avoiding competing with existing institutions.

It is through this process that blockchain is gradually becoming an IT/financial sector like any other.

11.2. Endogenous socialisation patterns

In the following section we examine the endogenous blockchain socialisation model, the movement from inside blockchain towards the outside. We explain how the technical structure of blockchain formalises certain modes of administration and imposes specific social behaviours to ensure its operation over time.

Project financing methods

The financing aspect is characteristic of the blockchain socialisation process in that its development led to the design of an ad hoc financing model: the ICO or Initial Coin Offering, a conceptual evolution in the investment field.

In January 2012, J.R. Willet revealed Mastercoin through a message on the Bitcointalk forum, which included a link to download a document entitled *The Second Bitcoin Whitepaper vs 0.5 (Draft for Public Comment)*. The document included a description of the technical system and a specific model for funding the project. The author explained that not being prepared to neglect his family by taking the time to explain his project to venture capitalists, he had created an alternative fund-raising model he called the Initial Distribution of Mastercoins. This model was intended to provide the funds required to pay developers to write the code and fully implement the protocol.

Following the prescriptions laid out in the model, an entity responsible for the Mastercoin project published a digital wallet address to collect Bitcoins when the Mastercoins were sold to the public. The entity also published the deadline before which Mastercoins could be purchased. Anyone sending Bitcoins to this address before the deadline was recognised by the protocol as having an equivalent number of Mastercoins. For example, if a person sent 100 Bitcoins to the address, they would have 100 Mastercoins after the deadline. The following year, Willet published version 1.0 of his whitepaper on BitcoinTalk, together with a call for funds for the Mastercoin project. As with the Genesis block from which the first Bitcoins were created, Mastercoins had a similar starting point called the 'Exodus Address'. Anyone who sent Bitcoins to this address between 31 July 2013 and 31 August 2013 received the equivalent number of Mastercoins as well as additional Mastercoins depending on the transaction date. The first Mastercoin transaction was recorded in early August, but the biggest wave of transactions occurred following its presentation to a group of cryptocurrency investors (known as Bitangels). The funding total reached 4,750 BTC, over US$ 500,000 at the time. This experiment created a precedent. Between July 2014 and August 2014, the Ethereum project financed its development through this model by collecting 31,500 Bitcoins, worth US$ 18.4 million at the time. This ICO enabled the Ethereum Foundation to be established in Zug, to supervise Ethereum software development.

The ICO model has enabled cryptocurrency projects to finance themselves on a global scale without going through the traditional financial intermediaries of banks and capital markets. The initiators of projects publish a document that is usually referred to as a 'whitepaper'. This whitepaper can have various characteristics depending on the intention of the holders. It describes the technical issues, but also covers business matters, seeking to be comprehensive and to anticipate the questions investors will typically pose. In the context of an ICO, the whitepaper supplements the due-diligence process by providing a full written explanation of the project's goals and how the funds will be spent. The initiators of ICOs issue tokens. Tokens are different from coins, which are the native tokens of a cryptocurrency, for example, a Bitcoin. Tokens are informational representations of assets. They are presented as having scarcity value, so it is best to acquire them early when this value is still low. They can be acquired by anyone during the ICO, in exchange for a cryptocurrency such as Bitcoin or Ether. The funds then generally go on to be used by the initiator of the ICO to finance research or protocol development.

On the investor side, the tokens have the function and utility described in the whitepaper, which may differ with each project. ICOs initially enabled regulations to be circumvented by creating a legal vacuum: Tokens had no value per se, not being associated with a financial counterpart, so the ICOs were not subject to regulation by national financial authorities.

The principle was based on an extension of the crowdfunding model, in which a pre-sale, represented by tokens, was organised offering the preferential use of goods or services in the future. The underlying idea was that if the project was successful, the tokens associated with it would gain in value and be traded in the marketplace. These unregulated tokens, akin to donations, went on to cause a good deal of speculative excitement. In 2018, the number and size of ICOs reached a peak, particularly with the Telegram messaging service and the EOS platform (TON US$ 1.7 billions, EOS US$ 4 billions).

The success of these types of financing projects (Figure 45) led to the proliferation of fanciful projects as well as attempts at fraud. Given the levels of excitement generated, some banks, such as Zuger Kantonalbank, refused to open bank accounts for companies whose funds came from ICOs, forcing some, like SwissBorg, to relocate their head offices. ICOs have also created categories of tokens, such as payment tokens, utility tokens, and security tokens. Payment tokens can be used as a means of payment, kept in a wallet by investors, or exchanged with other tokens or conventional currencies. Utility tokens provide access to services and are equivalent to pre-sales. Security tokens represent an investment in assets such as equity or membership rights.

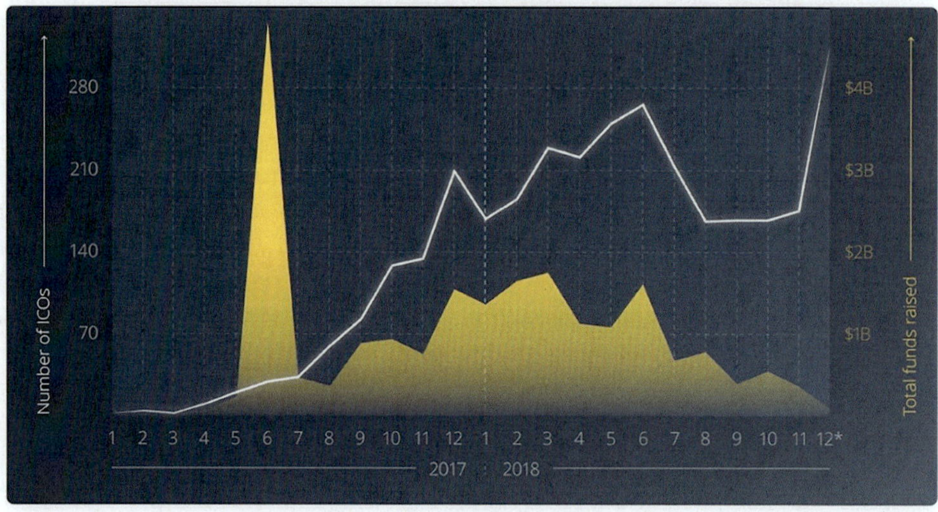

Figure 45. ICO Market 2017–2018. Source: CoinTelegraph.

The quality of the tokens issued prior to the division shown above remains unclear. In 2017, market supervisory and control bodies such as SEC, FINMA, and ESMA called on the players involved to take action. Individual countries were attempting to create standards to regulate the field, each in different ways. In Switzerland – a crypto-stronghold since the Ethereum tax office was set up in the canton of Zug – FINMA and the cantonal authorities published practical guidelines explaining how companies could register there. At the end of 2018, the Blockchain/ICO working group set up by the Federal Council published a report on the legal status of blockchain technology in Switzerland. The conclusions of this report served as the basis for a draft law submitted for consultation to the cantons, political parties, associations of municipalities as well as cities and regions, in order to adapt federal law to the development of blockchains as distributed ledger techniques. This project, entitled 'The Federal Act on the Adaptation of Federal Law to Developments in Distributed Ledger Technology', was not intended to introduce specific legislation on blockchain technology – the report states that 'the Swiss legal framework already covers business models based on *distributed ledger technology* (DLT) and blockchains'; rather, it was an attempt to integrate cryptoassets into substantive law by making quick, targeted changes. These included the right to return tokens in the event of insolvency and the creation of a new class of collective investment scheme (Limited Qualified Investment Funds, L-QIF) that would enable qualified investors to bring innovative products to market more quickly and without being subject to financial oversight by FINMA.

ICOs contributed to the 'blockchain hype' by diversifying the cryptocurrency offering and growing the number of application projects. After the initial frenzy, the sector has begun to calm down. Blockchain investment types have evolved to comply with regulatory standards such as STO and ISO. ICOs (Initial Coin Offerings) became TGEs (Token Generating Events), which provided secure investment models – sometimes even hybrid models in which ICOs were suitable for both the general public and professional investors.

Distribution policy

The socialisation of blockchain as a technology was also determined by the conditions under which its software was distributed. The first public version of the Bitcoin code was released in 2009 on the SourceForge platform, with a notice that the code was being distributed under the ownership conditions of the MIT/X11 licence. This meant the authors of the original code had agreed to grant certain rights to all persons receiving the code, including the right to sell it and to change its licence. Projects that grew out of Bitcoin, such as Namecoin, had the same characteristic. Most projects were published on the Github platform and distributed under various types of licence. The codes of the different Hyperledger projects were shared under the Apache 2.0 licence, which had initially been designed for denser projects. The Ethereum project, in a pragmatic spirit of resilience but also in an attempt to respect the diversity of ideas the contributors have brought to each programme, shares its codes under a number of different licences – GPL, MPL, and GNU.

The aspect common to all these licences is that they are compatible with the General Public Licence (GPL) developed by Richard Stallman and Eben Moglen in 1989. This means that all these pieces of software have been free and/or open source from the beginning. Free and open-source software licences are normative texts that set out the distribution rights for intellectual property (such as source code). Contrary to traditional approaches to IP, which grant the right to preclude certain uses, a free licence enables authors to permit certain uses of their work, including the right to study, modify, operate, and distribute it.

These types of contracts are particularly well suited to the development of computer code. A free licence regulates the relationships and responsibilities of a heterogeneous community of code developers, such as the Bitcoin developer community, to enable them to collectively manage a particular resource (the Bitcoin software) in good faith. Free licences have proven effective in software development with projects such as the Linux operating system, the Apache web server, and the Firefox web browser as well as with projects like Wikipedia. Today, development models for projects under free licences are taking the lead in innovation sectors like AI, BigData, and mobile. Leading IT industry players like Google, IBM, Facebook, and Microsoft recognise the importance of this model and have invested heavily in it through the release of code, support for specific projects, and development of products under free licences.

The increasing popularisation of free software led communities to produce specific software creation tools to help them coordinate their work and maintain quality levels as systems become more complex and the number of contributors increases. With free software, it is not just the end product that is freely available, but also the entire research and decision-making process. Having access to the source code of a piece of software means the developer can understand how it works and conduct tests during the release stage. Free and open-source software is therefore developed on the basis of the proposals, discussions, and arguments put forward by groups of individuals who are temporarily unified around a common goal.

A special set of tools and practices was developed to address these specific situations. Linus Torvald, the creator of Linux, developed the *Git* software – a decentralised source code versioning system, which is also a type of distributed ledger – to meet the specific needs of the Linux global developer community. The *Git* software was then used in the collective development of code for other applications. It is now the benchmark tool in the field of software development. The GitHub platform, which is based on *Git*, offers a number of features to aid the collective management of software development in areas such as version control and code management. In addition to these features, which were already available on the SourceForge platform initially used for Bitcoin, GitHub has become popular for its role in hosting free and open source projects. It also provides a number of functions to promote the socialisation of projects, such as task management, Wiki, flows and people, and project monitoring.

Splitting

Although not a unique attribute, the capacity to be forked is one of the salient features of software distributed under free and open-source licences. The term 'fork' refers to the splitting process, which leads to the continued development of the software independently of the community that had previously been in charge of it. Using the existing source code as the starting point, the two groups continue along independent development paths. A fork therefore results in the creation of two separate programmes (Figure 46). For example, contributors to Bitcoin's software worked on its GitHub repository by proposing (making 'pull requests') and confirming changes ('commits'). These were then discussed and possibly accepted ('merged') into the 'Bitcoin core', a central control point for the protocol. Some of the rejected changes created a fork which led to a new parallel blockchain. These various blockchains then cohabited with Bitcoin, gaining their own names, such as Litecoin and Bitcoin Cash.

Figure 46. The main forks of Bitcoin.

Though relatively rarely implemented, the fork is nevertheless an important mechanism in the world of open-source software. A fork is usually created when a community of developers cannot come to a consensus on an aspect deemed to be important. Someone who has never participated in a project can also fork it in order to use the existing source code as the basis for a project with technical similarities.

Forking is a way of proposing new social structures in order to develop new ideas, whether technical, organisational, or associated with legal issues. However, forking is viable only if a sufficiently large community forms around the new fork. The reputation of the developers and the benefits of their proposals are deciding factors in convincing enough people to come on board and make the fork viable. A balance must therefore be found between the need to experiment and the difficulty of finding sufficient community support to achieve and maintain a fork. It is common for one branch of a fork to be abandoned in favour of another that has demonstrated its usefulness after having contributed relevant innovations.

With a blockchain, the question is posed differently. The fact that blockchains are decentralised means the network participants must agree on a set of common rules. The network consists of nodes communicating in a collaborative manner. The nodes validate transactions, save them in their copy of the blockchain, and broadcast these additions to other nodes. A fork can therefore affect both the protocol and the data structure of the blockchain itself.

The term 'soft fork' is used when the proposed changes to the protocol prevent the validation of blocks and transactions that were formerly valid. In order to impose itself, this type of fork only requires most of the nodes to follow the new rule. An example of a soft fork might be the addition of a new type of transaction. Only blocks that contain the new type of transaction are rejected by the initial branch and the 'old miners' (Figure 47).

A Soft Fork

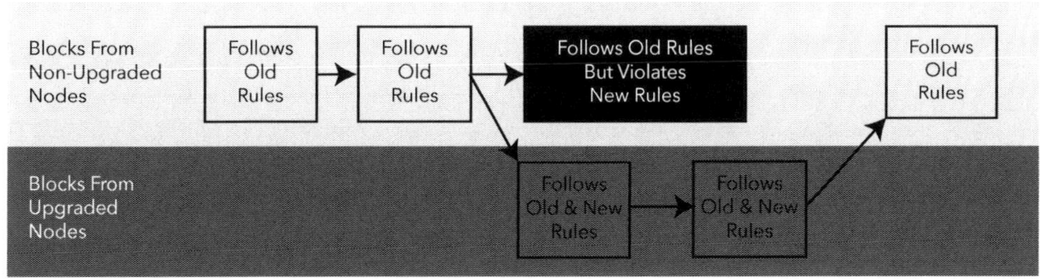

Figure 47. A soft fork: blocks violating new rules are made stale by the upgraded mining majority.

A 'hard fork' is considered more radical because it can validate blocks that were formerly invalid. Unlike a soft fork, a hard fork does not require all the nodes to follow the new rule in order to impose itself. The chains diverge to create two ledgers with the same history up to the fork and diverge from that moment on (Figure 48).

A Hard Fork

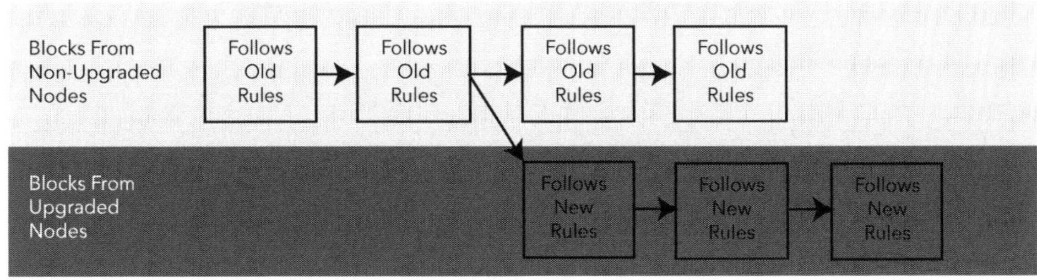

Figure 48. A hard fork: Non-upgraded nodes reject the new rules, diverging the chain.

A hard fork can be used to add new features, as in 2017, when a Bitcoin split occurred because some contributors wished to increase the capacity of the blockchain to deal with problems associated with the growth in the number of users. A hard fork can also be used to roll back certain operations. Following the hacking of The DAO (Decentralized Autonomous Organization), the vast majority of the Ethereum community favoured a hard fork to cancel the transactions on the tens of millions of dollars that had been diverted.

The network effect is essential in the adoption of a fork. The usefulness of a payment system lies in its adoption rate and therefore the number of people using it. For a network to be efficient, enough machines must be made available to digitally stamp the transactions to ensure their legitimacy (these machines are called miners in the case of Bitcoin).

A software community is therefore very similar to an institution: a social structure established over time and governed by certain rules, the purpose of which in this case is to develop a piece of software. A fork takes place when the institution cannot find common ground regarding the project's future. A fork enables the institution to divide itself and move in a new direction, creating a smaller community and a new distribution of responsibilities. Smaller groups allow members to communicate with each other more easily. The process can also be reversed if both groups decide it would be more advantageous to work together on the same project again.

Network-building Incentives

Here we explore how blockchain projects seek to continue their existence by motivating a variety of actors to participate and contribute to them.

Blockchains such as Bitcoin and Ethereum need resources to operate. In particular, transaction validation requires computing power. Participants freely choose to join the network, thus providing it with these resources. Each participant is a 'node' of the network. Strictly speaking, a node is a server running specific software.

One of the central ideas of public blockchains is that of rewarding nodes to encourage them to join the network. With Bitcoin, every time a node succeeds in validating a certain number of transactions (a block), it receives bitcoins in return.[142] In this manner, new bitcoins are created. This system rewards and incentivises the creation of new nodes, while allowing bitcoins to be distributed.

The intention is for a total of 22 million bitcoins to be created. Once this predefined number of bitcoins is in circulation, no new ones will be created. The subsidies are programmed to gradually decrease over time. This incentive system is therefore only temporary but was considered necessary during the first years of the system's operation in order to encourage the initial nodes to join.

A second incentive system involves the payment of transaction fees to nodes. Once the predefined number of Bitcoins is in circulation, no new ones are created, so the nodes only receive transaction fees.

The limitation on the number of Bitcoins in circulation has greatly encouraged the adoption of the system. If successful, Bitcoin should become a very rare asset. In its early stages, Bitcoin was extremely cheap: People bought it believing the system would continue to work, and that the currency's price would increase in the future.

There are therefore three mechanisms that motivate players to participate in the bitcoin network: node subsidies, Bitcoin scarcity, and transaction fees. Most blockchains rely on similar mechanisms. Different blockchains have different incentive systems that are often their unique selling points. The incentive mechanisms are based on the assumption that individuals exhibit economic rationality. In this case, it is assumed they are trying to maximise their utility as consumers and their profit as producers. This approach to human behaviour contrasts with concepts of behavioural economics, which examine cognitive biases and other irrational behaviours.

To retain their stability, public blockchains attempt to preserve their operations despite other players seeking to disrupt them. Most nodes act honestly in order to obtain the reward. Honest behaviour is rewarded, which helps to prevent hostile and/or incorrect behaviour.

---

[142] The current Block Reward for solving one block on the Bitcoin Blockchain is 12.5 BTC. Block Rewards gets halved after every 210,000 of blocks gets mined, and the average time for halving comes around 4 years.

The protocol specifies the size of the blocks and the frequency with which they are created. A block contains a limited number of transactions. The faster blocks are created, the harder it is to validate them.

Since the number of transactions per block is limited, a balance is sought using market mechanisms based on supply and demand. For example, a transaction fee can be associated with a transaction. Nodes seek to increase their profit by prioritising transactions with relatively high transaction fees. If the number of transactions saturates the network, the applicable transaction fees increase accordingly. Transactions with low fees are then executed later on, when the network is less busy. This price increase prevents congestion in the system by encouraging nodes to increase the resources available to the network, and by temporarily discouraging certain superfluous transactions.

The system uses these incentive mechanisms to maintain stability and to adapt to the level of demand. *Cryptoeconomics* refers to the study of these types of economic interactions. It seeks to create systems with certain desirable properties, such as durability over time. It focuses on the use of cryptography and financial incentives. Cryptography is used as a means of certifying the properties of the messages generated, while the economic incentives are defined within the system to encourage the desired properties to be maintained. The aim of *cryptoeconomics* is to take advantage of individual behaviours and the strategic interactions between the actors involved.

Cryptoeconomics is related to *mechanism design*, the discipline that seeks to create economic mechanisms and incentives to produce desired objectives in a context in which the actors behave rationally. *Mechanism design* lies at the crossroads of economics and game theory. With *mechanism design,* we start at the end *of the game* by defining the goals, then work backwards to define the rules. This is also known as reverse game theory. This approach aims to define the rules of a system to produce a given result.

Software demands a large amount of work on the part of its developers. With open-source software, the developers are not directly compensated when the software is commercialised. They have a diverse range of motives to work on it, as with any unpaid project. An interest in the technology is a predominant driver. However, blockchain has facilitated new self-financing methods such as ICOs, which now provide significant amounts of funding for these types of projects.

12. Designing Through Blockchain

The particular technical characteristics of blockchain technology, namely, decentralisation and auditability, have now entered the collective imagination and are changing the ways in which certain problems are approached. Some projects that were previously technically feasible but had not been applied have now been implemented thanks to an increasing awareness of the possibilities. We call this movement 'designing through blockchain'.

This chapter explores this phenomenon by analysing the evolution of blockchain technology and the way in which it has developed into its own economic sector. We explore two fields that have undergone major conceptual and formal upheaval as a result of being viewed through the prism of blockchain: regulatory techniques and identity recognition.

12.1. The emergence of a new sector

The development of blockchain has not been homogeneous. Two separate movements can be distinguished: projects that directly target the general public and mass markets and uses of blockchain aimed at the business sector.

Since 2017, blockchain technology has developed into a significant social phenomenon. Bitcoin in particular has been extensively discussed in the media. A large number of people have begun buying cryptocurrencies on trading platforms. In absolute terms, the amounts are dizzying, with market cap levels now exceeding US$ 100 billion (Figure 49). Beyond these initially impressive figures, it is still difficult to measure the true scope of the technology.

Figure 49. Total market capitalisation according to coinmarketcap.com.

Most of the funds raised by ICOs have been directed towards technical projects. Some of these have focused on technical improvements, others on entirely new blockchain systems. Some have promised to provide specific applications for end users, not just new tools for developers. According to the goals they have set for themselves, many of these projects are due to start delivering services soon. These future services can be expected to be made available for use by the public, albeit primarily as beta versions.

We can observe both economic models and a methodology based on a culture of 'perpetual prototyping', key features of the start-up culture of the information technology industry. In this sense projects have evaded responsibility for future technical issues as well as for defining the real value of the end use of their product. The language of prototypes and betas has its own marketing value in appealing to *early adopters* (the first users of a service). It also serves to protect companies in legal terms and to guard against disappointment from end users (Figure 50).

Important: Status is currently in beta testing. There are risks associated with testing a beta product, so when opting in you will be prompted to read and acknowledge you understand and accept these risks.

Though still a work in progress, we hope this beta shows the beginnings of a friendly, intuitive experience for Ethereum, and what will be hopefully the start of a fantastic client for the Ethereum network.

Figure 50. Warning message for the Status mobile app on Android PlayStore.

There is in fact a good deal of uncertainty surrounding the actual value and usefulness of these new services. While blockchain can be seen as an important social phenomenon, its use remains marginal. The few major exceptions are Bitcoin and a few other cryptocurrencies used for speculative purposes.

The latter are also used to store and transfer web-based assets. In countries in which significant, if perhaps temporary, capital control measures have been implemented, their use may increase significantly. Examples might be observed within the capital flow restrictions imposed in Venezuela in 2019 and in Greece in 2015. The same is true for countries experiencing high rates of inflation. When a country's financial infrastructure is experiencing difficulties, blockchain-based cryptocurrencies begin to find uses in the real economy.

Another possible use lies in humanitarian aid, such as when aid struggles to reach its destination due to corruption or is severely diminished by overheads and administrative costs charged by intermediaries. Blockchain technology provides a much more direct system, one that also allows transactions to be tracked. Its use is already being explored by organisations including the United Nations, World Economic Forum (WEF), UN Refugee Agency (UNHCR), World Food Programme (WFP), International Committee of the Red Cross (ICRC), and IBM. In 2017, the WFP launched a pilot project called Building Blocks, which began by assessing key assumptions around the capacity of blockchains to authenticate, record, and reconcile cash and food aid transactions in Pakistan. By 2018, the WFP reported that Building Blocks was able to facilitate money transfers while protecting beneficiary data, controlling financial risk and reducing costs by eliminating up to 98% of the fees charged by third-party institutions. The project is expected to speed up the implementation of emergency assistance operations.

These new opportunities are beginning to raise questions about monetary policy and sovereignty. The Open Money Initiative, an independent initiative funded by a number of blockchain players along with the Human Rights Foundation, examines how people use money in the context of closed economies and collapsing monetary systems, for instance in Venezuela (Figure 51).

Figure 51. Tweet from the Open Money Initiative showing a woman hiding money in her hair.

Some institutional actors with strong user bases, such as Facebook and Telegram, are creating their own cryptocurrencies for integration into their platforms. The marketing campaign for the Facebook consortium's cryptocurrency project Libra states that it will be aimed at people who do not have access to traditional financial services (the 'unbanked') and countries whose national currencies are weak. Libra will likely be pegged to the US dollar and made available as a payment tool on popular messaging applications such as Facebook, WhatsApp, and Messenger as well as the Instagram photo-sharing application. The Telegram app is also launching a cryptocurrency. The situation is similar to that of a highly financed market: Many promises have been made, but there are currently few deliverables available.

A wide range of actors, including companies and institutions, have attempted to take advantage of these new opportunities. The business sector has its own specific approach to blockchain. Solutions that were developed by and for private companies are primarily intended to improve existing processes and mostly involve permissioned blockchains. These types of blockchains can be distinguished according to their modes of governance, which can be centralised or by consortium.

In centrally controlled blockchains, each member must be approved by the central body, and transactions can only be validated by the central body. The database is shared between a number of different actors, but only the central body can regulate it. The use of blockchain in these cases does not constitute a major divergence from the use of existing technologies, but it does enable companies to familiarise themselves with the new technology. We do not focus further on this type of usage.

The situation is different where blockchains are governed by consortiums. In this case, each member owns and controls a node and can validate transactions. The structure imitates that of a public blockchain, but with a restricted number of selected members. This profoundly changes the ways in which co-operation is approached.

The consortium approach avoids responsibility being placed on a central actor. Conventional information exchange procedures without third parties often require data to be verified and reconciled by each participant, meaning the data structure must be standardised. When discrepancies are discovered, a tedious bureaucratic process is triggered, one which can sometimes end up in the courts.

In consortium blockchains, the blockchain modifies the relationship between actors by placing a distributed ledger system in the middle. The collaboration process is designed around this centralised element. The structure of the information recorded in the blockchain, as well as the validation rules, are therefore the primary focus of discussions. For example, organisations may decide that at least 70% of the nodes, not just a simple majority, must validate a block for it to be accepted.

This enables new situations to come about. One concrete example involved the declaration of bicycle thefts in Amsterdam: A common ledger for the owners, the insurance companies and the police was established using a blockchain to enable the various parties to manage their tasks in the event of a theft such as complaint filing, registration of the complaint, and insurance payout. The government could also have set up a centralised database and invited the other parties to use it, but this was not done before blockchains could be used to create ledgers of this type. Blockchain has brought many actors to the table and focused them on the modelling of transactions, processes, actors and objects.

Established IT industry players like IBM, Google, and Microsoft provided the infrastructure required to deploy these services. New actors like we.trade and sana.swiss modelled particular situations in attempts to provide turnkey services to companies, saving them from having to do the modelling and development work themselves. Thus, we are seeing the emergence of an industry that is changing the way companies approach relationships and information sharing with their partners.

12.2. New regulation techniques

Blockchain is prompting a re-assessment of responsibilities related to regulation. Here, we address the issue of responsibility from the point of view of service providers and regulatory institutions.

The ability to access content, whether in transit or in storage, carries with it a certain amount of responsibility. Encryption systems have already partially removed this burden in certain situations: Access providers are no longer aware of the content of TLS-protected web pages; chat services with 'end-to-end encryption' have no access to the content of the messages sent over their networks.

Where intermediaries are no longer able to read content, they no longer have to bear responsibility for that content. The end user of the service becomes the sole responsible party.

In the same way, a blockchain can be used to provide monetary services without having the capacity to discover the nature of each transaction. A dual phenomenon can therefore be observed: Users are lobbying for the protection of their privacy, while IT service providers are reluctant to take on the role of service regulator.

Censorship capabilities bring with them significant levels of responsibility, and there are costs associated with managing censorship rules and legislation. Reputational and political costs are associated with the use of platforms for some types of material, such as political or pornographic material. Third parties managing transactions are in direct competition with other systems that manage the same types of transactions without taking responsibility for them. In this context it might be advantageous for these third parties to reduce content regulation.

The United States has been considering abandoning the last few controls it exercises over domain names. This issue has been on the table since the 1990s. In 2012, China, India and Russia came together to demand equal rights in the regulation of the internet. Global pressure has increased in recent years, in particular following the Snowden affair. ICANN, the regulatory authority in charge of domain names, is itself demanding independence from the US government. The United States has recognised ICANN as an effective and mature multipartite organisation and has tasked it with bringing the global community together to address the process of transitioning to a global consensus mechanism. In this context, ICANN published a report in which it explores decentralised systems, possibly based on blockchain technology, using Bitcoin and Namecoin as examples.

New actors are also taking on new responsibilities. So-called oracle services, such as Chainlink and Provable, incorporate external data, including traditional financial information such as interest rates and prices, into blockchains. This means that commercial transactions implemented through smart contracts and executed on blockchains can have access to external data. These services allow for bidirectional operation: Information on blockchains is already available externally; through oracles, external data are now also available on a blockchain. The reliability of an oracle and the quality of the data it provides are therefore crucial factors.

Regulatory Technology (RegTech) is the fintech field that uses information technology to help businesses comply with regulatory requirements. The number of technical solutions available have multiplied rapidly, particularly following the financial crisis of 2008. The certification capabilities of blockchain systems are now enabling this industry to offer new services.

12.3. Identity paradigms

The concept of a person's identity can be understood as the principle of recognition, both by the person themselves and by others. Each individual is given a name at birth. Names, in conjunction with nationality, sex, and place and date of birth, constitute the basic elements of recognising a legal identity of each person.

Governments have established systems for proving one's legal identity, including passports and requirements for handwritten signatures. Most are now designing modern digital identification systems, such as ID that can be presented to prove one's identity on the internet, in similar ways.

Internet services, however, including blockchain-related services, are transforming the ways in which we conceive of a person's identity in a transaction. The identity of an individual is rarely verified. Most transactions dispense with a full legal identity check and only verify certain attributes, such as age, email address, or payment method. Identity management is gradually shifting towards the verification the attributes of individuals. There is a gradual shift from *who* someone is to *what* they are.

Accessing a public blockchain does not require specific identification procedures. Everyone is free to create a new account in order to receive and manage funds. Each account is associated with a key which is used to authenticate users and enables them to operate on the blockchain according to the established set of rules. Each operation, whether it is sending funds or adding a smart contract, is digitally signed by this account. This creates a chain of transactions related to a particular account.

Unlike traditional financial services, which demand that users provide formal identity documents before accessing the service, the members of a blockchain can use its services without authorisation from a third party. This is fairly common on the internet, where the creation of user accounts rarely requires strong identification. Most internet services have terms and conditions that must be accepted, and email addresses and phone numbers may also be requested to enable the person to be identified after the event, if necessary. Terms and conditions do not need to be accepted to use a public blockchain. Their technical configurations actually limit the actions available.

People's identities emerge through their actions. A person's activity on a merchant site like eBay or Airbnb can be established through their transaction history. Identities can be established on blockchains in the same way, through recognition.

A person can perform actions using multiple accounts on a number of different blockchains. The transactions performed through each account will be separate, but the different accounts can be unified under a single identity through the addition of a message recognising the person's activity on another system. The keybase.io service has already unified its users' identities using this principle by associating their social media identities with encryption keys. The person controlling the account digitally signs a message on each platform, proving that they are the same person.

This means that once someone has legally identified themselves on a blockchain, all transactions on this blockchain are legally identified. It also potentially enables them to legally prove their identity on other blockchains and other systems.

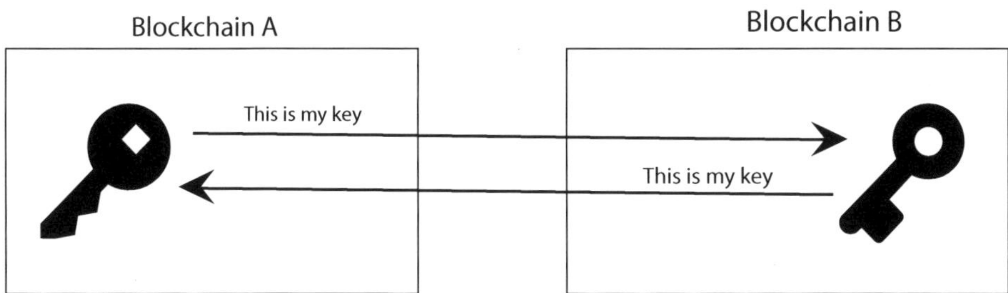

Figure 52. In each blockchain you write a message that identifies your key in the other blockchain. This proves you have access to both keys.

This distinction between an identity used on a network and an administrative identity endowed by a body external to the individual is extremely pertinent to discussions of the recognition bestowed on an individual and what that individual is authorised to do.

The shift towards the decentralised administration of identity makes this still more relevant. Identity can now be expressed in ways that are very different from its conventional legal expression. The most common digital identifiers used today are email addresses and usernames, such as Facebook and Twitter IDs. They place identification providers in a position of control over each of a person's digital transactions. Various proposals have been put forward in an attempt to change this situation, including the concept of self-sovereign identity. This administration technique gives individuals and organisations exclusive ownership of their digital and analogue identities as well as control over how their personal data are shared and used. Zero-knowledge proofs are also used to demonstrate the veracity of information without it being shared. For example, we can rent a car because we have the legal capacity to do so in terms of age and possession of the appropriate licence and insurance, but we simply attest to this capacity, without furnishing its details. This approach necessarily implies a change in the relationship between personal data and the identities associated with it. It generally questions the rights, recognition, responsibilities, and status of the individual in the public informational space.

Conclusions

Throughout this report we have observed the central but ambivalent role played by public actors in the construction of blockchain. We have seen how knowledge regarding cryptography, distributed systems, and, more generally, the architecture of the internet, is fundamentally structured by the relationships between governments, companies, and universities. We have observed how issues such as the security, privacy, auditability, storage, and ownership of information have frequently been problematised in the interest of maintaining independence from governments. The explicit intention of the Bitcoin project – to do away with all forms of trusted third parties (financial and governmental institutions and centralised servers) in the context of electronic financial transactions – follows a similar logic.

The Bitcoin project is entirely non-governmental in nature; it is an autonomous project with no centralised management and is conceptually uncontrollable. To illustrate this situation, we examined how Wikileaks used Bitcoin to counter the global financial blockade it found itself subjected to. More generally, we observed how the Bitcoin protocol was quickly integrated for use in global trade and finance. Although Bitcoin is not associated with any particular legal entity, it cannot avoid national regulations altogether. The desire of governments and companies to regulate Bitcoin and its derivatives and to control how they are used has given rise to some innovative normatives strategies.

We have seen how the financial involvement of major industrial and financial actors in Bitcoin's technical structure – its blockchain – has largely determined the ways in which it has evolved in terms of functionality, terminology, and outlook. Major industrial players have adapted blockchain to suit their own operational constraints and have created systems to address problems associated with permissions – in other words, how transactions are validated. The introduction of the distributed ledger concept made it possible to distinguish between different types of blockchain, such as public and consortium. We saw how this concept was quickly adopted by governments and other international institutions (see the governmental report titled *Distributed Ledger Technology: Beyond Blockchain*). The introduction of distributed ledgers has objectified and subsumed blockchain.

For their part, governments around the world are still seeking the perfect formula to approach the regulation and governance of the sector. These most often involve the implementation of measures to prevent certain uses of cryptocurrencies within national territories. The very design of blockchains can also be regulated through technical standardisation and the establishment of international legal frameworks. In order to gain a better understanding of blockchain technology, governments have also used case studies and experimental frameworks to test services and applications before putting legislation in place. An example of this is the usage of a regulatory sandbox. Some state actors have attempted to create their own infrastructure, which can then be adapted to their regulatory frameworks, such as the European Blockchain Services Infrastructure. No longer able to ignore the systemic transformations cryptocurrencies are engendering, countries like Russia, Iran, the UK, and China are assessing the possibility of creating their own national cryptocurrencies using blockchain technology.

Thus, the willingness of states to regulate the blockchain must be examined. We have noted that, in both concrete and conceptual terms, blockchain technology has created new situations that have called the prerogatives of national governments into question. As an illustration of this situation, we have seen how the technical ability to hold and transfer value through cryptocurrencies can go beyond the framework of national legal systems when the financial institutions of the countries in question find themselves in difficulty, as in Venezuela in 2019. Using domain-name management as an example, we have also seen how certain responsibilities can be transferred to the global community through distributed systems. Lastly, we noted that blockchain has posed profound questions about the conventional systems used by governments to manage identities. These examples demonstrate the ways in which blockchain technology and distributed systems are propelling certain activities beyond national and international jurisdiction. Some of these activities affect the global community and are out of step with legal systems designed and conceived at the level of sovereign states.

Since these states are unable to regulate activities at the global level, the regulation of blockchains must be looked at through the prism of new regulatory regimes. Embodied in global law and soft law, these regimes seek to create the conditions to regulate global phenomena, such as environmental risks. In the context of blockchain, this global, non-sovereign law is conceptualised through what we would term the private and advisory dimensions of standardisation. In other words, it is implemented through the development of technical standards such as ISO, or through the formulation of codes of conduct, charters and other advisory approaches. States are key players in establishing the normative architecture in this domain, but they do not pass laws in a vacuum; a whole series of private actors and non-governmental bodies are also involved.

The intention of this normalisation regime is to define a framework of constraints designed to regulate the use of blockchain technology, in order to guide behaviours in directions assumed to be the most correct. However, because they do not fall under the purview of national legislative bodies, these rules lack the legitimacy that would be conferred on them by democratic institutions. Within these new contexts, no single institution is capable of determining whether a particular decision safeguards the general interest. Nor can it determine, what constitutes fair behaviour, or who is to be responsible for taking decisions that will necessarily have an impact on society. As a last resort, some of those involved in this field have looked to the disciplines of ethics and morality to inspire new standardisation systems. Theories surrounding global administrative law raise questions regarding equity and justice in decision-making processes in order to attempt to make global legislators more accountable.

Blockchain was designed to bring about and manage activities which go beyond national government jurisdiction. These new, unlegislated activities can catch some actors by surprise, leaving them stunned and baffled, unable to respond to the change. We noted that governments are merely able to react to these situations by noting the effects of new services after the fact and attempting to contain those effects that seem to them to be detrimental. If we agree that the role of government is to act in the general interest within the public arena, the question then arises as to how it can continue in this role given the unprecedented social upheaval created by blockchain – and by digital and IT services more generally. How can governments not only anticipate, but also become involved in, the design and execution of these new activities?

Among the institutional instruments we have looked at in this study, the regulatory sandboxes produced by the financial sector appear to be the most advanced. The frameworks put in place by financial regulators to enable private firms to test small-scale applications in controlled environments, under the watchful eye of the legislator, appear to provide the necessary conditions for legislators to revise and adapt their regulatory frameworks with flexibility. We believe it will be necessary, at the very least, to roll out these types of systems in other sectors as well. This will involve the formalisation of sandboxes to experiment with and test a variety of regulatory environments, in sectors including agriculture, hospitality, and health. Sandboxes could also be created to explore, model, prototype, and test new democratic ways of designing and drafting normative texts.

These instruments, however effective, cannot remove the need for collective reflection on the new institutional frameworks that need to be modelled. As a society, we must address this issue as a matter of urgency to guard against greed and the risks posed by disruptive elements. The challenge is to guarantee – in a democratic and thoughtful manner – the general interest in a public space expanded by information.

Contributors

Alejandro Avilés, Software Engineer, Chief Technology Officer at Bitly.

Tom Boltshauser, Masters student in European studies. Research on Blockchain and European Institutions.

Eric Favre, Director General of Information Systems and Digital / State of Geneva.

Gilles Gravier, Director, Senior Open Source and Blockchain Strategy Advisor at Wipro.

Rachid Guerraoui, Professor at the School of Computer and Communication Sciences at EPFL, known for his contributions in the fields of concurrent and distributed computing.

Dirk Helbing, Professor of Computational Social Science at the Department of Humanities, Social and Political Sciences and affiliate of the Computer Science Department at ETH Zurich.

Anna Jobin, Researcher at the Health Ethics and Policy Lab at the Swiss Federal Institute of Technology (ETHZ) in Zurich.

Marcel Knecht, Head of Standardisation and International Affairs at SNV Swiss Association for Standardisation.

Michel Leonard, Emeritus Professor at University of Geneva, Institute of Service Science (ISS).

Nicolas Levrat, Director of the Global Studies Institute (GSI). Professor in the Faculty of Law at the University of Geneva.

Luzius Meisser, Bitcoin Association Switzerland.

Jean-Henry Morin, Associate professor of Information Systems, University of Geneva.

Alexandre Poltorak, Alsenet SA founder. Co-initiator of the candidacy of the city of Geneva for the 13th World Free Software Meetings.

Martin Rindlisbacher, Senior Business Architect, Executive Director at UBS.

Johan Rochel, Co-Founder and Co-Director of ethix: Lab for Innovation Ethics.

Alexis Roussel, Bitly CEO co-founder. Lawyer specialising in new technology. Served as E-Governance specialist for the United Nations. Was also the president of the Pirate Party of Switzerland.

Bernard Stiegler, French philosopher, head of the Institut de recherche et d'innovation at the Centre Georges-Pompidou.

Philippe Thévoz, Vice President of e-Government Systems at SICPA.

Glossary

Term	Definition
ASCII-8	American Standard Code for Information Interchange (ASCII) is a character encoding standard for electronic communication. ASCII-8 has a bit width of 8 bit.
ASIC	An application-specific integrated circuit (ASIC) is a piece of hardware specifically designed for a particular use.
Bitcoin (BTC)	Bitcoin (BTC) is the cryptocurrency of the Bitcoin blockchain. A Bitcoin is a token with a value derived from its use a for payment and wealth storage.
Blockchain	A blockchain is a database replicated on many servers or computers owned or governed by independent legal entities.
Block time	The average time is takes for new blocks (of transactions) to be added to the blockchain.
Chaincode	Smart contract in Hyperledger is called 'chaincode'.
Consensus protocol	A mechanism to decide which block of all the blocks mined is finally added to the blockchain.
CPU	Central processing unit (CPU), alternatively known as the processor. It carries out the instruction of computer programs by performing the basic arithmetic, logical, control, and input/output (I/O) operations specified by the instructions.
Cryptocurrency	A cryptocurrency (or crypto-currency) is a digital asset designed to work as a medium of exchange that uses cryptography to secure its transactions, to control the creation of additional units, and to verify the transfer of assets.
Cryptography	Cryptography is associated with the process of converting ordinary plain text into unintelligible text and

	vice versa. It is a method of storing and transmitting data in a particular form, so that only those for whom it is intended can read and process it. Cryptography not only protects data from theft or alteration, it can also be used for user authentication.
DAO Decentralised autonomous organisations	DAOs consist of multiple smart contracts, which are combined with a governance mechanism and interact with each other without (or with minimum) human intervention.
dApps Decentralised applications	A decentralised application or dApp is an application of a blockchain. More precisely, the backend code runs on a blockchain, while the frontend and user interface of the application can be written in any programming language.
Digital signature	A digital signature uses the private key to sign data, after which the corresponding public key of the signer can be used to verify that the signature is valid.
DVP Delivery vs payment	Delivery versus payment is a settlement procedure where the payment for a security is due at the time of delivery.
Ether (ETH)	Ether (ETH) is the cryptocurrency of the Ethereum platform.
Ethereum	Ethereum is an open-source, public, blockchain-based distributed computing platform featuring smart contract (scripting) functionality.
EVM	The Ethereum virtual machine (C38EVM) is responsible for code execution on the Ethereum network. Smart contracts are run by the EVM.
Fiat money/currency	Fiat money is a currency that a government has declared to be legal tender. Fiat money has no intrinsic value. Instead, its value depends on supply and demand of the currency.
Full nodes	see Miners

GPU	Graphics processing unit (GPU) is also known as the graphics card. It is designed to rapidly manipulate and alter memory to accelerate the creation of images to output to a display.
Hard fork	A hard fork is a radical way to update a blockchain protocol. It involves splitting the path of a blockchain by invalidating transactions confirmed by nodes that have not been updated to the new version of the protocol. This essentially creates two chains: one running the new protocol and one running the old protocol version.
Hash (value)	The output of a hash function is the hash value.
Hash Function	A hash function is an algorithm that converts data of any size into a fix length data string. As a one-way function, the output of the function does not indicate what the input was.
Hashing power	The hashing power is the computational power of a miner or mining pool. It represents the speed at which the cryptographic puzzle could be solved at a given difficulty level.
Hexadecimal system	Hexadecimal system or hex uses 16 symbols (numbers 0–9 and characters a-f). As each hexadecimal digit represents four binary digits (bits), it allows a more human-friendly representation of binary-coded values. One hexadecimal digit represents 4 bits, which is half of a byte (8 bits). For example, a single byte can have values ranging from 00000000 to 11111111 in binary form, but this may be more conveniently represented as 00 to FF in hexadecimal.
ICO	An initial coin offering (ICO) is a means of crowdfunding centred around cryptocurrency, which can be a source of capital for start-up companies. In an ICO, some quantity of the crowdfunded cryptocurrency is preallocated to investors in the form of 'tokens', in

	exchange for legal tender or other cryptocurrencies, such as Bitcoin or Ethereum. These tokens become functional units of currency if or when the ICO's funding goal is met, and the project launches.
IoT Internet of things	The Internet of Things is a network of physical objects (locks, vehicles, microwaves, and light bulbs) that use sensors and software to connect and exchange data over the Internet.
IPO	In an initial public offering (IPO), a private company raises investment capital by offering its stock to the public for the first time.
Merkle Tree	A Merkle or hash tree is a data structure that allows for the efficient and securing verification of large data structures. The data are divided into pairs and hashed. The resulting hash values are again paired and hashed together. This step is repeated until only a single hash remains representing the Merkle root or root hash.
Miners	Miners are nodes that validate transactions of a blockchain. They are paid for providing the computational power with transaction fees and mining rewards.
Mining pool	A mining pool is the pooling of resources by miners, who share their processing power over a network, to split the reward equally, according to the amount of work they contributed to the probability of finding a block.
Mining reward	Miners are rewarded for participating in the consensus protocol for adding blocks to the blockchain. In proof-of-work, the miner that solves the cryptographic puzzle first is given a reward and the transaction fees of all transaction included in his block.
Multisig/ multisignature (accounts)	Multisig or multisignature accounts require more than one private key to make a transaction. To allow for majorities, at least three private keys should be included in a multisignature account.

Node	Nodes are computers in a network that store a copy of a database and a set of rules (consensus protocol) that define the order in which nodes may take turns adding new changes to the database.
Nonce	Nonce is a random number used in the proof-of-work consensus protocol and stands for a number used once. It is a block component that is varied in the cryptographic puzzle to find a block hash having a certain number of leading zeros.
Parallel/orphaned/ uncled block	When two miners provide a valid proof-of-work at the same time, they both create a new block for the blockchain. Subsequent blocks are then added to either one of the two blocks, and two blockchains exist for a brief time. However, as the time in which a new block is mined varies (around the average block time), after a short period the longer chain prevails and the trans--actions, which have not been incorporated into the main chain, go back into the pool of non-validated transactions.
Permissioned	Permissioned refers to blockchains that restrict participation in consensus building/validation to a set of users.
Permissionless	Permissionless refers to blockchains that allow anyone to download and run a node. It is optional to participate in the validation/mining, or they may want a current copy of the blockchain.
PGP	Pretty Good Privacy (PGP) is an encryption program that provides cryptographic privacy and authentication for data communication. PGP is used for signing, encrypting, and decrypting texts, emails, files, directories, and whole disk partitions and to increase the security of email communications.

Power of Big Numbers/2256	An argument on why, although the uniqueness is not tested, identifiers such as the hash value are still considered to be unique due to the almost infinitesimally small probability of identical identifiers.
Private key	The private key allows the decryption of a message encrypted with the corresponding public key.
Proof-of-authority (PoA)	Proof-of-authority is a consensus mechanism where validators stake their identity and attached good reputation.
Proof-of-stake (PoS)	Proof-of-stake is a consensus protocol based on validators staking an amount of their wealth as collateral for the right to validate blocks of transactions. The probability they are assigned a block to validate is proportional to the size of their stake.
Proof-of-work (PoW)	Proof-or-work is a piece of data which is costly to produce but easy for others to verify and satisfies certain requirements. It is also a type of consensus protocol based on showing you have successfully produced a proof of work.
Public key	The public key allows encrypting messages that only owners of the corresponding private key can decrypt. The owner can publish the public key, and anyone can send messages only the owner can decrypt. The public key thereby functions as the public address of its owner.
Root hash	The root hash or Merkle root is the result of a hash/Merkle tree.
Scalability	Scalability refers to the ability of a blockchain to handle increased amounts of transactions.
Smart contracts	Smart contracts are self-executing contracts where the terms of the agreement between the contract parties are directly written in lines of code.

Smart lock	A smart lock is an electromechanical lock designed to perform locking and unlocking operations on a door when it receives such instructions from an authorised device using a wireless protocol and a cryptographic key to execute the authorisation process.
Soft fork	A soft fork is a way to update a blockchain protocol without creating a splitting of the network between nodes and clients that have updated their systems and those who have not. This means updated and none-updated nodes can still communicate.
Solidity	Solidity is a contract-oriented, high-level programming language for implementing smart contracts.
SSH	Secure Shell (SSH) is a cryptographic network protocol for operating network services securely over an unsecured network. SSH provides a secure channel over an unsecured network in a client-server architecture by connecting an SSH client application with an SSH server. Common applications include remote command-line login and remote command execution, but any network service can be secured with SSH
Sybil attacks	The Sybil attack in computer security is an attack wherein a reputation system is subverted by forging identities in peer-to-peer networks.
Token	A token is an object that represents something else. Cryptocurrency tokens are entries on the blockchain that can be reassigned to a new owner using a private key. Two main types of tokens can be differentiated into native tokens and asset-backed tokens. Native tokens have some value due to the utility they provide. Bitcoin on the Bitcoin blockchain and Ether on Ethereum are two examples of native tokens. Asset-backed tokens are claims on an underlying asset from a specific issuer.

Tokenisation	The process of linking an asset with a token on the blockchain.
Transaction fees	Transaction fees are the price of a transaction on the blockchain. This price can fluctuate depending on the demand for transactions given a fixed supply.
Validation	Validation is the process of checking whether the transactions sent are correct. The miner validating the transaction will check whether the sender has enough funds to execute the transaction.
Wallet	A cryptocurrency wallet is a software that stores the private keys that show the ownership of a public key representing a certain amount of cryptocurrency.
UTXO	UTXO or unspent transaction outputs are a concept used by Bitcoin to keep balances on the blockchain. Rather than using accounts, Bitcoin requires the user to have UTXO to make transactions. New UTXOs are created as the output of a transaction, and the same amount of UTXO used as input in the transaction (spent) are removed from the Bitcoin network.

References

The Technical Capabilities of Blockchain and its Economic Viability

ADB. (2016, September 16). Global Trade Finance Gap Reaches $1.6 Trillion, SMEs Hardest Hit. Retrieved from https://www.adb.org/news/global-trade-finance-gap-reaches-16-trillion-smes-hardest-hit-adb

Amati, F. (2016, January 1). Using the blockchain as a digital signature scheme. Retrieved 17 August 2018, from https://blog.signatura.co/using-the-blockchain-as-a-digital-signature-scheme-f584278ae826

Androulaki, E., Barger, A., Bortnikov, V., Cachin, C., Christidis, K., De Caro, A., ... Manevich, Y. (2018). Hyperledger fabric: a distributed operating system for permissioned blockchains (p. 30). Presented at the Proceedings of the Thirteenth EuroSys Conference, ACM

Antonopoulos, A. M. (2017a). *Bitcoin Q&A: Energy consumption*. Retrieved from https://www.youtubc.com/watch?v=2T0OUIW89lI

Antonopoulos, A. M. (2017b). *Mastering Bitcoin: Programming the Open Blockchain*. O'Reilly Media, Inc

AXPO. (2017, November 20). Electricity from the neighbourhood: Axpo launches a blockchain model for renewable energies. *Media Releases*. Retrieved from http://www.axpo.com/axpo/ch/en/news/news/medienmitteilungen/2017/electricity-from-the-neighbourhood--axpo-launches-a-blockchain-m.html

Back, A. (2017, December 11). Stop Talking About Bitcoin's Market Cap – WSJ. Retrieved 13 August 2018, from https://www.wsj.com/articles/stop-talking-about-bitcoins-market-cap-1513015626

Barinov, I. (2018, January 23). What is POA. Retrieved 17 August 2018, from https://github.com/poanetwork/wiki (Original work published 23 June 2017)

Ben-Sasson, E., Chiesa, A., Tromer, E., & Virza, M. (2015). Succinct Non-Interactive Zero Knowledge for a von Neumann Architecture

Besnainou, J. (2018, January 17). From the Brooklyn Microgrid to EXERGY – A Conversation with Lawrence Orsini, CEO of LO3 Energy | Cleantech Group. Retrieved 7 March 2018, from https://www.cleantech.com/from-the-brooklyn-microgrid-to-exergy-a-conversation-with-lawrence-orsini-ceo-of-lo3-energy/

Bitcoin Stack Exchange. (2013, January 12). How will multisig addresses work? Retrieved 17 August 2018, from https://bitcoin.stackexchange.com/questions/6100/how-will-multisig-addresses-work

Bitcoin Stack Exchange. (2015, July 2). Total amount of nodes and avarage active peer number. Retrieved 17 August 2018, from https://bitcoin.stackexchange.com/questions/38371/total-amount-of-nodes-and-average-active-peer-number

Bitcoin Stack Exchange. (2017, January 22). What's a Sybil attack? Retrieved 17 August 2018, from https://bitcoin.stackexchange.com/questions/50922/whats-a-sybil-attack

Bitcoin Wiki. (n.d.). Controlled supply. Retrieved 17 August 2018, from https://en.bitcoin.it/wiki/Controlled_supply

BitInfoCharts. (n.d.-a). Ethereum Avg. Transaction Fee chart. Retrieved 29 August 2017, from https://bitinfocharts.com/

BitInfoCharts. (n.d.-b). Top 100 Richest Bitcoin Addresses and Bitcoin distribution. Retrieved 13 August 2018, from https://bitinfocharts.com/

Blockchain.com. (n.d.-a). Average Block Size. Retrieved 17 August 2018, from https://www.blockchain.com/charts/avg-block-size

Blockchain.com. (n.d.-b). Bitcoin Block # 486913 [25.9.2017]. Retrieved 17 August 2018, from https://www.blockchain.com/btc/block/0000000000000000000df06024655affd28e5d506e5101a86eb0e6eb81f693deb

Blockgeek. (n.d.). Proof of Work vs Proof of Stake: Basic Mining Guide. Retrieved 17 August 2018, from https://blockgeeks.com/guides/proof-of-work-vs-proof-of-stake/

Blockgeeks.com. (n.d.). What is zkSNARKs: Spooky Moon Math. Retrieved 8 August 2018, from https://blockgeeks.com/guides/what-is-zksnarks/

Blocklink.info. (n.d.). Are you in the Bitcoin 1%? A New Model of the Distribution of Bitcoin Wealth. Retrieved 20 February 2018, from http://www.blocklink.info/distributions.html

Buterin, V. (2016, March 5). Serenity PoC2. Retrieved 17 August 2018, from https://blog.ethereum.org/2016/03/05/serenity-poc2/

Carle, G. (2018). Blockchain. Presented at the Energieforschungsgespräche Disentis, Disentis

CCN. (2014, August 4). How a Bitcoin Transaction Works. Retrieved 17 August 2018, from https://www.ccn.com/bitcoin-transaction-really-works/

Chase, B., & MacBrough, E. (2018). Analysis of the XRP Ledger consensus protocol. *ArXiv Preprint ArXiv:1802.07242*

Cohen, H. (2017, August). *BUILDING BLOCKS: The future of cash disbursements at the World Food Program.* Technovation Talks presented at the Blockchain Day: What is “The Blockchain” and why it matters to the UN & Member States?, UN Secretariat, conference room E. Retrieved from https://unite.un.org/techevents/blockchain

CoinDesk. (n.d.). CoinDesk ICO Tracker. Retrieved 13 August 2018, from https://www.coindesk.com/ico-tracker/

CoinDesk, Inc. (2018, January 9). Ethereum (ETH) Price. Retrieved from https://www.coindesk.com/ethereum-price/

CoinMarketCap. (n.d.). 24 Hour Volume Rankings (Exchange). Retrieved 16 May 2018, from https://coinmarketcap.com/exchanges/volume/24-hour/all/

Courtois, N., Song, G., & Castellucci, R. (2016). Speed Optimizations in Bitcoin Key Recovery Attacks. *Tatra Mountains Mathematical Publications*, *67*(1), 55–68. https://doi.org/10.1515/tmmp-2016-0030

Deloitte. (n.d.). Trade financing redefined using blockchain technology. Retrieved 16 August 2018, from https://www2.deloitte.com/in/en/pages/strategy/articles/trade-financing-redefined-using-blockchain-technology.html

Der Bundesrat. (n.d.). Faktenblatt – Vote électronique

Diffie, W., & Hellman, M. (1976). New directions in cryptography. *IEEE Transactions on Information Theory*, *22*(6), 644–654. https://doi.org/10.1109/TIT.1976.1055638

Digiconomist.net. (n.d.-a). Bitcoin Energy Consumption Index. Retrieved 9 August 2018, from https://digiconomist.net/bitcoin-energy-consumption

Digiconomist.net. (n.d.-b). Ethereum Energy Consumption Index (beta). Retrieved 9 August 2018, from https://digiconomist.net/ethereum-energy-consumption

Dwyer, B. (2011, September 1). Average Credit Card Processing Fees. Retrieved 13 August 2018, from https://www.cardfellow.com/blog/average-fees-for-credit-card-processing/

Earls, A. R. (2016, December 1). Blockchain not a panacea for supply chain traceability, transparency. Retrieved 4 January 2018, from http://searcherp.techtarget.com/feature/Blockchain-not-a-panacea-for-supply-chain-traceability-transparency

Economist. (2014, March 3). World Food Programme. Giving generously. Retrieved from https://www.economist.com/blogs/freeexchange/2014/03/world-food-programme

Eggen, M., Glarner, A., Hess, M., Iacangelo, S., Stengel, C., & Weber, R. H. (2018). *Positionspapier zur rechtlichen Einordnung von ICOs*. Blockchain Taskforce. Retrieved from http://web1897.login-12.loginserver.ch/wp-content/uploads/2018/04/Whitepaper-Anhang.pdf

Eidgenössische Spielbankenkommission ESBK. (2014). Online-Glücksspiele. Retrieved 27 December 2017, from https://www.esbk.admin.ch/esbk/de/home/illegal/online.html

Energate. (2017, December 27). Axpo startet Blockchain-Handel. *Energate Messenger.Ch*. Retrieved from http://www.energate-messenger.ch/news/179765/axpo-startet-blockchain-handel

Eperiesi-Beck, E. (2017, December 12). The threat quantum computers pose to modern security. Retrieved 8 August 2018, from https://beta.scmagazineuk.com/article/1473749

ESMT Berlin, & Grid Singularity. (2017). *Results of survey questions of the fist global summit on blockchain technology in the energy sector*. Vienna: Event Horizon. Retrieved from https://www.esmt.org/sites/default/files/eventhorizon_2017_survey.pdf

Essebier, J., & Bourgeois, J. (2018). Die Regulierung von ICOs. *Aktuelle Juristische Praxis*, (5)

Ethereum Stack Exchange. (2016, August 23). What is signing ethereum transaction? Retrieved 17 August 2018, from https://ethereum.stackexchange.com/questions/8238/what-is-signing-ethereum-transaction

Etherscan.io. (2017, July 3). Kovan Transaction 0x49414cabb0e592714e911ecbe0242532763e82f3ee239712e35d04dc0738dc08. Retrieved 17 August 2018, from https://kovan.etherscan.io/tx/0x49414cabb0e592714e911ecbe0242532763e82f3ee239712e35d04dc0738dc08

Etherscan.io. (n.d.-a). Ethereum Average Block Size Chart. Retrieved 17 August 2018, from https://etherscan.io/chart/blocksize

Etherscan.io. (n.d.-b). Ethereum Average Gas Price Chart. Retrieved 17 August 2018, from https://etherscan.io/chart/gasprice

Etherscan.io. (n.d.-c). Ethereum ChainData Size Growth – Fast Sync. Retrieved 17 August 2018, from https://etherscan.io/chart2/chaindatasizefast

Etherscan.io. (n.d.-d). Ethereum Transaction Growth Chart. Retrieved 17 August 2018, from https://etherscan.io/chart/tx

Etherscan.io. (n.d.-e). Kraken Exchange Ethreum account transaction list. Retrieved 17 August 2018, from https://etherscan.io/address/0xe853c56864a2ebe4576a807d26fdc4a0ada51919

Faggart, E. (2016). Tendermint – besser als Bitcoin und Ethereum? *Coinwelt*. Retrieved from http://coinwelt.de/2016/02/tendermint-besser-als-bitcoin-und-ethereum/

Fickling, D. (2018, January 4). Bitcoin's Cheap Energy Feast Is Ending. *Bloomberg.Com*. Retrieved from https://www.bloomberg.com/gadfly/articles/2018-01-04/bitcoin-s-cheap-energy-feast-is-ending

FINMA. (2017). *Regulatory treatment of initial coin offerings* (FINMA Guidance 04/2017). Bern

FINMA. (2018). *Guidelines for enquiries regarding the regulatory framework for initial coin offerings (ICOs)*

Gerard. (2017, November 26). The World Food Programme's much-publicised "blockchain" has one participant — i.e., it's a database. Retrieved 21 December

2017, from https://davidgerard.co.uk/blockchain/2017/11/26/the-world-food-programmes-much-publicised-blockchain-has-one-participant-i-e-its-a-database/

Germann, M., & Serdült, U. (2014). Internet Voting for Expatriates: The Swiss Case. *JeDEM – EJournal of EDemocracy and Open Government*, *6*(2), 197–215

Glarner, A., Müller, L., Linder, T., Furrer, A., Gschwend, C., Hofmann, D., … Meyer, S. (2018). *Switzerland's Financial Regulator Clears the Path for ICO's*. MME. Retrieved from https://www.mme.ch/fileadmin/files/documents/MME_Compact/2018/180228_Swiss_Financial_Regulator_clears_the_Path_for_ICOs.pdf

Glasl, D., & Maag, H. (2013, April). SIX Swiss Exchange – IPO Overview [www.legalink.ch/]. Retrieved 1 February 2018, from https://www.legalink.ch/xms/files/CROSS_BORDER_QUESTIONNAIRES/IPO/IPO_Zurich.pdf

Greenfield, R. (2017, July 24). Vulnerability: Proof of Work vs. Proof of Stake. Retrieved 17 August 2018, from https://medium.com/@robertgreenfieldiv/vulnerability-proof-of-work-vs-proof-of-stake-f0c44807d18c

Greenspan, G. (2016, November 3). Understanding zero-knowledge blockchains. Retrieved 8 August 2018, from https://www.multichain.com/blog/2016/11/understanding-zero-knowledge-blockchains/

GSMA. (2017). *State of the Industry Report on Mobile Money. Decade Edition: 2006 – 2016*. London. Retrieved from https://www.gsma.com/mobilefordevelopment/wp-content/uploads/2017/03/GSMA_State-of-the-Industry-Report-on-Mobile-Money_2016-1.pdf

Haig, S. (2018, January 4). Total Capitalization of the Crypto Markets Now Exceeds $750 Billion. Retrieved 13 August 2018, from https://news.bitcoin.com/total-capitalization-of-the-crypto-markets-now-exceeds-750-billion/

Helms, K. (2017a, July 4). Rollout of 260,000+ Bitcoin-Accepting Stores in Japan Begins – Bitcoin News. Retrieved 13 August 2018, from https://news.bitcoin.com/rollout-of-260000-bitcoin-accepting-stores-in-japan-begins/

Helms, K. (2017b, August 6). Major Japanese Department Store Chain Marui Accepts Bitcoin – Bitcoin News. Retrieved 13 August 2018, from https://news.bitcoin.com/japanese-department-store-chain-marui-accepts-bitcoin/

Herzog. (2014). *WFP's electronic vouchers: an innovative transfer modality for social safety net programmes in Lebanon* (OP_Reports – Operational Reports). World Food Program. Retrieved from http://documents.wfp.org/stellent/groups/public/documents/op_reports/wfp274669.pdf

Hidrobo, M., Hoddinott, J., Peterman, A., Margolies, A., & Moreira, V. (2014). Cash, food, or vouchers? Evidence from a randomized experiment in northern Ecuador. *Journal of Development Economics*, *107*(Supplement C), 144–156. https://doi.org/10.1016/j.jdeveco.2013.11.009

Hileman, G., & Rauchs, M. (2017). *Global cryptocurrency benchmarking study*. Cambridge Centre for Alternative Finance

Horwitz, A. (2018, January 2). Multisig: A beginner's guide. Retrieved 17 August 2018, from https://99bitcoins.com/multisig-a-beginners-guide/

Hübner, C. (2017, May 10). Blockchain und Klimaschutz. Retrieved 9 August 2018, from http://www.kas.de/wf/de/33.48842/

Jordan, R. (2018, January 10). How to Scale Ethereum: Sharding Explained. Retrieved 17 August 2018, from https://medium.com/prysmatic-labs/how-to-scale-ethereum-sharding-explained-ba2e283b7fce

Juskalian, R. (2017, April 1). You might not know what to do with it, but it's time to save up for a quantum computer. Retrieved 8 August 2018, from https://www.technologyreview.com/s/603495/10-breakthrough-technologies-2017-practical-quantum-computers/

Kasper, J. (2017). Evolution of Bitcoin: Volatility Comparisons with Least Developed Countries™ Currencies. *Journal of Internet Banking and Commerce*, *22*(3), 1–18

Keller, R. (2016, September 26). Wie geht eigentlich ein Börsengang? Retrieved 13 August 2018, from https://www.fuw.ch/article/ipo-wie-geht-das/

Keneally, M. (2018, February 7). Bitcoin is becoming more popular for political campaign donations – ABC News. Retrieved 13 August 2018, from https://abcnews.go.com/Politics/bitcoin-popular-political-campaign-donations/story?id=52873921

Kennedy, C. (2018, January 18). The Best Places In The World To Mine Bitcoin. Retrieved 13 August 2018, from https://oilprice.com/Finance/the-Markets/The-Best-Places-In-The-World-To-Mine-Bitcoin.html

Kharif, O. (2017, December 8). 1,000 People Own 40% of the Bitcoin Market. Retrieved 13 August 2018, from https://www.bloomberg.com/news/articles/2017-12-08/the-bitcoin-whales-1-000-people-who-own-40-percent-of-the-market

Kharpal, A. (2017, October 19). Bitcoin is not the new gold, Goldman Sachs says. Retrieved 13 August 2018, from https://www.cnbc.com/2017/10/19/bitcoin-is-not-the-new-gold-goldman-sachs-says.html

KPMG. (2017, April 19). Supply Chain Fraud. Retrieved from https://assets.kpmg.com/content/dam/kpmg/be/pdf/Markets/supply-chain-fraud.pdf

Kuo, M. A. (2017, April 20). China's Capital Controls: Politics or Policy? Retrieved 13 August 2018, from https://thediplomat.com/2017/04/chinas-capital-controls-politics-or-policy/

Kwon, J. (2014). *Tendermint: Consensus without Mining*. Retrieved from https://tendermint.com/static/docs/tendermint.pdf

Lee, S. (2018, February 7). Explaining Side Chains, The Next Breakthrough In Blockchain. Retrieved 17 August 2018, from https://www.forbes.com/sites/shermanlee/2018/02/07/explaining-side-chains-the-next-breakthrough-in-blockchain/#715cd62e52eb

Luke, M. N., Lee, S. J., Zdenek, P., & Dimitrova, A. (2018). *Blockchain in Electricity: a Critical Review of Progress to Date* (p. 36). Nera Economic Consulting / Eurelectric. Retrieved from https://cdn.eurelectric.org/media/3115/paper1_blockchain_eurelectric-h-BA73FBD9.pdf

Madeira, A. (2018, June 30). What Are Atomic Swaps? Retrieved 17 August 2018, from https://www.cryptocompare.com/coins/guides/what-are-atomic-swaps/

McMillan, R. (2014, March 3). The Inside Story of Mt. Gox, Bitcoin's $460 Million Disaster. *Wired*. Retrieved from https://www.wired.com/2014/03/bitcoin-exchange/

McWaters, R., Galaski, R., & Chatterjee, S. (2016). The future of financial infrastructure: An ambitious look at how blockchain can reshape financial services. Presented at the World Economic Forum

Mearian, L., & Maier, F. (2017). Microgrid in Brooklyn – Nie mehr Strompreisvergleich dank Blockchain. *Computerwoche*. Retrieved from https://www.computerwoche.de/a/nie-mehr-strompreisvergleich-dank-blockchain,3330627

Meisser, L. (2018). Welcher Weg zum digitalen Wertrecht? Überlegungen zur Übertragung von Wertrechten auf der Blockchain. Retrieved 28 April 2018, from https://docs.google.com/document/d/1WFusD3WcvQdbG_Ex9Sz4E1OaN_5RY2ETonbIKE2pvc8/edit#heading=h.yf82bz29mm1b

Mengelkamp, E., Gärttner, J., Rock, K., Kessler, S., Orsini, L., & Weinhardt, C. (2018). Designing microgrid energy markets: A case study: The Brooklyn Microgrid – ScienceDirect. *Applied Energy*, *210*, 870–880. http://dx.doi.org/10.1016/j.apenergy.2017.06.054

Mlynar, T., & Schaefer, I. (2016, December 10). Why Smart Contracts Will Need 'Smart Term Sheets' to Match – CoinDesk. Retrieved 19 March 2018, from https://www.coindesk.com/smart-contracts-will-need-smart-term-sheets-match/

Müller, Leo. Kryptowährungen. Besteht Handlungsbedarf?, Pub. L. No. Interpellation, 17.4144 (2017). Retrieved from https://www.parlament.ch/de/ratsbetrieb/suche-curia-vista/geschaeft?AffairId=20174144

Müller, Luk, Glarner, A., Linder, T., Meyer, S., Furrer, A., Gschwend, C., & Henschel, P. (2018). *Conceptual Framework for Legal & Risk Assessment of Blockchain Crypto Property (BCP)*. MME

Myrna, A., & Fletcher, C. I. (2012). *Analysis of World Bank Completed Cases of Fraud and Corruption from the Perspective of Procurement* (Background Paper). World Bank

Nordrum, A. (2016, March 3). Quantum Computer Comes Closer to Cracking RSA Encryption. Retrieved 8 August 2018, from https://spectrum.ieee.org/tech-talk/computing/hardware/encryptionbusting-quantum-computer-practices-factoring-in-scalable-fiveatom-experiment

Paralell.ru. (n.d.). 7. Обеспечение надежности в распределенных системах. Retrieved 17 August 2018, from http://parallel.ru/krukov/lec7.html

Parity Documentation. (n.d.). Aura – Authority Round. Retrieved 17 August 2018, from http://wiki.parity.io/Aura.html

Paynter, B. (2017, September 18). How Blockchain Could Transform The Way International Aid Is Distributed. *Fast Company*. Retrieved from https://www.fastcompany.com/40457354/how-blockchain-could-transform-the-way-international-aid-is-distributed

Peck, M. E. (2017, October 4). Why the Biggest Bitcoin Mines Are in China. Retrieved 13 August 2018, from https://spectrum.ieee.org/computing/networks/why-the-biggest-bitcoin-mines-are-in-china

Pickering, J., & Fraser, M. (2017, December 12). How China became a haven for people looking to cash in on the Bitcoin gold rush. Retrieved 9 August 2018, from http://uk.businessinsider.com/why-china-mines-more-bitcoin-than-any-other-country-2017-12

Pisa, M., & Juden, M. (2017). Blockchain and Economic Development: Hype vs. Reality. *Center For Global Development (CDG) Policy Paper, 107*. Retrieved from https://www.cgdev.org/publication/blockchain-and-economic-development-hype-vs-reality

PWC. (2016a). *Blockchain – an opportunity for energy producers and consumers?* Retrieved from https://www.pwc.com/gx/en/industries/assets/pwc-blockchain-opportunity-for-energy-producers-and-consumers.pdf

PWC. (2016b). *Blockchain – Chance für Energieverbraucher?* (Kurzstudie für die Verbraucherzentrale NRW, Düsseldorf). PWC

PwC. (2017). *Considering an IPO to fuel your company's future? Insight into the costs of going public and being public* (PwC Deals). Retrieved from www.pwc.com/us/iposervices

PwC, & Crypto Valley. (2017). *Initial Coin Offerings. A Strategic Perspective: Global and Switzerland*

Raju, A. (2018, August 17). Shardin FAQ. Retrieved 17 August 2018, from https://github.com/ethereum/wiki/wiki/Sharding-FAQs (Original work published 14 February 2014)

r/Bitcoin. (2014, July 6). What if a transaction gets mined in a orphaned block? Retrieved 17 August 2018, from https://www.reddit.com/r/Bitcoin/comments/29yzgf/what_if_a_transaction_gets_mined_in_a_orphaned/

r/ethereum. (2018, May 25). Rothschilds in crypto. Good/Bad/Neutral? Retrieved 17 August 2018, from https://www.reddit.com/r/ethereum/comments/8m3wj1/rothschilds_in_crypto_goodbadneutral/dzmspgv

Reynolds, E. (2015, December 9). Google's quantum computer is 100 million times faster than your PC. *Wired UK*. Retrieved from https://www.wired.co.uk/article/google-quantum-computing-d-wave

Ripple, R. (2017, July 29). 42,000 dormant bitcoin addresses. Retrieved 13 August 2018, from https://steemit.com/dormant/@rogerripple/42-000-dormant-bitcoin-addresses

Ripple Wiki. (n.d.). Introduction to Ripple for Bitcoiners. Retrieved 17 August 2018, from https://wiki.ripple.com/Introduction_to_Ripple_for_Bitcoiners

Roberts, J. J. (2017, April 15). Bitcoin Wallets Under Siege From 'Collider' Attack. Retrieved 8 August 2018, from http://fortune.com/2017/04/15/bitcoin-collider/

Roberts, J. J., & Rapp, N. (2017, November 25). Exclusive: Nearly 4 Million Bitcoins Lost Forever, New Study Says. Retrieved 13 August 2018, from http://fortune.com/2017/11/25/lost-bitcoins/

Schönenberger, Y. (2018, March 5). Experteninterview Tal.Markt/Elblox Projekt

Schor, L. (2018, March 23). On Zero-Knowledge Proofs in Blockchains. Retrieved 8 August 2018, from https://medium.com/@argongroup/on-zero-knowledge-proofs-in-blockchains-14c48cfd1dd1

Schweizer Casino Verband. (2017). *Jahresbericht 2016*. Bern

Sciarini, P., Cappelletti, F., Goldberg, A., Nai, A., & Tawfik, A. (2013). *Etude du vote par internet dans le canton de Genève*. Geneva: University of Geneva. Retrieved from http://ge.ch/vote-electronique/media/site_vote-electronique/files/imce/doc_rapports/rapport-final-sciarini-vote-par-internet.pdf

Scott Twombly. (2016). *Zero-knowledge Proofs*. Retrieved from https://www.youtube.com/watch?v=0Sy6nb72gCk

Sharma, N. (2017, November 5). Is Quantum Computing an Existential Threat to Blockchain Technology? Retrieved 8 August 2018, from https://singularityhub.com/2017/11/05/is-quantum-computing-an-existential-threat-to-blockchain-technology/

Shin, L. (2017, February 7). The First Government To Secure Land Titles On The Bitcoin Blockchain Expands Project. Retrieved 11 December 2017, from https://www.forbes.com/sites/laurashin/2017/02/07/the-first-government-to-secure-land-titles-on-the-bitcoin-blockchain-expands-project/

SIX Swiss Exchange. (n.d.). Needs-oriented listing standards – tailored to your requirements. Retrieved 13 August 2018, from https://www.six-swiss-exchange.com/issuers/equities/going_public/standards_en.html

Statista. (2017). Size of the online gambling market from 2009 to 2020. Retrieved 21 December 2017, from https://www.statista.com/statistics/270728/market-volume-of-online-gaming-worldwide/

Terazono, E. (2018, October 17). Bitcoin gets official blessing in Japan. Retrieved 13 August 2018, from https://www.ft.com/content/b8360e86-aceb-11e7-aab9-abaa44b1e130

The Economist. (2015, October 31). The trust machine. *The Economist*. Retrieved from https://www.economist.com/leaders/2015/10/31/the-trust-machine

Torres, C. (2017, December 13). Yellen Says Bitcoin Is a 'Highly Speculative Asset'. Retrieved 13 August 2018, from https://www.bloomberg.com/news/articles/2017-12-13/yellen-says-cryptocurrency-bitcoin-is-highly-speculative-asset

Tuan, C. (2017, July 27). The Rate of Blockchain Patent Applications Has Nearly Doubled in 2017. Retrieved 17 August 2018, from https://www.coindesk.com/rate-blockchain-patent-applications-nearly-doubled-2017/

Tunguz, T. (2017, January 31). How Much Does It Cost To Take Your Startup Public? Retrieved 31 January 2017, from tomtunguz.com

vDice. (2018, January 9). Retrieved from www.vdice.io

Verein für umweltgerechte Energie VUE. (2018). *Strom- und Biogasprodukte: Der Markt für erneuerbare Energieprodukte 2016*. Zürich: Bundesamt für Energie (BFE). Retrieved from http://www.bfe.admin.ch/themen/00612/00614/index.html?lang=de&dossier_id=06609

Visa. (n.d.). Small Business Retail | Visa. Retrieved 16 August 2018, from http://usa.visa.com/content/VISA/usa/englishlanguagemaster/en_US/home/run-your-business/small-business-tools/retail.html>

Wieczner, J. (2018, January 30). Why Bitcoin May Not Be Digital Gold After All. Retrieved 13 August 2018, from http://fortune.com/2018/01/30/bitcoin-gold-cryptocurrency-citi/#/

Wikipedia. (2018a). Post-quantum cryptography. In *Wikipedia*. Retrieved from https://en.wikipedia.org/w/index.php?title=Post-quantum_cryptography&oldid=853228537

Wikipedia. (2018b). Shard (database architecture). In *Wikipedia*. Retrieved from https://en.wikipedia.org/w/index.php?title=Shard_(database_architecture)&oldid=845931919

Wildau, G. (2018, January 9). Chinese regulators move to shutter bitcoin mines. Retrieved 13 August 2018, from https://www.ft.com/content/adfe7858-f4f9-11e7-88f7-5465a6ce1a00

Williams-Grut, O. (2018, March 12). Crypto exchanges are charging up to $1 million per ICO to list tokens: 'It's pure capitalism'. Retrieved 15 June 2018, from https://nordic.businessinsider.com/cryptocurrency-exchanges-listing-tokens-cost-fees-ico-2018-3/

Williamson, O. E. (1979). Transaction-Cost Economics: The Governance of Contractual Relations. *The Journal of Law & Economics*, *22*(2), 233–261

Wirdum, A. van. (2016, June 28). On Relay: How Different Bitcoin Developers Are Speeding Up the Network (Part 1). Retrieved 17 August 2018, from https://bitcoinmagazine.com/articles/on-relay-how-different-bitcoin-developers-are-speeding-up-the-network-part-1469724479/

Wong, J. I. (2017, November 3). The UN is using ethereum's technology to fund food for thousands of refugees. *Quartz*. Retrieved from https://qz.com/1118743/world-food-programmes-ethereum-based-blockchain-for-syrian-refugees-in-jordan/

Wood, R. T., & Williams, R. J. (2011). A Comparative Profile of the Internet Gambler: Demographic Characteristics, Game-play Patterns, and Problem Gambling Status, *13*(7), 1123–1141

WTO. (n.d.). The challenges of trade financing. Retrieved 14 February 2018, from https://www.wto.org/english/thewto_e/coher_e/challenges_e.htm

Zhang, C., Wu, J., Long, C., & Cheng, M. (2017). Review of Existing Peer-to-Peer Energy Trading Projects. *Energy Procedia*, *105*, 2563–2568. https://doi.org/10.1016/j.egypro.2017.03.737

Blockchain: A New Socio-Technical Environment

Blockchain as a historical construct

"A Declaration of the Independence of Cyberspace." Davos, 1996. https://www.eff.org/cyberspace-independence

Adrian, David, Luke Valenta, Benjamin VanderSloot, Eric Wustrow, Santiago Zanella-Béguelin, Paul Zimmermann, Karthikeyan Bhargavan, et al. "Imperfect Forward Secrecy: How Diffie-Hellman Fails in Practice." In *Proceedings of the 22nd ACM SIGSAC Conference on Computer and Communications Security – CCS '15*, 5–17. Denver, Colorado, USA: ACM Press, 2015. https://doi.org/10.1145/2810103.2813707

Back, Adam. "Hashcash – A Denial of Service Counter-Measure," 2002. http://www.hashcash.org/hashcash.pdf

Bertelloni, Maud Barret. "The Cypherpunk Vision of Techno-Politics." *St Anne's Academic Review*, December 4, 2017. http://st-annes-mcr.org.uk/staar/publications/staar-7-2017/barret-bertelloni-2017-the-cypherpunk-vision-of-techno-politics/

Blackman, Christine. "Stanford Encryption Pioneer Who Risked Career Becomes Hamming Medalist." *Stanford University* (blog), February 10, 2010. http://news.stanford.edu/news/2010/february8/hellman-encryption-medal-021010.html

Brodesser, Jens-Ingo. "First Monday Interviews: David Chaum." *First Monday* 4, no. 7 (July 5, 1999). https://doi.org/10.5210/fm.v4i7.683

Chaum, D. “A New Paradigm for Individuals in the Information Age.” In *1984 IEEE Symposium on Security and Privacy*, 99–99, 1984. https://doi.org/10.1109/SP.1984.10025

Chaum, David. “Blind Signatures for Untraceable Payments.” In *Advances in Cryptology*, edited by David Chaum, Ronald L. Rivest, and Alan T. Sherman, 199–203. Springer US, 1983

———. Cryptographic identification, financial transaction, and credential device. United States US4529870A, filed June 25, 1982, and issued July 16, 1985. https://patents.google.com/patent/US4529870A/en

———. “Security without Identification: Transaction Systems to Make Big Brother Obsolete.” *Communications of the ACM* 28, no. 10 (October 1, 1985): 1030–44. https://doi.org/10.1145/4372.4373

Chaum, David, Amos Fiat, and Moni Naor. “Untraceable Electronic Cash.” In *Advances in Cryptology — CRYPTO’ 88*, edited by Shafi Goldwasser, 319–27. Lecture Notes in Computer Science. Springer New York, 1990

Chaum, David L. “Untraceable Electronic Mail, Return Addresses, and Digital Pseudonyms.” *Commun. ACM* 24, no. 2 (February 1981): 84–90. https://doi.org/10.1145/358549.358563

Chu, Wesley W., ed. *Distributed Systems*. Dedham, MA: Artech House, 1986

Cormen, Thomas H., and Thomas H. Cormen, eds. *Introduction to Algorithms*. 2nd ed. Cambridge, Mass: MIT Press, 2001

Dai, wie. “B-Money,” 1998. http://www.weidai.com/bmoney.txt

Dennett, Stephen, Elizabeth J. Feinler, and Francine Perillo, eds. “ARPANET Information Brochure NIC-50003.” Defense Communication Agency, December 1985. https://drive.google.com/file/d/0B4GUEAtZeCNMS21LSUN6VmlrZm8/view

Diffie, W., and M. Hellman. “New Directions in Cryptography.” *IEEE Transactions on Information Theory* 22, no. 6 (November 1976): 644–54. https://doi.org/10.1109/TIT.1976.1055638

Diffie, Whitfield, and Martin E. Hellman. “Multiuser Cryptographic Techniques.” In *Proceedings of the June 7-10, 1976, National Computer Conference and*

Exposition on – AFIPS '76, 109. New York, New York: ACM Press, 1976. https://doi.org/10.1145/1499799.1499815

Dwork, Cynthia, and Moni Naor. "Pricing via Processing or Combatting Junk Mail." In *Advances in Cryptology — CRYPTO' 92*, edited by Ernest F. Brickell, 740:139–47. Berlin, Heidelberg: Springer Berlin Heidelberg, 1993. https://doi.org/10.1007/3-540-48071-4_10

Ellis, J H. "The Possibility of Non-Secret Secure Digital Encryption." Research Repport. CESG (Communications-Electronics Security Group), January 1970. https://web.archive.org/web/20160307205657/http://www.gchq.gov.uk/SiteCollectionDocuments/CESG_Research_Report_No_3006.pdf

Feistel, Horst. "Cryptography and Computer Privacy." *Scientific American* 228, no. 5 (1973): 15–23

Flichy, Patrice. "The Imaginary of Internet," n.d., 53

Gaston-Breton, Par Tristan. "Arpanet. Le monde en réseau," n.d., 6

Haber, Stuart, and W. Scott Stornetta. "How to Time-Stamp a Digital Document." *Journal of Cryptology* 3, no. 2 (January 1, 1991): 99–111. https://doi.org/10.1007/BF00196791

Hafner, Katie, and Matthew Lyon. *Where Wizards Stay up Late: The Origins of the Internet*. 1. Simon & Schuster paperback ed. New York: Simon & Schuster Paperbacks, 2006

Hellman, Martin E., and Thomas M. Cover. "Learning with Finite Memory." *The Annals of Mathematical Statistics* 41, no. 3 (1970): 765–82

Ian Grigg. "How DigiCash Blew Everything." *Next! Magazine*, January 1999. https://cryptome.org/jya/digicrash.htm

John Perry Barlow. "Crime and Puzzlement." Electronic Frontier Foundation, February 9, 2018. https://www.eff.org/fr/pages/crime-and-puzzlement

Jonnie Emsley. "Exclusive Interview: A Briefing with Scott Stornetta, Founding Father of Blockchain." *CryptoSlate* (blog), November 8, 2018. https://cryptoslate.com/exclusive-interview-a-briefing-with-scott-stornetta-founding-father-of-blockchain/

Kahn, David. *The Codebreakers: The Story of Secret Writing*. Rev. ed. New York: Scribner, 1996

Kelty, Christopher M. *Two Bits: The Cultural Significance of Free Software.* Durham: Duke University Press Books, 2008

Konheim, Alan G. "Horst Feistel: The Inventor of LUCIFER, the Cryptographic Algorithm That Changed Cryptology." *Journal of Cryptographic Engineering* 9, no. 1 (April 1, 2019): 85–100. https://doi.org/10.1007/s13389-018-0198-5

Lamport, Leslie, Robert Shostak, and Marshall Pease. "The Byzantine Generals Problem." *ACM Transactions on Programming Languages and Systems* 4, no. 3 (July 1, 1982): 382–401. https://doi.org/10.1145/357172.357176

Leiner, Barry M., Vinton G. Cerf, David D. Clark, Robert E. Kahn, Leonard Kleinrock, Daniel C. Lynch, Jon Postel, Larry G. Roberts, and Stephen Wolff. "Brief History of the Internet." Internet Society, 1997. https://www.internetsociety.org/wp-content/uploads/2017/09/ISOC-History-of-the-Internet_1997.pdf

Mahoney, Michael S. "The History of Computing in the History of Technology." *IEEE Annals of the History of Computing* 10, no. 2 (April 1988): 113–25. https://doi.org/10.1109/MAHC.1988.10011

Margaret Rouse. "What Is Bellcore (Bell Communications Research)?" SearchNetworking. Accessed May 3, 2019. https://searchnetworking.techtarget.com/definition/Bellcore

Markoff, John. "In Retreat, U.S. Spy Agency Shrugs at Found Secret Data." *The New York Times*, November 28, 1992, sec. U.S.https://www.nytimes.com/1992/11/28/us/in-retreat-us-spy-agency-shrugs-at-found-secret-data.html

Mcluhan, Marshall. *Pour Comprendre Les Medias: Les Prolongements Technologiques De l'homme.* Place of publication not identified: Points, 2015

Merkle, Ralph C. "A Digital Signature Based on a Conventional Encryption Function." In *Advances in Cryptology — CRYPTO '87*, edited by Carl Pomerance, 369–78. Lecture Notes in Computer Science. Springer Berlin Heidelberg, 1988

———. "Secure Communications over Insecure Channels." *Communications of the ACM* 21, no. 4 (Spring 1978): 294–99. https://doi.org/10.1145/359460.359473

Mockapetris, P. V. "RFC883: Domain Names: Implementation Specification," November 1983. https://tools.ietf.org/html/rfc883

Mockapetris, P.V. "RFC1034: Domain Names – Concepts and Facilities." RFC Editor, November 1987. https://doi.org/10.17487/rfc1034

"Nick Szabo -- Smart Contracts: Building Blocks for Digital Markets." Accessed August 13, 2019. http://www.fon.hum.uva.nl/rob/Courses/InformationInSpeech/CDROM/Literature/LOTwinterschool2006/szabo.best.vwh.net/smart_contracts_2.html

pet3rpan. "Before Bitcoin Pt.1 — 70s 'Public Key Saga.'" *Pet3rpan* (blog), March 24, 2018. https://medium.com/@pet3rpan/history-of-things-before-bitcoin-cryptocurrency-part-one-e199f02ca380

———. "Before Bitcoin Pt.2 — 'The Origins of Decentralisation.'" *Medium* (blog), April 4, 2018. https://medium.com/@pet3rpan/history-of-things-before-bitcoin-cryptocurrency-part-two-94c4576005

Richissin, Todd. "Bellcore Says It Has Time-Stamp To Protect Records, Settle Patent Disputes." *AP NEWS*, November 20, 1990. https://apnews.com/fafed65be37183cb1b7412a83c6d3cbc

Rid, Thomas. *Rise of the Machines: A Cybernetic History*. 1 edition. New York: W. W. Norton & Company, 2016

Rivest, R L, A Shamir, and L Adleman. "A Method for Obtaining Digital Signatures and Public- Key Cryptosystems." *Communications of the ACM* 21, no. 2 (1978): 7

Shannon, C. E. "A Mathematical Theory of Communication." *Bell System Technical Journal* 27, no. 3 (July 1948): 379–423. https://doi.org/10.1002/j.1538-7305.1948.tb01338.x

———. "A Mathematical Theory of Cryptography," September 1, 1945. https://www.iacr.org/museum/shannon/shannon45.pdf

———. "Communication Theory of Secrecy Systems." *The Bell System Technical Journal* 28, no. 4 (October 1949): 656–715. https://doi.org/10.1002/j.1538-7305.1949.tb00928.x

Sherman, Alan T., Farid Javani, Haibin Zhang, and Enis Golaszewski. "On the Origins and Variations of Blockchain Technologies." *IEEE Security & Privacy* 17, no. 1 (January 2019): 72–77. https://doi.org/10.1109/MSEC.2019.2893730

"Smart Contracts." Accessed May 26, 2019. http://www.fon.hum.uva.nl/rob/Courses/InformationInSpeech/CDROM/Literatur e/LOTwinterschool2006/szabo.best.vwh.net/smart.contracts.html

Stuart Haber. "Stuart Haber Bio." World Crypto Index. Accessed May 3, 2019. https://www.worldcryptoindex.com/creators/stuart-haber/

Su, Zaw-Sing. "RFC830: Distributed System for Internet Name Service," October 1982. https://tools.ietf.org/html/rfc830

Théry, Gérard. "Les autoroutes de l'information," 1994

Tim Gihring. "The Rise and Fall of the Gopher Protocol." MinnPost, August 11, 2016. https://www.minnpost.com/business/2016/08/rise-and-fall-gopher-protocol/

Williamson, M J. "Non-Secret Encryption Using a Finite Field," 1974

Yann Verdo. "Leslie Lamport, l'homme qui a appris aux ordinateurs à travailler ensemble." *Les Echos*, May 30, 2014. https://www.lesechos.fr/2014/05/leslie-lamport-lhomme-qui-a-appris-aux-ordinateurs-a-travailler-ensemble-303924

Zimmermann, Philip. "Why I Wrote PGP," 1991. https://www.philzimmermann.com/EN/essays/WhyIWrotePGP.html

The design and implementation of the Bitcoin protocol

Albrechtslund, Anders. "Online Social Networking as Participatory Surveillance." *First Monday* 13, no. 3 (2008). https://doi.org/10.5210/fm.v13i3.2142

Antonopoulos, Andreas M. *Mastering Bitcoin: Programming the Open Blockchain*. Second edition. Sebastopol, CA: O'Reilly, 2017

Back, Adam. "[ANNOUNCE] Hash Cash Postage Implementation." Accessed June 3, 2019. http://www.hashcash.org/papers/announce.txt

Barlow, John Perry. "A Not Terribly Brief History of the Electronic Frontier Foundation." *Electronic Frontier Foundation* (blog), November 8, 1990. https://www.eff.org/fr/pages/not-terribly-brief-history-electronic-frontier-foundation

Bercy Infos. “Crypto-monnaies, crypto-actifs... Comment s’y retrouver ?” Le portail des ministères économiques et financiers, April 7, 2018. https://www.economie.gouv.fr/particuliers/cryptomonnaies-cryptoactifs

“Bitcoin.” SourceForge. Accessed May 26, 2019. https://sourceforge.net/projects/bitcoin/

“Bitcoin Forum – Index.” Bitcoin Talk. Accessed May 26, 2019. https://bitcointalk.org/

Bitcoin Wiki contributors. “Contract – Bitcoin Wiki.” Wiki, 2012. https://en.bitcoin.it/wiki/Contract

Caprettini, Bruno, and Hans-Joachim Voth. “Rage against the Machines: New Technology and Violent Unrest in Industrializing England.” UBS International Center of Economics in Society, University of Zurich, 2018. https://doi.org/10.5167/uzh-158743

Christin, Nicolas. “Traveling the Silk Road: A Measurement Analysis of a Large Anonymous Online Marketplace.” *ArXiv:1207.7139 [Cs]*, July 30, 2012. http://arxiv.org/abs/1207.7139

Danezis, George, and Claudia Diaz. “A Survey of Anonymous Communication Channels.” *Journal of Privacy Technology*, no. 46 (February 2008)

Davis, Joshua. “The Crypto-Currency,” October 3, 2011. https://www.newyorker.com/magazine/2011/10/10/the-crypto-currency

Finney, Hal. Letter to cypherpunks@al-qaeda.net. “RPOW – Reusable Proofs of Work,” August 15, 2004. https://nakamotoinstitute.org/rpow/

Jakobsson, Markus, and Ari Juels. “Proofs of Work and Bread Pudding Protocols(Extended Abstract).” In *Secure Information Networks: Communications and Multimedia Security IFIP TC6/TC11 Joint Working Conference on Communications and Multimedia Security (CMS’99) September 20–21, 1999, Leuven, Belgium*, edited by Bart Preneel, 258–72. IFIP — The International Federation for Information Processing. Boston, MA: Springer US, 1999. https://doi.org/10.1007/978-0-387-35568-9_18

jtimon. “List of Bitcoin-like Proposed Currencies and Chains,” May 2011. https://bitcointalk.org/index.php?topic=7500

kdawson. “Bitcoin Releases Version 0.3 – Slashdot.” *Slashdot*, July 11, 2010. https://news.slashdot.org/story/10/07/11/1747245/bitcoin-releases-version-03

Krause, Max J., and Thabet Tolaymat. “Quantification of Energy and Carbon Costs for Mining Cryptocurrencies.” *Nature Sustainability* 1, no. 11 (November 2018): 711. https://doi.org/10.1038/s41893-018-0152-7

Matonis, Jon. “Bitcoin Foundation Launches to Drive Bitcoin’s Advancement.” *Forbes*, September 27, 2012.https://www.forbes.com/sites/jonmatonis/2012/09/27/bitcoin-foundation-launches-to-drive-bitcoins-advancement/

Nagy, Béla, J. Doyne Farmer, Quan M. Bui, and Jessika E. Trancik. “Statistical Basis for Predicting Technological Progress.” *PLOS ONE* 8, no. 2 (February 28, 2013): e52669. https://doi.org/10.1371/journal.pone.0052669

Nagy, Béla, J. Doyne Farmer, Jessika E. Trancik, and John Paul Gonzales. “Superexponential Long-Term Trends in Information Technology.” *Technological Forecasting and Social Change*, Contains Special Section: Economic Hard Times: Impact on Innovation and Innovation Potential, 78, no. 8 (October 1, 2011): 1356–64. https://doi.org/10.1016/j.techfore.2011.07.006

Nakamoto, Satoshi. “Bitcoin: A Peer-to-Peer Electronic Cash System Bitcoin: A Peer-to-Peer Electronic Cash System,” 2008

———. “Bitcoin Open Source Implementation of P2P Currency.” *P2P Foundation*, February 11, 2009. http://p2pfoundation.ning.com/forum/topics/bitcoin-open-source

———. “Bitcoin P2P E-Cash Paper,” October 31, 2008. http://www.metzdowd.com/pipermail/cryptography/2008-October/014810.html

———. “Bitcoin v0.1 Released,” January 8, 2009. http://www.metzdowd.com/pipermail/cryptography/2009-January/014994.html

———. “Transactions and Scripts: DUP HASH160 ... EQUALVERIFY CHECKSIG.” *Bitcointalk.Org*, July 17, 2010. https://bitcointalk.org/index.php?topic=195.msg1617#msg1617

Philippas, Dionisis. “Media Attention and Bitcoin Prices.” *SSRN Electronic Journal*, 2019. https://doi.org/10.2139/ssrn.3313866

Popper, Nathaniel. *Digital Gold: Bitcoin and the inside Story of the Misfits and Millionaires Trying to Reinvent Money*. First Harper Paperback edition. New York: Harper, 2016

Powell, Alvin. “Creating a Computer Currency.” *Harvard Gazette* (blog), August 29, 2007. https://news.harvard.edu/gazette/story/2007/08/creating-a-computer-currency/

Ray Dillinger. “If I'd Known What We Were Starting | LinkedIn,” September 20, 2017. https://www.linkedin.com/pulse/id-known-what-we-were-starting-ray-dillinger/

Reitman, Rainey. “Bitcoin – a Step Toward Censorship-Resistant Digital Currency.” *Electronic Frontier Foundation* (blog), January 20, 2011. https://www.eff.org/deeplinks/2011/01/bitcoin-step-toward-censorship-resistant

Satoshi Nakamoto. “Welcome to the New Bitcoin Forum!” *Bitcoin Forum*, November 22, 2009. https://bitcointalk.org/index.php?topic=5

SourceForge. “Clarifying SourceForge.Net's Denial of Site Access for Certain Persons in Accordance with US Law.” *SourceForge Community Blog* (blog), January 25, 2010. https://sourceforge.net/blog/clarifying-sourceforgenets-denial-of-site-access-for-certain-persons-in-accordance-with-us-law/

Thomas, Keir, PCWorld | December 10, and 2010 04:30 PM PT About | Smart tech advice for your small business. “Could the Wikileaks Scandal Lead to New Virtual Currency?” PCWorld, December 10, 2010. https://www.pcworld.com/article/213230/could_wikileaks_scandal_lead_to_new_virtual_currency.html

“Transcript of #bitcoin-Dev (IRC) Primary Discussion on Namecoin,” November 18, 2010.https://web.archive.org/web/20101118020511/http://veritas.maximilianeum.ch/bitcoin/irc/logs/2010/11/14#l1150

vinced. “[Announce] Namecoin – a Distributed Naming System Based on Bitcoin.” *Bicoin Talk*, April 18, 2011. https://bitcointalk.org/index.php?topic=6017

Vranken, Harald. “Sustainability of Bitcoin and Blockchains.” *Current Opinion in Environmental Sustainability*, Sustainability governance, 28 (October 1, 2017): 1–9. https://doi.org/10.1016/j.cosust.2017.04.011

Vries, Alex de. “Bitcoin's Growing Energy Problem.” *Joule* 2, no. 5 (May 16, 2018): 801–5. https://doi.org/10.1016/j.joule.2018.04.016

Blockchain as a distributed ledger technology

Androulaki, Elli, Artem Barger, Vita Bortnikov, Christian Cachin, Konstantinos Christidis, Angelo De Caro, David Enyeart, et al. "Hyperledger Fabric: A Distributed Operating System for Permissioned Blockchains." *Proceedings of the Thirteenth EuroSys Conference on – EuroSys '18*, 2018, 1–15. https://doi.org/10.1145/3190508.3190538

Arthur, Charles, and Josh Halliday. "WikiLeaks Fights to Stay Online after US Company Withdraws Domain Name." *The Guardian*, December 3, 2010, sec. Media. https://www.theguardian.com/media/blog/2010/dec/03/wikileaks-knocked-off-net-dns-everydns

Assia, Yoni, Vitalik Buterin, Hakim liorhakiLior, Meni Rosenfeld, and Rotem Lev. "Colored Coins whitepaper – Digital Assets," 2013. https://docs.google.com/document/d/1AnkP_cVZTCMLIzw4DvsW6M8Q2JC0llz rTLuoWu2z1BE/edit?usp=embed_facebook

"Bitcoin Energy Consumption Index." Digiconomist. Accessed March 12, 2019. https://digiconomist.net/bitcoin-energy-consumption

Bodó, Balázs, and Alexandra Giannopoulou. "The Logics of Technology Decentralization – The Case of Distributed Ledger Technologies." In *Blockchain and Web 3.0 Social, Economic, and Technological Challenges*. Routledge, 2020. https://papers.ssrn.com/sol3/papers.cfm?abstract_id=3330590##

Buterin, Vitalik. "A Prehistory of the Ethereum Protocol." *Vitalik Buterin's Website* (blog), September 14, 2017. https://vitalik.ca/general/2017/09/14/prehistory.html

———. "Bootstrapping A Decentralized Autonomous Corporation: Part I." *Bitcoin Magazine* (blog), September 20, 2013. https://bitcoinmagazine.com/articles/bootstrapping-a-decentralized-autonomous-corporation-part-i-1379644274/

———. "On Public and Private Blockchains." *Ethereum Foundation Blog* (blog), August 6, 2015. https://blog.ethereum.org/2015/08/07/on-public-and-private-blockchains/

Chase, Brad, and Ethan MacBrough. "Analysis of the XRP Ledger Consensus Protocol." *ArXiv.Org*, February 21, 2018. http://arxiv.org/abs/1802.07242

Dalton, David, and Paolo Gianturco. "Blockchain : de la frénésie au prototype." Deloitte, Mai 2016. https://www2.deloitte.com/fr/fr/pages/services-financier/articles/efma-blockchain-de-la-frenesie-au-prototype.html

Edmund L. Andrews. "Chris Larsen: Money Without Borders." *Stanford Graduate School of Business* (blog), September 24, 2013. http://stanford.io/1qRRzpd

Epicenter Podcast. *EB84 – Tim Swanson: Permissioned Ledgers and the Case for Blockchains Without Bitcoin*, 2015. https://www.youtube.com/watch?v=k3pM8vB2QYc

"Exclusive: Blockchain Platform Developed by Banks to Be Open-Source." *Reuters*, October 20, 2016. https://uk.reuters.com/article/us-banks-blockchain-r3-exclusive-idUKKCN12K17E

Finley, Klint. "Out in the Open: Teenage Hacker Transforms Web into One Giant Bitcoin Network." *Wired*, January 27, 2014. https://www.wired.com/2014/01/ethereum/

Foley, Ian. "Blockchains and Enterprise: The Hybrid Approach to Adoption | Distributed.Com/." *Distributed* (blog). Accessed July 30, 2019. https://distributed.com/news/blockchains-and-enterprise-hybrid-approach-adoption

Gatteschi, V., F. Lamberti, C. Demartini, C. Pranteda, and V. Santamaría. "To Blockchain or Not to Blockchain: That Is the Question." *IT Professional* 20, no. 2 (March 2018): 62–74. https://doi.org/10.1109/MITP.2018.021921652

Great Britain, and Treasury. *Digital Currencies: Response to the Call for Information*. London: HM Treasury, 2015. https://www.gov.uk/government/uploads/system/uploads/attachment_data/file/414040/digital_currencies_response_to_call_for_information_final_changes.pdf

Guegan, Dominique. "The Digital World: II – Alternatives to the Bitcoin Blockchain?" June 2018. https://halshs.archives-ouvertes.fr/halshs-01832002

Hearn, Mike. "Corda Technical Whitepaper – Corda: A Distributed Ledger," November 2016

hperretta, Author. "Private vs. Public and Permissioned vs. Permissionless." *Blocktonite* (blog), June 27, 2017. https://blocktonite.com/2017/06/27/private-vs-public-and-permissioned-vs-permissionless/

Hyperledger. "Linux Foundation's Hyperledger Project Announces 30 Founding Members and Code Proposals to Advance Blockchain Technology." *Hyperledger* (blog), February 10, 2016. https://www.hyperledger.org/announcements/2016/02/09/linux-foundations-hyperledger-project-announces-30-founding-members-and-code-proposals-to-advance-blockchain-technology

Jones, Paul, and Albert Szmigielski. "An Open Letter to Banks and Financial Institutions." *CryptoIQ* (blog), March 23, 2016. https://medium.com/@CryptoIQ.ca/an-open-letter-to-banks-and-financial-institutions-ab5b0674444d

Koens, Tommy, and Erik Poll. "The Drivers Behind Blockchain Adoption: The Rationality of Irrational Choices." In *Euro-Par 2018: Parallel Processing Workshops*, edited by Gabriele Mencagli, Dora B. Heras, Valeria Cardellini, Emiliano Casalicchio, Emmanuel Jeannot, Felix Wolf, Antonio Salis, et al., 11339:535–46. Cham: Springer International Publishing, 2019. https://doi.org/10.1007/978-3-030-10549-5_42

Narayanan, Arvind, Joseph Bonneau, Edward Felten, Andrew Miller, and Steven Goldfeder. *Bitcoin and Cryptocurrency Technologies: A Comprehensive Introduction*. Princeton: Princeton University Press, 2016

Oliver Belin. "The Difference Between Blockchain and Distributed Ledger Technology." *TradeIX* (blog), January 30, 2018. https://tradeix.com/distributed-ledger-technology/

Pahl, Claus, Nabil EL Ioini, and Sven Helmer. "A Decision Framework for Blockchain Platforms for IoT and Edge Computing," 105–13, 2019. https://www.scitepress.org/PublicationsDetail.aspx?ID=TqT447y14pE=&t=1

Passlack, Markus. "On the Disruptive Potential of Distributed Ledger Technologies." Universidade Católica Portuguesa, 2019. https://repositorio.ucp.pt/handle/10400.14/26961

Peter, Kimberley, and Michael Schaus. "Understanding Bitcoin Currency and Blockchain Technology as a Media System," 22, 2016

R3. "Corda Developer Documentation." R3, July 17, 2019. https://docs.corda.net/

Schueffel, Patrick. "Alternative Distributed Ledger Technologies Blockchain vs. Tangle vs. Hashgraph – A High-Level Overview and Comparison." Rochester,

NY: Social Science Research Network, December 15, 2017. https://papers.ssrn.com/abstract=3144241

Shin, Laura. "Here's the Man Who Created ICOs and This Is the New Token He's Backing." *Forbes*, September 21, 2017. https://www.forbes.com/sites/laurashin/2017/09/21/heres-the-man-who-created-icos-and-this-is-the-new-token-hes-backing/

Straus, Ryan. "The Last Straw for Bitcoin." *American Banker*, June 5, 2013. https://www.americanbanker.com/opinion/the-last-straw-for-bitcoin

Swanson, Tim. "A Brief History of R3 – the Distributed Ledger Group." *Great Wall of Numbers* (blog), February 27, 2017. https://www.ofnumbers.com/2017/02/27/a-brief-history-of-r3-the-distributed-ledger-group/

———. "Consensus-as-a-Service: A Brief Report on the Emergence of Permissioned, Distributed Ledger Systems," n.d., 66

Vujičić, D., D. Jagodić, and S. Ranđić. "Blockchain Technology, Bitcoin, and Ethereum: A Brief Overview." In *2018 17th International Symposium INFOTEH-JAHORINA (INFOTEH)*, 1–6, 2018. https://doi.org/10.1109/INFOTEH.2018.8345547

Wolfson, Rachel. "IBM Launches A Blockchain-Based Global Payments Network Using Stellar's Cryptocurrency." *Forbes*, March 18, 2019. https://www.forbes.com/sites/rachelwolfson/2019/03/18/ibm-launches-a-blockchain-based-global-payments-network-using-stellars-cryptocurrency/

Blockchain socialisation patterns

Anthamatten, Jennifer, and Pascal Lago. "Après la frénésie de la blockchain." Avenir Suisse, June 4, 2019. https://www.avenir-suisse.ch/fr/publication/apres-la-frenesie-de-la-blockchain/

Auer, Raphael. "Beyond the Doomsday Economics of 'Proof-of-Work' in Cryptocurrencies." BIS Working Papers. Bank for International Settlements, January 21, 2019. https://www.bis.org/publ/work765.htm

Auer, Raphael, and Stijn Claessens. "Regulating Cryptocurrencies: Assessing Market Reactions." BIS Quarterly Review. Bank for International Settlements, September 23, 2018. https://www.bis.org/publ/qtrpdf/r_qt1809f.htm

Bank of international Settlements. “V. Cryptocurrencies: Looking beyond the Hype.” In *Annual Economic Report 2018*. Bank of international Settlements, 2018. https://www.bis.org/publ/arpdf/ar2018e5.htm

Bishr, Aisha Bin. “Dubai: A City Powered by Blockchain.” *Innovations: Technology, Governance, Globalization* 12, no. 3–4 (December 28, 2018): 4–8. https://doi.org/10.1162/inov_a_00271

BlockchainsforSchools.com. “Differences Between a Whitepaper, Yellow Paper, and Beige Paper.” *Medium* (blog), August 1, 2018. https://medium.com/@hello_38248/differences-between-a-white-paper-yellow-paper-and-beige-paper-ad173f982237

Buterin, Vitalik. “DLS • Vitalik Buterin • Cryptocurrencies and Blockchains: Combining Mechanism Design and Computation.” Faculty of Mathematics, University of Waterloo. Accessed June 9, 2019. https://www.youtube.com/watch?v=EFlg-a4Klf4&app=desktop

———. “Mastercoin: A Second-Generation Protocol on the Bitcoin Blockchain.” *Bitcoin Magazine* (blog), November 4, 2013. https://bitcoinmagazine.com/articles/mastercoin-a-second-generation-protocol-on-the-bitcoin-blockchain-1383603310

Catalini, Christian, and Joshua S. Gans. “Some Simple Economics of the Blockchain.” *SSRN Electronic Journal*, December 2016. https://doi.org/10.2139/ssrn.2874598

Cheung, Chun Yin, and Kevin Feng. “2018 Market Survey Report for (Non-Financial) Application of Blockchain in China.” PwC, 2018. https://www.pwccn.com/en/services/risk-assurance/publications/2018-china-blockchain-survery-report.html

Chiu, Jonathan, and Thorsten V. Koeppl. “The Economics of Cryptocurrencies Bitcoin and Beyond.” *SSRN Electronic Journal*, 2017. https://doi.org/10.2139/ssrn.3048124

Corradi, Fiammetta, and Philipp Höfner. “The Disenchantment of Bitcoin: Unveiling the Myth of a Digital Currency.” *International Review of Sociology* 28, no. 1 (January 2, 2018): 193–207. https://doi.org/10.1080/03906701.2018.1430067

De Filippi, Primavera. "Bitcoin." In *A History of Intellectual Property in 50 Objects*. Cambridge University Press, 2019. https://hal.archives-ouvertes.fr/hal-02046688

———. "Repenser Le Droit à l'ère Numérique : Entre La Régulation Technique et La Gouvernance Algorithmique." In *Droit et Machine*, edited by V. Gautrais and P. E. Moyse, Vol. 3. Éditions Thémis, 2017. https://hal.archives-ouvertes.fr/hal-01676890

De Filippi, Primavera, and Michel Reymond. "La Blockchain: comment réguler sans autorité." In *Numérique : reprendre le contrôle*, 81–96, 2016. https://archive-ouverte.unige.ch/unige:90735

De Filippi, Primavera, and Aaron Wright. *Blockchain and the Law: The Rule of Code*. Cambridge, Massachusetts: Harvard University Press, 2018

Doerr, Audrey D. "The Role of Whitepapers in the Policy-Making Process: The Experience of the Government of Canada: The Experience of the Government of Canada." Carleton University, 1973. https://curve.carleton.ca/6c511929-de0c-4a39-903a-55a282577f96

entethalliance. "Enterprise Ethereum Alliance," 2019. https://entethalliance.org/

Farshid, Simon, Andreas Reitz, and Peter Roßbach. "Design of a Forgetting Blockchain: A Possible Way to Accomplish GDPR Compatibility," 2019. http://scholarspace.manoa.hawaii.edu/handle/10125/60145

Frankenfield, Jake. "Hard Fork." Investopedia, February 6, 2019. https://www.investopedia.com/terms/h/hard-fork.asp

———. "Soft Fork." Investopedia, February 6, 2019. https://www.investopedia.com/terms/s/soft-fork.asp

Gasull, Clement. "Des racines libertariennes à la bienveillance du monde économique : aperçu des idéologies dans le développement des blockchains." In *Les enjeux des blockchains*. 6: France Stratégie, 2018. https://halshs.archives-ouvertes.fr/halshs-01967287/document

Hacker, Philipp, Ioannis Lianos, Georgios Dimitropoulos, and Stefan Eich. "Regulating Blockchain: Techno-Social and Legal Challenges – An Introduction." SSRN Scholarly Paper. Rochester, NY: Social Science Research Network, September 10, 2018. https://papers.ssrn.com/abstract=3247150

Halaburda, Hanna. "Blockchain Revolution without the Blockchain?" *Communications of the ACM* 61, no. 7 (June 25, 2018): 27–29. https://doi.org/10.1145/3225619

Harrington, Joseph Emmett. *Games, Strategies, and Decision Making*. New York: Worth, 2009

Harry, Brian. "The Largest Git Repo on the Planet." *Brian Harry's Blog* (blog), May 24, 2017. https://devblogs.microsoft.com/bharry/the-largest-git-repo-on-the-planet/

Herian, Robert. *Regulating Blockchain: Critical Perspectives in Law and Technology*. Routledge, 2018. https://www.routledge.com/Regulating-Blockchain-Critical-Perspectives-in-Law-and-Technology/Herian/p/book/9781138592766

International Monetary Fund, and World Bank. "The Bali Fintech Agenda." Policy Report. International Monetary Fund, October 2018

"ISO/TC 307 – Blockchain and Distributed Ledger Technologies." ISO. Accessed June 20, 2019. https://www.iso.org/committee/6266604.html

Iwata, Hideyuki, Takeshi Morikawa, and Takashi Tominaga. "Trends in Standardization of Blockchain Technology by ISO/TC 307." *NTT Technical Review*, May 5, 2018. https://www.ntt-review.jp/archive/ntttechnical.php?contents=ntr201805gls.html

Iwata, Hideyuki, Takashi Tominaga, and Takeshi Morikawa. "Trends in Standardization of Blockchain Technology by ISO/TC 307." *NTT Technical Review* 16, no. 5 (2018): 5

La Raudière, Laure de, and Jean-Michel Mis. "Rapport d'information des travaux de la mission d'information commune sur les chaînes de blocs (blockchains)." Rapports d'information. Assemblée Nationale, décembre 2018. http://www.assemblee-nationale.fr/15/rap-info/i1501.asp

Le Conseil fédéral. "Bases juridiques pour la distributed ledger technology et la blockchain en Suisse – État des lieux avec un accent sur le secteur financier." Rapport du Conseil fédéral. Bern: Confédération suisse, December 14, 2018

"L'émergence du bitcoin et autres crypto-actifs : enjeux, risques et perspectives." Focus. Banque de France, March 5, 2018. https://publications.banque-france.fr/lemergence-du-bitcoin-et-autres-crypto-actifs-enjeux-risques-et-perspectives

Lyons, Tom, Ludovic Courcelas, and Ken Timsit. “Scalability, Interoperability and Sustainability of the Blockchain.” European Union Blockchain Observatory & Forum, March 2019. https://www.eublockchainforum.eu/sites/default/files/reports/report_scalaibility_06_03_2019.pdf

Mann, Richard P., and Dirk Helbing. “Optimal Incentives for Collective Intelligence.” *Proceedings of the National Academy of Sciences*, April 26, 2017, 201618722. https://doi.org/10.1073/pnas.1618722114

Mark Walport. “Distributed Ledger Technology: Beyond Block Chain.” Government Office for Science, January 2016. https://www.gov.uk/government/publications/distributed-ledger-technology-blackett-review

Massachusetts Institute of Technology. “The MIT License,” 1980. https://opensource.org/licenses/MIT

May, Timothy C. “Enough with the ICO-Me-So-Horny-Get-Rich-Quick-Lambo Crypto.” *CoinDesk* (blog), October 19, 2018. https://www.coindesk.com/enough-with-the-ico-me-so-horny-get-rich-quick-lambo-crypto

Mead, George Herbert, Charles W. Morris, Daniel R. Huebner, and Hans Joas. *Mind, Self, and Society*. The definitive edition. Chicago ; London: University of Chicago Press, 2015

Mnohoghitnei, Irina, Simon Scorer, and Khushali Shingala. “Embracing the Promise of Fintech.” Quarterly Bulletin. Bank of England, 2019. https://www.bankofengland.co.uk/quarterly-bulletin/2019/2019-q1/embracing-the-promise-of-fintech

Möslein, Florian. “Legal Boundaries of Blockchain Technologies: Smart Contracts as Self-Help?” SSRN Scholarly Paper. Rochester, NY: Social Science Research Network, October 17, 2018. https://papers.ssrn.com/abstract=3267852

Munster, Ben. “Confessions of a Whitepaper Writer.” *Decrypt* (blog), April 22, 2019. https://decrypt.co/6643/confessions-of-a-white-paper-writer

Nash, John F. “Equilibrium Points in N-Person Games.” *Proceedings of the National Academy of Sciences* 36, no. 1 (January 1, 1950): 48–49. https://doi.org/10.1073/pnas.36.1.48

Natarajan, Harish, Solvej Karla Krause, and Helen Luskin Gradstein. "Distributed Ledger Technology (DLT) and Blockchain." The World Bank, December 1, 2017. http://documents.worldbank.org/curated/en/177911513714062215/Distributed-Ledger-Technology-DLT-and-blockchain

"[Necro Thread] It's Here: The Second Bitcoin Whitepaper." Accessed June 5, 2019. https://bitcointalk.org/index.php?topic=56901.0

"Omni Protocol Specification (Formerly Mastercoin)." 2013. Reprint, Omni, May 15, 2019. https://github.com/OmniLayer/spec

Orcutt, Mike. "In 2019, Blockchains Will Start to Become Boring." MIT Technology Review. Accessed June 13, 2019. https://www.technologyreview.com/s/612687/in-2019-blockchains-will-start-to-become-boring/

O'Rourke, Morgan. "Believing the Blockchain Hype." *Risk Management*, 2019. Expanded Academic ASAP

Pellegrini, François, and Sébastien Canevet. *Droit Des Logiciels: Logiciels Privatifs et Logiciels Libres*. 1re édition. Paris: Presses universitaires de France, 2013

Perez, Yessi Bello. "A Brief History of Cryptocurrency and Blockchain Whitepapers." *Hard Fork | The Next Web* (blog), February 21, 2019. https://thenextweb.com/hardfork/2019/02/21/a-brief-history-of-cryptocurrency-and-blockchain-white-papers/

Pignon, Vincent. "Preuve de concept blockchain appliquee au registre du commerce." Compte-rendu de projet. République et Canton de Genève, January 2018

Porta, Donatella Della. "Critical Trust: Social Movements and Democracy in Times of Crisis." *Cambio. Rivista Sulle Trasformazioni Sociali* 2, no. 4 (2012): 33-43–43. https://doi.org/10.13128/cambio-19432

Quintais, João Pedro, Balázs Bodó, Valeria Ferrari, and Alexandra Giannopoulou. "Blockchain And The Law: A Critical Evaluation." *Amsterdam Law School Legal Studies Research Paper*, December 18, 2018. https://ssrn.com/abstract=3317404

Qureshi, Haseeb. "Blockchain Fees Are Broken. Here Are 3 Proposals to Fix Them." *Hacker Noon* (blog), June 3, 2019. https://hackernoon.com/blockchain-fees-are-broken-here-are-3-proposals-to-fix-them-1f772e1530dd

Raymond, Eric Steven. "Homesteading the Noosphere," 1998. http://www.catb.org/esr/writings/homesteading/homesteading/

Rozas, David, Antonio Tenorio-Fornés, Silvia Díaz-Molina, and Samer Hassan. "When Ostrom Meets Blockchain: Exploring the Potentials of Blockchain for Commons Governance." SSRN Scholarly Paper. Rochester, NY: Social Science Research Network, July 30, 2018. https://papers.ssrn.com/abstract=3272329

Shipley, Luke. "The Whitepaper Revolution ~ the Good, the Bad and the Sickening." *Hacker Noon* (blog), November 24, 2017. https://hackernoon.com/the-whitepaper-revolution-the-good-the-bad-and-the-sickening-438b51333fa

"'Sovereign' Cryptocurrencies Serve Governments, Not People." *VentureBeat* (blog), August 11, 2018. https://venturebeat.com/2018/08/11/sovereign-cryptocurrencies-serve-governments-not-people/

Staff of Global Legal Research Directorate. "Regulation of Cryptocurrency Around the World." The Law Library of Congress, Global Legal Research Center, June 2018. https://www.loc.gov/law/help/cryptocurrency/world-survey.php

Stiegler, Bernard, and Alain Jugnon. *Dans La Disruption: Comment Ne Pas Devenir Fou?* Paris: Éditions Les Liens qui libèrent, 2016

"Strategic Business Plan ISO/TC 307." Accessed June 20, 2019. https://isotc.iso.org/livelink/livelink/fetch/2000/2122/687806/ISO_TC_307__Blockchain_and_distributed_ledger_technologies_.pdf?nodeid=19772644&vernum=-2

Strobel, Volker. Pold87/Academic-Keyword-Occurrence: First Release. Zenodo, 2018. https://doi.org/10.5281/zenodo.1218409.

Swartz, Lana. "What Was Bitcoin, What Will It Be? The Techno-Economic Imaginaries of a New Money Technology." *Cultural Studies* 32, no. 4 (July 4, 2018): 623–50. https://doi.org/10.1080/09502386.2017.1416420

Swiss Financial Supervisory Authority FINMA. "Guide pratique pour les questions d'assujettissement concernant les initial coin offerings (ICO)," février 2018

"The Rule of Code vs. The Rule of Law." *Harvard University Press Blog* (blog), April 10, 2018. https://harvardpress.typepad.com/hup_publicity/2018/04/blockchain-and-the-law.html

Transform Group, LLC. "BitAngels." BitAngels, 2019. http://bitangels.io/

Turinetti, Alice. *La Normalisation: Etude en droit économique*. Editions Publibook, 2018

Vergne, Jean-Philippe, and Gautam Swain. "Categorical Anarchy in the U.K.? The British Media's Classification of Bitcoin and the Limits of Categorization." SSRN Scholarly Paper. Rochester, NY: Social Science Research Network, June 24, 2016. https://papers.ssrn.com/abstract=2800329

Vitalik Buterin. "Intro to Cryptoeconomics." February 23, 2017. https://vitalik.ca/files/intro_cryptoeconomics.pdf

———. *Introduction to Cryptoeconomics – Vitalik Buterin*, 2017. https://www.youtube.com/watch?v=pKqdjaH1dRo

Walch, Angela. "The Path of the Blockchain Lexicon (and the Law)." SSRN Scholarly Paper. Rochester, NY: Social Science Research Network, March 24, 2017. https://papers.ssrn.com/abstract=2940335

Wang, Junyao, Shenling Wang, Junqi Guo, Yanchang Du, Shaochi Cheng, and Xiangyang Li. "A Summary of Research on Blockchain in the Field of Intellectual Property." *Procedia Computer Science*, 2018 International Conference on Identification, Information and Knowledge in the Internet of Things, 147 (January 1, 2019): 191–97. https://doi.org/10.1016/j.procs.2019.01.220

Weber, Steve. *The Success of Open Source*. Cambridge, MA: Harvard University Press, 2004

Willett, J.R. "MasterCoin Buyer/Seller Thread," September 2013. https://bitcointalk.org/index.php?topic=287145.0

———. "MasterCoin Specification 1.1," September 2013. https://e33ec872-a-62cb3a1a-s-sites.googlegroups.com/site/2ndbtcwpaper/MasterCoin%20Specification%201.1.pdf

———. "The Second Bitcoin Whitepaper vs. 0.5 (Draft for Public Comment)," January 2012. https://e33ec872-a-62cb3a1a-s-sites.googlegroups.com/site/2ndbtcwpaper/2ndBitcoinWhitepaper.pdf

Wolla, Scott A. “Bitcoin: Money or Financial Investment?” PAGE ONE Economics. Federal Reserve Bank of St. Louis, March 2018. https://www.stlouisfed.org/education/page-one-economics-classroom-edition/bitcoin-money-or-financial-investment

“Workshop Report at 25/Mar/2016 | Blockchain Community Group.” Accessed June 20, 2019. https://www.w3.org/community/blockchain/workshop-report-at-25mar2016/

Zynis, Dominik. “A Brief History Of Mastercoin.” *Omni* (blog), November 29, 2013. https://blog.omni.foundation/2013/11/29/a-brief-history-of-mastercoin/

Designing through blockchain

Alizart, Mark. *Cryptocommunisme*. 1re édition. Perspectives Critiques. Paris: PUF, 2019

Anderson, Mally. “Exploring Decentralization: Blockchain Technology and Complex Coordination.” *Journal of Design and Science (JoDS)*, February 7, 2019. https://jods.mitpress.mit.edu/pub/7vxemtm3

Arner, Douglas W., Janos Nathan Barberis, and Ross P. Buckley. “FinTech, RegTech and the Reconceptualization of Financial Regulation.” SSRN Scholarly Paper. Rochester, NY: Social Science Research Network, October 1, 2016. https://papers.ssrn.com/abstract=2847806

Arthur, W. Brian. *The Nature of Technology: What It Is and How It Evolves*. Place of publication not identified: Free Press, 2014. http://www.myilibrary.com?id=894342

Atzori, Marcella. “Blockchain Technology and Decentralized Governance: Is the State Still Necessary?” SSRN Scholarly Paper. Rochester, NY: Social Science Research Network, December 1, 2015. https://papers.ssrn.com/abstract=2709713

Barkai, D. “Technologies for Sharing and Collaborating on the Net.” In *Proceedings First International Conference on Peer-to-Peer Computing*, 13–28. Linkoping, Sweden: IEEE Comput. Soc, 2002. https://doi.org/10.1109/P2P.2001.990419

Bauerle, Nolan, and Peter Ryan. "State of Blockchains Q32018." State of Blockchains. Coindesk, 2018. https://www.coindesk.com/research/state-of-blockchains-q3-2018

Bennett, Vicki E. Review of *Review of Learning Race and Ethnicity: Youth and Digital Media, Everett, Anna, ed*, by Anna Everett ed. *Children, Youth and Environments* 18, no. 2 (2008): 264–67

Berman, Ana. "China Introduces New Anti-Anonymity Regulations for Blockchain-Related Companies." *Cointelegraph* (blog), January 10, 2019. https://cointelegraph.com/news/china-introduces-new-anti-anonymity-regulations-for-blockchain-related-companies

Bhardwaj, Shweta, and Manish Kaushik. "Blockchain—Technology to Drive the Future." In *Smart Computing and Informatics*, edited by Suresh Chandra Satapathy, Vikrant Bhateja, and Swagatam Das, 78:263–71. Singapore: Springer Singapore, 2018. https://doi.org/10.1007/978-981-10-5547-8_28

Blackshear, Sam, Evan Cheng, David L Dill, Victor Gao, Ben Maurer, Todd Nowacki, Alistair Pott, et al. "Move: A Language With Programmable Resources," n.d., 26

Burg, John, Christine Murphy, and Jean Paul Pétraud. "Blockchain for International Development: Using a Learning Agenda to Address Knowledge Gaps." *MERL Tech* (blog), November 29, 2018. http://merltech.org/blockchain-for-international-development-using-a-learning-agenda-to-address-knowledge-gaps/

Chiu, Jonathan, and Thorsten V. Koeppl. "The Economics of Cryptocurrencies Bitcoin and Beyond." *SSRN Electronic Journal*, 2017. https://doi.org/10.2139/ssrn.3048124

Chohan, Usman W. "God in the Machine: The Use of Blockchain Technology in Organized Religious Praxis." SSRN Scholarly Paper. Rochester, NY: Social Science Research Network, February 8, 2019. https://papers.ssrn.com/abstract=3331823

De Filippi, Primavera, and Samer Hassan. "Blockchain Technology as a Regulatory Technology: From Code Is Law to Law Is Code." *First Monday* 21, no. 12 (November 14, 2016). https://doi.org/10.5210/fm.v21i12.7113

De, Filippi Primavera, and Aaron Wright. *Blockchain and the Law, The Rule of Code*. Cambridge: Harvard University Press, 2018. https://doi.org/10.4159/9780674985933

Durov, Nikolai. "Telegram Open Network Blockchain," March 26, 2019

Federal Reserve Bank of St. Louis, and David Andolfatto. "Blockchain: What It Is, What It Does, and Why You Probably Don't Need One." *Review* 100, no. 2 (2018): 87–95. https://doi.org/10.20955/r.2018.87-95

Feige, Uriel, Amos Fiat, and Adi Shamir. "Zero-Knowledge Proofs of Identity." *Journal of Cryptology* 1, no. 2 (June 1, 1988): 77–94. https://doi.org/10.1007/BF02351717

"Forrester: Total Economic Impact of IBM Blockchain." Forrester, July 2018. https://www.themsphub.com/content/forrester-report-the-total-economic-impact-of-ibm-blockchain/

Fusaro, Teddy, and Matt Hougan. "Bitwise Asset Management." presented at the Presentation to the U.S. Securities and Exchange Commission, March 19, 2019. https://www.sec.gov/comments/sr-nysearca-2019-01/srnysearca201901-5164833-183434.pdf

Gaggioli, Andrea. "Blockchain Technology: Living in a Decentralized Everything." *Cyberpsychology, Behavior, and Social Networking* 21, no. 1 (January 1, 2018): 65–66. https://doi.org/10.1089/cyber.2017.29097.csi

Goulet, Jean. "Revalorisation du droit et jurimétrie." *Les Cahiers de droit* 9, no. 1 (1967): 9. https://doi.org/10.7202/1004340ar

Guerraoui, Rachid, Petr Kuznetsov, Matteo Monti, Matej Pavlovic, and Dragos-Adrian Seredinschi. "AT2: Asynchronous Trustworthy Transfers." *ArXiv.Org*, March 5, 2019. http://arxiv.org/abs/1812.10844

Guerraoui, Rachid, and Jingjing Wang. "On the Unfairness of Blockchain." In *Networked Systems*, edited by Andreas Podelski and François Taïani, 36–50. Lecture Notes in Computer Science. Springer International Publishing, 2019

Hamilton, David. "China Announces New Blockchain Lab Initiative." *CoinCentral* (blog), August 30, 2018. https://coincentral.com/china-blockchain-lab-initiative/

Helbing, Dirk, ed. *Towards Digital Enlightenment: Essays on the Dark and Light Sides of the Digital Revolution*. Cham: Springer International Publishing, 2019. https://doi.org/10.1007/978-3-319-90869-4

James, Laura. "Oaths, Pledges and Manifestos: A Master List of Ethical Tech Values." *Medium* (blog), March 7, 2018. https://medium.com/doteveryone/oaths-pledges-and-manifestos-a-master-list-of-ethical-tech-values-26e2672e161c

Joosten, Rieks. "A Conceptual Analysis on Sovrin." *10536*, 2018. https://doi.org/10.13140/rg.2.2.10518.04160

Kirilova, D., N. Maslov, and A. Reyn. "Blockchain as a new technology for development." *International Journal of Open Information Technologies* 7, no. 1 (January 8, 2019): 34–38

Lapointe, Cara, and Lara Fishbane. "The Blockchain Ethical Design Framework." *Innovations: Technology, Governance, Globalization* 12, no. 3–4 (December 28, 2018): 50–71. https://doi.org/10.1162/inov_a_00275

Li, M., J. Weng, A. Yang, W. Lu, Y. Zhang, L. Hou, J. Liu, Y. Xiang, and R. Deng. "CrowdBC: A Blockchain-Based Decentralized Framework for Crowdsourcing." *IEEE Transactions on Parallel and Distributed Systems*, 2018, 1–1. https://doi.org/10.1109/TPDS.2018.2881735

Lum, Heather Christina, ed. *Critical Issues Impacting Science, Technology, Society (STS), and Our Future:* Advances in Human and Social Aspects of Technology. IGI Global, 2019. https://doi.org/10.4018/978-1-5225-7949-6

Nitot, Tristan, and Nina Cercy. *Numérique: reprendre le contrôle*, 2016

O'Neil, Cathy. *Weapons of Math Destruction: How Big Data Increases Inequality and Threatens Democracy*. London: Penguin Books, 2017

Owen, Taylor. *Disruptive Power: The Crisis of the State in the Digital Age*. Oxford Studies in Digital Politics. Oxford ; New York: Oxford University Press, 2015

Polys. "How Blockchain-Based Online Elections Can Save Democracy." Blog. *Polys – Medium* (blog), February 26, 2018. https://medium.com/@polysvote/how-blockchain-based-online-elections-can-save-democracy-6f7920c1f7cc

Prinz, Wolfgang. “Blockchain and CSCW – Shall We Care?,” 2018. https://doi.org/10.18420/ecscw2018_13

Reijers, Wessel, and Mark Coeckelbergh. “The Blockchain as a Narrative Technology: Investigating the Social Ontology and Normative Configurations of Cryptocurrencies.” *Philosophy & Technology* 31, no. 1 (March 2018): 103–30. https://doi.org/10.1007/s13347-016-0239-x

Scardovi, Claudio. *Restructuring and Innovation in Banking*. Springer, 2016

Schmidt, Eric, and Jared Cohen. *The New Digital Age: Transforming Nations, Businesses, and Our Lives*. First Vintage Books Edition. New York: Vintage Books, A Division of Random House LLC, 2014

Schon, Donald A. “Designing as Reflective Conversation with the Materials of a Design Situation.” *Research in Engineering Design* 3, no. 3 (September 1, 1992): 131–47. https://doi.org/10.1007/BF01580516

Taleb, Nasser. “Prospective Applications of Blockchain and Bitcoin Cryptocurrency Technology.” *TEM Journal; Vol 8* No 1 (2019): 2019. ISSN 2217-8309. https://doi.org/10.18421/tem81-06

Tapscott, Don, and Alex Tapscott. *Blockchain Revolution: How the Technology Behind Bitcoin and Other Cryptocurrencies Is Changing the World*. Penguin Publishing Group, 2018

Tobin, Andrew. “Sovrin: What Goes on the Ledger?” Evernym, 2018. https://www.evernym.com/wp-content/uploads/2017/07/What-Goes-On-The-Ledger.pdf

Vangulick, David, Bertrand Cornélusse, and Damien Ernst. “Blockchain: A Novel Approach for the Consensus Algorithm Using Condorcet Voting Procedure.” In *Proceedings of the IEEE International Conference on Decentralized Applications and Infrastructures*. San Francisco, 2019. http://hdl.handle.net/2268/232444

Vigna, Paul, and Michael J. Casey. *The Truth Machine: The Blockchain and the Future of Everything*. New York: St. Martin’s Press, 2018

Werbach, Kevin. *The Blockchain and the New Architecture of Trust*. Information Policy Series. Cambridge, MA: MIT Press, 2018

Wilson, Steve. "Identity Is Dead." Constellation Research Inc., June 6, 2019. https://www.constellationr.com/blog-news/identity-dead

Witzig, Pascal. "Cutting out the Middleman: A Case Study of Blockchain Technology Induced Reconfigurations in the Swiss Financial Services Industry." In *Blockchains, Smart Contracts, Decentralised Autonomous Organisations and the Law*, by Daniel Kraus, Thierry Obrist, and Olivier Hari, 18–48. Edward Elgar Publishing, 2019. https://doi.org/10.4337/9781788115131.00008

World Economic Forum. "Globalization 4.0: Shaping a New Global Architecture in the Age of the Fourth Industrial Revolution." World Economic Forum, April 2019. https://www.weforum.org/whitepapers/globalization-4-0-shaping-a-new-global-architecture-in-the-age-of-the-fourth-industrial-revolution/

Wüst, K., and A. Gervais. "Do You Need a Blockchain?" In *2018 Crypto Valley Conference on Blockchain Technology (CVCBT)*, 45–54, 2018. https://doi.org/10.1109/CVCBT.2018.00011

Zuboff, Shoshana. *The Age of Surveillance Capitalism: The Fight for the Future at the New Frontier of Power*. London: Profile Books, 2018

Zwitter, Andrej, and Mathilde Boisse-Despiaux. "Blockchain for Humanitarian Action and Development Aid." *Journal of International Humanitarian Action* 3, no. 1 (December 2018). https://doi.org/10.1186/s41018-018-0044-5

Conclusions

Benyekhlef, Karim. "Une introduction au droit global," January 8, 2017. https://www.karimbenyekhlef.ca/blogue/2017/01/08/une-introduction-au-droit-global/

Benyekhlef, Karim, and Centre de recherche en droit public, eds. *Vers un droit global?* Montréal, Québec: Les Éditions Thémis, 2016

Benyekhlef, Karim, Antonia Pereira de Sousa, Mathieu Amouroux, and Karim Seffar. *Une Possible Histoire de La Norme: Les Normativités Émergentes de La Mondialisation*. 2e édition. Montréal: Les Éditions Thémis, 2015

Cassese, Sabino, ed. *Research Handbook on Global Administrative Law*. Research Handbooks on Globalisation and the Law. Cheltenham, UK Northampton, MA: Edward Elgar Publishing, 2016

Castells, Manuel. *The Power of Identity*. 2nd ed., with a new preface. The Information Age: Economy, Society, and Culture. Malden, MA: Wiley-Blackwell, 2010

Dubuisson-Quellier, Sophie, ed. *Gouverner les conduites*. Domaine Gouvernances, n.d

Flueckiger, Alexandre. "(Re)faire la loi : traité de légistique à l'ère du droit souple," 2019. https://archive-ouverte.unige.ch/unige:116477

Fromageau, Edouard. "La théorie des institutions du droit administratif global : étude des interactions avec le droit international public." University of Geneva, 2014. https://archive-ouverte.unige.ch/unige:72810

Frydman, Benoit. "Droit global et régulation. Quels points de contrôle pour une régulation de l'économie de marché ?" *Revue d'études benthamiennes*, no. 14 (December 30, 2018). https://doi.org/10.4000/etudes-benthamiennes.846

Frydman, Benoît. *Petit manuel pratique du droit global.* Bruxelles: Académie Royale de Belgique, 2014

Held, David. *Models of Democracy*. Stanford University Press, 2006

Hennebel, Ludovic. "Droit Administratif Global (Global Administrative Law)." SSRN Scholarly Paper. Rochester, NY: Social Science Research Network, December 14, 2012. https://papers.ssrn.com/abstract=2189312

Kingsbury, B. "The Concept of 'Law' in Global Administrative Law." *European Journal of International Law* 20, no. 1 (February 1, 2009): 23–57. https://doi.org/10.1093/ejil/chp005

Kingsbury, Benedict, Nico Krisch, and Richard B. Stewart. "L'émergence du droit administratif global." *Revue internationale de droit économique* (t. XXVII), no. 1 (2013): 37. https://doi.org/10.3917/ride.259.0037

Rosanvallon, Pierre. *La Légitimité Démocratique: Impartialité, Réflexivité, Proximité*. Livres Du Nouveau Monde. Paris: Seuil, 2008

Zittrain, Jonathan. *The Future of the Internet and How to Stop It*. New Haven, [Conn.]: Yale University Press, 2008

Supervisory Group

Dr. Olivier Glassey, Member steering committee TA-SWISS and head of supervisory group, University of Lausanne UNIL

Raphael Bucher, Federal Office for the Environment

Prof. Christian Cachin, University of Bern

Hannes Gassert, crstl

Anja Wyden Guelpa, civiclab

Dr. Uwe Heck, Federal IT Steering Unit

Luzius Meisser, meissereconomics

Marine Pasquier-Beaud, Swiss Federal Office of Energy

Martin Rindlisbacher, UBS

Dr. Fabian Schnell, Avenir Suisse

Antoine Verdon, Swiss Legal Tech Association

Project Management TA-SWISS

Dr. rer. soc. Elisabeth Ehrensperger, Managing director TA-SWISS

Dr. Catherine Pugin, Project manager TA-SWISS

Weitere Publikationen von TA-SWISS

Markus Christen et al.

Wenn Algorithmen für uns entscheiden: Chancen und Risiken der künstlichen Intelligenz

2020, 360 Seiten, zahlr. Abb. (z. T. farbig)
Format 16 x 23 cm, broschiert
ISBN 978-3-7281-4001-2
als eBook (Open Access) erhältlich

Fabienne Perret, Tobias Arnold, Remo Fischer, Peter de Haan, Ueli Haefeli

Automatisiertes Fahren in der Schweiz: Das Steuer aus der Hand geben?

2020, 328 Seiten, zahlr. Abb. (z. T. farbig)
Format 16 x 23 cm, broschiert
ISBN 978-3-7281-3995-5
als eBook (Open Access) erhältlich

Sarah Fässler et al.

Social Freezing – Kinderwunsch auf Eis

2019, 294 Seiten, zahlr. Abb. und Tabellen
Format 16 x 23 cm, broschiert
ISBN 978-3-7281-3962-7
als eBook (Open Access) erhältlich

Alexander Lang et al.

Genome Editing – Interdisziplinäre Technikfolgenabschätzung

2019, 472 Seiten, zahlr. Abb. (z. T. farbig)
Format 18,5 x 26,5 cm, broschiert
ISBN 978-3-7281-3981-8
als eBook (Open Access) erhältlich

vdf Hochschulverlag AG an der ETH Zürich, Voltastrasse 24, VOB D, CH-8092 Zürich